Poetry Focus 2021

Leaving Certificate poems and notes for **English Higher Level**

Martin Kieran & Frances Rocks

GILL EDUCATION

124423762

Gill Education
Hume Avenue
Park West
Dublin 12
www.gilleducation.ie

Gill Education is an imprint of M.H. Gill & Co.

ISBN: 978-0-7171-83906

Design: Graham Thew
Print origination: Carole Lynch

For permission to reproduce photographs, the authors and publisher gratefully acknowledge the following:

© Alamy: 20, 23, 36, 81, 84, 89, 96, 100, 112, 156, 158, 161, 164, 187, 189, 191, 194, 196, 199, 204, 206, 207, 208, 214, 216, 218, 239, 243, 246, 264, 267, 275, 296, 299, 300, 307, 311, 312, 314, 317, 325, 329, 332, 389, 390, 395, 398, 403, 406, 407, 410, 420, 424, 426, section header: Paul Durcan, Gerard Manley Hopkins, John Keats; © Bridgeman Images: 116, 118, 366, 368; © E+/Getty Premium: 120, 123; Courtesy of Faber & Faber Ltd: section header: Seamus Heaney; © Francine Scialom Greenblatt: 135, 140; © Getty Images: 5,7, 11, 16, 19, 40, 43, 45, 48, 51, 65, 73, 75, 92, 124, 145, 172, 175, 234, 237, 279, 281, 392, 412, section header: Sylvia Plath; © 248, 400; © iStock: 31, 34, 79, 94, 68, 71, 211, 271, 274, 318, 319, 347, 350, 352, 372, 415, 418, section header: Unseen Poetry; © Minden Pictures/Getty Premium: 25, 29, 304, 306; © Photodisc/Getty Premium: 321, 324; © RTE: section header: Eavan Boland; © Shutterstock: 128, 131, 167, 342, 344, 362, 375, 378; © Sportsfile: 151, 154; © Stockbyte/ Getty Images: 256; Courtesy of The Josef and Yaye Breitenbach Charitable Foundation, New York: section header: Elizabeth Bishop; © Topfoto: 77, 223, 252, 260, 261, 283, section header: Robert Frost; © Zoonar/ Getty Images Plus: 268, 270.

The authors and publisher have made every effort to trace all copyright holders, but if any have been inadvertently overlooked we would be pleased to make the necessary arrangement at the first opportunity.

The paper used in this book is made from the wood pulp of managed forests. For every tree felled, at least one tree is planted, thereby renewing natural resources.

Contents

*(OL) indicates poems that are also prescribed for the Ordinary Level course.

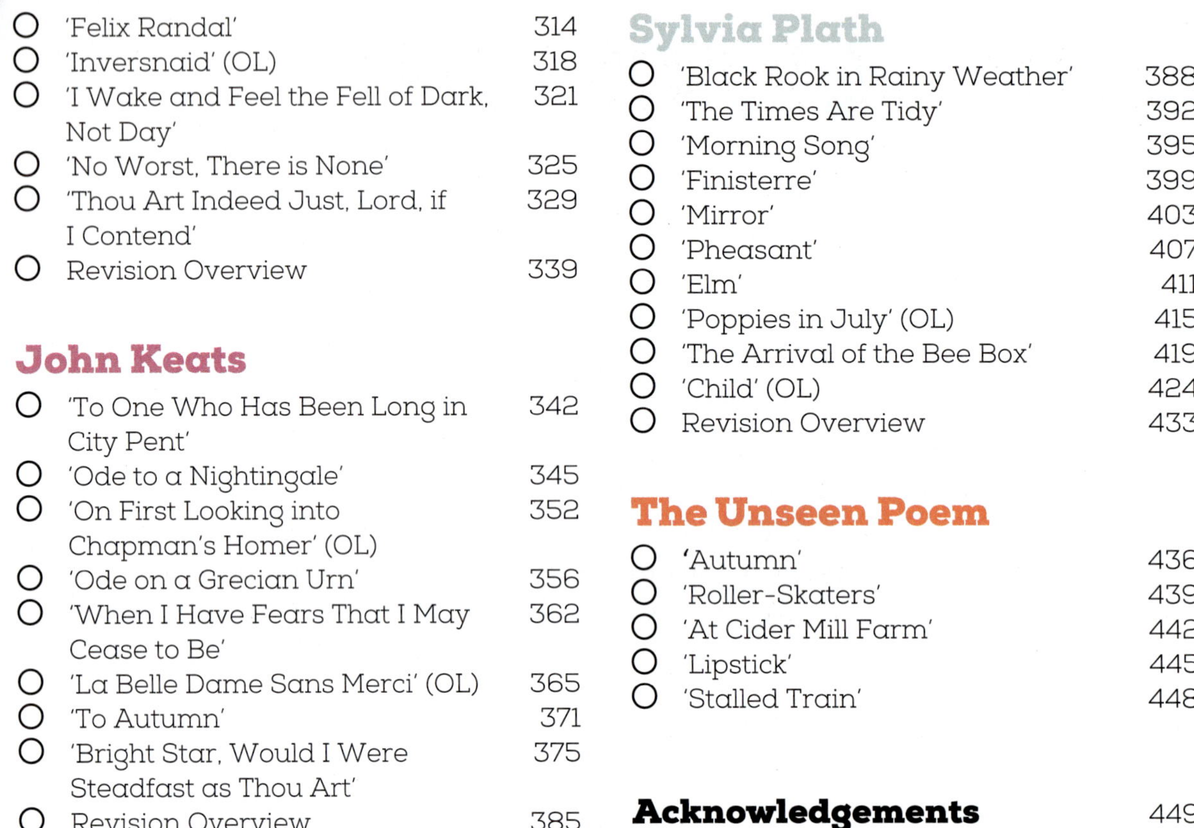

John Keats

Sylvia Plath

The Unseen Poem

*(OL) indicates poems that are also prescribed for the Ordinary Level course.

Introduction

Poetry Focus is a modern poetry textbook for Leaving Certificate Higher Level English. It includes all the prescribed poems for the 2021 exam as well as succinct commentaries on each one. Well-organised study notes allow students to develop their own individual responses and enhance their skills in critical literacy. There is no single 'correct' approach to answering the poetry question. Candidates are free to respond in any appropriate way that shows good knowledge of and engagement with the prescribed poems.

- **Concise poet biographies** provide context for the poems.
- **List of prescribed poems** gives a brief introduction to each poem.
- **Personal response** questions follow the text of each poem. These allow students to consider their first impressions before any in-depth study or analysis. These questions provide a good opportunity for written and/or oral exercises.
- **Critical literacy** highlights the main features of the poet's subject matter and style. These discussion notes will enhance the student's own critical appreciation through focused group work and/or written exercises. Analytical skills are developed in a coherent, practical way to give students confidence in articulating their own personal responses.
- **Analysis (writing about the poem) is provided using graded sample paragraphs** which aid students in fluently structuring and developing valid points, using fresh and varied expression. These model paragraphs also illustrate effective use of relevant quotations and reference.
- **Class/homework exercises** for each poem provide focused practice in writing personal responses to examination-style questions.
- **Summary points** provide a memorable snapshot of the key aspects to remember about each poem.
- **Full sample Leaving Certificate essays** are accompanied by marking-scheme guidelines and examiners' comments. These show the student exactly what is required to achieve a successful top grade in the Leaving Cert. The examiner's comments illustrate the use of the PCLM marking scheme and are an invaluable aid for the ambitious student.
- **Sample essay plans** on each poet's work illustrate how to interpret a question and recognise the particular nuances of key words in examination questions. Student evaluation of these essay plans increase confidence in developing and organising clear response to exam questions.
- **Sample Leaving Cert questions** on each poet are given at the end of their particular section.
- **Revision Overviews** provide a concise and visual summary of each poet's work, through highlighting and interlinking relevant themes.
- **Unseen Poetry** provides guidelines for this 20-mark section of the paper. Included are numerous sample questions and answers, which allow students to practise exam-style answers.

 **The FREE eBook contains:**

- **Investigate Further** sections which contain **useful weblinks** should you want to learn more.
- **Pop-up key quotes** to encourage students to select their own individual combination of references from a poem and to write brief commentaries on specific quotations.
- Additional sample graded paragraphs called '**Developing your personal response**'.
- Audio of a selection of the poetry as read by the poets, including audio of all Eavan Boland, Paul Durcan and Seamus Heaney poetry.

Further material can also be found on GillExplore.ie:

- **A glossary of common literary terms** provides an easy reference when answering questions.
- **A critical analysis checklist** offers useful hints and tips on how to show genuine engagement with the poetry.

How is the Prescribed Poetry Question Marked?

Marking is done (ex. 50 marks) by reference to the PCLM criteria for assessment.

- Clarity of purpose (P): 30% of the total (15 marks)
- Coherence of delivery (C): 30% of the total (15 marks)
- Efficiency of language use (L): 30% of the total (15 marks)
- Accuracy of mechanics (M): 10% of the total (5 marks)

Each answer will be in the form of a response to a specific task requiring candidates to:

- Display a clear and purposeful engagement with the set task (P)
- Sustain the response in an appropriate manner over the entire answer (C)
- Manage and control language appropriate to the task (L)
- Display levels of accuracy in spelling and grammar appropriate to the required/chosen register (M)

General

'Students at Higher Level will be required to study a representative selection from the work of eight poets: a representative selection would seek to reflect the range of a poet's themes and interests and exhibit his/her characteristic style and viewpoint. Normally the study of at least six poems by each poet would be expected.' (DES English Syllabus, 6.3)

The marking scheme guidelines from the State Examinations Commission state that in the case of each poet, the candidates have **freedom of choice** in relation to the poems studied. In addition, there is **not a finite list of any 'poet's themes and interests'**.

Note that in responding to the question set on any given poet, the candidates must refer to the poem(s) they have studied but are not required to refer to **any specific poem(s), nor are they expected to discuss or refer to all the poems they have chosen to study**.

In each of the questions in **Prescribed Poetry**, the underlying nature of the task is the invitation to the candidates to **engage with the poems themselves**.

Exam Advice

- **You are not expected to write about any set number of poems** in the examination. You might decide to focus in detail on a small number of poems, or you could choose to write in a more general way on several poems.
- Most candidates write one or two well-developed **paragraphs** on each of the poems they have chosen for discussion. In other cases, a paragraph will focus on one specific aspect of the poet's work. When discussing recurring themes or features of style, appropriate cross-references to other poems may also be useful.
- Reflect on central **themes** and viewpoints in the poems you discuss. Comment also on the use of language and the poet's distinctive **style**. Examine imagery, tone, structure, rhythm and rhyme. Be careful not to simply list aspects of style, such as alliteration or repetition. There's little point in mentioning that a poet uses sound effects or metaphors without discussing the effectiveness of such characteristics.
- Focus on **the task** you have been given in the poetry question. Identify the key terms in the wording of the question and think of similar words for these terms. This will help you develop a relevant and coherent personal response in keeping with the PCLM marking scheme criteria.
- Always root your answers in the text of the poems. Support the points you make with **relevant reference and quotation**. Make sure your own expression is fresh and lively. Avoid awkward expressions, such as 'It says in the poem that ...'. Look for alternatives: 'There is a sense of ...', 'The tone seems to suggest ...', 'It's evident that ...', etc.
- Neat, **legible handwriting** will help to make a positive impression on examiners. Corrections should be made by simply drawing a line through the mistake. Scored-out words distract attention from the content of your work.
- Keep the emphasis on why particular poets **appeal to you**. Consider the continuing relevance or significance of a poet's work. Perhaps you have shared some of the feelings or experiences expressed in the poems. Avoid starting answers with prepared biographical sketches. Brief reference to a poet's life are better used when discussing how the poems themselves were shaped by such experiences.
- Remember that the examination encourages **individual engagement** with the prescribed poems. Poetry can make us think and feel and imagine. It opens our minds to the wonderful possibilities of language and ideas. Your interaction with the poems is what matters most. **Commentary notes and critical interpretations are all there to be challenged.** Read the poems carefully and have confidence in expressing your own personal response.

Elizabeth Bishop 1911–1979

'The armored cars of dreams, contrived to let us do so many a dangerous thing.'

Elizabeth Bishop was born in Worcester, Massachusetts, in 1911. She spent part of her childhood with her Canadian grandparents following her father's death and mother's hospitalisation. She then lived with various relatives who, according to Bishop, took care of her because they felt sorry for her. These unsettling events, along with the memories of her youth, inspired her to read poetry – and eventually to write it. After studying English at university, she travelled extensively and lived in New York, Florida and, for 17 years, Brazil. She also taught at several American colleges. Throughout her life she suffered from ill health and depression. As a poet, she wrote sparingly, publishing only five slim volumes in 35 years. However, her work received high acclaim. 'I think geography comes first in my work,' she told an interviewer, 'and then animals. But I like people, too. I've written a few poems about people.' Bishop died suddenly in her Boston apartment on 6 October 1979. She was 68 years old. Her poetry continues to gain widespread recognition and study.

Investigate Further

To find out more about Elizabeth Bishop, or to hear readings of her poems, you could search some useful websites, such as YouTube, BBC poetry, poetryfoundation.org and poetryarchive.org, or access additional material on this page of your eBook.

Prescribed Poems

Note that Bishop uses American spellings and punctuation in her work.

*(OL) indicates poems that are also prescribed for the Ordinary Level course.

POETRY FOCUS

1 The Fish

I caught a tremendous fish
and held him beside the boat
half out of water, with my hook
fast in a corner of his mouth.
He didn't fight.
He hadn't fought at all.
He hung a grunting weight,
battered and venerable
and homely. Here and there
his brown skin hung in strips
like ancient wallpaper,
and its pattern of darker brown
was like wallpaper:
shapes like full-blown roses
stained and lost through age.
He was speckled with barnacles,
fine rosettes of lime,
and infested
with tiny white sea-lice,
and underneath two or three
rags of green weed hung down.
While his gills were breathing in
the terrible oxygen
—the frightening gills,
fresh and crisp with blood,
that can cut so badly—
I thought of the coarse white flesh
packed in like feathers,
the big bones and the little bones,
the dramatic reds and blacks
of his shiny entrails,
and the pink swim-bladder
like a big peony.
I looked into his eyes
which were far larger than mine
but shallower, and yellowed,
the irises backed and packed
with tarnished tinfoil
seen through the lenses
of old scratched isinglass.

tremendous: huge, startling, fearsome.

venerable: ancient, worthy of respect.

homely: comfortable, easy-going, unpretentious, plain.

rosettes: rose-shaped decorations made of ribbon, often awarded as prizes.

sea-lice: small parasites that live on the skin of fish.

gills: breathing organs of fish.

entrails: internal organs.

peony: large, flamboyant flower, usually pink.

irises: coloured parts of an eye.

isinglass: gelatine-like substance obtained from the bodies of fish, opaque.

They shifted a little, but not
to return my stare.
—It was more like the tipping
of an object toward the light.
I admired his sullen face,
the mechanism of his jaw,
and then I saw
that from his lower lip
—if you could call it a lip—
grim, wet, and weaponlike,
hung five old pieces of fish-line,
or four and a wire leader
with the swivel still attached,
with all their five big hooks
grown firmly in his mouth.
A green line, frayed at the end
where he broke it, two heavier lines,
and a fine black thread
still crimped from the strain and snap
when it broke and he got away.
Like medals with their ribbons
frayed and wavering,
a five-haired beard of wisdom
trailing from his aching jaw.
I stared and stared
and victory filled up
the little rented boat,
from the pool of bilge
where oil had spread a rainbow
around the rusted engine
to the bailer rusted orange,
the sun-cracked thwarts,
the oarlocks on their strings,
the gunnels—until everything
was rainbow, rainbow, rainbow!
And I let the fish go.

sullen: bad-tempered, sulky.
mechanism: workings.

leader: wire connecting fishhook and line.

crimped: pressed into ridges.

frayed: unravelled, worn.

bilge: dirty water that collects in the bottom of a boat.

bailer: bucket that scoops water out of a boat.
thwarts: rowers' benches.

oarlocks: metal devices for holding oars.
gunnels: upper edges of the side of a boat.

'He hung a grunting weight'

Personal Response

1. List two details that appealed to you in the description of the fish in lines 1–15. Why did they make an impact on you? Were they unusual or did they appeal to your senses? Support your response with quotation from the poem.
2. What is the poet's attitude towards the fish? Where does it change as the poem progresses? Give a reason for this change. Refer closely to the poem in your response.
3. Who had the 'victory' in this situation – the fish or Bishop? Why did you come to this conclusion? Support your discussion with clear references to the poem.

Critical Literacy

'The Fish' is from Elizabeth Bishop's first published collection, *North and South* (1946). She lived in Florida during the 1930s and the poem is based on her experience of catching a large jewfish at Key West. Bishop once said, 'I like painting probably better than I like poetry' and 'The Fish' is certainly a very visual poem. Bishop uses the fish as a way of exploring a 'green' awareness, the respect for nature and all living things.

The poem's opening line is direct and forceful ('I caught a tremendous fish'). Bishop's use of the personal pronoun 'I' gives a sense of immediacy and intimacy. The adjective 'tremendous' reflects the **poet's breathless excitement and awe at this magnificent specimen of fish**. The act of catching the fish is described in a personal, down-to-earth way. Bishop once said, 'I always tell the truth in my poems ... that's exactly how it happened.' The fish is 'half out of water', no longer in its natural habitat.

In line 5, the focus shifts from the person who caught the fish to the fish itself. **It is now given a personality**: 'He didn't fight.' The onomatopoeic 'grunting' allows us to be part of this scene, as we hear the distressed noises from the gasping, ugly ('homely'), exhausted ('battered') fish. Then another aspect of the fish is presented to us: it is 'venerable', ancient and worthy of reverence. Bishop the participant is giving way to Bishop the observer. While in college, Bishop met Marianne Moore, a famous American poet whose focus was on the accurate description of a particular thing. This poetic movement was known as **imagism**. We can see the similarity of style between the two poets in Bishop's description of the fish: 'Here and there/ his brown skin hung in strips/like ancient wallpaper'.

The surface **detail is painstakingly and imaginatively described** ('like full-blown roses'). There seems to be an attempt to domesticate the creature, but the sordid reality of the blotches on the skin is also noted ('stained and lost through age'). The texture of the fish is described

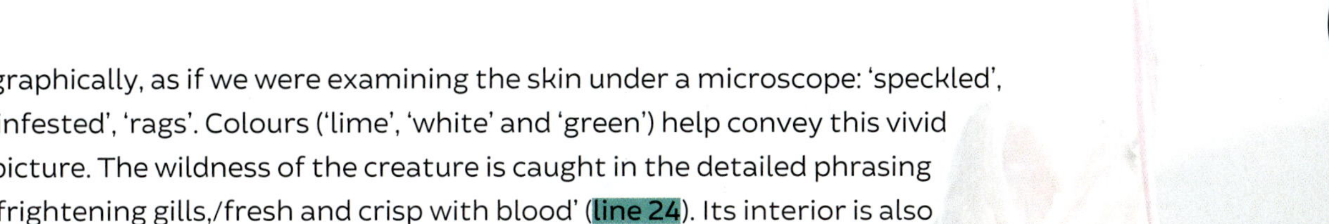

graphically, as if we were examining the skin under a microscope: 'speckled', 'infested', 'rags'. Colours ('lime', 'white' and 'green') help convey this vivid picture. The wildness of the creature is caught in the detailed phrasing 'frightening gills,/fresh and crisp with blood' (line 24). Its interior is also imagined ('pink swim-bladder/like a big peony'). These original and striking images appeal to both our visual and tactile senses.

Bishop's delight in catching this fine specimen soon gives way to an **emotional involvement with the fish** and his struggle for survival (line 34). She compares his eyes to her own ('far larger'). She notes the wear and tear from a long, hard life ('yellowed'). The irises are 'backed and packed/with tarnished tinfoil'. Here, assonance and alliteration give emphasis to the image. However, the fish's eyes are unresponsive, so there seems to be no interplay between creature and poet. This suggests both the independence and the vulnerability of the fish.

Progression in the poem is shown in the verbs: 'I caught', 'I thought', 'I looked' and, in line 45, 'I admired'. The **poet admires the resolute nature of the fish** ('his sullen face'). This fish has survived previous battles ('five big hooks/ grown firmly in his mouth'). Precise detail emphasises the severity of these battles ('A green line, frayed at the end/where he broke it'). Military language highlights the effort the fish has made to survive: 'weaponlike', 'medals'. Bishop's sympathy is clear as she notes the fish's 'aching jaw'. For the fish, it is clear that the pain of battle remains.

Line 65 shows the poet transfixed ('I stared and stared'). Now the scene expands from a single fisher in a 'little rented boat' to something of **universal significance** ('victory' fills up the boat). Ordinary details (the 'bilge', the 'thwarts' and the 'gunnels') are transformed. The oil has 'spread a rainbow'. Everything is coloured and Bishop's relationship with the fish changes. She exercises mercy. A moment of epiphany occurs and she lets 'the fish go'. All the tension in the poem is finally released. The underlying drama contained between the opening line ('I caught a tremendous fish') and the closing line ('And I let the fish go.') has been resolved. **Victory belongs to both the poet and the fish**. The fish is free; the poet has seen and understood.

This poem is a long narrative with a clear beginning, middle and end. Bishop has chosen a suitably unrhymed form. The metre is appropriate for the speaking voice: dimeter (two stresses) and trimeter (three stresses). Short run-on lines suggest the poet excitedly examining her catch and the recurring use of dashes indicates her thought process as she moves from delight to wonder, empathy and, finally, comprehension. The concluding rhyming couplet brings a definite and satisfying resolution to the dramatic tension.

Writing About the Poem

Elizabeth Bishop has been praised for her 'painterly eye'. Discuss this aspect of her style in 'The Fish'. Support your views with close reference to the poem.

Sample Paragraph

An artist looks, then sees, re-creates and leads both themselves and their viewers to a new insight. I think Elizabeth Bishop accomplishes all this in her poem 'The Fish'. The poet looks at the event ('I caught a tremendous fish') and then moves to describe the fish, using striking images ('brown skin hung in strips/like ancient wallpaper'). Like a camera, she pans this way and that, making us see also 'its pattern of darker brown' with 'shapes like full-blown roses'. She leads us to imagine the interior of the fish, its 'coarse white flesh/ packed in like feathers'. If Bishop were painting this fish, I could imagine it in glistening oil colours. In her poem, she paints with words: 'the pink swim-bladder/like a peony'. She engages with her subject: 'I looked into his eyes'. She acknowledges this veteran as she notes his 'medals', the 'five big hooks/grown firmly in his mouth'. They have been there so long that the skin has grown over them and she draws our attention to the fish's 'aching jaw'. Just like a painter, Bishop orders her picture so that we can see the 'five-haired beard of wisdom/trailing' from the fish. The poem concludes with a burst of colour ('rainbow, rainbow, rainbow!'). The rainbow from the oil-soaked bilge water has transformed the poet's relationship with the fish. Like Bishop, we now see the proper relationship between people and nature – one of respect. So the 'painterly eye' has led us to see the drama, the fish and what it really was, and finally our correct response to the earth and its creatures.

EXAMINER'S COMMENT

A mature and interesting interpretation of the question. The top-grade response is very well focused and there is a sustained personal perspective throughout. Judicious use of quotations rounds off the answer. With the exception of the last sentence, expression is generally fluent and assured.

Class/Homework Exercises

1. Bishop often structures her poems like a mini-drama. Examine the poem 'The Fish' and comment on how a dramatic effect is achieved. Consider setting, characterisation, conflict, the interior debate, tension building to climax, and resolution. Refer closely to the text of the poem in your response.
2. 'Elizabeth Bishop has commented that she simply tried "to see things afresh" in her poetry.' To what extent is this true of her poem, 'The Fish'? Support your answer with reference to the text.

Summary Points

- **Themes include endurance and the relationship between nature and human nature.**
- **Observational details, vibrant language, personification, striking comparisons.**
- **Engaging first-person narrative voice.**
- **Varying tones – joyful, admiring, celebratory.**
- **Memorable sound effects – assonance, alliteration, sibilance, repetition.**
- **Dramatic development that ends in a moment of insight.**

2 The Bight

On my birthday

At low tide like this how sheer the water is.
White, crumbling ribs of marl protrude and glare
and the boats are dry, the pilings dry as matches.
Absorbing, rather than being absorbed,
the water in the bight doesn't wet anything,
the color of the gas flame turned as low as possible.
One can smell it turning to gas; if one were Baudelaire
one could probably hear it turning to marimba music.
The little ocher dredge at work off the end of the dock
already plays the dry perfectly off-beat claves.
The birds are outsize. Pelicans crash
into this peculiar gas unnecessarily hard,
it seems to me, like pickaxes,
rarely coming up with anything to show for it,
and going off with humorous elbowings.
Black-and-white man-of-war birds soar
on impalpable drafts
and open their tails like scissors on the curves
or tense them like wishbones, till they tremble.
The frowsy sponge boats keep coming in
with the obliging air of retrievers,
bristling with jackstraw gaffs and hooks
and decorated with bobbles of sponges.
There is a fence of chicken wire along the dock
where, glinting like little plowshares,
the blue-gray shark tails are hung up to dry
for the Chinese-restaurant trade.
Some of the little white boats are still piled up
against each other, or lie on their sides, stove in,
and not yet salvaged, if they ever will be, from the last bad storm,
like torn-open, unanswered letters.
The bight is littered with old correspondences.
Click. Click. Goes the dredge,
and brings up a dripping jawful of marl.
All the untidy activity continues,
awful but cheerful.

The Bight: refers to a wide bay or inlet.

marl: rich clay soil.

pilings: heavy beams supporting a jetty.

Baudelaire: Charles Baudelaire (1821–67), French symbolist poet.

marimba: wooden instrument similar to a xylophone, played by African and Central American jazz musicians.

ocher: ochre; orange-brown colour.

claves: clefs; musical keys.

impalpable drafts: slight air currents.

frowsy: shabby, foul-smelling.

retrievers: hunting dogs.

bristling: shining.

jackstraw gaffs: splinters used as hooks on fishing rods.

bobbles: trimmings.

plowshares: ploughing blades.

stove in: storm-damaged.

salvaged: repaired.

dredge: a dredger is a machine for digging underwater.

Personal Response

1. Using close reference to the text, describe the atmosphere in the first six lines of the poem.
2. Choose one simile that you think is particularly effective in the poem. Briefly explain your choice.
3. Although the poem is not directly personal, what does it suggest to you about Elizabeth Bishop herself? Refer to the text in your answer.

Critical Literacy

'The Bight' showcases Elizabeth Bishop's aesthetic appreciation of the world around her. The setting for this poem is Garrison Bight in Florida. In describing the small, untidy harbour, Bishop displays a characteristically keen eye for observation and an expert use of metaphor. The subtitle, 'On my birthday', suggests a special occasion and, perhaps, a time for reflection and reappraisal of life.

The poem begins with an introduction to the bight at 'low tide' and gradually constructs a **vivid picture of an uninviting place**: 'White, crumbling ribs of

marl protrude and glare'. Grim personification and a sharp 'r' sound effect emphasise the unsettling atmosphere. There is a sense of unreality about sea water that 'doesn't wet anything'. The description in these opening lines is typically detailed, sensual and precise – all carefully shaped by the poet's own personal vision of the world. References to 'the pilings dry as matches' and the 'gas flame' water are rather disturbing, implying that something dangerous might be about to happen.

Bishop's mention of the French poet Charles Baudelaire (line 7) would suggest that she shares his belief in expressing human experience through objects and places around us. The poet imagines Baudelaire being able to 'hear' the water 'turning to marimba music'. She also finds an unexpected jazz rhythm ('perfectly off-beat claves') coming from the machine that is dredging 'off the end of the dock'. In lines 11–19, Bishop depicts the 'outsize' birds through a series of vigorous images. They seem awkward and out of place in this busy, built-up location. **Figurative language illustrates their mechanical movements**: pelicans 'crash' into the sea 'like pickaxes', while man-of-war birds 'open their tails like scissors'. An underlying sense of disquiet can be detected in the detailed observations of these 'tense' birds as they 'tremble' in flight.

The poet's portrayal of the bight is quite realistic: 'frowsy sponge boats keep coming in' to harbour. With wry humour, she acknowledges their unlikely beauty, 'bristling with jackstraw gaffs' and 'decorated with bobbles of sponges'. The cluttered dockside is a busy working environment where 'blue-gray shark tails are hung up to dry' (line 26). The 'little white boats' are a reminder of the local fishing community and its dependence on the sea. Bishop compares the small fishing boats to 'torn-open, unanswered letters'. The bight suddenly reminds her of a cluttered writing-desk – her own, presumably – 'littered with old correspondences'.

This metaphor is developed in lines 33–36. Bishop returns to sharp sounds: the 'Click. Click.' noise of the dredger (compared to an animal unearthing the wet clay) as it 'brings up a dripping jawful of marl'. The ending is highly symbolic of the poet's own impulse to dig deep into personal memories. Drawing a close comparison between her own life and the 'untidy activity' of the bight, she concludes that both are 'awful but cheerful'. **The matter-of-fact tone of these closing lines is derisive but good humoured**. It reflects her realistic approach to the highs and lows of human experience – and the thoughts that are likely to have crossed her mind as she celebrated yet another birthday.

Writing About the Poem

'Closely observed description and vivid imagery are striking features of Elizabeth Bishop's poems.' Discuss this statement in relation to 'The Bight'. Refer to the poem in support of your views.

Sample Paragraph

I think 'The Bight' is a good example of how Elizabeth Bishop slowly builds up a picture of a fairly inhospitable place. At first, she describes the 'sheer' water and the 'crumbling ribs of marl', personifying the soil as an emaciated body. This is a vivid image that suggests that the bay is bleak and unattractive. We get a sense of the sounds she hears – the 'dredge at work' pounding away in the background. Bishop uses dramatic imagery to bring the birds to life – particularly the vicious man-of-war birds whose tails are 'like scissors' and 'tense' as wishbones. We also see the poet's eye for precise detail in her description of the damaged fishing boats that lie on the shore 'like torn-open, unanswered letters'. Bishop uses colour imagery very effectively – 'blue-gray shark tails' are hanging out to dry for the local restaurant. Her descriptions appeal to other senses, particularly sound. The poem ends with the rasping sound of the dredger – 'Click. Click.' digging up 'a dripping jawful of marl'. This remarkable image suggests to me how the bight keeps bringing back memories to the poet, both pleasant and unpleasant. It is an impressive way of rounding off the poem, as she associates the untidy harbour with her own life – 'awful but cheerful'.

EXAMINER'S COMMENT

A very well-focused, high-grade response, making excellent use of numerous accurate quotations. The various elements of the question are addressed and there is evidence of good personal engagement with the text. Expression throughout is also fluent and controlled.

Class/Homework Exercises

1. 'Elizabeth Bishop's poetry is both sensuous and reflective.' To what extent is this true of 'The Bight'? Support the points you make with suitable reference to the text of the poem.
2. 'In many of her poems, Elizabeth Bishop begins with vivid visual and aural details which lead to moments of intense understanding.' Discuss this statement with reference to 'The Bight'.

Summary Points

- **Descriptive details give a clear picture of the littered bay at low tide.**
- **Enduring personal upheavals and disappointments are central themes.**
- **Bishop relates to the untidy location as she reappraises her own disorderly life.**
- **Striking metaphorical language, memorable patterns of unusual imagery.**
- **Contrasting tones – pessimistic, reflective, insightful, upbeat.**

3 At the Fishhouses

Although it is a cold evening,
down by one of the fishhouses
an old man sits netting,
his net, in the gloaming almost invisible,
a dark purple-brown,
and his shuttle worn and polished.
The air smells so strong of codfish
it makes one's nose run and one's eyes water.
The five fishhouses have steeply peaked roofs
and narrow, cleated gangplanks slant up
to storerooms in the gables
for the wheelbarrows to be pushed up and down on.
All is silver: the heavy surface of the sea,
swelling slowly as if considering spilling over,
is opaque, but the silver of the benches,
the lobster pots, and masts, scattered
among the wild jagged rocks,
is of an apparent translucence
like the small old buildings with an emerald moss
growing on their shoreward walls.
The big fish tubs are completely lined
with layers of beautiful herring scales
and the wheelbarrows are similarly plastered
with creamy iridescent coats of mail,
with small iridescent flies crawling on them.
Up on the little slope behind the houses,
set in the sparse bright sprinkle of grass,
is an ancient wooden capstan,
cracked, with two long bleached handles
and some melancholy stains, like dried blood,
where the ironwork has rusted.
The old man accepts a Lucky Strike.
He was a friend of my grandfather.
We talk of the decline in the population
and of codfish and herring
while he waits for a herring boat to come in.
There are sequins on his vest and on his thumb.
He has scraped the scales, the principal beauty,
from unnumbered fish with that black old knife,
the blade of which is almost worn away.

gloaming: twilight, evening.

shuttle: tool used for weaving and mending fishing nets.

cleated: wooden projections nailed to a ladder to prevent slipping.

gangplanks: removable ramps used for boarding or leaving boats.

opaque: murky, dark, difficult to see through.

translucence: semi-transparent, light shining partially through.

iridescent: glittering, changing colours.

coats of mail: armour made of metal rings.

capstan: round machine used for winding or hauling rope.

Lucky Strike: American cigarette.

sequins: small, shiny discs used for decorating clothes.

Down at the water's edge, at the place
where they haul up the boats, up the long ramp
descending into the water, thin silver
tree trunks are laid horizontally
across the gray stones, down and down
at intervals of four or five feet.

Cold dark deep and absolutely clear,
element bearable to no mortal,
to fish and seals . . . One seal particularly
I have seen here evening after evening.
He was curious about me. He was interested in music;
like me a believer in total immersion,
so I used to sing him Baptist hymns.
I also sang 'A Mighty Fortress Is Our God.'
He stood up in the water and regarded me
steadily, moving his head a little.
Then he would disappear, then suddenly emerge
almost in the same spot, with a sort of shrug
as if it were against his better judgment.
Cold dark deep and absolutely clear,
the clear gray icy water . . . Back, behind us,
the dignified tall firs begin.
Bluish, associating with their shadows,
a million Christmas trees stand
waiting for Christmas. The water seems suspended
above the rounded gray and blue-gray stones.
I have seen it over and over, the same sea, the same,
slightly, indifferently swinging above the stones,
icily free above the stones,
above the stones and then the world.
If you should dip your hand in,
your wrist would ache immediately,
your bones would begin to ache and your hand would burn
as if the water were a transmutation of fire
that feeds on stones and burns with a dark gray flame.
If you tasted it, it would first taste bitter,
then briny, then surely burn your tongue.
It is like what we imagine knowledge to be:
dark, salt, clear, moving, utterly free,
drawn from the cold hard mouth
of the world, derived from the rocky breasts
forever, flowing and drawn, and since
our knowledge is historical, flowing, and flown.

total immersion: completely covered in liquid; a form of baptism.

associating: linking.

transmutation: changing shape.

briny: very salty.

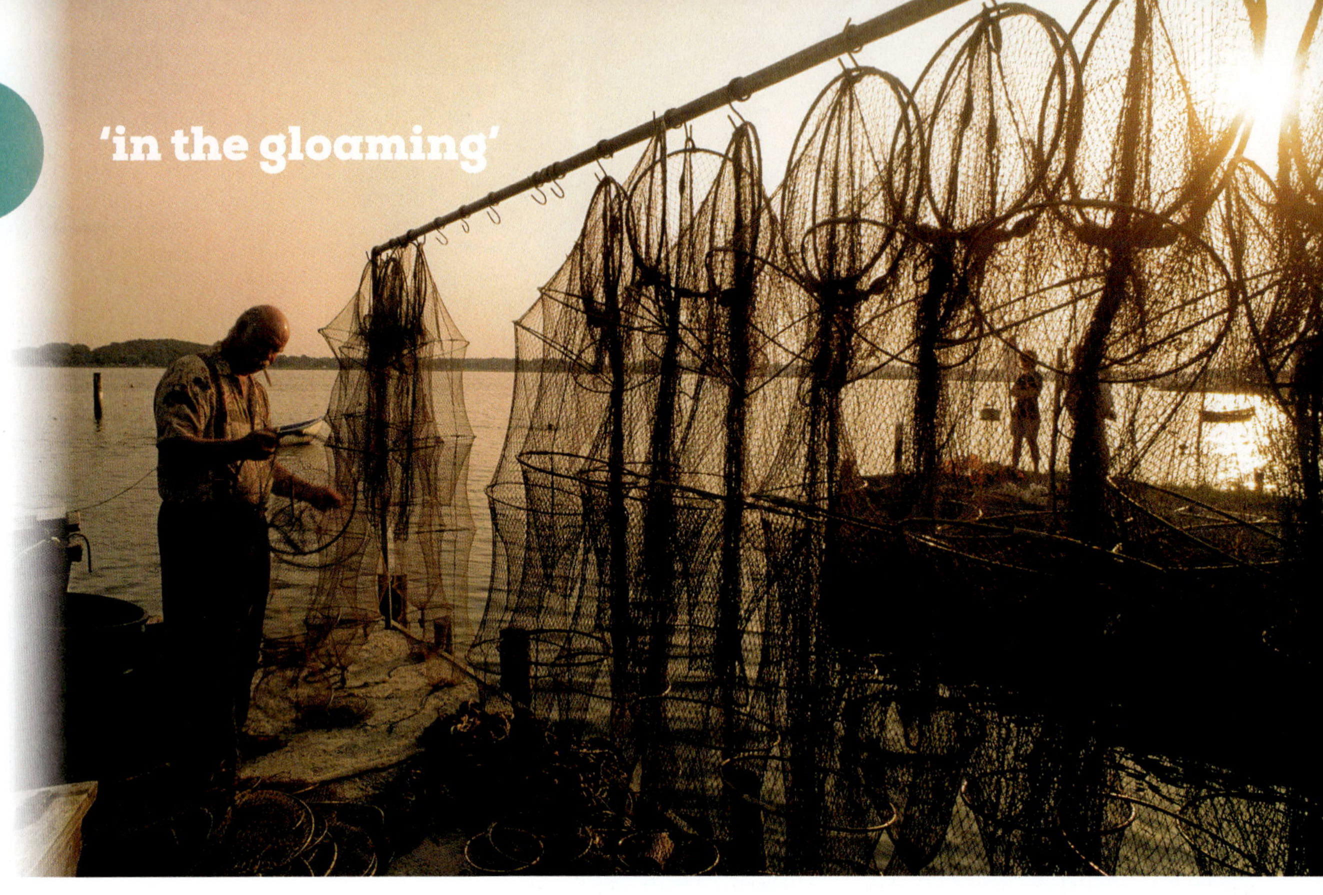

Personal Response

1. In your opinion, what role has the old fisherman in the poem? Is he a link with the past, a person in harmony with his environment or something else? Refer closely to the text in your response.
2. Bishop uses a chilling maternal image at the conclusion of the poem. What effect has this startling metaphor on the poem's tone? Support your discussion with clear references from the text.
3. Did you find 'At the Fishhouses' thought-provoking? What questions did the poem raise about the poet and her attitudes? Refer to the text in your answer.

Critical Literacy

'At the Fishhouses' comes from Elizabeth Bishop's award-winning second collection, *A Cold Spring* (1965). What Bishop sees is never quite what the rest of us see. She challenges us to look again. She gives us poetry as 'normal as sight ... as artificial as a glass eye'. An ordinary sight of an old fisherman 'in the gloaming' mending nets in Nova Scotia becomes a strange, exact hallucination examining the essence of knowledge. Bishop saw; now we see. She changes the view.

The poem's opening section (lines 1–40) gives us a **detailed, sensuous description** of a scene from Nova Scotia. Bishop has an unerring sense of place. The fishhouses are described so vividly that we can almost smell the fish ('it makes one's nose run and one's eyes water'), see the fish tubs

('completely lined/with layers of beautiful herring scales') and hear the sea ('swelling slowly as if considering spilling over'). The poet draws us right into the scene with microscopic detail, making us pore over the surface of 'benches', 'lobster pots' and 'masts'. We experience the 'apparent translucence' of the weathered, silvered wood, which matches the cold, opaque, silver sea. Musical language lends beauty to this timeless scene. The long 'o' sound in 'Although' (in the opening line) is echoed in 'cold', 'old' and 'gloaming'. All is harmony. The colours of the fisherman's net, 'dark purple-brown', become 'almost invisible'. Nothing jars. The rhythmic work is conveyed in the pulsating phrase 'for the wheelbarrows to be pushed up and down on'. Physical effort is suggested by the assonance of 'u' and 'o'. In lines 23–25, the wheelbarrows are described in minute detail ('plastered/with creamy iridescent coats of mail'). The small, circular fish scales are like the metal rings on a medieval knight's coat of armour. Bishop moves in closer to show us similarly coloured little flies, also 'iridescent', moving on the scales.

The poet's eye focuses on 'the little slope behind the houses' and an 'ancient wooden capstan'. Here is a **forlorn reminder of the tough physical work** of the past. The discarded cylinder is 'cracked' and has 'melancholy stains, like dried blood'; the ironwork has also 'rusted'. In line 32, a human connection is made when the 'old man accepts a Lucky Strike' cigarette. The personal detail ('a friend of my grandfather') gives a surface intimacy to this chilling poem. But there are hidden depths. The man is described as having 'sequins on his vest and on his thumb'. This decorative detail is more usually associated with glamorous ball gowns than an old fisherman's jersey. Does the image of the man's black knife, 'almost worn away', suggest an ebbing life?

In the poem's short second section (lines 41–46), we are at the water's edge and the repetition of 'down' draws us nearer the element of water as we note the 'long ramp/descending'. **The movement seems symbolic of Bishop's own descent into her subconscious mind**. As before, the graceful fish scales have transformed the wooden ramp into 'thin silver/tree trunks'.

The third section (lines 47–83) **changes the view**. We are now not merely looking, but seeing. We are **entering the interior**. We journey with Bishop to examine an element that is 'bearable to no mortal', yet is home 'to fish and seals'. No human can survive in the icy waters of the North Atlantic Sea: 'Cold dark deep and absolutely clear'. Another figure, a seal, appears in this bleak, surreal sequence. In this compelling episode, seal and poet are linked by a shared belief in 'total immersion'. For the seal, this is into water. Is it some form of baptism for Bishop? The poet, however, finds no comfort in religion, despite singing hymns for the seal ('A Mighty Fortress Is Our God'). Religion, like the distant fir trees, is behind her, waiting to be cut down.

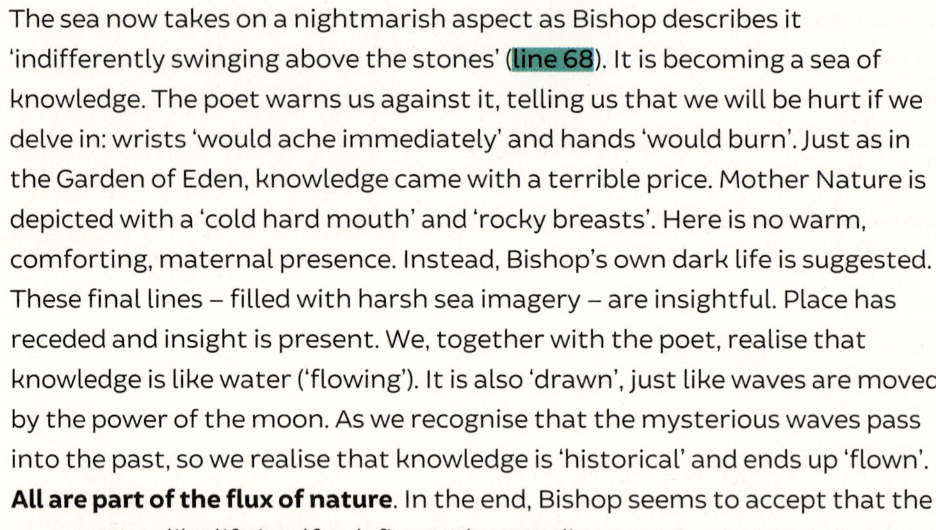

The sea now takes on a nightmarish aspect as Bishop describes it 'indifferently swinging above the stones' (line 68). It is becoming a sea of knowledge. The poet warns us against it, telling us that we will be hurt if we delve in: wrists 'would ache immediately' and hands 'would burn'. Just as in the Garden of Eden, knowledge came with a terrible price. Mother Nature is depicted with a 'cold hard mouth' and 'rocky breasts'. Here is no warm, comforting, maternal presence. Instead, Bishop's own dark life is suggested. These final lines – filled with harsh sea imagery – are insightful. Place has receded and insight is present. We, together with the poet, realise that knowledge is like water ('flowing'). It is also 'drawn', just like waves are moved by the power of the moon. As we recognise that the mysterious waves pass into the past, so we realise that knowledge is 'historical' and ends up 'flown'. **All are part of the flux of nature**. In the end, Bishop seems to accept that the vast ocean – like life itself – defies understanding.

Writing About the Poem

'Bishop gives us facts and minute details, sinking or sliding giddily off into the unknown.' Discuss this statement with reference to the poem 'At the Fishhouses'. Support your views with close reference to the text.

Sample Paragraph

I certainly agree that Elizabeth Bishop gives us 'facts and minute details'. The 'five fishhouses' are clearly described, with their characteristic 'steeply peaked roofs' and their walkways, 'narrow, cleated' to enable the wheelbarrows to move smoothly. The exchange between the poet and the old man ('a friend of my grandfather') is realistically shown, with even the brand of cigarette identified ('Lucky Strike'). We not only see the fish scales, 'coats of mail', but we also note the 'crawling' flies on the scale-splattered wheelbarrows. Then the poem turns from this detailed scrutiny of the actual to an abstract meditation. Here, the poet is 'sliding giddily off into the unknown'. From observing the icy North Atlantic Sea ('Cold dark deep and absolutely clear'), Bishop starts to explore the essence of knowledge – and even of life itself. Knowledge is not comfortable; the world is not a nice place, with its 'cold hard mouth'. Experience and knowledge come with an expensive price tag. The last two lines, for me, are dreamlike and surreal. I imagine a sea of knowledge that has been gained in the past ('historical'). This knowledge is always changing and 'flowing' as new discoveries are made.

EXAMINER'S COMMENT

A precise discussion that deals directly with both aspects of the statement: 'facts and minute details' and 'sliding ... into the unknown'. Some good personal engagement and a clear understanding of the poem are evident in this top-grade response. There is also effective use of apt quotation.

Class/Homework Exercises

1. How does Bishop's style contribute to the communication of her themes? Refer to two literary techniques used by the poet in 'At the Fishhouses' and comment on their effectiveness in each case. Refer closely to the text in your response.
2. 'Elizabeth Bishop is known for her skill at creating an authentic sense of place.' To what extent is this true of her poem, 'At the Fishhouses'? Support your answer with reference to the text.

Summary Points

- **Poet's return to her childhood home allows Bishop to reflect on life.**
- **Conversational language, descriptive details and sensuous imagery add authenticity.**
- **Assonant effects echo the deep reflective mood.**
- **Alliterative and sibilant sounds evoke a realistic sense of the sea.**
- **Surreal, nightmarish view of nature.**
- **Visionary conclusion that the ocean – like life itself – is beyond understanding.**

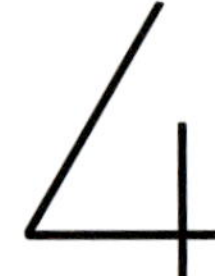

The Prodigal

Title: the biblical parable of the Prodigal Son is about a young man who wasted his inheritance on drunkenness and ended up working as a swineherd. The word 'prodigal' refers to a spendthrift or wastrel.

The brown enormous odor he lived by
was too close, with its breathing and thick hair,
for him to judge. The floor was rotten; the sty
was plastered halfway up with glass-smooth dung.
Light-lashed, self-righteous, above moving snouts,
the pigs' eyes followed him, a cheerful stare—
even to the sow that always ate her young—
till, sickening, he leaned to scratch her head.
But sometimes mornings after drinking bouts
(he hid the pints behind a two-by-four),
the sunrise glazed the barnyard mud with red;
the burning puddles seemed to reassure.
And then he thought he almost might endure
his exile yet another year or more.

But evenings the first star came to warn.
The farmer whom he worked for came at dark
to shut the cows and horses in the barn
beneath their overhanging clouds of hay,
with pitchforks, faint forked lightnings, catching light,
safe and companionable as in the Ark.
The pigs stuck out their little feet and snored.
The lantern—like the sun, going away—
laid on the mud a pacing aureole.
Carrying a bucket along a slimy board,
he felt the bats' uncertain staggering flight,
his shuddering insights, beyond his control,
touching him. But it took him a long time
finally to make his mind up to go home.

odor: odour, smell.

sty: pig-shed.

snouts: pigs' noses.

bouts: sessions.

companionable: comfortable.

the Ark: Noah's Ark. In the Bible story, Noah built a boat to save animals from a great flood.

aureole: circle of light.

'the pigs' eyes followed him'

Personal Response

1. In your opinion, is Elizabeth Bishop sympathetic to the central character in this poem? Give reasons for your answer, using close reference to the text.
2. Choose two images that you found particularly memorable in the poem. Comment briefly on the effectiveness of each.
3. Write your personal response to the poem, referring to the text in your answer.

Critical Literacy

In 'The Prodigal', published in 1951, Elizabeth Bishop returns to the well-known Bible parable of the Prodigal Son. She imagines the squalor and degradation this wayward youth endured when he was forced to live among the pigs he looked after. The poet herself had experienced depression and alcoholism in her own life and could identify with the poem's marginalised central figure. Bishop uses a double-sonnet form to trace the prodigal's struggle from wretchedness to eventual recovery.

The poem's opening lines present the repugnant living conditions of the exiled prodigal's everyday life: 'The brown enormous odor' engulfs him. The abhorrent stench and filth of the pig-sty is the only life he knows. Immersed in this animal-like state, he has lost all sense of judgement. Even the odour, 'with its breathing and thick hair', is beyond his notice. **Bishop's graphic imagery is typically precise**, describing the foul-smelling sty's shiny walls as 'plastered halfway up with glass-smooth dung'.

In lines 5–8, the 'Light-lashed' pigs are given human traits ('self-righteous', 'a cheerful stare'). The poet conveys a **disturbing sense of the young man's confused and drunken grasp on reality**. In his sub-human state, overwhelmed by nausea and isolation, he now seems almost at home among the pigs. Although he is 'sickening', he can still show odd gestures of affection towards them – 'even to the sow that always ate her young'.

Bishop delves deeper into the alcoholic's secretive world in lines 9–14. Ironically, the morning hangovers are not entirely without their compensations: 'burning puddles seemed to reassure'. Despite the ugliness and deprivation of his diminished existence, **he can occasionally recognise unexpected beauty in nature**, such as when 'the sunrise glazed the barnyard mud with red'. It is enough to give him hope: 'then he thought he almost might endure/his exile'. Emphatic broad vowel sounds add a further dimension of pathos to this line.

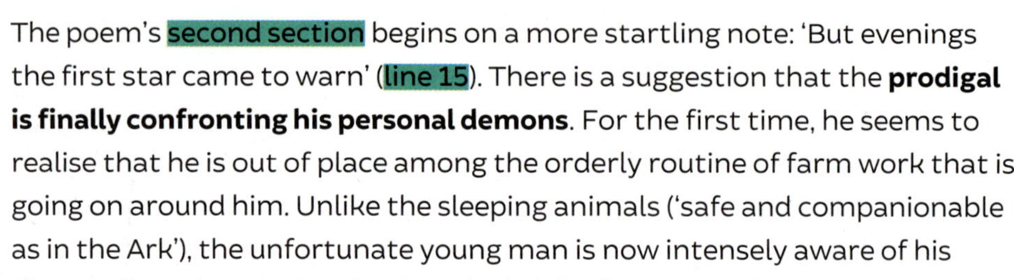

The poem's second section begins on a more startling note: 'But evenings the first star came to warn' (line 15). There is a suggestion that the **prodigal is finally confronting his personal demons**. For the first time, he seems to realise that he is out of place among the orderly routine of farm work that is going on around him. Unlike the sleeping animals ('safe and companionable as in the Ark'), the unfortunate young man is now intensely aware of his dismal alienation. He is poised on the brink of coming to his senses.

For the frustrated prodigal, a defining moment occurs when he finally disassociates himself from the snoring pigs. Yet ironically, it seems as though he almost envies their simple comfort and security 'beneath their overhanging clouds of hay'. Vivid images of routine farm life, such as 'The lantern – like the sun, going away' (line 22), take on a new symbolic significance for the unhappy exile. Is he finally considering the transience of life? Is there still a possibility of regaining his humanity? For an instant, **the young man seems to find a vague kind of hope** in the beautiful 'pacing aureole' of lamplight reflected on the mud.

A renewed vigour and purpose mark the poem's final lines. Bishop identifies exactly when the prodigal experiences 'shuddering insights'. This defining instant is symbolised by his acute awareness of 'the bats' uncertain staggering flight'. Taking his cue from nature, **he slowly accepts responsibility for his own destiny**: 'But it took him a long time/finally to make his mind up to go home'. This crucial decision to return from exile is a powerful illustration of human resilience. The poem's affirmative ending is emphasised by the importance placed on 'home' (the only unrhymed end word in the poem). Bishop's reworking of the well-known Biblical tale carries a universal message of hope, offering the prospect of recovery not just from alcoholism, but from any form of human debasement.

Writing About the Poem

'Elizabeth Bishop's mood can vary greatly – from deep depression to quiet optimism.' Discuss this statement, with particular reference to 'The Prodigal'.

Sample Paragraph

Bishop's poem, 'The Prodigal', is extremely grim. The early mood, describing the 'brown enormous odor' (American spelling) is clearly meant to capture the terrible living conditions of the young alcoholic son who had left his home, partied non-stop and fallen on hard times. The description of the outhouse is extremely repulsive. Bishop's tone is one of despair. The prodigal has fallen as low as any person, living among the pigs he looks after. The images are negative – 'rotten', 'sickening',

'barnyard mud'. The stench makes him queasy. But the mood changes when the alcoholic becomes more aware of himself and dares to hope that he will get it together and return to a decent life. Images of light and beauty suggest this – 'catching light', 'a pacing aureole'. The turning point is when the prodigal stumbles on 'shuddering insights' – which refers to his belief that he can regain his dignity and humanity if he really wants to. Although this is extremely difficult and 'took him a long time', he succeeds in the end. The last line emphasises his optimistic mood – as he decides to 'make his mind up to go home'.

EXAMINER'S COMMENT

A well-focused response that addresses the question. Effective use of accurate quotation throughout. The answer would have benefitted from some discussion on the restrained ('quiet') nature of the final optimism. Expression is weakened by slang and over-use of the word 'extremely', which leaves it below top-grade standard.

Class/Homework Exercises

1. 'Bishop's poetry often goes beyond description to reveal valuable insights about people's courage and resilience.' Discuss this statement with particular reference to 'The Prodigal'. Refer to the poem in your response.
2. 'While Elizabeth Bishop's poems can appear deceptively simple, they often contain underlying themes of universal significance.' Discuss this view with close reference to 'The Prodigal'.

Summary Points

- **Themes include the alcoholic's alienation, human determination and resilience.**
- **Odd glimpses of beauty exist in the most unexpected of circumstances.**
- **Effective descriptive details, personification and startling metaphorical language.**
- **Vivid picture of the prodigal's unhappy life and living conditions.**
- **Striking images of light and darkness.**
- **Varying tones, contrasting moods – despair and hope.**

Questions of Travel

There are too many waterfalls here; the crowded streams
hurry too rapidly down to the sea,
and the pressure of so many clouds on the mountaintops
makes them spill over the sides in soft slow-motion,
turning to waterfalls under our very eyes.
—For if those streaks, those mile-long, shiny, tearstains,
aren't waterfalls yet,
in a quick age or so, as ages go here,
they probably will be.
But if the streams and clouds keep travelling, travelling,
the mountains look like the hulls of capsized ships,
slime-hung and barnacled.

here: Brazil.

hulls: main sections of ships.

capsized: overturned in the water.

barnacled: covered with small shellfish.

Think of the long trip home.
Should we have stayed at home and thought of here?
Where should we be today?
Is it right to be watching strangers in a play
in this strangest of theatres?
What childishness is it that while there's a breath of life
in our bodies, we are determined to rush
to see the sun the other way around?
The tiniest green hummingbird in the world?
To stare at some inexplicable old stonework,
inexplicable and impenetrable,
at any view,
instantly seen and always, always delightful?
Oh, must we dream our dreams
and have them, too?
And have we room
for one more folded sunset, still quite warm?

the sun the other way around: the view of the sun in the southern hemisphere.

inexplicable: incomprehensible, mysterious.

But surely it would have been a pity
not to have seen the trees along this road,
really exaggerated in their beauty,
not to have seen them gesturing
like noble pantomimists, robed in pink.
—Not to have had to stop for gas and heard
the sad, two-noted, wooden tune

pantomimists: people taking part in a pantomime, a slapstick comedy.

ELIZABETH BISHOP

of disparate wooden clogs
carelessly clacking over
a grease-stained filling-station floor.
(In another country the clogs would all be tested.
Each pair there would have identical pitch.)
—A pity not to have heard
the other, less primitive music of the fat brown bird
who sings above the broken gasoline pump
in a bamboo church of Jesuit baroque:
three towers, five silver crosses.

—Yes, a pity not to have pondered,
blurr'dly and inconclusively,
on what connection can exist for centuries
between the crudest wooden footwear
and, careful and finicky,
the whittled fantasies of wooden cages.
—Never to have studied history in
the weak calligraphy of songbirds' cages.
—And never to have had to listen to rain
so much like politicians' speeches:
two hours of unrelenting oratory
and then a golden silence
in which the traveller takes a notebook, writes:

'Is it lack of imagination that makes us come
to imagined places, not just stay at home?
Or could Pascal have been not entirely right
about just sitting quietly in one's room?

Continent, city, country, society:
the choice is never wide and never free.
And here, or there ... No. Should we have stayed at home,
wherever that may be?'

disparate: very different, separate.

church of Jesuit baroque: ornately decorated 17th-century churches, often found in Brazil.

finicky: excessively detailed, elaborate.

whittled: carved.

fantasies: amazing creations.

calligraphy: decorative handwriting (in this case, the swirling design of the carved birdcages).

unrelenting: never stopping, endless.

Pascal: Blaise Pascal, a 17th-century mathematician and philosopher who wrote that 'man's misfortunes spring from the single cause that he is unable to stay quietly in his room'.

'the pressure of so many clouds on the mountaintops'

Personal Response

1. From your reading of lines 1–12, describe Bishop's reaction to the landscape spread before her. How does she feel about this abundance of nature? Is she delighted, unhappy, awestruck? Support your response with quotation from the text.
2. Choose two examples of repetition in the poem. Briefly explain what each example contributes to Bishop's treatment of the poem's theme.
3. Would you consider the ending of the poem conclusive or inconclusive? How does Bishop really feel about travel? Refer closely to the text in your response.

Critical Literacy

This is the title poem of Elizabeth Bishop's 1965 collection, *Questions of Travel*. Bishop herself was a great traveller, aided by an inheritance from her father. In this poem, she questions the need for travel and the desire that people have to see the world for themselves. The poet provokes the reader by posing a series of questions about the ethics of travel. She places her original observations of Brazil before us and wonders whether it would be better if we simply imagined these places while sitting at home. Finally, she challenges us to consider where our 'home' is.

The poem's opening line is an **irritable complaint** about Brazil: 'There are too many waterfalls here'. In the first section (lines 1–12), Bishop observes the luxuriant, fertile landscape spread out before her. She finds fault with the 'crowded streams' that 'hurry too rapidly' and the 'pressure of so many clouds'. The richness of the misty equatorial landscape is caught in a series of soft sibilant 's' sounds ('spill', 'sides', 'soft slow-motion'). Clouds melt into the 'mile-long, shiny, tearstains'. Everything is on the move, changing position and shape. Both Bishop and the water are 'travelling, travelling'. **Repetition emphasises this restless movement**. The circular motion suggests that neither traveller nor clouds have any real purpose or direction. An original and striking image of a mountain range ('like the hulls of capsized ships') catches our attention. The vegetation is 'slime-hung'; the outcrops of rocks are like the crustaceans of shellfish ('barnacled'). As always, the poet's interest lies in the shape and texture of the words.

A more **reflective mood is found in the poem's second section** (lines 13–29). Bishop presents readers with a **series of challenging questions** for consideration. In all, eight 'questions of travel' are posed. Should we remain 'at home' and imagine 'here'? Bishop is uneasy at the prying scrutiny of tourists 'watching strangers in a play'. She is aware that this is how people live; it is not a performance for public consumption. The emphasis here is on the 'childishness' of the tourists as they rush around, greedily consuming sights, viewing the sun from its other side in southern countries, such as

Brazil. But as far as Bishop is concerned, historic ruins and 'old stonework' do not speak to the visitor. The repetition of 'inexplicable' stresses the inaccessibility of foreign cultures. The bland, unknowing response of tourists is captured in the conversational phrase 'always delightful'. Their selfish desire for more and more experiences is vividly shown in the image of the traveller nonchalantly packing views, as if they were clothes or souvenirs being placed in a bag at the end of a trip: 'And have we room/for one more folded sunset, still quite warm?' Perhaps Bishop is asking whether any famous sight ever actually touched the traveller, or was it skimmed over in a frenzy to pack in as much as possible?

Justification for travel is the dominant theme of the third section (lines 30–59): 'But surely it would have been a pity/not to have seen'; '– A pity not to have heard'; 'a pity not to have pondered'; '– Never to have studied'; 'never to have had to listen'. The repetition of 'pity' beats out a tense rhythm as the poet seeks to condone travel. Bishop's well-known 'painterly eye' provides the evidence, as she presents a series of fresh, first-hand illustrations, e.g. the trees 'gesturing/like noble pantomimists, robed in pink'. The flowing movement of the trees, their flamboyant colour and their suggestion of Brazil's mime plays would be hard to imagine if not really experienced. The sound of this easy-going, carefree society is conveyed in the hard 'c' sound of 'carelessly clacking', which evokes the slovenly walk of local peasants. The Brazilian love of music is evident in 'clacking', a sound usually associated with the rhythmic castanets. The difference in cultures is wryly noted: 'In another country the clogs would all be tested./Each pair there would have identical pitch.' Elsewhere, all would be sanitised uniformity.

Are these the experiences the traveller would miss by not being in another country? The locals' casual attitude to functionality is shown in the contrasting images of the 'broken gasoline pump' and the intricate construction of a 'bamboo church' with 'three towers, five silver crosses'. **The spirit of the people soars in 'Jesuit baroque'**. A similar contrast is seen in wooden carving – the 'crudest wooden footwear' does not have the same importance for these free-spirited people as the 'careful and finicky ... fantasies of wooden cages' (line 51). Another unstoppable force, that of equatorial rainstorms, is likened to the endless rant of a politician bellowing out his 'unrelenting oratory'. Could any of this be imagined from afar?

Lines 58–67 begin in 'golden silence', as Bishop attempts to clarify her own thinking on the value of travel. In the final lines, she **wonders if we travel because we lack the imagination to visualise these places**. However, in the previous section, the poet has graphically shown that nothing can surpass a person **actually hearing and seeing** a place and its people. A reference is made to the 17th-century philosopher Blaise Pascal, who preferred to remain at home. The poet feels that he was not 'entirely right' about this, and by sharing her whimsical images of Brazil with us, she has led us to agree

with her. Another interesting question is posed: How free are we to go where we wish? Bishop states that the choices are 'never wide and never free'; there are always constraints on the traveller. But an emphatic 'No' tells us that this does not take away from the authenticity of the experience.

In the poem's concluding lines, Bishop returns to the question of whether or not people should stay at home. She then teases the reader with the follow-up, 'wherever that may be?' (line 67). This is a much deeper, philosophical reflection, which reverberates in our minds. **Home is a place of belonging**, from which travellers set out and to which they return. The visited countries are not secure bases; the tourist does not belong there, but is merely a visitor en route to somewhere else. In short, the traveller's role is one of an outsider – observing, but not participating. Bishop's own life experience is revealed here. Perhaps she travelled so extensively because she never felt truly at home in any single place.

Writing About the Poem

'Elizabeth Bishop's poems are not only delightful observations, but are also considered meditations on human issues.' Discuss this statement with reference to the poem 'Questions of Travel'. Support your views with close reference to the text.

Sample Paragraph

Elizabeth Bishop was a tireless traveller and in 'Questions of Travel', she presents the reader with evocative images from the misty equatorial landscape of Brazil, where clouds 'spill over the sides' of mountains 'in soft slow-motion'. The giant mountain ranges are imaginatively compared to upturned ships, and their vegetation likened to the 'slime-hung and barnacled' appearance of the bottoms of these ships. The sounds of the people intrude – disparate clogs 'carelessly clacking'. The harsh alliteration mimics the sound of wood hitting floor. No detail is too minute to escape her famous 'eye': 'the broken gasoline pump', 'the 'three towers' and 'five silver crosses' of the small bamboo church. These are Bishop's delightful observations. But the poet also addresses moral questions surrounding travel, particularly relevant in our times. What right have we to watch people's private lives, as if they were performing in public? Why are we rushing around, 'travelling, travelling'? Why do we not 'just stay at home'? These issues have a modern resonance, as we are aware nowadays of the effect of our carbon footprint on the environment. The poem concludes with a curious question on the meaning of 'home'. Bishop asks us to consider where it is ('home,/wherever that may be'). Suddenly an accepted certainty becomes as hard to define as the disintegrating clouds at the start of the poem.

EXAMINER'S COMMENT

A careful top-grade examination of both parts of the statement – the poet's 'delightful observations' and her treatment of issues – is presented by the candidate. The thoughtful approach is referenced accurately with pertinent quotations from the poem.

Class/Homework Exercises

1. Comment on the different tones in 'Questions of Travel'. Refer closely to the text in your response.
2. 'Elizabeth Bishop's poetry explores interesting aspects of home and belonging.' To what extent do you agree with this statement? Support your answer with suitable reference to 'Questions of Travel'.

Summary Points

- **The stunning Brazilian landscape prompts Bishop to reconsider the value of travel.**
- **Other themes include the natural world, home, and the creative imagination.**
- **Memorable onomatopoeic effects – assonance, alliteration, sibilance.**
- **Descriptive language, effective use of powerful metaphors and similes.**
- **Reflective, philosophical tone; inconclusive ending.**

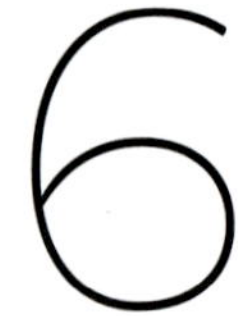

The Armadillo

For Robert Lowell

Dedication: Elizabeth Bishop dedicated 'The Armadillo' to her friend and fellow poet, Robert Lowell. An armadillo is a nocturnal burrowing creature found mainly in South America. It rolls up into a ball to protect itself from danger.

This is the time of year
when almost every night
the frail, illegal fire balloons appear.
Climbing the mountain height,

time of year: St John's Day (24 June).

fire balloons: helium-filled balloons carrying colourful paper boxes.

rising toward a saint
still honored in these parts,
the paper chambers flush and fill with light
that comes and goes, like hearts.

a saint: St John.

these parts: Rio de Janeiro, Brazil.

chambers: hollow boxes.

Once up against the sky it's hard
to tell them from the stars—
planets, that is—the tinted ones:
Venus going down, or Mars,

tinted: shaded.

or the pale green one. With a wind,
they flare and falter, wobble and toss;
but if it's still they steer between
the kite sticks of the Southern Cross,

the pale green one: probably the planet Uranus.

kite sticks of the Southern Cross: cross-shaped constellation of stars.

receding, dwindling, solemnly
and steadily forsaking us,
or, in the downdraft from a peak,
suddenly turning dangerous.

Last night another big one fell.
It splattered like an egg of fire
against the cliff behind the house.
The flame ran down. We saw the pair

of owls who nest there flying up
and up, their whirling black-and-white
stained bright pink underneath, until
they shrieked up out of sight.

The ancient owls' nest must have burned.
Hastily, all alone,
a glistening armadillo left the scene,
rose-flecked, head down, tail down,

and then a baby rabbit jumped out,
short-eared, to our surprise.
So soft! – a handful of intangible ash
with fixed, ignited eyes.

Too pretty, dreamlike mimicry!
O falling fire and piercing cry
and panic, and a weak mailed fist
clenched ignorant against the sky!

intangible: flimsy, insubstantial.

ignited: lit up.

mimicry: imitation.

weak mailed fist: the animal's bony armour (defenceless against fire).

'chambers flush and fill with light'

Personal Response

1. Based on your reading of the first four stanzas, how does the poet present the fire balloons? Are they mysterious, beautiful, threatening? Refer to the text in your answer.
2. Comment on Bishop's use of interesting verbs in the poem.
3. In your view, is this an optimistic or pessimistic poem? Give reasons for your response.

Critical Literacy

'The Armadillo' describes St John's Day (24 June) in Brazil, where Elizabeth Bishop lived for more than 15 years. On this annual feast day, local people would celebrate by lighting fire balloons and releasing them into the night sky. Although this custom was illegal – because of the fire hazard – it still occurred widely.

The opening lines introduce us to an exotic, night-time scene. The sense of drama and excitement is palpable as Bishop observes these 'illegal' balloons 'rising toward a saint'. They are also presented as fragile ('frail') but beautiful: 'the paper chambers flush and fill with light'. There is something magical and majestic about their ascent towards the heavens. **The language is simple and conversational**, reflecting the religious faith of the local people. Bishop compares the flickering light of the 'paper chambers' to 'hearts', perhaps suggesting the unpredictability of human feelings and even life itself.

Lines 9–20 associate the drifting balloons with distant planets, adding to their romantic air of mystery. The unsteady rhythm and alliterative description ('With a wind,/they flare and falter') suggest an irregular, buoyant movement. The poet is **increasingly intrigued by the fire balloons** as they 'wobble' out of sight. She notes that they sometimes 'steer between' the stars. Although she appears to be disappointed that the balloons are 'steadily forsaking us', she also worries about them 'suddenly turning dangerous' as a result of downdrafts buffeting and igniting them.

The tone changes dramatically in line 21, as Bishop recalls the destructive force of one exploding balloon that fell to earth near her house: 'It splattered like an egg of fire'. This characteristically stirring simile and the onomatopoeic verb highlight the sense of unexpected destruction. The shock is immediately felt by humans and animals alike. Terrified owls – desperate to escape the descending flames – 'shrieked up out of sight' (line 28). Contrasting **colour images emphasise the garish confusion**: the 'whirling black-and-white' bodies of the owls are 'stained bright pink underneath'.

The poet suddenly notices 'a glistening armadillo', isolated and alarmed. Determined to escape the fire, it scurries away: 'rose-flecked, head down, tail down' (line 32). Amid the chaos, a baby rabbit 'jumped out', its urgent movement reflecting the lethal atmosphere. Bishop expresses her intense shock at seeing its burnt ears: 'So soft! – a handful of intangible ash'. **This graphic metaphor emphasises the animal's weakness and suffering**. Its 'fixed, ignited eyes' reflect the fire falling from the sky.

Bishop's emotive voice emerges forcefully in the poem's closing lines. She rejects her earlier description of the elegant fire balloons as being 'Too pretty'. Having witnessed the horrifying reality of the tormented animals, she castigates all her earlier romantic notions about the colourful festivities. Such thoughts are suddenly seen as 'dreamlike mimicry'. **The final image of the trapped armadillo is highly dramatic**. Its 'piercing cry' is harrowing. Bishop imagines the terrified creature in human terms ('a weak mailed fist'). Although the armadillo's helpless body is 'clenched ignorant against the sky', it is unlikely that its coat of armour will save it from fire. The irony of this small creature's last futile act is pitiful. Despite its brave defiance, the armadillo is doomed.

Some critics have commented on the **symbolism** in the poem, seeing the victimised creatures as symbols for powerless and marginalised people everywhere. It has been said that the careless fire balloons signify warfare, mindless violence and ignorant destruction. Is Bishop indicating that people's fate is beyond their control? It has also been suggested that the fire balloons signify love ('that comes and goes, like hearts') or even the creative impulse itself – beautiful, elusive and sometimes tragic. As with all poems, readers must decide for themselves.

Writing About the Poem

Describe the tone in 'The Armadillo'. Does it change during the course of the poem? Refer to the text in your answer.

Sample Paragraph

The opening section of 'The Armadillo' is dramatic and filled with anticipation. Bishop sets the night-time scene during the noisy Brazilian festival to honour St John. 'This is the time of year' suggests a special occasion. The tone is celebratory and excited as the local community release countless 'illegal fire balloons' which light up the skies. The poet seems in awe of the wonderful spectacle, watching the 'paper chambers flush and fill with light'. The tone changes slightly to sadness as she watches the colourful

EXAMINER'S COMMENT

A focused top-grade response that traces the development of tone in the poem. There is a real sense of well-informed engagement with the text. Short, accurate quotations are used effectively to illustrate the different changes in tone. The expression is clear, varied and controlled throughout.

balloons rise and disappear among the stars, 'steadily forsaking us'. A more dramatic transformation occurs when the exploding balloons start 'turning dangerous'. Due to careless human activity, fire falls from the air, causing mayhem for the vulnerable animals below. Terrified owls 'shrieked', a young rabbit is burnt to 'intangible ash' and the armadillo is reduced to 'panic'. Bishop's personal voice is filled with anger and disgust as she rages against the 'falling fire'. The italics and exclamation marks in the final stanza highlight her frustrated tone as she identifies with the unfortunate armadillo whose 'weak mailed fist/clenched ignorant against the sky' represents a useless gesture of resistance.

Class/Homework Exercises

1. 'In reading the poetry of Elizabeth Bishop, readers can discover moments of quiet reflection and shocking truth.' Discuss this statement in relation to 'The Armadillo', supporting the points you make with reference to the poem.
2. 'In her poems, Elizabeth Bishop often connects the twin themes of cruelty and vulnerability.' Discuss this view with suitable reference to 'The Armadillo'.

Summary Points

- **Both humans and animals are victims of man's thoughtless actions.**
- **Precise sense of place, detailed description of exotic atmospheres and experiences.**
- **Reflective tone reveals the poet's personal feelings and attitudes.**
- **Lack of judgemental comment allow us to find our own interpretation.**
- **Rich visual imagery, striking metaphors, onomatopoeia and end rhyme.**

Sestina

ELIZABETH BISHOP

September rain falls on the house.
In the failing light, the old grandmother
sits in the kitchen with the child
beside the Little Marvel Stove,
reading the jokes from the almanac,
laughing and talking to hide her tears.

She thinks that her equinoctial tears
and the rain that beats on the roof of the house
were both foretold by the almanac,
but only known to a grandmother.
The iron kettle sings on the stove.
She cuts some bread and says to the child,

It's time for tea now; but the child
is watching the teakettle's small hard tears
dance like mad on the hot black stove,
the way the rain must dance on the house.
Tidying up, the old grandmother
hangs up the clever almanac

on its string. Birdlike, the almanac
hovers half open above the child,
hovers above the old grandmother
and her teacup full of dark brown tears.
She shivers and says she thinks the house
feels chilly, and puts more wood in the stove.

It was to be, says the Marvel Stove.
I know what I know, says the almanac.
With crayons the child draws a rigid house
and a winding pathway. Then the child
puts in a man with buttons like tears
and shows it proudly to the grandmother.

But secretly, while the grandmother
busies herself about the stove,
the little moons fall down like tears
from between the pages of the almanac
into the flower bed the child
has carefully placed in the front of the house.

Title: a sestina is a traditional poetic form of six six-line stanzas followed by a final stanza of three lines. In Bishop's 'Sestina', the same six words recur at the ends of lines in each stanza: tears, almanac, stove, grandmother, house and child. The final three-line stanza contains all six words.

the Little Marvel Stove: a heater or cooker that burns wood or coal.

almanac: calendar giving important dates, information and predictions.

equinoctial: the time when day and night are of equal length (22 September, 20 March approximately).

Time to plant tears, says the almanac.
The grandmother sings to the marvellous stove
and the child draws another inscrutable house.

inscrutable: secret; impossible to understand or interpret.

'the child draws a rigid house'

Personal Response

1. Describe the atmosphere in the house. Is it happy, unhappy, relaxed, secretive? Support your response with quotation from the text.
2. Choose one image that you find particularly interesting and effective in the poem. Briefly explain your choice.
3. Write your personal response to the poem, supporting your views with reference to the text.

Critical Literacy

'Sestina' was written between 1960 and 1965. For Elizabeth Bishop, the creative act of writing brought shape and order to experience. This poem is autobiographical, as it tells of a home without a mother or father. It is one of Bishop's first poems about her childhood and she was in her fifties, living in Brazil, when she wrote it. The complicated, restrictive structure of the poem can be seen as the poet's attempt to put order on her early childhood trauma.

The poem's opening stanza paints a domestic scene, which at first seems cosy and secure. The child and her grandmother sit in the evening light beside a stove. They are reading 'jokes from the almanac' and 'laughing and talking'. However, on closer observation, sadness is layered onto the scene with certain details: 'September rain', 'failing light' and the old grandmother hiding 'her tears'. Bishop adopts the point of view of adult reminiscence. She recollects; she is an observer of her own childhood and the poem's **tone is disturbing and challenging**. We are introduced to someone who is concealing deeply rooted feelings of sorrow. The six end-words echo alarmingly throughout the poem. This is a house full of tears with a grandmother and child together, alone.

In stanza two the grandmother believes that her autumn tears and the rain were 'foretold by the almanac'. There is a sense of inevitability and tired resignation in the opening lines. But normality enters: 'The iron kettle sings on the stove'. Homely domesticity is seen when the grandmother cuts some bread and says to the child: 'It's time for tea now'. **Bishop suddenly switches from being an observer to being an interpreter**, as she lets the reader see the workings of the child's mind in the third stanza: 'but the child/is watching the teakettle's small hard tears'. The child interprets sorrow everywhere; even droplets of steam from a kettle are transformed into the unwept tears of the grandmother. The phrase 'dance like mad' strikes a poignant note as we remember that Bishop's own mother was committed to a psychiatric hospital when Bishop was just five years old; they never met again. A cartoon-like image of the almanac ends this stanza. We view it through the child's eyes, as 'the clever almanac'.

Stanza four focuses closely on the almanac. It is a **sinister presence**, personified as a bird of ill-omen: 'Birdlike' it hovers, suspended 'half open'. This mood of misgiving is heightened when we are told that the grandmother's cup is not full of tea, but of 'dark brown tears'. However, normality asserts itself again – the grandmother 'shivers' and puts wood on the fire.

Stanza five opens with the eerie personification of the Marvel Stove and the almanac. A **sense of inevitability** ('It was to be') and hidden secrets ('I know what I know') is absorbed by the child. Just as the older Bishop puts order on her traumatic childhood experiences by arranging them into the tightly knit form of the sestina, the child in the poem attempts to order her experiences by drawing houses. But the house is tense, 'rigid', inflexible. The unhappy history of this childhood cannot be changed; the situation was as it was. This house can only be reached by a 'winding pathway'. Does this echo Bishop's later travels, as she searches for home? The sadness of Bishop's situation focuses on the drawing now, as the child sketches a man with 'buttons like tears'.

In stanza six, the tears continue to fall, now 'into the flower bed' in the child's drawing. **Fantasy and reality are mixed** in the innocent perception of the child, who feels but does not understand. The final three lines contain all six key words as the almanac instructs that it is 'Time to plant tears'. Is the time for regret over? Is the child planting tears that will be wept in the future? Should the grandmother and child be shedding tears now? The 'child draws another inscrutable house'. The secrecy continues. Nothing is as it seems. The future looks chilling.

Writing About the Poem

Elizabeth Bishop's poetry is an emotional journey. To what extent do you agree with this? Support your views with close reference to 'Sestina'.

Sample Paragraph

I agree that the reader goes on an emotional journey with Bishop in the poem 'Sestina' as Bishop struggles to come to terms with her traumatic childhood. Our hearts go out to the small, motherless and fatherless little girl, caught in an almost nightmare scenario, as the almanac hangs 'Birdlike' above her. The child senses, but does not comprehend the awful tragedy in the house. Bishop allows us to see the workings of the little mind as the child blends reality and fantasy, as stoves and books talk. Everything seems to know except the child. The chaotic experiences of Bishop's childhood are strictly contained in the formal structure of the sestina, with six stanzas containing six lines ending with the same six end-words: house, grandmother, child, stove, almanac and tears. This mirrors the 'rigid' house of the little girl's drawings. Both the older and the younger Bishop are trying desperately to put order and control on this overwhelming situation. The reader experiences the poignancy through the details of the 'failing light', 'the rain that beats on the roof of the house' and the teacup 'full of dark brown tears'. Finally, the reader, like Bishop, is not left comforted, but is faced with one last mystery as yet another 'inscrutable' house is drawn.

EXAMINER'S COMMENT

A top-grade, insightful answer focusing on the emotional journey undertaken by both the poet and reader. There is a clear sense of engagement with the poem. Quotations are used effectively throughout.

Class/Homework Exercises

1. Some critics have said that 'Sestina' is a sentimental poem. Do you agree with this? Support your views with close reference to the poem.
2. 'Elizabeth Bishop's most compelling poems often address painful memories of the poet's childhood.' To what extent is this true of her poem, 'Sestina'? Support your answer with reference to the text.

Summary Points

- **Adult poet reflects on troubled childhood and the desire for security of home.**
- **Disturbing sinister tone, sense of inevitability.**
- **Ominous personification and surreal imagery blur reality.**
- **Tear imagery patterns emphasise sorrow-filled scene.**
- **Strict form of sestina contains and controls overflowing emotions.**
- **Vivid imagery, powerful metaphorical language.**

ELIZABETH BISHOP

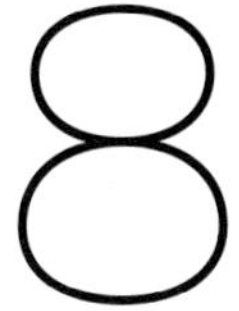

First Death in Nova Scotia

In the cold, cold parlor
my mother laid out Arthur
beneath the chromographs:
Edward, Prince of Wales,
with Princess Alexandra,
and King George with Queen Mary.
Below them on the table
stood a stuffed loon
shot and stuffed by Uncle
Arthur, Arthur's father.

Since Uncle Arthur fired
a bullet into him,
he hadn't said a word.
He kept his own counsel
on his white, frozen lake,
the marble-topped table.
His breast was deep and white,
cold and caressable;
his eyes were red glass,
much to be desired.

'Come,' said my mother,
'Come and say good-bye
to your little cousin Arthur.'
I was lifted up and given
one lily of the valley
to put in Arthur's hand.
Arthur's coffin was
a little frosted cake,
and the red-eyed loon eyed it
from his white, frozen lake.

Arthur was very small.
He was all white, like a doll
that hadn't been painted yet.
Jack Frost had started to paint him
the way he always painted

parlor: room set aside for entertaining guests.

chromographs: coloured copies of pictures.
Edward: British Royal (1841–1910).
Alexandra: Edward's wife.

King George: King George V (1865–1936).
Queen Mary: wife of King George V (1867–1953).
loon: great crested grebe, an aquatic diving bird.

counsel: opinion.

frosted: iced.

the Maple Leaf (Forever).
He had just begun on his hair,
a few red strokes, and then
Jack Frost had dropped the brush
and left him white, forever.

The gracious royal couples
were warm in red and ermine;
their feet were well wrapped up
in the ladies' ermine trains.
They invited Arthur to be
the smallest page at court.
But how could Arthur go,
clutching his tiny lily,
with his eyes shut up so tight
and the roads deep in snow?

the Maple Leaf: Canadian national emblem.

ermine: white fur.

page: boy attendant.

'the roads deep in snow'

Personal Response

1. With reference to lines 1–20 of the poem, describe the mood and atmosphere in the 'parlor'.
2. The poet uses several comparisons in this poem. Select one that you found particularly interesting and comment on its effectiveness.
3. Write your personal response to this poem, referring to the text in your answer.

Critical Literacy

'First Death in Nova Scotia' was published when Elizabeth Bishop was in her early fifties. Written entirely in the past tense, it is an extraordinarily vivid memory of a disturbing experience. In the poem, Bishop's young narrator recounts the circumstances of an even younger cousin's death.

From the outset, we visualise Cousin Arthur's wake through a child's eyes. Characteristically, Bishop sets the scene in stanza one using **carefully chosen** descriptive details. It is winter in Nova Scotia. The dead child has been laid out in a 'cold, cold parlor'. Above the coffin are old photographs of two deceased royal couples. Fragmented memories of unfamiliar objects add to the dreamlike atmosphere. A stuffed loon sits on the marble-topped table. The young girl is suddenly confronted with strange signs of life and death. In her confusion, she takes refuge in the unfamiliar objects she sees around her.

The dead boy and the 'dead' room soon become real for the reader, as does the dilemma faced by the **living child, who seems increasingly unsettled**. Stanza two focuses on the young narrator's fixation with the stuffed bird. By thinking hard about the death of this 'cold and caressable' loon, she is trying to find a possible explanation for death. She is fascinated by the loon – perhaps an escape mechanism from the unfamiliar atmosphere in the parlour. In any case, the bird – with its spellbinding 'red glass' eyes – might be less threatening than the dead body in the casket. Suddenly, somewhere in the child's imagination, Cousin Arthur and the personified bird become closely associated. Both share an impenetrably cold stillness, suggested by the 'marble-topped table', which is compared to a 'white, frozen lake'.

In stanza three the child's mother lifts her up to the coffin so that she can place a lily of the valley in the dead boy's hand. Her mother's insistent invitation ('Come and say good-bye') is chillingly remote. We sense the young girl's vulnerability ('I was lifted up') as she is forced to place the flower in Arthur's hand. In a poignantly childlike image, she compares her cousin's white coffin to 'a little frosted cake'. **The mood turns progressively surreal** when the apprehensive narrator imagines the stuffed bird as a predator ('the red-eyed loon eyed it'). As always, Bishop's imagery is direct, brisk and to the point.

Bishop continues to explore childhood innocence in stanza four. Using the simplest of language, the child narrator describes her dead cousin: 'He was all white, like a doll'. In a renewed burst of imagination, she creates her own 'story' to explain what has happened to Arthur. His death must be caused by the winter frost that 'paints' the autumn leaves, including the familiar maple leaf. This thought immediately brings to mind the Canadian song 'The Maple Leaf Forever'. To the child, it seems that Jack Frost started to paint Arthur, but 'dropped the brush/and left him white, forever'. This creative **stream of consciousness highlights the child's efforts to make sense of death's mysterious reality**.

The imagery of childhood fairytales continues in stanza five when the narrator pictures Arthur in the company of the royal families whose pictures hang on the parlour walls. He is now 'the smallest page at court'. For the first time, the cold has disappeared and the royals are 'warm in red and ermine'. This fantasy, however, is short-lived. Still shaken by the strangeness of the occasion, the young narrator questions how this could have happened – especially as Arthur could not travel anywhere 'with his eyes shut up so tight/and the roads deep in snow'. The poem's final, tender image reflects both the child's naivety and a genuine concern for her cousin. Ironically, all around are symbols of immortality – the heavenly royal images of Arthur's entrance into a new, more glorious life. But the narrator's **enduring uncertainty remains central to the poem**.

Writing About the Poem

'The unknowable nature of life and death is a central concern of Elizabeth Bishop's poetry.' Discuss this statement with reference to 'First Death in Nova Scotia'. Support the points you make by referring to the poem.

Sample Paragraph

In several poems I have studied, it's clear that Elizabeth Bishop addresses life's mysteries. Sometimes she does this through the eyes of a child, as in 'First Death in Nova Scotia'. The poem describes her first experience of a death and how she struggled to understand it. It is an elegy for her young cousin, Arthur, and Bishop's memories of his funeral are extraordinarily clear. Everything about it confuses her. The formal, domestic setting is uninviting – a 'cold, cold parlor' has strange chromographs of the British Royal Family on the walls and a stuffed loon bird on the marble table. As a young girl, Bishop recalls being forced to place a lily in her dead cousin's cold hand. These objects add to her

EXAMINER'S COMMENT

A focused and sustained response, showing good engagement with the text. Starting with a succinct overview, the paragraph traces the progress of thought through the poem, using apt and accurate quotations effectively. Clear expression and a convincing personal approach also contribute to this top-grade response.

insecurity. Nothing is explained to her and she escapes into her own imaginary world, comparing Arthur's casket to 'a little frosted cake'. She tries to tell herself that 'Jack Frost' is responsible for leaving Arthur 'white forever'. In the last verse, she imagines her dead cousin in an afterlife – not in heaven, but in a magical royal castle, 'the smallest page at court'. However, the young Elizabeth is caught between make-believe and reason. Her final thoughts challenge her own fantasy about life after death. Common sense tells her that Arthur, 'with his eyes shut up so tight', could not go out into 'roads deep in snow'. I thought Bishop really captured the uncertainty of a young child's mind in this poem. I also got the impression that she was making the point that life and death can never be fully understood, no matter what age a person is.

Class/Homework Exercises

1. In your opinion, does 'First Death in Nova Scotia' present a realistic view of death? Support your argument with reference to the text of the poem.
2. 'Elizabeth Bishop often makes effective use of simple language and childlike images to convey disturbing childhood experiences.' Discuss this statement with close reference to 'First Death in Nova Scotia'.

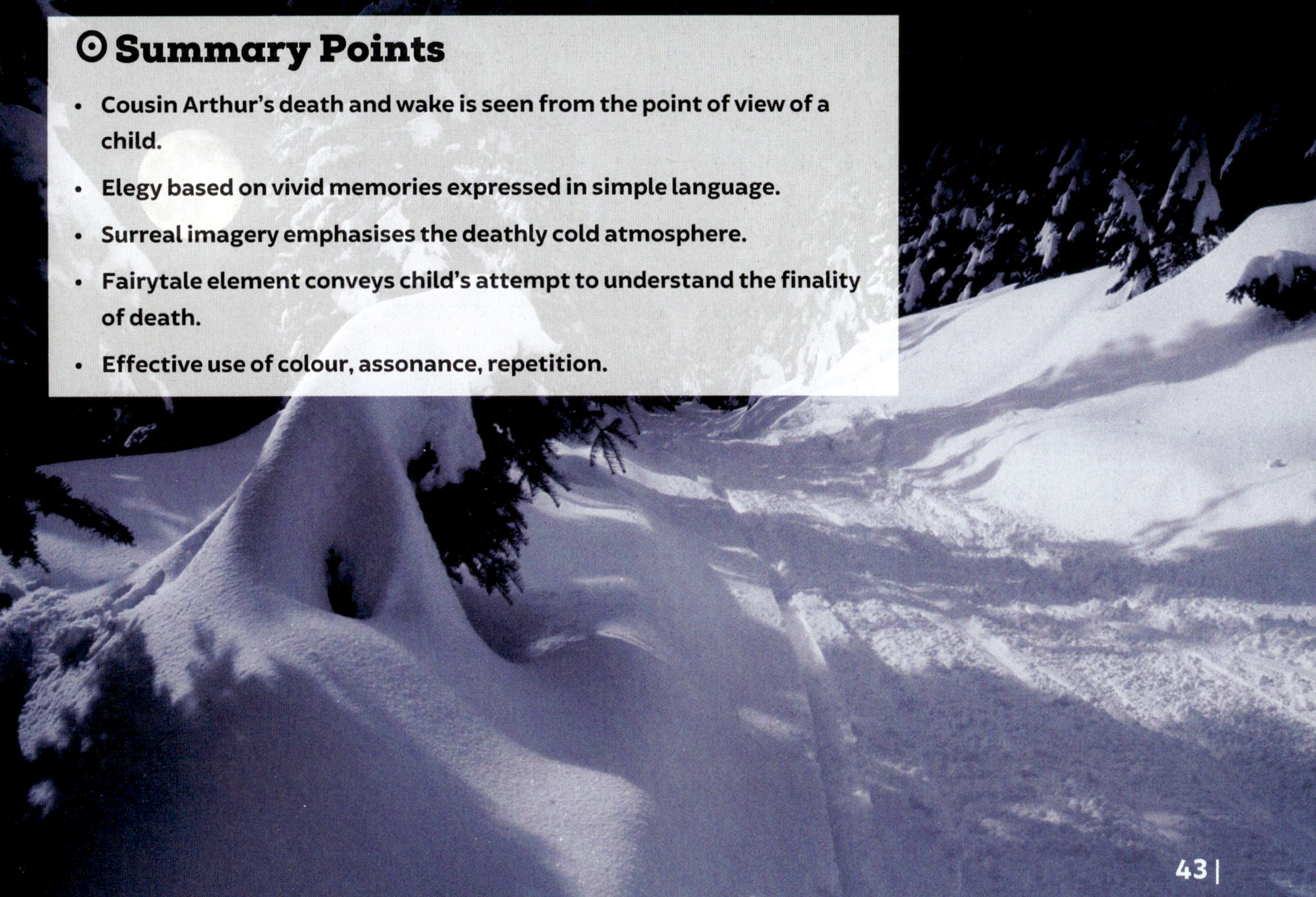

Summary Points

- **Cousin Arthur's death and wake is seen from the point of view of a child.**
- **Elegy based on vivid memories expressed in simple language.**
- **Surreal imagery emphasises the deathly cold atmosphere.**
- **Fairytale element conveys child's attempt to understand the finality of death.**
- **Effective use of colour, assonance, repetition.**

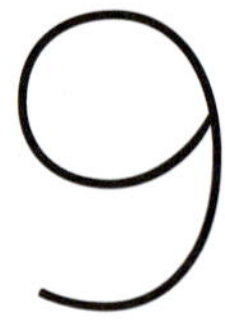

Filling Station

Oh, but it is dirty!
– this little filling station,
oil-soaked, oil-permeated
to a disturbing, over-all
black translucency.
Be careful with that match!

oil-permeated: soaked through with oil.

translucency: shine, glow.

Father wears a dirty,
oil-soaked monkey suit
that cuts him under the arms,
and several quick and saucy
and greasy sons assist him
(it's a family filling station),
all quite thoroughly dirty.

monkey suit: dungarees; all-in-one working clothes.

saucy: cheeky, insolent.

Do they live in the station?
It has a cement porch
behind the pumps, and on it
a set of crushed and grease-
impregnated wickerwork;
on the wicker sofa
a dirty dog, quite comfy.

impregnated: saturated.

Some comic books provide
the only note of color –
of certain color. They lie
upon a big dim doily
draping a taboret
(part of the set), beside
a big hirsute begonia.

doily: ornamental napkin.

taboret: drum-shaped low seat; a stool.

hirsute: hairy.

begonia: house plant with large multicoloured leaves.

Why the extraneous plant?
Why the taboret?
Why, oh why, the doily?
(Embroidered in daisy stitch
with marguerites, I think,
and heavy with gray crochet.)

extraneous: unnecessary, inappropriate.

daisy stitch: stitch pattern used in embroidery.

marguerites: daisies.

crochet: intricate knitting patterns.

Somebody embroidered the doily.
Somebody waters the plant,
or oils it, maybe. Somebody
arranges the rows of cans
so that they softly say:
ESSO–SO–SO–SO
to high-strung automobiles.
Somebody loves us all.

ESSO-SO-SO: Esso is a brand of oil; reference to the careful arrangement of oil cans.

Personal Response

1. In your opinion, how does Bishop make the opening two stanzas of this poem dynamic and interesting? Comment on her use of punctuation, direct speech and compound words, which draw us into the world of the poem. Support your response with quotation from the text.
2. Trace the development of the poet's attitude to the filling station throughout the poem. Does it change from being critical and patronising to being more positive? Illustrate your answer with close reference to the text.
3. Comment on the effectiveness of Bishop's use of repetition in lines 34–41. Refer to the text in your response.

Critical Literacy

Elizabeth Bishop was strongly influenced by a poetic movement called imagism, which was concerned with the accurate description of a particular thing. In this poem, she gives us an iconic description of a familiar American scene, the small-town gas station. Bishop found the new culture in 1960s California bewildering and it is noteworthy that the voice in this poem is that of an outsider trying to make sense of what is observed.

'it's a family filling station'

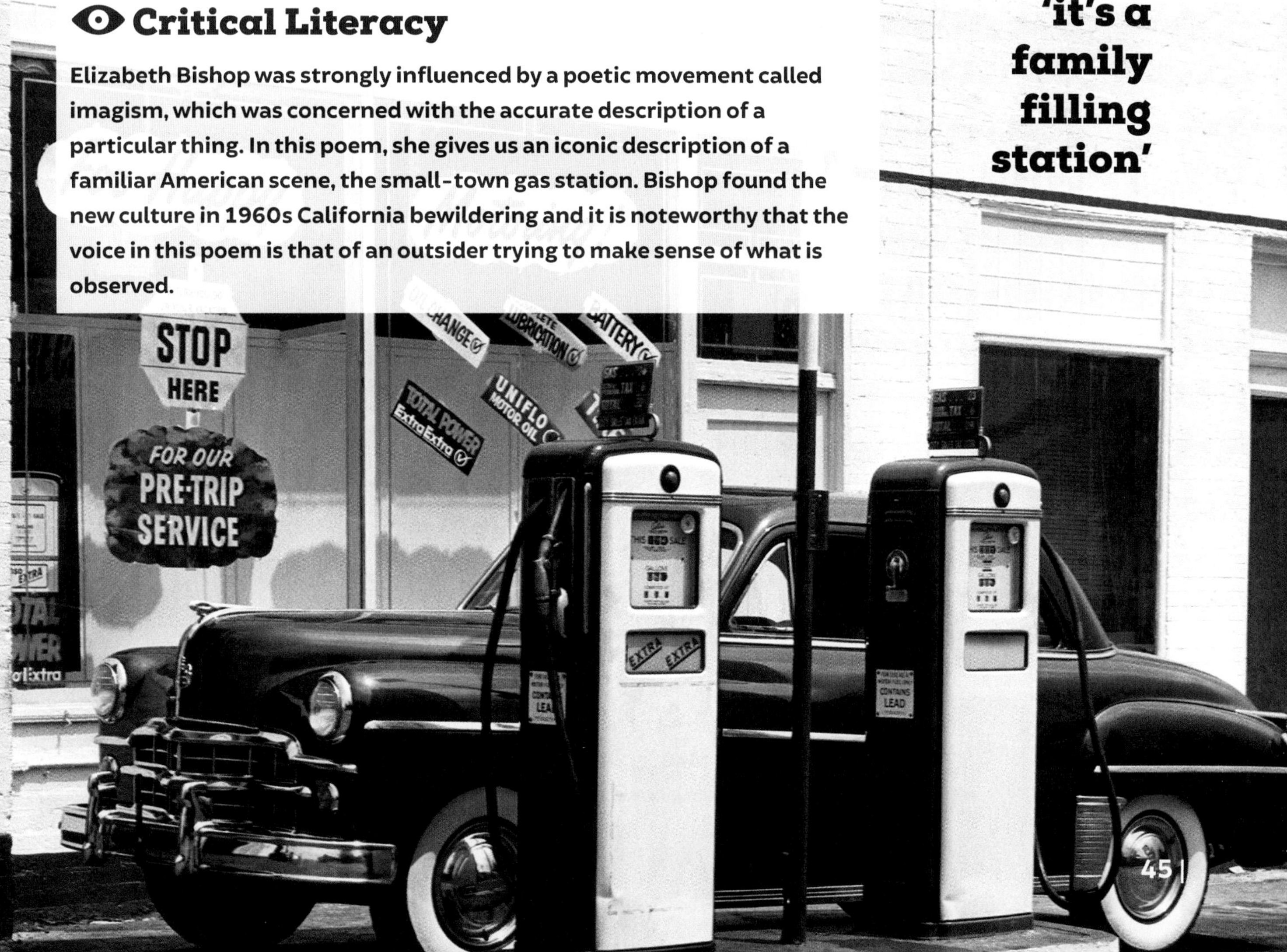

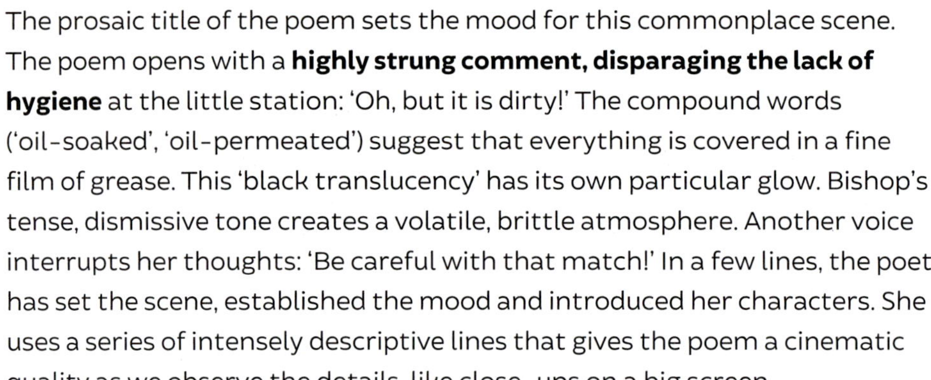

The prosaic title of the poem sets the mood for this commonplace scene. The poem opens with a **highly strung comment, disparaging the lack of hygiene** at the little station: 'Oh, but it is dirty!' The compound words ('oil-soaked', 'oil-permeated') suggest that everything is covered in a fine film of grease. This 'black translucency' has its own particular glow. Bishop's tense, dismissive tone creates a volatile, brittle atmosphere. Another voice interrupts her thoughts: 'Be careful with that match!' In a few lines, the poet has set the scene, established the mood and introduced her characters. She uses a series of intensely descriptive lines that gives the poem a cinematic quality as we observe the details, like close-ups on a big screen.

The busy little station is captured in the second stanza through the poet's critical observations as she watches the family go about their business. The father is wearing a 'dirty,/oil-soaked monkey suit' that is too small for him ('cuts him under the arms'). The sons are described using alliteration of the letter 's', which suggests their fluid movements as well as their oily appearance ('several quick and saucy/and greasy sons assist'). Like the poet, we also become fascinated by this unremarkable spot. Bishop's critical tone becomes more strident as she comments on the sons' insolence ('saucy') and their lack of hygiene ('all quite thoroughly dirty'). **We can hear the contempt in her voice**.

The third stanza questions, in a disbelieving tone, whether anyone could actually reside in such an awful place: 'Do they live in the station?' The poet's eye seems to pan around her surroundings **like a camera, picking up on small details** as she tries to piece the scene into some kind of order. She lingers on the porch and its set of 'crushed and grease-/impregnated wickerwork'. Her disdain is obvious to the reader. The dog is described as a 'dirty dog' – it is almost as if it, too, has been smeared in oil. The repetition of the 'd' sound emphasises the unkempt appearance of everything. Then, suddenly, the poem turns on the homely word 'comfy'. The poet is surprised to note that the dog is quite content here. We are reminded that because of the harrowing circumstances of her own childhood, Bishop never fully knew what home was; we are left wondering if she longed to be 'comfy' too.

In stanzas four and five, she begins to notice evidence of a woman's hand in this place, particularly 'a big dim doily' on the 'taboret'. She notes the colourful 'comic books' and her eye is caught by the incongruous sight of 'a big hirsute begonia'. Even the plant has masculine qualities, being big and hairy. Bishop is observing the extraordinary in the ordinary; **in the most unlikely places, there is beauty and love**. We understand her bemusement as she reflects, almost in exasperation: 'Why, oh why, the doily?' We, like the narrator, have to reassess our initial view of this cluttered gas station. On closer observation, there is care and attention to detail, including artistic embroidery. We are brought up close to examine this marvellous 'daisy stitch'. The critical, conversational tone of the poem clearly belongs to

someone who is an observer, someone who does not belong. Is this the role Bishop was forced to adopt in her own life?

The poet's disturbed tone gives way in the final stanzas to one of comfort. The lines whisper softly with sibilant 's' sounds. 'Somebody' cares for things, arranging the cans in order 'so that they softly say: ESSO–SO–SO–SO'. Bishop commented that 'so–so–so' was a phrase used to calm highly strung horses. It is used here to calm herself, just as the oil in the cans is used to make the engines of 'high-strung automobiles' run smoothly. The tone relaxes and a touch of humour creeps in: she notes that 'Somebody waters the plant,/or oils it, maybe'. The use of repetition is also soothing as we, like Bishop, come to realise that there is 'Somebody' who cares. The **poem concludes on a quiet note of assurance that everybody gets love from somewhere: 'Somebody loves us all'**. This is a particularly poignant ending when we consider that Elizabeth Bishop's parents were both absent from her childhood.

Writing About the Poem

'Elizabeth Bishop's poems are often described as deceptively casual.' Discuss this view of the poet's work, with particular reference to 'Filling Station'. Support your response with close reference to the text.

Sample Paragraph

'Filling Station' deals with a central concern of all human beings, the need to feel cared for, the need to belong. Instead of a heavy tone, Bishop adopts a deceptively casual tone in this poem from the start, with its conversational opening: 'Oh, but it is dirty!' However, the carefully selected phrases ('oil-soaked, oil-permeated') show a carefully crafted poem. The use of repetition of 'why' to suggest the increasing puzzlement of the poet as she tries to make sense of this scene also convinces me that Bishop is a craftsperson at work. Similarly, the repetition of 'Somebody' leaves a sense of reassurance not only for the high-strung cars and their drivers, but also for us, as the poet states that 'Somebody loves us all'. The tone is that of a parent soothing a contrary child who won't go to sleep. The word 'comfy' is also deceptively casual as, suddenly, the critical tone of the poem changes when the poet realises that the dog is content to be living there. I thought it was clever of the poet to use such a homely word as 'comfy' to totally change the mood of the poem. Finally, I think that Bishop shows

EXAMINER'S COMMENT

This is a mid-grade answer, which competently addresses the question. There is some very good engagement with the poem and effective use is made of apt references. The expression is reasonably well controlled, although slightly repetitive at times, leaving this short of being a high-grade standard.

her skill in the use of the sibilant 's' at the conclusion of the poem. Just as the oil stops the gears in a car from making noise, the carefully arranged oil cans in the filling station send their message of comfort to the narrator and to us: 'Somebody loves us all'.

Class/Homework Exercises

1. 'A sense of homelessness pervades Bishop's poetry'. Comment on this statement, referring to both the content and stylistic techniques used in 'Filling Station'. Support your discussion with reference to the poem.
2. 'Elizabeth Bishop succeeds in conveying her themes through effective use of striking visual imagery and powerful aural effects.' Discuss this view with reference to 'Filling Station'.

Summary Points

- **Bishop attempts to comprehend the significance of a run-down filling-station.**
- **Vivid picture of homely petrol station through closely observed visual detail.**
- **Cinematic techniques, conversational and colloquial language, flashes of humour.**
- **Contemptuous tone gives way to a concluding note of reassurance.**
- **Realisation that love and beauty can be found anywhere.**

10 In the Waiting Room

In Worcester, Massachusetts,
I went with Aunt Consuelo
to keep her dentist's appointment
and sat and waited for her
in the dentist's waiting room.
It was winter. It got dark
early. The waiting room
was full of grown-up people,
arctics and overcoats,
lamps and magazines.
My aunt was inside
what seemed like a long time
and while I waited I read
the *National Geographic*
(I could read) and carefully
studied the photographs:
the inside of a volcano,
black, and full of ashes;
then it was spilling over
in rivulets of fire.
Osa and Martin Johnson
dressed in riding breeches,
laced boots, and pith helmets.
A dead man slung on a pole
—'Long Pig,' the caption said.
Babies with pointed heads
wound round and round with string;
black, naked women with necks
wound round and round with wire
like the necks of light bulbs.
Their breasts were horrifying.
I read it right straight through.
I was too shy to stop.
And then I looked at the cover:
the yellow margins, the date.
Suddenly, from inside,
came an *oh!* of pain
—Aunt Consuelo's voice—
not very loud or long.
I wasn't at all surprised;

Worcester: much of the poet's childhood was spent here.

arctics: waterproof overshoes.

***National Geographic*:** international geography magazine.

Osa and Martin Johnson: well-known American explorers.

pith helmets: sun helmets made from dried jungle plants.

'Long Pig': term used by Polynesian cannibals for human flesh.

even then I knew she was
a foolish, timid woman.
I might have been embarrassed,
but wasn't. What took *me*
completely by surprise
was that it was *me*:
my voice, in my mouth.
Without thinking at all
I was my foolish aunt,
I—we—were falling, falling,
our eyes glued to the cover
of the *National Geographic*,
February, 1918.

I said to myself: three days
and you'll be seven years old.
I was saying it to stop
the sensation of falling off
the round, turning world
into cold, blue-black space.
But I felt: you are an *I*,
you are an *Elizabeth*,
you are one of *them*.
Why should you be one, too?
I scarcely dared to look
to see what it was I was.
I gave a sidelong glance
—I couldn't look any higher—
at shadowy gray knees,
trousers and skirts and boots
and different pairs of hands
lying under the lamps.
I knew that nothing stranger
had ever happened, that nothing
stranger could ever happen.
Why should I be my aunt,
or me, or anyone?
What similarities—
boots, hands, the family voice
I felt in my throat, or even
the *National Geographic*
and those awful hanging breasts –
held us all together
or made us all just one?
How—I didn't know any
word for it—how 'unlikely' ...

Elizabeth: the poet is addressing herself.

How had I come to be here,
like them, and overhear
a cry of pain that could have
got loud and worse but hadn't?

The waiting room was bright
and too hot. It was sliding
beneath a big black wave,
another, and another.

Then I was back in it.
The War was on. Outside,
in Worcester, Massachusetts,
were night and slush and cold,
and it was still the fifth
of February, 1918.

The War: First World War (1914–18).

'then it was spilling over'

Personal Response

1. In your view, what image of women is presented in the poem? Support your answer with reference to the text.
2. Select two images that have a surreal or dreamlike impact in the poem. Comment on the effectiveness of each image.
3. Write your personal response to the poem, using textual reference.

Critical Literacy

'In the Waiting Room' describes a defining coming-of-age experience for the poet when she was just six years old. While her aunt receives dental treatment, the child narrator browses through the pages of a *National Geographic* magazine and observes what is happening around her. In the powerful and provocative moments that follow, she begins to acknowledge her individual sense of being female.

The poem opens with a specific setting recalled in vivid detail by the child narrator. She flicks through a *National Geographic* magazine in the dentist's office while her aunt is in the patients' surgery. Familiar images of 'grown-up people,/arctics and overcoats' seem to convey a sense of well-being. It is the winter of 1918 in Worcester, Massachusetts. **The language is direct and uncomplicated, mirroring the candid observations of a young girl** as filtered through the adult poet's mature interpretation. Short sentences establish the fragmented flashback, allowing the reader to identify immediately with the narrative: 'It was winter. It got dark/early'. In addition to the unguarded tone, Bishop's short lines give the poem a visual simplicity, even though the first stanza is composed of 35 lines.

The mood changes from line 18 onwards, as the young girl studies the dramatic magazine photographs of an active volcano 'spilling over/in rivulets of fire'. For the first time, **she recognises the earth's destructive force**. In contrast to the earlier feeling of security in the waiting room, the atmosphere becomes uneasy. Disturbing pictures ('A dead man slung on a pole' and 'Babies with pointed heads') are as intriguing as they are shocking. The child is drawn further into an astonishingly exotic scene of cannibalism and violence. Graphic images of ornamental disfigurement seem horrifying: 'naked women with necks/wound round and round with wire'. The repetition of 'round and round' emphasises the young girl's spiralling descent into an enthralling world. Caught between fascination, repulsion and embarrassment ('too shy to stop'), she concentrates on the magazine's cover in an effort to regain control of her feelings.

The child is unexpectedly startled by a voice 'from inside' (line 36). At first, she presumes that the sound ('an *oh!* of pain') has been made by her aunt. But then something extraordinary happens and she realises that she has made the sound herself: 'it was *me*'. This sudden awareness that the cry has come from within herself prompts a **strange, visionary experience** in which she identifies closely with her 'foolish aunt'. The scene is dramatic and dreamlike: 'I – we – were falling, falling'.

In the surreal sequence that follows, the child focuses on her approaching birthday as she tries to resist the sensation of fainting: 'three days/and you'll be seven years old' (line 54). Ironically, it is at this crucial point (on the edge of 'cold, blue-black space') that she gains an astonishing insight into her own sense of self: 'you are an *Elizabeth*,/you are one of *them*'. The idea of sharing a common female identity with her aunt and the unfamiliar women in the magazine is overwhelming: 'nothing stranger/had ever happened' (line 72). It seems as though **all women have lost their individuality and have merged into a single female identity**. Although she attempts to stay calm, she is plagued by recurring questions and confusion: 'Why should I be my aunt,/or me, or anyone?' The young Elizabeth's awakening to adulthood is obviously painful. In attempting to come to terms with her destiny as both an individual and also as part of a unified female gender, she makes this hesitant statement: 'How – I didn't know any/word for it – how "unlikely" ...'.

Before she can return to reality, the young girl must endure further discomfort. Her surroundings feel 'bright/and too hot' (line 90) and she imagines being submerged 'beneath a big black wave', a startling metaphor for helplessness and disorientation. In the final stanza, she regains her composure in the waiting room's apparent safety, where she lists the certainties of place and time. But there is a distinct sense of life's harshness: 'The War was on' and Massachusetts is encountering 'slush and cold' (line 97). Such **symbols are central to our understanding of this deeply personal poem**. Just as the image of the erupting volcano seemed to signify Bishop's development, the waiting room itself marks a transition point in her self-awareness.

Writing About the Poem

'An unsettling sense of not being fully in control is a central theme in the poetry of Elizabeth Bishop.' To what extent is this true of 'In the Waiting Room'? Support your answer with reference to the text of the poem.

Sample Paragraph

The theme of growing up is central to 'In the Waiting Room'. It's unlike nostalgic poems. They often describe childhood experiences in a sentimental way. The atmosphere at the start is relaxed as the child passes time by reading the magazine. However, the photographs of a volcano 'full of ashes' and of cannibals carrying a dead man ('Long Pig') are upsetting. The mood becomes nervous. Photographs of native women terrify the child as some of them wear wire necklaces. The poet compares them to 'light bulbs' – an image which frightens her. The outside world is so violent and unexpected that she then goes into a trance-like state and cries out in agony. Her experience is more unsettled as she struggles to keep a grip on reality. Instead, she faints into 'cold, blue-black space'. The image suggests how out of control she is. However, what really unsettles her is the discovery that she herself is a young woman and she shares this with every other female. The photos of the women suggest her own future and she becomes terrified. Her uneasy feelings are summed up when she describes being overcome by the heat in the waiting room, 'beneath a big black wave'. This leaves me feeling sympathy for this girl who is unsure about her life and future role as a woman.

EXAMINER'S COMMENT

A reasonably focused and sustained mid-grade response, which addresses the question competently. Good use is made of quotations. The expression could be more controlled in places, particularly in the opening section.

Class/Homework Exercises

1. 'Bishop's reflective poems combine precise observation with striking imagery.' Discuss this view with reference to 'In the Waiting Room'. Refer to the poem in your answer.
2. 'In many of her poems, Elizabeth Bishop offers interesting insights into how children struggle to make sense of the adult world.' Discuss this statement with reference to 'In the Waiting Room'.

Summary Points

- **Themes include loss of innocence, coming-of-age experience, lack of belonging.**
- **Realisation of unique individuality and common female identity.**
- **Conversational language relays candid observations of young girl.**
- **Contrasting tones of alarm, dismay and disgust.**
- **Unnerving imagery used to explore comprehension of the wider world.**
- **Dreamlike atmosphere – surreal, nightmarish.**

Sample Leaving Cert Questions on Bishop's Poetry

1. **From your study of the poetry of Elizabeth Bishop on your course, select the poems that, in your opinion, best show her effective use of specific places to communicate a sense of separation and loss. Justify your selection by showing how Bishop's effective use of specific places communicates a sense of separation and loss.**
2. **'Bishop's reflective poetry is defined largely by tranquil observation, precise descriptive language and deep compassion.' Discuss this view, supporting your answer with reference to both the thematic concerns and poetic style in the poetry of Elizabeth Bishop on your course.**
3. **'Bishop's powerful portrayal of the world of nature is conveyed through vibrant imagery and energetic expression.' To what extent do you agree or disagree with this view? Support your answer with reference to Bishop's subject matter and writing style in her prescribed poems.**

How do I organise my answer?

(Sample question 2)

'Bishop's reflective poetry is defined largely by tranquil observation, precise descriptive language and deep compassion.' Discuss this view, supporting your answer with reference to both the thematic concerns and poetic style of the poetry of Elizabeth Bishop on your course.

Sample Plan 1

Intro: (*Stance: agree with viewpoint in the question*) Bishop's poetry is distinguished by her position as the permanent outsider. Poems thinly conceal her estrangement as orphan, woman and troubled adult. Recurring themes of identity, endurance and man's relationship with nature explored through detailed language and warm tones of care and concern.

Point 1: (*Endurance/epiphany – visual details*) 'The Fish' explores themes of endurance and hope through the precise description of a caught fish. Striking imagery conveys the unique wonder of the fish ('brown skin hung in strips', 'pink swim-bladder'). Details reveal the fish's astonishing beauty and tenacity; compels compassion from poet and reader.

Understanding the Prescribed Poetry Question

Marks are awarded using the PCLM Marking Scheme:
P = 15; C = 15; L = 15; M = 5
Total = 50

- **P** (Purpose = 15 marks) refers to the set question and is the launch pad for the answer. This involves engaging with all aspects of the question. Both theme and language must be addressed, although not necessarily equally.
- **C** (Coherence = 15 marks) refers to the organisation of the developed response and the use of accurate, relevant quotation. Paragraphing is essential.
- **L** (Language = 15 marks) refers to the student's skill in controlling language throughout the answer.
- **M** (Mechanics = 5 marks) refers to spelling and grammar.
- Although no specific number of poems is required, students usually discuss at least 3 or 4 in their written responses.
- Aim for at least 800 words, to be completed within 45–50 minutes.

NOTE

In keeping with the PCLM approach, the student has to take a stance – agreeing, disagreeing or partially agreeing – with the statement that:

- **Bishop's reflective observation** (childhood, loss of innocence, coming-of-age experiences, belonging/alienation, endurance, man's relationship with nature, etc.)

... is defined through:

- **precise descriptive language and deep compassion** (observational detail, startling personification, striking comparisons, surreal imagery, sound effects, sympathetic tones, etc.)

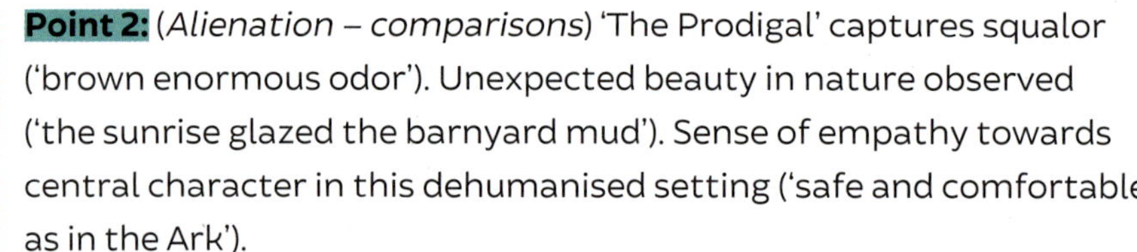

Point 2: (*Alienation – comparisons*) 'The Prodigal' captures squalor ('brown enormous odor'). Unexpected beauty in nature observed ('the sunrise glazed the barnyard mud'). Sense of empathy towards central character in this dehumanised setting ('safe and comfortable as in the Ark').

Point 3: (*Childhood experience – striking imagery*) 'First Death in Nova Scotia' is a powerful and perceptive observation of coming-of-age. Startling dreamlike imagery ('Arthur's coffin was a little frosted cake'), odd personification and fairy-tale language suggest an understanding of child's terrifying experience ('Jack Frost had dropped the brush/and left him white, forever').

Point 4: (*Identity – surreal imagery*) 'In the Waiting Room' also uses bizarre imagery ('Babies with pointed heads') to show child's struggle with nature's destructive forces ('rivulets of fire'). Dramatic otherworldly sequence signals the end of childhood ('falling, falling'). Sensitive tone, realisation of common identity ('you are one of them').

Conclusion: Poems reveal hidden beauty found in ordinary places. Bishop succeeds in 'making the familiar strange' through her carefully crafted poetry and sympathetic point of view.

Sample Paragraph: Point 1

'The Fish' is a detailed description of a close encounter between man and nature. It is full of vivid imagery and figurative language. A first-person narrative enables Bishop to bring the reader with her, 'I caught', 'I looked', 'I stared'. Through her well-known painterly language, the poet conveys the large patterns on the fish's skin, 'shapes like full-blown roses'. The sibilant sounds and compound word emphasise its lush markings. Tranquil observation shows a deeply felt regard for the battle-scarred creature, 'I admired his sullen face'. The fish's admirable endurance is detailed, 'five big hooks grown firmly in his mouth'. He has earned his 'medals'. Bishop's compassionate eye notes his 'aching jaw'. We share the poet's reflective moment of heightened awareness with the description of the universal symbol of hope, 'a rainbow'. The excitement is captured in short run-on lines. However, the rhyming couplet brings the poem to a harmonious conclusion – a respectful relationship between human beings and nature is expressed in the simple final line, 'And I let the fish go'.

EXAMINER'S COMMENT

This well-written top-grade response carefully considers all the main aspects of the question. There is a clear sense of engagement with the poem, particularly in the succinct analysis of how Bishop's themes are communicated through stylistic features, such as the first-person narrative, vivid imagery and sound effects. Textual support is excellent throughout and the final point on the use of rhythm is impressive.

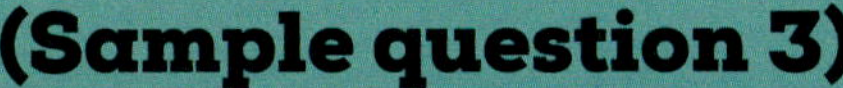

(Sample question 3)

'Bishop's powerful portrayal of the world of nature is conveyed through vibrant imagery and energetic expression.' To what extent do you agree or disagree with this view? Support your answer with reference to Bishop's subject matter and writing style in her prescribed poems.

Sample Plan 2

Intro: (*Stance: partially agree with viewpoint in the question*) Bishop not only provides a powerful portrayal of nature, but also examines people and their circumstances through vigorous imagery and lively language.

Point 1: (*Nature – coastal scene at low tide*) 'The Bight' gives a vivid view of a compelling scene that stimulates Bishop's imagination. Vibrant details and rich metaphors describe the small coastal bay's dilapidated scenery ('crumbling ribs of marl', 'frowsy sponge boats').

Point 2: (*Human nature – child, grandmother*) 'Sestina' examines early childhood trauma through ominous personification ('birdlike, the almanac/hovers') and surreal imagery ('a man with buttons like tears'). Poem's structure mirrors child's drawing of 'rigid' house, both trying to contain tremendous grief.

Point 3: (*Nature – Brazilian landscape*) 'Questions of Travel' is a painterly description of the luxuriant, equatorial landscape. Bishop wonders why people are so interested in foreign places. Effective use of emphatic verbs ('hurry', 'spill'), surreal simile of exotic trees ('gesturing/like noble pantomimists robed in pink') and huge mountains ('like the hulls of capsized ships').

Point 4: (*Nature – environment, animals*) 'The Armadillo' details tragic consequences on nature of man's unthinking actions. Oral and descriptive imagery reflect the poet's frustration and compassion ('piercing cry/and panic').

Conclusion: Bishop makes 'the familiar strange' in her portrayals of both people and nature through her 'forever flowing' precise imagery and powerful language use.

NOTE

In keeping with the PCLM approach, the student has to take a stance by agreeing and/or disagreeing that Bishop's poetry conveys:

- **a powerful portrayal of the world of nature** (relationship between nature and human nature, beauty, power, vulnerability of nature, etc.)

... conveyed through:

- **vibrant imagery and energetic expression** (vivid details, sensuous imagery, striking comparisons, strong verbs, energetic sound effects, dramatic encounters, engaging conversational language, evocative tones, etc.)

Sample Paragraph: Point 4

Bishop's dramatic portrayal of nature is vivid and precise. 'The Armadillo' highlights her ecological outlook, exploring the tragic consequences of man's thoughtless actions. The damaging effects of the 'fragile' fire balloons, lit as celebrations for a Brazilian festival, are shown through a powerful simile – one balloon 'splattered like a fire egg'. The poem slows down to focus on the distinctive beauty of each animal affected. The young rabbit is described in the sibilant phrase, 'so soft'. Individual animals' responses are carefully noted. The owls 'shrieked', the 'baby rabbit jumped out'. The poet is compelling readers to be aware of the unique beauty under threat. The rabbit has been 'ignited' into 'intangible ash', only its eyes remain, red and fixed. The horrific danger of the lanterns is depicted in the alliterative phrase, 'falling fire'. This results in the 'glistening' armadillo scurrying 'head down, tail down' to find safety. The concluding italicised lines force us to see just how vulnerable nature is – its 'weak mailed fist' raised against the powerful man-made forces of destruction.

EXAMINER'S COMMENT

Excellent response that focuses on all elements of the question. The 'powerful portrayal' aspect is effectively tackled ('dramatic', 'highlights', 'force us'). Informed and insightful views are presented in an argument seamlessly interwoven with textual support, employing critical terms with skill. Impressive expression throughout. Top-grade standard.

MARKING SCHEME GUIDELINES

Candidates are free to agree and/or disagree with the statement, but they should engage with how various stylistic features effectively communicate compelling insights into the harshness and cruelty of life. Reward responses that include clear analysis of both themes and language use (though not necessarily equally) in Bishop's poetry.

INDICATIVE MATERIAL

Bishop's effective stylistic features:

- striking use of places, people, sound effects, vivid imagery, structure, precise tones/moods, etc.

... to communicate:

- compelling insights into life's harshness and cruelty
- engaging awareness into traumatic childhood experiences, unexpected natural beauty, empathy with nature, degradation, dramatic visionary moments, etc.

Leaving Cert Sample Essay

'Bishop makes effective use of various stylistic features to communicate compelling insights into the harshness and cruelty of life.' To what extent do you agree or disagree with this statement? Support your answer with reference to the poetry of Elizabeth Bishop on your course.

Sample Essay

1. Elizabeth Bishop's poems are often based on personal experiences. Many of them refer back to her childhood and painful memories. These often lead to insights about life. Her writing style is precise and dramatic. Poems like 'The Prodigal', 'Sestina', 'First Death in Nova Scotia' and 'The Fish', show her awareness of human nature and nature. She reflects on the confusion of growing up and experiences such as human suffering and grief. Bishop is also noted for her detailed descriptive language – especially her use of startling imagery and ability to create atmosphere.

2. In 'The Prodigal', she retells a Bible story about a man who sinks low in society as a result of alcohol. Bishop focuses on the bleaker side of life. The opening lines show her skill at setting the degrading farmyard scene. The youth is living with the pigs in dehumanised conditions. The imagery highlights the foul atmosphere – 'brown enormous odor', 'breathing and thick hair'. Bishop gives us a very disturbing insight into alcoholism.

In the early morning, the situation does not seem as bad to the youth as it is seen through a cloud of alcohol. He can even find the beauty in nature – 'the sunrise glazed over farmyard mud with red'. However, the hiding of the pint bottles shows how addiction has left him isolated. In his degradation, the truth about his sad life is beginning to be understood by him and he feels he may be able to 'go home'.

3. One of Bishop's poetic techniques is her detailed descriptions. This is found in 'Sestina', one of her personal poems and one that is filled with hidden unhappiness. She describes a familiar event, a grandmother sits in the kitchen as September rain falls outside and the light fades. She is making tea and reading to her young granddaughter. However, as the poem progresses, this cosy domestic scene begins to change in tone. All is not what it seems. There is a sense of uncertainty and an underlying sadness associated with the passing of time.

4. The poet shows her controlled writing skill by using the sestina. This consists of six 6-line stanzas plus a final 3-line stanza. Key words are repeated in each stanza. Everything takes place in the kitchen. In 'Sestina', the atmosphere has mystery and magic. It's also a little dark and secretive – like a fairytale. In the final lines, a very surprising thing happens, unnoticed by the grandmother. The buttons in the child's drawing become 'little moons that fall down like tears into the flower bed' in the drawing. The whole focus is on these tears as if Bishop is saying that life will bring pain and sadness to everyone, old and young. Bishop gets an insight into the disappointments of life and is suggesting that such moments of awareness can happen at any time.

5. 'First Death in Nova Scotia' is told from the point-of-view of a child experiencing death for the first time. Her mother has brought her to see the body of her cousin Arthur. She observes the portraits of royalty hanging around the body and begins to imagine that they have called him to be a pageboy in court. Bishop creates a disturbing scene, using surreal images. Near the body stands a stuffed loon bird on a 'marble-topped table'. The dead body appears 'all white, like a doll' and 'Jack Frost had started to paint him'. The poet contrasts Arthur with the royal couples in their warm red and ermine fur. The young girl is very confused about death and wonders how Arthur could possibly get to court 'with his eyes shut up tight and the roads deep in snow'. This is the key insightful moment in the poem, suggesting that the child – and perhaps Bishop herself – is questioning the existence of heaven and the possibility of going there after death.

6. Bishop's similes and metaphors are very effective. She uses these features to show an awareness of the suffering of animals – e.g. in 'The Fish'. Her description of the 'tremendous fish' is very detailed. Its 'brown skin hung down like old wallpaper'. Bishop shows the blotched skin – 'like full-blown roses' and gives a close-up picture of the colours, 'dramatic blacks and reds'. We are shown how the fish suffered – with 'five hooks' still stuck in its mouth. Other very powerful images show its 'sullen face' and 'aching mouth'. She begins to admire the fish for its beauty and for putting up a fight – and this leads to her showing her great respect for nature – 'I then let the fish go'.

7. Elizabeth Bishop shows a wide variety of stylistic features to communicate compelling insights into cruelty. The people in her poems are often associated with loss or suffering. Many of the insights show her facing up to life's realities – and her themes of death, pain and loss of innocence are universal.

(815 words)

EXAMINER'S COMMENT

The essay includes some authentic engagement with the question, with most discussion rooted in the texts of the poems. Good commentary on the poet's style in 'First Death' and 'The Fish'. Analysis of insights could have been clearer and more developed at times, however, for example, in paragraph 3. Despite some misquotes and repetitive expression, this is a solid mid-grade response that interacted well with Bishop's themes and writing style.

GRADE: H3
P = 11/15
C = 10/15
L = 11/15
M = 5/5
Total = 37/50

Class/Homework Exercise

1. **Rewrite paragraph 6. (Aim for at least 130 words.)**

PROMPT!

- *Maintain the focus on the full question.*
- *Highlight the poet's compelling insights.*
- *Use accurate quotations.*
- *Vary expression, avoiding repetition of 'very' and 'show'.*

Revision Overview

'The Fish'
Nature is a central theme. After surviving previous struggles against adversity, the fish gains Bishop's respect.

'The Bight'
A beautifully conceived poem that reflects on the chaotic nature of everyday existence.

'At the Fishhouses'
Detailed observation of the relationship between people and nature leads to insight and a sense of belonging.

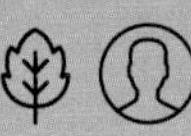

'The Prodigal'
Compelling presentation of the power of the human spirit to endure hardship and to retain hope.

'Questions of Travel'
Reflective poem raises issues about the meaning and necessity of travel – and the morality of tourism.

'The Armadillo'
Powerful depiction of man-made disasters and careless violence signified by the suffering of defenceless animals.

'Sestina'
Unsettling story of a grandmother and a child living with loss addresses poignant themes of grief and coming-of-age.

'First Death in Nova Scotia'
In this recollection of childhood and loss of innocence, Bishop transforms the child's uncertainty into a dynamic poetic vision.

'Filling Station'
Closely observed description of a small family filling station where the nurturing influence of women is evident.

'In the Waiting Room'
Recalls a dramatic scene that highlights the difficult transition from childhood to adulthood.

Last Words

'Bishop was spectacular at being unspectacular.'
Marianne Moore

'Bishop disliked the swagger and visibility of literary life.'
Eavan Boland

'The sun set in the sea ... and there was one of it and one of me.'
Elizabeth Bishop

NATURE

TRAVEL/ JOURNEYS

IDENTITY

MEANING OF LIFE

CONFICT

SUFFERING

HISTORY/ MEMORY

DEATH

LOVE

BEAUTY

Eavan Boland

1944–

'Poetry begins – as all art does – where certainties end.'

Eavan Boland has been one of the most prominent voices in Irish poetry and is the author of many highly acclaimed poetry collections. Born in Dublin but raised in London, she had early experiences with anti-Irish racism that gave her a strong sense of heritage and a keen awareness of her identity. She later returned to attend school and university in Dublin, where she published a pamphlet of poetry after her graduation. Boland received her BA from Trinity College in 1966. Since then she has held numerous teaching positions and has published poetry, books of criticism and articles. She married in 1969 and has two children. Her experiences as a wife and mother have influenced her to recognise the beauty and significance of everyday living. Boland writes plainly and eloquently about her experiences as a woman, mother and exile. She has taught at several colleges in America where she has been a professor of English at Stanford University, California. In addition to traditional Irish themes, Eavan Boland explores a wide range of subjects, including incisive commentaries on contemporary subjects and intensely personal poems about history, womanhood and relationships.

Investigate Further

To find out more about Eavan Boland, or to hear readings of her poems not available in your eBook, you could search some useful websites, such as YouTube, BBC Poetry, poetryfoundation.org and poetryarchive.org, or access additional material on this page of your eBook.

Prescribed Poems

○ **1 'The War Horse'**
A runaway horse in a quiet suburban estate is the starting point for Boland's explorations of attitudes to warfare and violence throughout Irish history. **Page 64**

○ **2 'Child of Our Time' (OL)**
Written in response to a newspaper photograph of a child killed in the 1974 Dublin bombings, this poem tries to draw some kind of meaning from the tragedy. **Page 68**

○ **3 'The Famine Road'**
The poet dramatically recreates a tragic period in Irish history. Boland also links the Famine with another traumatic experience, the story of a woman diagnosed as infertile by her doctor. **Page 72**

○ **4 'The Shadow Doll'**
Boland considers the changing nature of marriage since Victorian times. The silence and submission of women are signified by the porcelain doll in its airless glass dome. **Page 76**

○ **5 'White Hawthorn in the West of Ireland'**
The poet's journey into the West brings her into contact with a wildly beautiful landscape where she can explore Irish superstitions and a strange, unspoken language. **Page 80**

○ **6 'Outside History'**
Another poem addressing the experience of the marginalised ('outsiders') and reflecting Boland's own humanity as a female Irish poet. **Page 84**

○ **7 'The Black Lace Fan My Mother Gave Me'**
This poem was inspired by the first gift given by the poet's father to her mother back in 1930s Paris. The souvenir is a symbol of young love and the mystery of changing relationships. **Page 88**

○ **8 'This Moment' (OL)**
In this short lyric, Boland unobtrusively captures the mystery and magic of the natural world and the beauty of loving relationships. **Page 92**

○ **9 'The Pomegranate'**
Another personal poem in which Boland uses mythical references to examine the complexity of feelings experienced in mother-daughter relationships. **Page 95**

○ **10 'Love' (OL)**
This reflective poem is addressed to the poet's husband, and considers the changing nature of romantic love. In developing her themes, Boland draws on Greek mythology. **Page 99**

*(OL) indicates poems that are also prescribed for the Ordinary Level course.

1 The War Horse

The War Horse: a powerful horse ridden in war by a knight or cavalry soldier.

This dry night, nothing unusual
About the clip, clop, casual

Iron of his shoes as he stamps death
Like a mint on the innocent coinage of earth.

I lift the window, watch the ambling feather
Of hock and fetlock, loosed from its daily tether

In the tinker camp on the Enniskerry Road,
Pass, his breath hissing, his snuffling head

Down. He is gone. No great harm is done.
Only a leaf of our laurel hedge is torn –

Of distant interest like a maimed limb,
Only a rose which now will never climb

The stone of our house, expendable, a mere
Line of defence against him, a volunteer

You might say, only a crocus its bulbous head
Blown from growth, one of the screamless dead.

But we, we are safe, our unformed fear
Of fierce commitment gone; why should we care

If a rose, a hedge, a crocus are uprooted
Like corpses, remote, crushed, mutilated?

He stumbles on like a rumour of war, huge,
Threatening; neighbours use the subterfuge

Of curtains; He stumbles down our short street
Thankfully passing us. I pause, wait,

Then to breathe relief lean on the sill
And for a second only my blood is still

With atavism. That rose he smashed frays
Ribboned across our hedge, recalling days

Of burned countryside, illicit braid:
A cause ruined before, a world betrayed.

mint: a place where money is made; a machine for making money.
coinage: collection of coins. Here it refers to imprints the horse makes on the suburban gardens.
ambling: walking at a leisurely pace.
hock: joint in the back of a horse's leg.
fetlock: tuft of hair that grows above and behind the hoof.
tether: rope for tying an animal.
tinker camp: travellers' halting-site.
snuffling: breathing noisily.

expendable: can be done without, can be sacrificed to achieve an object.

mutilated: prevented from having a limb.

subterfuge: trick used to avoid an argument or an awkward situation.

atavism: the recurrence of a trait present in distant ancestors.
frays: is strewn, ragged.
illicit braid: illegal ribbon, a reference to a 19th-century popular movement of poor Catholics in Ireland. The Ribbonmen wore a green ribbon in opposition to the Orangemen.

Personal Response

1. Describe the atmosphere in the first ten lines of the poem. Is it edgy or relaxed? Refer to the text in your response.
2. Choose one image from the poem that is particularly vivid and dramatic. Briefly explain your choice.
3. Write your own personal response to the poem, highlighting the impact it made on you.

Critical Literacy

'The War Horse' was written in 1972 by Eavan Boland after she had moved to the suburbs at the foothills of the Dublin Mountains. It was an icy winter and the 'sounds of death from the televisions were heard almost nightly' as the news about the Northern Ireland Troubles was broadcast. In this poem, Boland questions ambivalent attitudes towards war.

This poem is based on a **real event**, **the appearance of a 'loosed' Traveller horse**, described in lines 1–9. Boland has said, 'It encompassed a real event. It entered a place in my heart and moved beyond it.' An aural description of the innocuous noise, 'nothing unusual', heralds the arrival of the animal. The horse, a menacing intruder that suggests the opposition between force and formality, wreaked havoc on the neat order of **suburban gardens**. The rigid control of the rhyming couplets mirrors the desire for order in the suburbs.

Onomatopoeia and the alliteration of the hard 'c' vividly echo the horse's walk, like something out of a young child's story: 'clip, clop, casual'. The second couplet counteracts this sense of ordinariness as it describes the damage the animal inflicts. The brutal verb 'stamps' jolts the reader as the garden, **'the innocent coinage of earth'**, is being destroyed. The simile of a mint, which puts an indelible mark on metal to make coins, is used to highlight the destruction. The **consequences of war** are also permanent – people are wounded or killed ('stamps death').

The **poet is an observer**: 'I lift the window, watch'. A detailed description of the horse's leg, 'ambling feather/Of hock and fetlock', conceals its capacity for

violence. There then follows an explanation of where the horse came from, the 'tinker camp on the Enniskerry Road'. The **random nature of violence** is aptly contained in the verbs 'ambling', 'loosed' and also in the long run-on line 'loosed ... Road'. The sounds the animal makes are vividly conveyed using onomatopoeia: 'hissing', 'snuffling'. The moment of danger passes: 'He is gone'. We can feel the palpable relief: 'No great harm is done'. Colloquial language reduces the event to a trivial disruption.

Lines 10–16 show that the poet has adopted a **sensible approach** as she surveys the **damage**, minimising it with an emphasis on the word 'only': 'Only a leaf is torn', 'Only a crocus', 'Only a rose'. These are all 'expendable'; they can be done without. The language becomes more unsettling as violent descriptions are used to show the mangled blooms: 'like a maimed limb ... which now will never climb', 'Blown from growth'. All describe a world that will never be the same again, potential that will never be realised and life that is cut short. From Boland's perspective, 'the screamless dead' can no longer command attention.

And who cares anyway? It is of 'distant interest'. This apathetic view can be taken by people as they watch atrocities in other countries. The **language of war** is prominent: 'a mere/Line of defence', 'a volunteer', the head is 'Blown'. The poet's focus has now shifted away from the horse and is concentrated on conflict, its consequences and the vulnerability of victims.

In lines 17–21, Boland realises that 'we are safe'. War calls for commitment; people must choose to take sides, to fight. This is frightening: 'our unformed fear'. It is there but not expressed, nor given substance or form. Here in this domestic incident is war in miniature, the entry of an intruder who perpetrates damage. The poet asks why the community should care about something so insignificant as a damaged rose or a crushed crocus. She is challenging people who are blasé and examining their **insularity**: 'why should we care ... corpses, remote, crushed, mutilated?' Are there consequences if people do not care?

Boland criticises her own community in lines 22–30, with the neighbours described as hiding behind curtains ('subterfuge'). This 'I don't want to know' attitude reflects the **ambivalence** about the Northern Troubles in the Irish Republic during the 1970s. The tension, 'I pause, wait', is followed by release: 'breathe relief'. At the conclusion, there are two insightful views. One is the suburban woman's; the other is an Irish person's awareness of connecting with past history. There is an ancestral memory, 'atavism', which associates the smashed rose with Ireland's history. The ribbon trails back to the violence of English colonialism. Boland and her neighbours chose not to confront the horse, just as generations of Irish people did not successfully confront the invaders. The intruder (the horse, the British) destroyed something beautiful and precious (the rose, Irish culture and freedom). The mood here is one of regret. Should both intruders have been challenged? How right is it to live so indifferently? The poem ends on a bleak note, a lament for **'a world betrayed'**.

Writing About the Poem

'We are collectively involved in violence which occurs in our land.' Discuss how 'The War Horse' reflects this statement. Illustrate your response with reference to the poem.

Sample Paragraph

Boland uses an ordinary, domestic incident, the arrival of a tinker's horse into a suburban Dublin garden, to explore the ambivalent attitude to wars that seem distant. The colloquial phrase 'No great harm is done' and the neighbours who use 'the subterfuge/Of curtains' both illustrate this insular approach. Everything is all right so long as 'we' are safe. The consequences of war are listed as Boland itemises them: 'maimed limb', 'now will never climb', 'expendable', 'screamless dead'. The vulnerability of the innocent victims is exposed. Can we afford to be so indifferent? The implicit statement is that we should care. She then conveys the ancestral memory of how Ireland was invaded by the British. The word 'Ribboned' recalls the Ribbonmen, a secret society that was active against the invaders for a while. We are left feeling that perhaps due to the majority of Irish people's indifference and through a lack of commitment, 'A cause' was lost. The poem ends with a lament, 'a world betrayed', with its long echoing vowel sound. I think Boland is upset at people's lack of commitment in a time of trouble.

EXAMINER'S COMMENT

This response succinctly addresses the task through a discussion on the theme and style of the poem. It ranges from the local incident to war's inevitable consequences and people's indifference. Close engagement with the text is evident in the discussion of colloquial language and sound effects. Good use is made of the rhetorical question, 'Can we afford to be so indifferent?' This well-controlled answer merits the top grade.

Class/Homework Exercises

1. Is 'The War Horse' a private poem, or does it have a wider significance? Use reference to the text in your answer.
2. Eavan Boland creates an underlying sense of threat throughout 'The War Horse'. Discuss this view using close reference to the poem.

Summary Points

- **Themes include attitudes to conflict and violence throughout Irish history.**
- **Inclusive personal pronouns and rhetorical questions used to involve readers.**
- **Use of observational details, vibrant language, striking comparisons.**
- **Contrasting atmospheres and tones – reflective, accusatory.**
- **Memorable onomatopoeic effects – assonance, alliteration, internal rhyme.**

2 Child of Our Time (for Aengus)

Yesterday I knew no lullaby
But you have taught me overnight to order
This song, which takes from your final cry
Its tune, from your unreasoned end its reason,
Its rhythm from the discord of your murder
Its motive from the fact you cannot listen.

We who should have known how to instruct
With rhymes for your waking, rhythms for your sleep,
Names for the animals you took to bed,
Tales to distract, legends to protect,
Later an idiom for you to keep
And living, learn, must learn from you, dead,

To make our broken images rebuild
Themselves around your limbs, your broken
Image, find for your sake whose life our idle
Talk has cost, a new language. Child
Of our time, our times have robbed your cradle.
Sleep in a world your final sleep has woken.

discord: lack of harmony among people; harsh, confused sounds; conflict.

idiom: turn of phrase; words which when used together have a different meaning from when used singly.

'our times have robbed your cradle'

Personal Response

1. Boland believes that the 'murder of the innocent' is one of the greatest obscenities. How is this explored in the poem? Refer to the text in response.
2. Where are the two feelings, tenderness and outrage, evident in the poem? Use reference to the text in your response.
3. What is Boland implying about 'our times'? Is she satisfied or dissatisfied with what is happening? Refer closely to the text in your answer.

Critical Literacy

'Child of Our Time' was written in 1974 at the height of the Troubles in Northern Ireland. It was prompted by a harrowing newspaper picture of a fireman tenderly carrying a dead child from the rubble of a bomb explosion in Dublin. The poem is dedicated to Aengus, the infant son of the poet's friend, who had suffered cot death. This lyric is a response to the sudden and unexpected deaths of all young children. It also challenges adults to change their ways.

The title of this poem places the little child in a wider context than that of family and town – he is a child of 'our time'. He is our responsibility; he belongs to us. A child should be a **symbol of innocence**, growth, love, potential and the future, but this has been savagely and tragically cut short by 'our time'. Boland did not have children when she wrote this poem ('Yesterday I knew no lullaby'), but in the first stanza she describes how she has been taught to sing a lullaby which is different: 'you have taught me overnight to order/This song'.

The child's violent and tragic death demands a response, so she will form and order and 'reason' a poem from the child's 'unreasoned end'. It is a song made of harsh sounds, 'discord'. The tone moves from tender compassion ('lullaby') to indignation ('the fact you cannot listen'). There is no escaping the finality of death, yet the poet is a balanced, reasonable person trying to make **order out of disorder** in a poem that uses simple language and is carefully arranged in three stanzas.

The poem is also charged with both **sadness and awareness**. The compassionate voice of the poet is heard in 'rhythms for your sleep,/Names for the animals you took to bed'. However, Boland is aware of the awfulness of the event: 'final cry', 'end', 'murder'. The language is formal, as befits such a solemn occasion: 'We who should have known', 'Child/Of our time'. This poem has several elements of an elegy (a poem for the dead): it laments, praises and consoles. The poem's many half-rhymes mimic this discordant time: 'idle'/'cradle', 'order'/'murder'.

The collective 'We' in the second stanza is used to show the true context of the child as a member of the human family. **It is 'We' who are responsible** for not making society safer so that childhood could consist of 'Tales to distract, legends to protect'. The repetitive sound of 'rhymes' and 'rhythms' imitates the rocking sound of a mother nursing her child. Boland's aim is clear: we must learn from our mistakes and reconstruct a better world out of 'our broken images'.

In the third stanza, the poet is insistent that **society takes on this responsibility**, that we 'find ... a new language'. We have to engage in dialogue, not 'idle/Talk', so that we can deliver a safer world for our children. Ironically, it is the little child, who 'our time' has 'robbed' from his cradle, who will form the scaffold around which we can build a new and better society: 'rebuild/Themselves around your limbs'. The final line of the poem is a **prayer and a hope**: 'Sleep in a world your final sleep has woken'. It is a wish that the little child be at rest now and that the world may be woken to its senses by his death.

Writing About the Poem

'Eavan Boland is a "sensitive poet" who is "rarely thrown off balance by anger".' Discuss this view of the poet in relation to the poem, 'Child of Our Time'. Support your answer with reference to the text.

Sample Paragraph

'Child of Our Time' is an example of Boland's control in the face of what must be the most horrific event that humanity can witness: the brutal and senseless murder of an innocent child. The poem is carefully ordered into three that act as balanced paragraphs in an argument. The first stanza emphasises the meaningless atrocity of 'your unreasoned end'. The second places responsibility where it belongs, on the adult society that should have provided a safe environment for the young: 'We who should have known'. The third stanza urges the adults to do something now, to 'find for your sake whose life our idle/Talk has cost, a new language'. Boland's language is formal and controlled, appropriate for an elegy. The child has taught the poet a lullaby with his death. The adults must learn from this tragedy – they have to learn to talk. The balance is impressive, as the poet makes order out of disorder rather than letting her anger explode. The poem lacks sentimentality or even consolation. Instead, the quiet, insistent voice states that 'we' 'must learn'. Sometimes a soft voice

EXAMINER'S COMMENT

Boland's careful management of ideas is explored in this answer to advance the view that she explores the tragic event in a controlled, sensitive way. Attention is paid to the form of the poem: 'The poem is carefully ordered into three stanzas that act as balanced paragraphs in an argument.' The insightful critical commentary shows good personal engagement. Clear expression and effective use of accurate quotation enhances this highly successful top-grade response.

delivers a more powerful message. Boland sensitively deals with a tragic event with an absence of anger and with an insistence that, as a result, lessons must be learned.

Class/Homework Exercises

1. There is a 'difficult sort of comfort' in literature. Discuss this statement in relation to 'Child of Our Time'. Support the points you make with reference to the poem.
2. In 'Child of Our Time', Boland explores the universal experience of tragic violence. To what extent do you agree with this view? Support the points you make with reference to both the themes and language use in the poem.

Summary Points

- **Addresses issues surrounding the tragic death of a child.**
- **Striking images of innocence, poignant mood, repetition.**
- **Universal significance of random violence and tragedy.**
- **Solemn, didactic tone emphasised by extended uninterrupted lines.**
- **Simple childlike language and gentle sound effects.**

POETRY FOCUS

3 The Famine Road

Title: during the Irish Famine of 1845–48, the British authorities organised various relief schemes. The hungry were given a small wage to buy food for participating in road building and other community projects. Many of the new roads were constructed in remote areas and served little purpose other than controlling the starving population.

'Idle as trout in light Colonel Jones,
these Irish, give them no coins at all; their bones
need toil, their characters no less.' Trevelyan's
seal blooded the deal table. The Relief
Committee deliberated: 'Might it be safe,
Colonel, to give them roads, roads to force
from nowhere, going nowhere of course?'

'one out of every ten and then
another third of those again
women – in a case like yours.'

Sick, directionless they worked; fork, stick
were iron years away; after all could
they not blood their knuckles on rock, suck
April hailstones for water and for food?
Why for that, cunning as housewives, each eyed –
as if at a corner butcher – the other's buttock.

'anything may have caused it, spores,
a childhood accident; one sees
day after day these mysteries.'

Dusk: they will work tomorrow without him.
They know it and walk clear; he has become
a typhoid pariah, his blood tainted, although
he shares it with some there. No more than snow
attends its own flakes where they settle
and melt, will they pray by his death rattle.

'You never will, never you know
but take it well woman, grow
your garden, keep house, good-bye.'

'It has gone better than we expected, Lord
Trevelyan, sedition, idleness, cured
in one; from parish to parish, field to field,
the wretches work till they are quite worn,
then fester by their work; we march the corn
to the ships in peace; this Tuesday I saw bones
out of my carriage window, your servant Jones.'

'Barren, never to know the load
of his child in you, what is your body
now if not a famine road?'

Colonel Jones: army officer and Chairman of the Board of Works.

Trevelyan: Charles Trevelyan, a senior civil servant in overall charge of famine relief.

Relief Committee: groups usually consisting of landlords, the clergy and influential people were set up to distribute food.

deliberated: considered, discussed.

spores: germs.

typhoid pariah: someone shunned because of this deadly blood disease.

death rattle: last sound of the dying.

sedition: subversion, treachery.

corn/to the ships: throughout the famine years, corn was exported from Ireland.

Personal Response

1. Describe the tone of voice in the opening stanza, using close reference to the text.
2. The poet links the abuse of famine victims with the mistreatment of women in modern society. Is this convincing? Explain your answer.
3. In your view, how chillingly pessimistic are the last three lines of the poem? Give reasons for your answer.

Critical Literacy

The poem raises interesting questions about marginalised people, a favourite theme in Boland's work. Here she makes a connection between a famine road in the 1840s and an infertile woman in modern times. Boland presents the poem as a series of dramatic moments featuring a variety of characters.

Stanza one begins with the voice of Colonel Jones, a British official, reading from a letter written by Lord Trevelyan, who had overall responsibility for famine relief. The boorish tone of the opening comments about 'these Irish' is explicitly offensive. Trevelyan's generalised insults reflect the **depth of prejudice and suspicion** felt towards an entire population, who are 'Idle as trout in light'. Such ruthless disregard is further underlined by the vivid image of the official blood-red seal. The proposed solutions – 'toil' or hard labour building roads 'going nowhere' – could hardly be more cynical and are all the more ironic coming from the 'Relief Committee'.

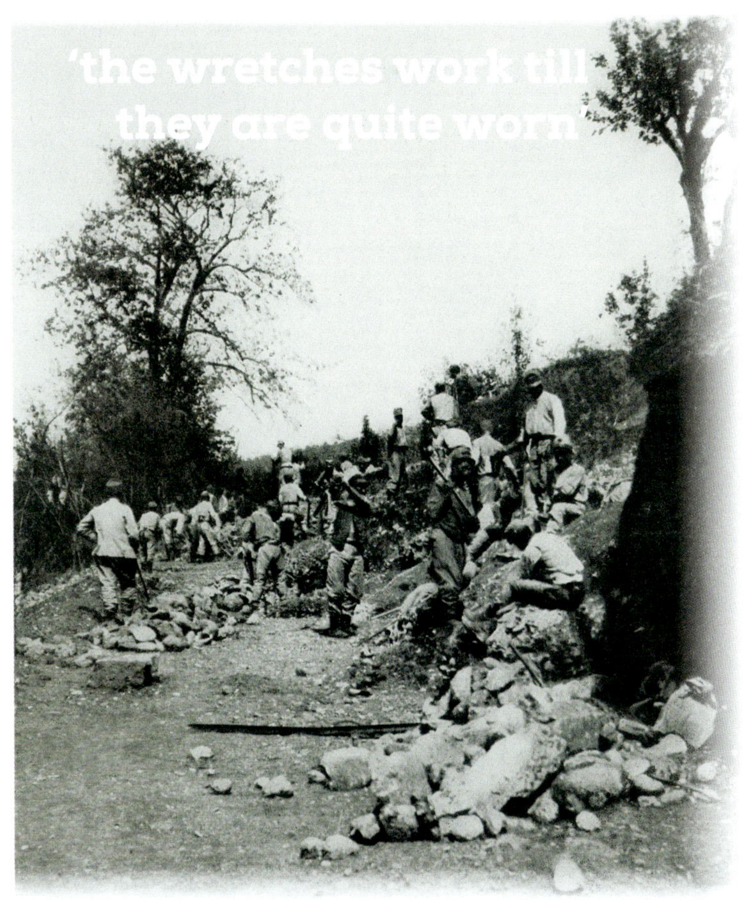

Stanza two (like stanzas four and six) is italicised and introduces another speaker, the authoritative voice of a consultant doctor. The unidentified voice quoting statistics to an unnamed woman is casually impersonal. The situation becomes clearer as the poem continues: the medical expert is discussing the woman's failure to have children. Boland portrays him as insensitive and patronising: 'anything may have caused it'. His tone becomes increasingly **unsympathetic as he dismisses her disappointment**: 'You never will, never you know'. He almost seems to take delight in repeating the word 'never'. The doctor's final comments are as severe as some of the remarks made by any of the British officials: 'take it well woman, grow/your garden, keep house'.

In stanza three, the poet herself imagines the terrible experiences of the famine victims. The

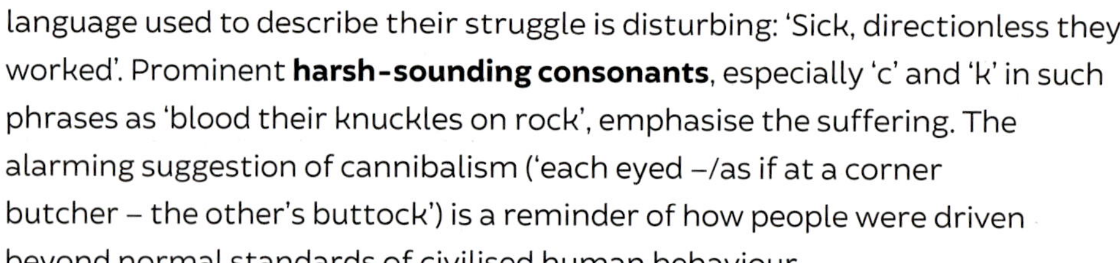

language used to describe their struggle is disturbing: 'Sick, directionless they worked'. Prominent **harsh-sounding consonants**, especially 'c' and 'k' in such phrases as 'blood their knuckles on rock', emphasise the suffering. The alarming suggestion of cannibalism ('each eyed –/as if at a corner butcher – the other's buttock') is a reminder of how people were driven beyond normal standards of civilised human behaviour.

Stanza five focuses on the prevalence of death throughout the long famine years. Attitudes harden as widespread disease becomes commonplace. The poet's direct description, steady rhythm and resigned tone combine to reflect the awful reality of the times: 'they will work tomorrow without him'. Boland illustrates the **breakdown of communities** with the tragic example of one 'typhoid pariah' abandoned to die without anyone to 'pray by his death rattle'.

This great human catastrophe is made all the more pathetic in stanza seven, which begins with an excerpt from Colonel Jones's response to Trevelyan: 'It has gone better than we expected'. **The offhand tone is self-satisfied** as he reports that the road-building schemes have succeeded in their real purpose of controlling the peasant population ('the wretches'). The horrifyingly detached admission – without the slightest sense of irony – of allowing the starving to 'fester' while 'we march the corn/to the ships' is almost beyond comprehension. The colonel's matter-of-fact comment about seeing 'bones/out of my carriage window' is a final reminder of the colossal gulf between the powerful and the powerless.

In the final stanza, Boland's **own feelings of revulsion** bring her back to the present when she sums up the 'Barren' reality of the childless woman 'never to know the load/of his child'. The famine road is reintroduced as a common symbol for the shared tragedies of both the victims of mass starvation and infertility. The concluding rhetorical question leaves us to consider important issues of authority and the abuse of power, whatever the circumstances.

Writing About the Poem

'Eavan Boland uses evocative symbols to address important issues.' Discuss this statement in relation to 'The Famine Road', supporting your points with suitable quotation or reference.

Sample Paragraph

The deserted famine road in Boland's poem is a haunting symbol through which we can examine aspects of power. The poet blends two narratives, one of a country road in the 1840s and the other of a modern-day visit to a doctor, in a series of dramatic scenes. Lord Trevelyan and the doctor

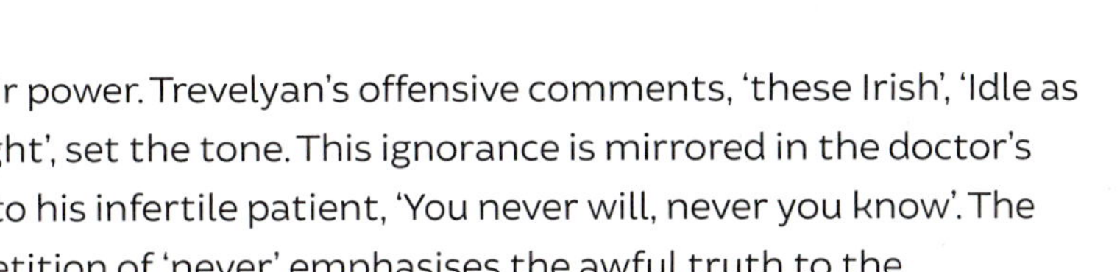

abuse their power. Trevelyan's offensive comments, 'these Irish', 'Idle as trout in light', set the tone. This ignorance is mirrored in the doctor's response to his infertile patient, 'You never will, never you know'. The harsh repetition of 'never' emphasises the awful truth to the unfortunate woman. Severe remedies are handed out to both the famine workers and the woman: the workers will 'toil' to build roads 'going nowhere', the woman will 'grow/your garden, keep house' for a non-existent family. The superior, patronising attitude of those in charge is captured in snippets of direct speech, 'It has gone better than we expected', 'but take it well woman'. Boland often focuses on the marginalised in society. None of the famine victims' voices are heard in this poem, and this omission emphasises their lack of power and their vulnerability. Instead, the 'wretches work till they are quite worn'. The alliterative 'w' stresses the futile never-ending effort. The workers cannot produce food to feed themselves, the barren woman cannot have a child. Nothing changes.

EXAMINER'S COMMENT

This top-grade response traces the two interconnected narratives, focusing on the dramatic significance of these events. The similar tones of those in charge are well explored: Trevelyan's 'offensive' remarks are mirrored in 'the doctor's response to his infertile patient'. An interesting point is made about the omission of the victims' voices. Expression is controlled and confident throughout.

Class/Homework Exercises

1. To what extent does 'The Famine Road' show Eavan Boland's sympathies for the outsiders and the marginalised in society? Refer to the poem in your answer.
2. Eavan Boland makes effective use of several dramatic techniques in 'The Famine Road'. Discuss this view, supporting your points with close reference to the poem.

Summary Points

- **Dramatic recreation of famine suffering and exploitation.**
- **Updated comparison with the experience of an infertile woman.**
- **Authentic language, descriptive details, stark imagery, symbols.**
- **Sound effects echo the harsh, cynical atmosphere.**

4 The Shadow Doll

Title: a shadow doll was sent to the bride-to-be in Victorian times by her dressmaker. It consisted of a Victorian figurine under a dome of glass modelling the proposed wedding dress.

They stitched blooms from ivory tulle
to hem the oyster gleam of the veil.
They made hoops for the crinoline.

Now, in summary and neatly sewn –
a porcelain bride in an airless glamour –
the shadow doll survives its occasion.

Under glass, under wraps, it stays
even now, after all, discreet about
visits, fevers, quickenings and lusts

and just how, when she looked at
the shell-tone spray of seed pearls,
the bisque features, she could see herself

inside it all, holding less than real
stephanotis, rose petals, never feeling
satin rise and fall with the vows

I kept repeating on the night before –
astray among the cards and wedding gifts –
the coffee pots and the clocks and

the battered tan case full of cotton
lace and tissue-paper, pressing down, then
pressing down again. And then, locks.

tulle: fine net fabric.

oyster: off-white colour.

crinoline: hooped petticoat.

discreet: careful to avoid embarrassment by keeping confidences secret; unobtrusive.

quickenings: sensations; a woman's awareness of the first movements of the child in the womb.

bisque: unglazed white porcelain.

stephanotis: scented white flowers used for displays at both weddings and funerals.

Personal Response

1. What style of language is used to describe the doll? Do you consider it beautiful or stifling, or both? Illustrate your response with reference to the poem.
2. Choose two phrases from the poem that you found particularly interesting. Explain the reasons for your choice.
3. Do you think marriage has changed for the modern bride in today's world? Refer to the last two stanzas in your answer.

Critical Literacy

'The Shadow Doll' is taken from the 1990 collection of poems, *Outside History*. The shadow doll wore a model of the wedding dress for the bride-to-be. Boland uses the doll as a symbol to explore the submission and silence surrounding women and women's issues by placing the late-twentieth century and Victorian times side by side.

The first two stanzas describe the doll vividly, with her 'ivory tulle' and 'oyster gleam'. The 'porcelain doll' is a **beautiful, fragile object**, but the 'ivory' and 'oyster' colours are lifeless. Passivity and restriction are being shown in the phrase 'neatly sewn'. The pronoun 'it' is used – the woman is seen as an object, not a real flesh-and-blood human being. Her community is described in the preparations: 'They stitched', 'They made'. Are they colluding in the constraint? The phrase 'airless glamour' conveys an allure that has been deprived of life-giving oxygen. The occasion of the marriage is long gone, but the doll remains as a reminder, a shadow of what was.

'a porcelain bride'

The **language of containment** and imprisonment is continued in stanza three: 'Under glass, under wraps'. The doll is silent and 'discreet'; it knows but does not tell. The bride would have kept the doll throughout her life, so the doll would have been present at all major events such as marriage, childbirth, sickness and intimate moments, 'visits, fevers, quickenings and lusts'. These experiences are not explored in poetry, which is why women and their issues are 'outside history'. They are neither recorded nor commented on.

Stanza four sees the **pronoun change to 'she'** as the poet imagines the Victorian bride considering her own wedding: 'she could see herself/inside it all'. It is as if she becomes like the doll, assuming a mask of 'bisque features' and unable to feel real life: 'holding less than real/stephanotis', 'never feeling/satin rise and fall with the vows'. The only remnant of her life is the silent doll. Stanza five ends with the word 'vows', and this is the link into the next stanza, which is a view from the modern-day bride where the narrative voice becomes 'I'.

The poet is 'repeating' the same vows as the Victorian bride. Are these entrapping and imprisoning women? Like the Victorian bride, the modern bride is surrounded by things ('cards and wedding gifts'), yet she is 'astray' (stanza six), with the same **sense of disorientation** coming over her. Is she feeling this because she is losing her individual identity as she agrees to become part of a couple?

Stanza seven increases the **feelings of restriction** when the suitcase is described as 'battered', and there is the added emphatic repetition of 'pressing down'. Finally, the single monosyllable 'locks' clicks the poem to an end. The onomatopoeic sound echoes through the years as Boland voices the silence in the depressing ending. For some women, little has changed since Victorian times.

Writing About the Poem

'Boland's poems often end on a bleak note.' Discuss how 'The Shadow Doll' reflects this statement. Illustrate your response with reference to the text.

Sample Paragraph

The onomatopoeia of the word 'locks' echoes with frightening intensity at the end of 'The Shadow Doll'. It suggests to me the clang of a prison door as the prisoner is denied freedom. This poem explores the nature and meaning of marriage for women. It starts with the description of the Victorian doll with its wedding dress, which seems to become a stifling mask fitted on a living, breathing woman, 'airless glamour', 'Under glass', 'under wraps'. The modern bride is 'astray'. Marriage is shown as confining and silencing, 'discreet'. The repetition of the phrase 'pressing down' has an almost nightmarish sense of claustrophobia. Both the Victorian bride and the modern bride are surrounded by objects, 'seed pearls', 'stephanotis', 'the cards and wedding gifts'. I find it strange that there is no mention of the groom, or friends or families. Instead there is a growing sense of isolation and intimidation culminating in the echoing phrase 'And then, locks'. What or who is locked in? What or who is locked out?

EXAMINER'S COMMENT

This short response carefully considers the effect of the poem's ending and Boland's exploration of the theme of marriage as a repressive and restricting force in women's lives. The paragraph also touches on interesting questions about the narrow views expressed in the poem. A real sense of individual engagement is evident, particularly in the comment about the final two rhetorical questions. Top-grade standard.

Class/Homework Exercises

1. 'In her poetry, Boland uses concrete images of objects, colours and textures to explore themes.' In your opinion, how valid is this statement? Use reference to 'The Shadow Doll' in your answer.
2. In 'The Shadow Doll', Boland succeeds in highlighting the experience of women in patriarchal societies. Discuss this view using close reference to the poem.

Summary Points

- **Themes include the changing nature of marriage and the oppression of women.**
- **Effective concrete details, symbolism, confinement imagery, repetition.**
- **Dreamlike sense of disorientation.**
- **Varying tones – reflective, sympathetic, critical and hopeful.**

5 White Hawthorn in the West of Ireland

Title: hawthorn is a flowering tree that blossoms in springtime. It is associated with fairy tales and superstitions in Irish folklore. People believed that it was unlucky to cut hawthorn or to keep it indoors.

I drove West
in the season between seasons.
I left behind suburban gardens.
Lawnmowers. Small talk.

Under low skies, past splashes of coltsfoot,
I assumed
the hard shyness of Atlantic light
and the superstitious aura of hawthorn.

All I wanted then was to fill my arms with
sharp flowers,
to seem, from a distance, to be part of
that ivory, downhill rush. But I knew,

I had always known
the custom was
not to touch hawthorn.
Not to bring it indoors for the sake of

the luck
such constraint would forfeit –
a child might die, perhaps, or an unexplained
fever speckle heifers. So I left it

stirring on those hills
with a fluency
only water has. And, like water, able
to re-define land. And free to seem to be –

for anglers,
and for travellers astray in
the unmarked lights of a May dusk –
the only language spoken in those parts.

the season: between spring and summer.

coltsfoot: wild plant with yellow flowers.
assumed: became part of.
Atlantic light: unsettled weather causes the light to vary.
superstitious aura: disquiet associated with hawthorn stories.

forfeit: lose, risk.

heifers: cows which have not yet had calves.

Personal Response

1. Describe the poet's changing mood as she travels from her suburban home to the West. Refer to the text in your answer.
2. There are many beautiful images in the poem. Choose two that you find interesting and briefly explain their appeal.
3. What is the significance of the white hawthorn? What might it symbolise? Refer closely to the poem in your answer.

Critical Literacy

In this poem, the folklore associated with hawthorn in rural Ireland is seen as symbolic of an ancient 'language' that has almost disappeared. Boland structures her themes around the image of a journey into the West. It seems as though she is hoping to return to her roots in the traditional landscape of the West of Ireland.

The poem opens on a conversational note. Boland's clear intention is to leave the city behind: 'I drove West/in the season between seasons'. Her tone is determined, dismissing the **artificial life of suburbia** ('Lawnmowers. Small talk.') in favour of the freedom awaiting her. Stanza one emphasises the poet's strong desire to get away from her cultivated suburban confines, which seem colourless and overly regulated. The broken rhythm of line 4 adds to the abrupt sense of rigidity.

'the superstitious aura'

This orderly landscape is in stark contrast with the world of 'Atlantic light' Boland discovers on her journey. Stanzas two and three contain **striking images of energy and growth**. The 'splashes of coltsfoot' suggest a fresh enthusiasm for the wide open spaces as she becomes one with this changing environment. The prominent sibilant 's' underpins the rich stillness of the remote countryside.

She seems both fearful and fascinated by the hawthorn's 'superstitious aura'. The experience is similar to an artist becoming increasingly absorbed in the joy of painting. Run-on lines and the frequent use of the pronoun 'I' accentuate our appreciation of the **poet's own delight** in 'that ivory, downhill rush'.

Stanzas four and five focus on the mystery and superstition associated with hawthorn in Irish folk tradition. Boland's awareness of the **possible dangers** check her eagerness as she considers the stories that have been handed down: 'a child might die, perhaps'. The poet is momentarily caught between a desire to fill her arms with these wild flowers and her own disquieting belief in the superstitions. Eventually, she decides to follow her intuition and respect the customs of the West: 'So I left it'.

The personification ('stirring') of the hawthorn in stanza six reinforces Boland's regard for this unfamiliar landscape as a **living place**. The poet's imagination has also been stirred by her journey. In comparing the hawthorn to water, she suggests its elemental power. Both share a natural 'fluency' which can shape and 're-define land'.

The poet links the twin forces of superstition and landscape even more forcibly in stanza seven. They both defy time and transcend recorded history. The hawthorn trees give the poet a **glimpse of Ireland's ancient culture**. Although nature remains elusive, Boland believes that for outsiders like herself – visiting 'anglers' and tourists – it is 'the only language spoken in these parts'. Her final tone is one of resignation as she accepts that she can never fully understand Ireland's unique landscape or the past.

Writing About the Poem

'Boland uses a variety of poetic techniques to create poems which allow readers to contemplate the beauty and mystery of nature.' Discuss this statement, with particular reference to 'White Hawthorn in the West of Ireland'.

Sample Paragraph

Eavan Boland creates vivid word pictures of two contrasting landscapes, the ordered urban and the wild rural. She decisively sets off on her journey, 'I left behind suburban gardens'. Suddenly the view opens out to the big western skyline, full of variable weather, 'the hard shyness of Atlantic light'. The magic of the countryside is conveyed in the 'superstitious aura of hawthorn'. The lush assonance of this line's broad vowels contrasts abruptly with the sharp sounds of the town's descriptive details. The short lines of the first stanza are replaced by long run-on lines mirroring the energy of nature, 'that ivory downhill rush', and the poet's delight, 'All I wanted then was to fill my arms/with sharp flowers'. But there is another aspect to nature foreshadowed in the adjective, 'sharp'. Cutting the hawthorn is considered bad luck in the countryside and Boland respects the local tradition, 'So I left it'. She, like the other tourists, may enjoy, but not fully understand the wild beauty of nature, 'the only language spoken in those parts'. Because of Boland's remarkable poetic skills, readers are left appreciating nature's beauty, 'astray in/the unmarked lights of a May dusk'.

EXAMINER'S COMMENT

This answer focuses on how aspects of Boland's style contribute to communicating her message that nature may be appreciated but never entirely understood. A developed discussion encompasses the poet's use of varying tones and sound effects: 'The lush assonance of this line's broad vowels contrast sharply with the sharp sounds of the town's descriptive details.' Accurate quotation supports the discussion throughout. A confident top-grade standard.

Class/Homework Exercises

1. What do you think Eavan Boland has learned from her journey to the West of Ireland? Refer to the poem, 'White Hawthorn in the West of Ireland', in your answer.
2. Boland makes effective use of both visual and aural imagery to celebrate the Irish landscape in this poem. Discuss this statement, using close reference to the text.

Summary Points

- **Beauty of the native landscape and Irish traditions are central themes.**
- **Contrast between urban and rural landscapes.**
- **Reflective tone reveals the poet's personal feelings and attitudes.**
- **Vivid visual imagery, free rhythm, striking onomatopoeia and sibilant effects.**

Outside History

There are outsiders, always. These stars –
these iron inklings of an Irish January,
whose light happened

thousands of years before
our pain did: they are, they have always been
outside history.

They keep their distance. Under them remains
a place where you found
you were human, and

a landscape in which you know you are mortal.
And a time to choose between them.
I have chosen:

out of myth into history I move to be
part of that ordeal
whose darkness is

only now reaching me from those fields,
those rivers, those roads clotted as
firmaments with the dead.

How slowly they die
as we kneel beside them, whisper in their ear.
And we are too late. We are always too late.

inklings: slight idea or suspicion; clues.

history: record or account of past events and developments; the study of these.

mortal: destined to die.

myth: tale with supernatural characters; untrue idea or explanation; imaginary person; story with a germ of truth in it.
ordeal: painful experience.

clotted as: clogged up.

firmaments: sky or heavens.

'These stars'

Personal Response

1. How are the stars 'outsiders'? Do you think they are an effective symbol for those who are marginalised and regarded as being of no importance? Discuss, using reference from the poem.
2. In your opinion, what does Boland mean by the final line of the poem?
3. Write a short personal response to 'Outside History', highlighting the impact the poem made on you.

Critical Literacy

'Outside History' was written in 1990 as part of a collection of poems that were arranged to reflect the changing seasons. This poem is set in January. Boland believes that it is important to remember the experiences of those who have not been recorded in history. These are the outsiders, 'the lost, the voiceless, the silent' to whom she gives a hauntingly beautiful voice.

Lines 1–6. The poem opens with an **impersonal statement**: 'There are outsiders, always'. The poet is referring to those who have not been recorded in history. The stars are also outsiders, standing outside and above human history. At their great distance, they are shown as cold and distant ('iron', 'Irish January'). They have a permanence and longevity that are in contrast to human life: 'whose light happened/thousands of years before/our pain did'. The run-on line suggests the light that travels thousands of years to reach us. The phrase 'outside history' is placed on its own to emphasise how the stars do not belong to human history.

Lines 7–10. The poet stresses **the remoteness of the stars**: 'They keep their distance'. They don't want to be involved. Now she turns to 'you', a member of the human race, and places 'you' in context with the words 'place' and 'landscape'. This is where 'you found/you were human' and 'mortal'. Unlike the stars; 'you' are a suffering member of the human race who is subject to ageing and death. The line 'And a time to choose between them' could refer to choosing between the perspective of the stars, i.e. remaining at an uninvolved distance, or the perspective of a member of the human race, i.e. involved and anguished.

Lines 11–18. The phrase 'I have chosen' marks a **turning point** in the poem. Boland has made a deliberate decision, moving away from 'myth' and tradition. She felt that myth obscures history. She regarded figures like Caitlín Ní Houlihán and Dark Rosaleen, female symbols for Ireland, as 'passive', 'simplified' and 'decorative' emblems in male poems. For the poet, history was laced with myths, which, in her opinion, were as unreal, cold and distant as the stars are from reality. She regarded these mythic emblems as false and limiting, 'a corruption'. Boland is trying to achieve a sense of belonging and wholeness by unwinding the myth and the stereotype. She wanted reality rather than the glittering image of the stars: 'out of myth into history I move to be/part of that ordeal'.

Just as the stars' light travelled vast distances to reach us, so the darkness of unwritten history is travelling to reach her 'only now'. The run-on stanza again suggests great distances that had to be covered for the poet to connect with the past. There follows a description that recalls the **Irish famine**: 'those fields', 'those rivers', 'those roads' which were covered with 'the dead'. The paradoxical phrase 'clotted as/firmaments' uses the language of the stars to describe the numberless bodies strewn everywhere as a result of the famine. This condensed image evokes a poignant sense of the unmarked graves of countless victims, as numberless as the stars.

Lines 19–21. The concluding stanza changes to the collective 'we'. Is this referring to the Irish people accepting responsibility for **honouring the dead** and being part of history? The rite of contrition is being said: 'As we kneel beside them, whisper in their ear'. It was believed that the person's soul would go to rest in heaven as he or she had made their peace with God, but the repetition of the last line stresses that the words of comfort have come 'too late'. The people don't know they are being honoured by the poet. Nevertheless, the poem stands as a testament to them and their unrecorded history. Has Boland changed her attitude from the beginning of the poem: 'There are outsiders, always'? Has she brought them in from the cold sidelines, including them into history? Or has she (and we) left it too late?

Writing About the Poem

'Eavan Boland's poetry gives a haunting voice to the marginalised and dispossessed in society.' Discuss this statement, with particular reference to 'Outside History'.

Sample Paragraph

A stark statement opens the poem, 'There are outsiders, always', reminiscent of Christ's statement that the poor are always with us. I found the symbol of the stars effective because they represented the cold distance the outsiders must feel as they look in, but don't belong, 'they have always been/outside history'. The sympathetic tone and the alliterative phrase, 'iron inklings of an Irish January' capture the predicament facing marginalised people. The stars show no human empathy with the dispossessed, 'They keep their distance'. But Boland has 'chosen' to embrace her humane side. She will be 'part of that ordeal' in order to give a voice to those forgotten. The run-on stanza indicates how long it has taken. She gives them an unforgettable voice, recalling their tragic story, 'those roads clotted as/firmaments with the dead'. The verb 'clotted' suggests the obscenity of what happened to the victims, evoking abandoned mounds of earth where they lay. The poem ends with the melancholy realisation, 'And we are too late'. They won't know that they are being remembered. The dispossessed may not, but Boland has given them a voice.

EXAMINER'S COMMENT

As part of a full essay this perceptive reading of Boland's poem addresses the task directly in a series of accurately referenced arguments. Excellent use of quotation throughout supports the thoughtful discussion points. Expression is also clear and impressive, 'But Boland has chosen to embrace her humane side'. An informed exploration of the poet's language also ensures the top-grade standard.

Class/Homework Exercises

1. Does 'Outside History' make a compelling case on behalf of voiceless and marginalised people? Support your answer with close reference to the text of the poem.
2. In your opinion, what does the dominant tone throughout the poem reveal about Eavan Boland as a person? Support your answer with close reference to the text.

Summary Points

- **Key themes – exclusion of the marginalised.**
- **Boland's distrust of myth, history and stereotypes.**
- **Varying tones – reflective, regretful, didactic.**
- **Effective use of repetition, striking imagery.**

7 The Black Lace Fan My Mother Gave Me

It was the first gift he ever gave her,
buying it for five francs in the Galeries
in pre-war Paris. It was stifling.
A starless drought made the nights stormy.

They stayed in the city for the summer.
They met in cafés. She was always early.
He was late. That evening he was later.
They wrapped the fan. He looked at his watch.

She looked down the Boulevard des Capucines.
She ordered more coffee. She stood up.
The streets were emptying. The heat was killing.
She thought the distance smelled of rain and lightning.

These are wild roses, appliquéd on silk by hand,
darkly picked, stitched boldly, quickly.
The rest is tortoiseshell and has the reticent,
clear patience of its element. It is

a worn-out, underwater bullion and it keeps,
even now, an inference of its violation.
The lace is overcast as if the weather
it opened for and offset had entered it.

The past is an empty café terrace.
An airless dusk before thunder. A man running.
And no way now to know what happened then –
none at all – unless, of course, you improvise:

The blackbird on this first sultry morning,
in summer, finding buds, worms, fruit,
feels the heat. Suddenly she puts out her wing –
the whole, full, flirtatious span of it.

Galeries: Galeries Lafayette is a store in Paris.

appliquéd: trimming.

tortoiseshell: clear decorative material.
reticent: reserved, restrained.

bullion: treasure.

improvise: make up, imagine.

flirtatious: enticing, playful.
span: extent, measure.

Personal Response

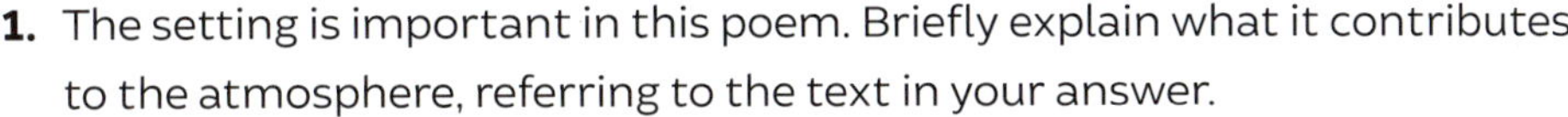

1. The setting is important in this poem. Briefly explain what it contributes to the atmosphere, referring to the text in your answer.
2. Comment on the effect of the short sentences and irregular rhythms in the first three stanzas.
3. Did you like this poem? Give reasons for your response, referring to the text of the poem in your answer.

Critical Literacy

Set in pre-war Paris in the 1930s, the incident that occurs is the giving of a gift, a black lace fan that the poet's father gave to her mother. A fan was usually seen as a sign of romantic love and desire. However, its significance here is never entirely explained to us. Maybe this is in recognition of our inability to fully understand other people's relationships or to recall the past and the effect it has on us. Boland's poem is one of those attempts.

Stanza one begins on a narrative note as the poet recreates a significant moment in her parents' lives back in the 1930s. **The fan was a special symbol of young love** and was important because it was 'the first gift' from her father to her mother. Other details of the precise cost and the 'stifling' weather add to the importance of the occasion. Although the Parisian

'And no way now to know what happened then'

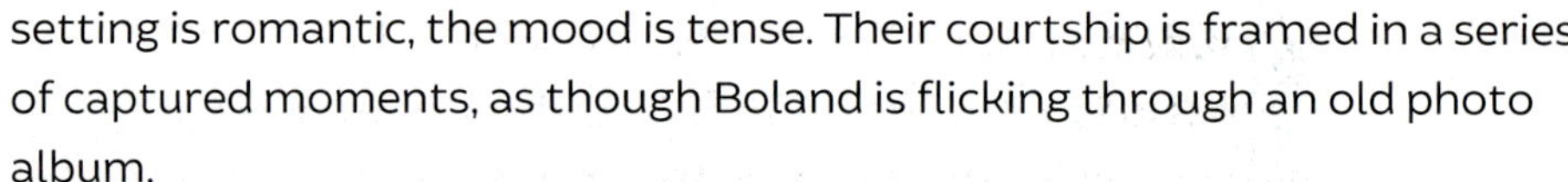

setting is romantic, the mood is tense. Their courtship is framed in a series of captured moments, as though Boland is flicking through an old photo album.

In stanzas two and three, short sentences and the growing unevenness of the rhythm add to this cinematic quality: 'They met in cafés. She was always early'. The hesitant relationship between the lovers is conveyed repeatedly through their nervous gestures: 'He looked at his watch', 'She stood up'. Boland builds up the tension through references to the heat wave: 'the distance smelled of rain and lightning'. The image might also suggest the **stormy nature of what lay ahead** for the couple.

Stanzas four and five focus on the elegant lace fan in **vivid detail**. The poet notes its decorative qualities, carefully embroidered with the most romantic 'wild roses' and fine 'tortoiseshell'. She seems fascinated by the painstaking craft ('stitched boldly') involved in creating this beautiful token of love. But the poet's appreciation of the fan becomes diminished with guilt. The tortoiseshell has suffered 'violation' at the expense of the gift. In Boland's mind, the delicate colours decorating the fan came from 'a worn-out, underwater bullion'. The tone is suddenly downbeat as the thought throws a shadow ('The lace is overcast') on her parents' relationship.

In stanza six, the poet imagines the romantic Parisian drama of the 'empty café terrace', but admits that she can never know what really happened that fateful evening in the 'airless dusk before thunder'. Instead, she must 'improvise' it. But at least the romantic moment is preserved in her imagination. Not for the first time, however, there is an underlying suggestion of the reality of relationships over time, and the balance of joy and disappointment that is likely. For Boland, the fan is only a small part of her parents' story. Perhaps she realises that **the past can never be completely understood**.

The striking image of a blackbird dominates the final stanza. The poet returns to the present as she observes the bird 'in summer, finding buds'. The movement of the blackbird's wing is an unexpected link with the black lace fan all those years ago. While the souvenir is old, its significance as a symbol of youthful romance can still be found elsewhere. For the first time, **Boland now seems to understand the beauty of her parents' love** for each other. The last lines are daring and appear to describe both the blackbird and her mother as a young girl holding her new gift: 'Suddenly she puts out her wing –/the whole, full, flirtatious span of it'. The energetic pace of the lines combine with the alliterative sounds and sibilant music to produce a lively sense of celebration at the end.

Writing About the Poem

'Eavan Boland takes a balanced, unsentimental view of relationships.' To what extent is this true of 'The Black Lace Fan My Mother Gave Me'? Support your answer with reference to the poem.

Sample Paragraph

This poem is not a typical love poem. It is out of the ordinary. The poet does not try to glorify the relationship. Indeed, they seem unsure of each other. The poet tries to work out the story behind their relationship by looking at the lace fan. She imagines the intense heat of Paris: 'It was stifling.' References to the weather hint at an uncomfortable relationship: 'The heat was killing.' Boland might be referring indirectly to the future problems in the couple's marriage over the years. The fact that the Second World War was about to break out is also a bad sign. Having said that, the gift of the fan is a symbol of the attraction the couple felt. It is a traditional image of true romance. Eavan shows the reality of the relationship by noting the unsentimental details: 'He was late', 'She stood up'. There was nervousness when they were first infatuated with each other, but their love was to change over time. She also compares the fan to a blackbird's wing which excites the poet. This gives us a final impression that Boland is happy to imagine the love between her parents back in the 1930s. In a way, the poem is as much about the love Boland herself feels for her parents as about their love.

EXAMINER'S COMMENT

This paragraph focuses well on the way love is presented throughout the poem. The answer would have been improved by a less note-like commentary at the beginning. Good use is made of suitable quotations and this high-grade response is well-rounded off with an effective point about the poet's own enduring love for her parents.

Class/Homework Exercises

1. Comment on Eavan Boland's use of symbolism in 'The Black Lace Fan My Mother Gave Me', referring to the text in your answer.
2. What does Boland's poem reveal about her parents' relationship? Support the points you make with reference to both the subject matter and language use in the poem.

Summary Points

- **Themes include romantic love and changing family relationships.**
- **Striking language – central symbol of the fan, dramatic image of the blackbird.**
- **Evocative atmosphere of 1930s Paris.**
- **Vivid detail; varying tones – reflective, nostalgic, realistic.**

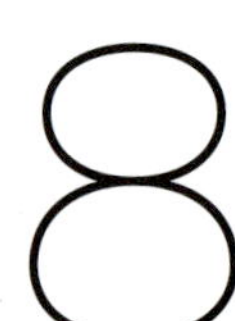

This Moment

A neighbourhood.
At dusk.

Things are getting ready
to happen
out of sight.

Stars and moths.
And rinds slanting around fruit.

But not yet.

One tree is black.
One window is yellow as butter.

A woman leans down to catch a child
who has run into her arms
this moment.

Stars rise.
Moths flutter.
Apples sweeten in the dark.

rinds: peels.

Personal Response

1. Choose either one visual or one aural image from the poem, and briefly comment on its effectiveness. Support your answer by referring to the text.
2. Comment on how Boland manages to create drama within the poem.
3. What do you think is the central theme in the poem? Refer closely to the text in your answer.

Critical Literacy

In this short lyric poem, Eavan Boland captures the experience of a passing moment in time. It is clear that she is moved by the ordinariness of suburban life, where she glimpses the immeasurable beauty of nature and human nature. The occasion is another reminder of the mystery and wonder of all creation, as expressed by the American poet Walt Whitman, who wrote, 'I know of nothing else but miracles'.

The poem's opening lines introduce a suburban area in any part of the world. Boland pares the scene down to its essentials. All we learn is that it is dusk, a time of transition. The atmosphere is one of quiet intensity. Full stops break the rhythm and force us to evaluate what is happening. Although we are presented with an **anonymous setting**, it seems strangely familiar. The late evening – especially as darkness falls – can be a time for reflecting about the natural world.

The stillness and dramatic anticipation intensify further in lines 3–8. Something important is about to happen 'out of sight'. Boland then considers some of nature's wonders: 'Stars and moths'. In the twilight, everything seems mysterious, even 'rinds slanting around fruit'. The poet's eye for detail is like that of an artist. The rich, sensory image of the cut fruit is exact and tactile. She uses simple language precisely to create a **mood of natural calmness** that is delayed for a split second ('But not yet').

There is time for two more **vivid images** in lines 9–10. The startling colour contrast between the 'black' tree and the window that is 'yellow as butter' has a cinematic effect. The simile is homely, in keeping with the domestic setting. Repetition of 'One' focuses our attention as the build-up continues. Again, Boland presents the sequence of events in a series of brief glimpses. It is as if she is marking time, preparing us for the key moment of revelation.

This occurs in lines 11–13. The central image of the mother and child intuitively reaching out for each other is a powerful symbol of unconditional love. It is every bit as wonderful as any of life's greatest mysteries. The three lines become progressively condensed as the child reaches her mother. The syntax suggests their eagerness to show their love for each other. Boland's decision to generalise ('A woman' and 'a child') emphasises the **universal significance** of 'this moment'. The crucial importance of people's feelings transcends time and place.

There is a slight tone of anti-climax about the last three lines. However, Boland rounds off her description of the moment by placing it within a wider context. The constant expression of family love is in harmony with everything else that is beautiful in nature. This feeling is suggested by the recurring sibilant 's' sounds and the carefully chosen verbs ('rise', 'flutter' and 'sweeten'), all of which celebrate the excitement and **joy of everyday human relationships**.

Writing About the Poem

'Eavan Boland's poetry deals effectively with important contemporary issues.' Discuss this statement, with particular reference to her poem, 'This Moment'.

Sample Paragraph

Boland places her poem in a contemporary setting, a Dublin suburb at dusk. The short lines, 'A neighbourhood./At dusk', set a modern tone for this anonymous, yet familiar scene which is played out worldwide. The mystery of this transition time between day and night is caught in the economical run-on lines, 'Things are getting ready/to happen/out of sight'. In this 'not yet' moment, the mysterious powers of nature are observed, 'rinds slanting around fruit'. Yet, I also feel there is a slight tinge of danger, reminding me of the serpent in the Garden of Eden waiting to pounce. Boland's famous painterly eye precisely captures this moment at dusk, the silhouetted tree, the window lit by its electric lamp, 'One tree is black./ One window is yellow as butter'. Suddenly a child runs into a waiting mother's arms, 'A woman leans down to catch a child'. The general terms used emphasise the universal significance of this experience of a child returning to the security of a mother's arms. The tension of the moment is relaxed as if nature exhales, all is now in its rightful place. A series of gentle verbs, 'rise', 'flutter' and 'sweeten', trace its movement. Boland's poem describes a common social issue – how in this uncertain modern world, every parent gives a sigh of relief when a child returns safely home.

EXAMINER'S COMMENT

This competent response addresses both the theme and style of the poem. A developed discussion deals with Boland's use of free verse and economical language. An interesting personal reading of the poem is given in the line, 'I also feel there is a slight tinge of danger ...'. This well-written, successful answer engages closely with the text of the poem. Top-grade standard.

Class/Homework Exercises

1. Comment on the poet's tone in 'This Moment'. Refer to the text in your discussion.
2. A sense of intense mystery is often found in Boland's poetry. To what extent is this true of 'This Moment'? Support your answer with close reference to the poem.

Summary Points

- **Themes include the mystery of nature and the beauty of loving relationships.**
- **Effective use of simple language and succinct dramatic style.**
- **Vivid, sensuous imagery; sibilant and assonant effects.**
- **Varying moods – subdued, reflective, celebratory.**

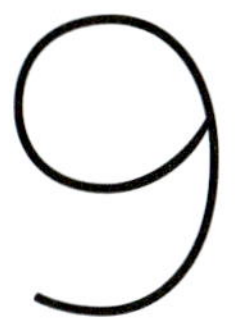

 The Pomegranate

EAVAN BOLAND

Title: the pomegranate (from a French word meaning an apple with many seeds) is a pulpy oriental fruit.

The only legend I have ever loved is
the story of a daughter lost in hell.
And found and rescued there.
Love and blackmail are the gist of it.
Ceres and Persephone the names.
And the best thing about the legend is
I can enter it anywhere. And have.
As a child in exile in
a city of fogs and strange consonants,
I read it first and at first I was
an exiled child in the crackling dusk of
the underworld, the stars blighted. Later
I walked out in a summer twilight
searching for my daughter at bed-time.
When she came running I was ready
to make any bargain to keep her.
I carried her back past whitebeams
and wasps and honey-scented buddleias.
But I was Ceres then and I knew
winter was in store for every leaf
on every tree on that road.
Was inescapable for each one we passed.
And for me.
            It is winter
and the stars are hidden.
I climb the stairs and stand where I can see
my child asleep beside her teen magazines,
her can of Coke, her plate of uncut fruit.
The pomegranate! How did I forget it?
She could have come home and been safe
and ended the story and all
our heart-broken searching but she reached
out a hand and plucked a pomegranate.
She put out her hand and pulled down
the French sound for apple and
the noise of stone and the proof
that even in the place of death,
at the heart of legend, in the midst
of rocks full of unshed tears
ready to be diamonds by the time

Ceres and Persephone: mythological figures. Ceres was the goddess of earth and motherhood. Persephone was her beautiful daughter who was forced by Pluto to become his wife and was imprisoned in Hades, the underworld. Ceres was determined to find Persephone and threatened to prevent anything from growing on the earth until she was allowed to rescue her daughter. But because Persephone had eaten sacred pomegranate seeds in Hades, she was condemned forever to spend part of every year there.

city of fogs: London, where the poet once lived.

buddleias: ornamental bushes with small purple flowers.

the story was told, a child can be
hungry. I could warn her. There is still a chance.
The rain is cold. The road is flint-coloured.
The suburb has cars and cable television.
The veiled stars are above ground.
It is another world. But what else
can a mother give her daughter but such
beautiful rifts in time?
If I defer the grief I will diminish the gift.
The legend will be hers as well as mine.
She will enter it. As I have.
She will wake up. She will hold
the papery flushed skin in her hand.
And to her lips. I will say nothing.

rifts: gaps, cracks.
defer: delay.

Personal Response

1. Boland conveys a sense of the city of London in this poem. How does she succeed in doing this? Refer closely to the text in your answer.
2. From your reading of this poem, what do you learn about the relationship between the poet and her daughter? Refer to the text in your answer.
3. Comment on the poet's mood in the last five lines of the poem.

Critical Literacy

In the poem, narrated as one unrhymed stanza, Boland explores the theme of parental loss by comparing her own experiences as a mother and daughter with the myth of Ceres and Persephone. Although it is a personal poem, it has a much wider relevance for families everywhere.

'my chil
asleep'

Boland presents this exploration of the mother–child relationship as a dramatic narrative. In the opening lines, the poet tells us that she has always related to 'the story of a daughter lost in hell'. This goes back to her early experience as 'a child in exile' living in London. Her **sense of displacement** is evident in the detailed description of that 'city of fogs and strange consonants'. Like Persephone trapped in Hades, Boland yearned for home. But the myth has a broader relevance to the poet's life – she 'can enter it anywhere'. Years later, she recalls a time when, as a mother, she could also identify with Ceres, 'searching for my daughter'.

Lines 13–18 express the intensity of Boland's feelings for her child: she was quite prepared 'to make any bargain to keep her'. The **anxious tone** reflects the poet's awareness of the importance of appreciating the closeness between herself and her teenage daughter while time allows. She expresses her maternal feelings through rich natural images: 'I carried her back past whitebeams'. But she is also increasingly aware that both she and her daughter are getting older. This is particularly evident in line 20, as she anticipates an 'inescapable' change in their relationship: 'winter was in store for every leaf'.

Line 24 marks a defining moment ('It is winter') for them both. Observing her daughter asleep in her bedroom, Boland now sees herself as Ceres and the 'plate of uncut fruit' as the pomegranate. This marks the realisation that **her child has become an adult**. The poet imagines how different it might have been had Persephone not eaten the fruit – 'She could have come home' and ended all the 'heart-broken searching'. But Persephone deliberately made her choice, a decision that is emphasised by the repeated mention of her gesture ('she reached/out a hand', 'She put out her hand'). Significantly, Boland is sympathetic: 'a child can be/hungry'.

In line 42, the poet considers alerting her daughter ('I could warn her') about the dangers and disappointments that lie ahead. **Harsh imagery** suggests the difficulties of modern life: 'The rain is cold. The road is flint-coloured'. Boland wonders if 'beautiful rifts in time' are the most a mother can offer. Such delaying tactics may only postpone natural development into adulthood.

In the end, she decides to 'say nothing'. There is a clear sense of resignation in the final lines. The poet accepts the reality of change. Boland's daughter will experience the same stages of childhood and motherhood as the poet herself: 'The legend will be hers as well as mine'. This truth is underlined by the recurring use of 'She will', a recognition that her daughter's destiny is in her own hands. The **poem ends on a quietly reflective note** as Boland respectfully acknowledges the right of her daughter to mature naturally and make her own way in life.

Writing About the Poem

'Eavan Boland's use of mythical references vividly illuminates her own personal experiences.' Discuss this statement, with particular reference to Boland's poem, 'The Pomegranate'.

Sample Paragraph

Eavan Boland has been very successful in blending her own life as a child and mother with Persephone and Ceres. The fact that she uses an ancient legend adds a touch of mystery to the theme of mother–daughter relationships. This gives the poem a universal quality. First, she compares herself to Persephone, the exiled child in London. This links the grimy city life to the underworld of Hades. But Boland is more concerned with the present and her fears of losing her own daughter who is growing up fast. By describing her fears through the old story of Ceres, she increases our understanding of how anxious she was feeling. Both parents were 'searching' desperately. Together, the legend and the true life story of the poet and her reluctance to come to terms with her daughter growing up really show how parents have to let go of their children and give them the freedom to make their own mistakes and learn for themselves. Most parents find it hard to give their children freedom. Overall, the mythical references emphasise the universality of Boland's natural feelings for her daughter. I thought they were very effective in conveying the poem's central theme.

EXAMINER'S COMMENT

There are some very good points here in response to a challenging question. Although the answer shows personal engagement, it could be rooted more thoroughly in the text through a more extensive use of quotation. Some sentences are overlong and the expression is repetitive at times (with overuse of the words 'fears' and 'freedom'). Points would need to be more developed to achieve the top grade.

Class/Homework Exercises

1. What image of Eavan Boland herself emerges from 'The Pomegranate'? Refer closely to the text in your answer.
2. Boland manages to create a series of powerfully evocative moods throughout this poem. Discuss this statement, supporting your answer with close reference to the text.

Summary Points

- **Boland considers the complexity of mother-daughter relationships.**
- **Striking images – nature, family and the difficulties of modern life.**
- **Mythical references reflect a timeless, universal sense of loss.**
- **Tones vary – empathetic, anxious, resigned.**

EAVAN BOLAND

10 Love

Dark falls on this mid-western town
where we once lived when myths collided.
Dusk has hidden the bridge in the river
which slides and deepens
to become the water
the hero crossed on his way to hell.

Not far from here is our old apartment.
We had a kitchen and an Amish table.
We had a view. And we discovered there
love had the feather and muscle of wings
and had come to live with us,
a brother of fire and air.

We had two infant children one of whom
was touched by death in this town
and spared: and when the hero
was hailed by his comrades in hell
their mouths opened and their voices failed and
there is no knowing what they would have asked
about a life they had shared and lost.

I am your wife.
It was years ago.
Our child was healed. We love each other still.
Across our day-to-day and ordinary distances
we speak plainly. We hear each other clearly.

And yet I want to return to you
on the bridge of the Iowa river as you were,
with snow on the shoulders of your coat
and a car passing with its headlights on:

I see you as a hero in a text –
the image blazing and the edges gilded –
and I long to cry out the epic question
my dear companion:

mid-western town: In 1979, Boland lived in the United States and attended the prestigious Iowa Writers' Workshop.

myths: fictitious tales with supernatural characters and events.

hero: Aeneas was a hero in the Aeneid. He visited the underworld by crossing the River Styx where he saw his dead companions, but they could not communicate with him.

Amish: strict American religious sect that makes functional, practical furniture without decoration.

epic: great, ambitious.

Will we ever live so intensely again?
Will love come to us again and be
so formidable at rest it offered us ascension
even to look at him?

But the words are shadows and you cannot hear me.
You walk away and I cannot follow.

formidable: very impressive.

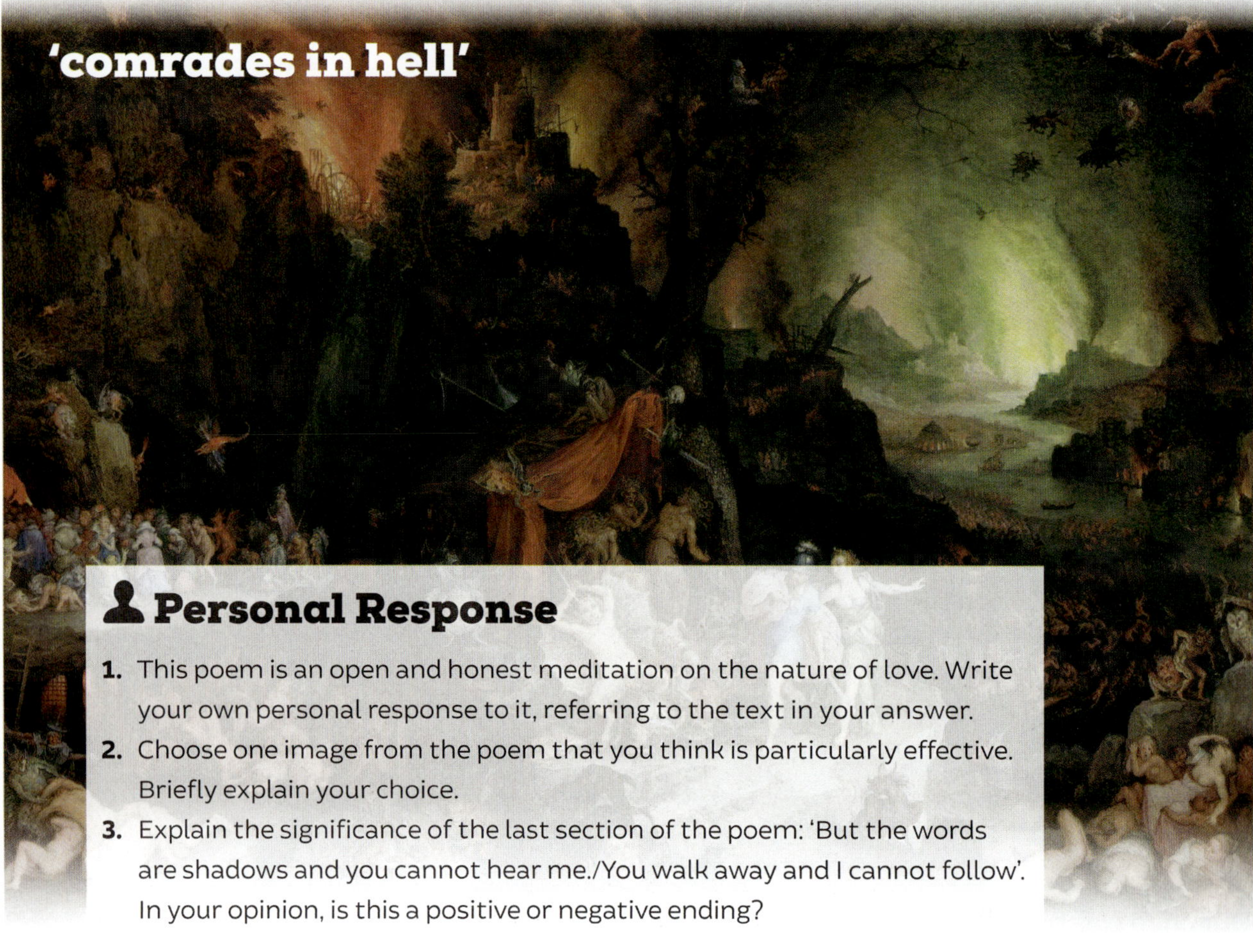

Personal Response

1. This poem is an open and honest meditation on the nature of love. Write your own personal response to it, referring to the text in your answer.
2. Choose one image from the poem that you think is particularly effective. Briefly explain your choice.
3. Explain the significance of the last section of the poem: 'But the words are shadows and you cannot hear me./You walk away and I cannot follow'. In your opinion, is this a positive or negative ending?

Critical Literacy

'Love' is part of a sequence of poems called 'Legends' in which Boland explores parallels between myths and modern life. She records her personal experience of family life in Iowa at a time when her youngest daughter was seriously ill and came close to death. This is interwoven with the myth of Aeneas returning to the underworld. The narrative poem explores the nature of human relationships and how they change over time. It also shows the unchanging nature of human experience down through the ages.

Lines 1–6. The poem opens in darkness, **remembering the past**. Boland's personal experience was in 'this mid-western town' in Iowa, and she connects this with the myth of Aeneas visiting the underworld. Aeneas crosses the bridge on the River Styx to reach Hades, the land of the Shades ('the hero crossed on his way to hell'). Boland and her husband were also experiencing their own hell as they visited their very sick little girl in hospital.

Lines 7–12. These lines give us a **clear, detailed picture of their domestic life**: 'a kitchen', 'an Amish table', 'a view'. The poem is written in loose, non-rhyming stanzas, which suits reminiscences. The couple's internal emotional life is shown in the **striking metaphor** 'love had the feather and muscle of wings'. Love was beating, alive, vibrant. The word 'feather' suggests it could soar to great heights, while 'muscle' signifies that it was extraordinarily powerful. This natural, graceful love was palpable, substantial, elemental, 'a brother of fire and air'.

Lines 13–19. The **personal drama** of the sick daughter who 'was touched by death' is recalled. But Boland did not lose her child. The verb 'spared' links us with the myth again. Aeneas is in the underworld, but because his comrades are shadows, they cannot ask the questions they are longing to ask about the life they once shared. This mythical reference reflects the couple's inability to express their intense feelings at such a critical time. The moment of communication is lost: 'there is no knowing what they would have asked'.

Lines 20–36. The poet goes on to consider the **changing nature of love**. The 'we' becomes 'I'– 'I am your wife'. Do they, as husband and wife, communicate as deeply as they did before? Her tone is matter-of-fact, almost businesslike. She wants to recapture the intensity of their love and shared times, when she saw her husband as 'a hero in a text'. In her memory of him, he is outlined by the cars' lights as they pass on the bridge. Described as 'blazing' and 'gilded', he is contrasted to the darkness of the night, as Aeneas is contrasted with the darkness of the underworld. Boland longs to experience that special time, that transcendence, again.

The closing lines are dominated by rhetorical questions: 'Will we ever live so intensely again?' The inference is no. She can imagine asking these questions about the life they shared, but she cannot actually articulate them. This is **similar to Aeneas's dilemma** – his comrades wished to ask questions about the life they shared with him, but 'their voices failed'. Neither Boland nor the 'comrades' could express their feelings. The words of the questions remain unformed, unspoken, 'shadows'.

Lines 37–38. The poem ends with a two-line stanza in which the poet accepts that the **gap cannot be bridged**: 'You walk away and I cannot follow'. There is a real sense of loss and resignation in Boland's final tone.

Writing About the Poem

Memory is one of the central themes in Boland's poem, 'Love'. In your opinion, does the poet convey this theme effectively? Refer to the text in your answer.

Sample Paragraph

By blending myth and personal experience, Boland gives her poems a true sense of universality. But she also blends timelines, the past and the present tenses to give a quality of timelessness. In 'Love', the freshness of a strong memory is captured by her use of the present tense: 'Dark falls', 'here is our old apartment'. The recent past is shown in the past tense as she recalls: 'We had a view', 'love ... had come to live with us', 'We had two infant children'. In the past they had a life together which was lived very intensely. Are they missing any of this now? The tense then changes to the present as Boland states: 'I am your wife'. Here she honestly explores her concerns about the changing nature of love. Their moment of crisis is over: 'Our child was healed'. Realistically she reviews the current situation and notes 'words are shadows', 'you cannot hear me'. The intense personal nature of their love has changed. Like Aeneas's comrades, she cannot express her question ('voices failed'), and her husband, like Aeneas, cannot hear. The changing tenses add a compelling timeless quality to the experience of memory, as time shared is recalled. The poem ends with the never-changing realisation that time cannot be relived.

EXAMINER'S COMMENT

An unusual approach is taken as the response focuses on the use of tenses as a stylistic feature to communicate theme: 'The changing tenses add a compelling timeless quality to the experience of memory'. There is evidence of close reading of the poem and effective use of quotation throughout. Expression is varied and fluent. This assured response, e.g. 'The poem ends with the never-changing realisation that time cannot be relived', deserves a high grade.

Class/Homework Exercises

1. The poem, 'Love', illustrates Boland's subtle skill in conveying significant universal truths through her exploration of personal relationships. Discuss this view, supporting your points with close reference to the text.
2. 'When myths collided.' Do you consider Boland's use of myths in her work effective in exploring her themes? Discuss, referring closely to the poem, 'Love'.

Summary Points

- **The changing nature of romantic love is a central theme.**
- **References to Greek mythology used to explore parallels with modern life.**
- **Use of detailed description, striking metaphors, rhetorical questions.**
- **Contrasting tones of relief, nostalgia, reflection and resignation.**

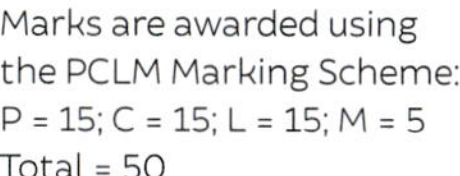

Sample Leaving Cert Questions on Boland's Poetry

1. **'Eavan Boland's poetic narratives often examine contemporary themes through effective comparisons from the shadowlands of myth and history.' Discuss this statement, supporting your answer with reference to the poetry of Eavan Boland on your course.**
2. **'Boland's intensely personal poems address issues that have a timeless quality and a universal significance.' To what extent do you agree or disagree with this statement? Support your answer with reference to the poetry of Eavan Boland on your course.**
3. **From your study of the poetry of Eavan Boland on your course, select the poems that, in your opinion, best demonstrate her skilful use of language and imagery to explore aspects of identity and human rights. Justify your selection by demonstrating Boland's skilful use of language and imagery to explore aspects of identity and human rights in the poems you have chosen.**

Understanding the Prescribed Poetry Question

Marks are awarded using the PCLM Marking Scheme: P = 15; C = 15; L = 15; M = 5 Total = 50

- **P** (Purpose = 15 marks) refers to the set question and is the launch pad for the answer. This involves engaging with all aspects of the question. Both theme and language must be addressed, although not necessarily equally.
- **C** (Coherence = 15 marks) refers to the organisation of the developed response and the use of accurate, relevant quotation. Paragraphing is essential.
- **L** (Language = 15 marks) refers to the student's skill in controlling language throughout the answer.
- **M** (Mechanics = 5 marks) refers to spelling and grammar.
- Although no specific number of poems is required, students usually discuss at least 3 or 4 in their written responses.
- Aim for at least 800 words, to be completed within 45–50 minutes.

How do I organise my answer?

(Sample question 1)

'Eavan Boland's poetic narratives often examine contemporary themes through effective comparisons from the shadowlands of myth and history.' Discuss this statement, supporting your answer with reference to the poetry of Eavan Boland on your course.

Sample Plan 1

Intro: (*Stance: agree with viewpoint in the question*) Boland explores modern and universal issues – e.g. changing nature of relationships and marginalised victims – through powerful references to history and myth.

Point 1: (*Myth – Ceres and Persephone*) 'The Pomegranate' acknowledges difficulty for parents to give children their freedom ('I will say nothing').

Point 2: (*History – Irish Famine*) 'The Famine Road' connects a modern-day infertile woman with an 1840s famine road to show the gap between power and powerlessness. Both are 'Barren', incapable of supporting life. Contrasting voices illustrate the cold sense of dismissal.

Point 3: (*History – Unrecorded Irish Victims*) 'Outside History' honours the 'outsiders' place in history through vivid imagery ('roads clotted as/ firmaments with the dead'). The excluded are finally included.

NOTE

In keeping with the PCLM approach, the student has to take a stance by agreeing and/or disagreeing that Boland's poetic stories examine:

- **present-day issues** (love, war, death, oppression, marginalisation, transition, identity, tradition, victimisation, etc.)

... examined through:

- **comparisons from myth and history** (references to myth and the mysterious past, symbolism and powerful imagery, offering new perspectives on modern themes; enhancing tones, etc.)

Point 4: (*Myth – Aeneas and the Underworld*) 'Love' examines difficulties of communication in a relationship through dramatic metaphors ('the words are shadows and you cannot hear me').

Conclusion: Effective references to myth/history explore specific personal moments that transcend the particular. Boland often highlights the universality of human experience.

Sample Paragraph: Point 1

In 'The Pomegranate', Boland explores the protectiveness of the modern mother towards her child. But the dramatic narrative uses the myth of Ceres and Persephone to show the universal experience of the intense loss experienced when a child moves to 'another world'. The vivid image of the 'plate of uncut fruit' reminds the poet of the pomegranate seeds that Persephone ate in Hades which caused her tragic separation from her mother. The timeless experience of the desperate mother 'searching for my daughter', eager to 'make any bargain to keep her' is vividly recalled. Ceres entered into a bitter-sweet agreement with Pluto to allow her daughter to return to earth for six months of the year. Boland too has to accept the loss of her daughter to adult maturity. With quiet resignation, she realises that she must suffer like Ceres to grant freedom, 'If I defer the grief I will diminish the gift'. In this intensely personal moment of transition and loss, vividly captured in the poet's subdued, reflective tone, Boland respectfully comes to terms with the reality that some things are beyond her control, 'I will say nothing'.

EXAMINER'S COMMENT

This well-written high-grade response succinctly addresses the question through focusing on the central myth used in the poem. Close engagement with the text is evident in the critical discussion which draws comparisons between the mythical references and Boland's own maternal feelings. Comments on tone and imagery respond to the 'poetic' element of the question.

NOTE

In keeping with the PCLM approach, the student has to take a stance by justifying his/her selection of Boland's poems which best demonstrate the poet's:

- **skilful use of language** (carefully crafted observational details, striking imagery and symbolism, memorable aural effects, engaging tones, etc.)

... to explore:

- **features of identity and basic human rights** (uniqueness of self, nationality, belonging, freedom, power, submission, violence, innocent suffering, victimisation, etc.)

(Sample question 3)

From your study of the poetry of Eavan Boland on your course, select the poems that, in your opinion, best demonstrate her skilful use of language and imagery to explore aspects of identity and human rights. Justify your selection by demonstrating Boland's skilful use of language and imagery to explore aspects of identity and human rights in the poems you have chosen.

Sample Plan 2

Intro: (*Stance: agree with viewpoint in the question*) Boland explores aspects of identity and human rights – importance of self, innocent victims of violence – through evocative language, symbolism, forceful verbs, poetic structure and varying tones.

Point 1: (*Identity – woman*) 'The Shadow Doll' demonstrates through the dreamlike description of a Victorian doll modelling a bride's confined position in society ('airless glamour', 'under wraps'). Repetition ('pressing down') and strong verbs ('locks') emphasise suppression.

Point 2: (*Identity – woman*) 'The Black Lace Fan' is a symbol of freedom and romance ('flirtatious span') and is contrasted with the 'stifling' Parisian atmosphere. The couple's uncertain relationship is subtly explored.

Point 3: (*Human rights – innocent victim*) 'Child of Our Time' powerfully reflects on an innocent death during the Northern Ireland Troubles. Tone varies from compassion ('rhymes for your waking') to indignation ('you cannot listen'). A didactic voice ('must learn') completes a poem whose carefully ordered 3-stanza structure mirrors Boland's attempt to put order on disorder.

Point 4: (*Human rights – innocent victim*) 'The War Horse' also examines the brutal consequences of war and aspects of national identity, using emphatic verbs, rhetorical questions and vivid imagery ('screamless dead').

Conclusion: Poet memorably explores the themes of woman's identity and the human rights of innocent victims. Through skilful use of language and imagery, Boland creates visionary moments to enrich the reader's experience.

Sample Paragraph: Point 4

'The War Horse' addresses the obliteration of innocent victims' human rights through Boland's detailed observation of a 'loosed' Traveller horse wreaking havoc on suburban gardens. The brutal consequences of the actions of a warlike intruder is conveyed through powerfully dramatic language – the horse 'stamps death' on the 'innocent coinage of the earth'. It 'smashed' a rose. Boland's historical reference ('illicit braid') to the secret society of the Ribbonmen recalls the destruction caused by another earlier intruder, the British, who invaded Ireland. A chilling rhetorical question ('why should we care/If a rose, a hedge, a crocus are uprooted/Like corpses, remote, crushed, mutilated?') and repetitive personal pronouns ('we, we are safe') seek to implicate readers in these terrible events. The poet wishes us to consider why no-one challenged the intruder. She provokes us to ask whether it is right to be a passive bystander when destruction is happening. Does indifference cause a 'world' to be 'betrayed'?

EXAMINER'S COMMENT

Top-grade response showing close engagement with the poet's use of language in conveying powerfully held views on aspects of Irish history. Excellent expression ('obliteration', 'implicate') and effective use of key quotes, well integrated into the commentary add to the impressive quality of the answer. The paragraph is rounded off effectively with two thought-provoking questions.

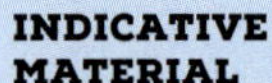

INDICATIVE MATERIAL

Boland's fascinating world, influenced by both history and the present day:

- engaging exploration of Irish history, superstition, past and present relationships, power/ powerlessness, enduring natural beauty, etc.

... is created through:

- a carefully controlled style
- striking use of places, people, precise tones/ moods, sound effects, detailed imagery, structure, etc.

Leaving Cert Sample Essay

'Boland creates a fascinating world that is often influenced by both history and the present day, in a carefully controlled poetic style.' To what extent do you agree or disagree with this statement? Support your answer with reference to the poetry of Eavan Boland on your course.

Sample Essay

1. In a recent interview, Eavan Boland said she believed that 'the past is a place of shadows where peoples' names disappear'. I agree completely that Boland creates a very interesting poetic world through her precisely controlled language and imagery. But I do not fully agree that she is influenced by both the present day and history. In many poems, she identifies herself only with the marginalised and dispossessed, those written out of history. She gives a compelling voice to these unrecorded victims in poems like 'Outsiders' and 'The Famine Road'. Boland also creates moments of intense beauty in her celebration of family relationships, nature and tradition.

2. In 'This Moment', Boland writes about a moment when she records a common experience. It's a moment of love in an ordinary, suburban setting. She presents us with the love between a mother and young child. The poet uses a lot of onomatopoeia, including sibilant sounds, 'Star and moths and rinds'. This is an image of nature. She uses very simple language, 'One window is yellow as butter', and this paints a homely scene. The mood is harmonious, 'Stars rise. Moths flutter. Apples sweeten'. This is a very dramatic poem that is influenced by the modern world. We should appreciate the simple things in family life. The poem records a special time and offers a welcome moment of relief and security in our tense modern world.

3. 'White Hawthorn in the West of Ireland' is a reflection on the differing relationships Boland has with the orderly suburban world and the wild, mystical country landscape. Her exact phrases describe the tidy, modern, urban environment, 'I left suburban gardens. Lawnmowers. Small talk'. In contrast, flowing lines and dynamic images of growth portray the abundant countryside. She glories in being 'Part of/that ivory downhill rush'. She intrigues her readers with the unlucky 'sharp flowers' of the hawthorn. In Irish folklore, hawthorn was believed to bring misfortune to those who cut it or keep it indoors, 'for the sake of/the luck such constraint would forfeit'. The run-on lines and stanzas capture the wild spirit of the countryside where the hawthorn stirs 'on those hills/with a fluency only water has'. Boland describes a fascinating world shaped by the present day and Irish folklore in her meticulous style.

4. In both 'Outside History' and 'The Famine Road', the record of the past focuses on those dispossessed not only in life but in history. It is with these marginalised victims that Boland empathises. Her critical eye forms vivid, condensed imagery forcing us to confront the uncomfortable reality of the victims' experience in the past ('roads clotted as firmaments with the dead'). She makes a deliberate conscious effort to 'move to be part of that ordeal', to shed light on the 'darkness' which obliterates the memory of those who 'have always been outside history'. She wishes to move 'out of myth', away from the historical, passive myths of Caitlín Ní Houliháin and Dark Rosaleen. While Boland admits that those dead won't be aware that they are now honoured in her repetitive phrase, 'and we are too late. We are always too late', the poet has brought the victims in from 'outside history' – those in the present and the future – through her elegiac poem.

5. Boland also focuses on the marginalised victims of the Irish Famine. In her dramatic recreation of this terrible time, we never hear the voices of these 'Sick, directionless' people. Harsh consonant 'c' and 'k' sounds compel her readers to experience the suffering of these unrecorded victims ('blood on their knuckles on rock, suck April hailstones for water and for food'). She quotes the recorded words in the letter of the British civil servant, Trevelyan, to Colonel Jones, 'Idle as trout in light Colonel Jones, these Irish'. The ironically named 'Relief Committee' decided to have the starving Irish build roads 'going nowhere of course'. Boland has deliberately excluded the voices of the 'wretches' in a chilling account of how the suffering of the Famine victims was omitted. Instead they will 'fester by their work' while the British remove food from the land, 'March the corn to the ships in peace'. That was what was important.

6. In this poem, Boland also records the experiences of a modern-day infertile woman who is disempowered. She does not allow the woman's voice to be heard. Instead, the tone of the doctor dominates, 'take it well woman, grow your garden'. Similar tones are heard from both the British and the doctor. Boland's voice now interrupts the two narratives. She uses the adjective 'Barren' to link the two experiences.

7. Eavan Boland has constructed an absorbing depiction of a world which is affected by modern times and the past. She has said, 'The rich and interesting part, for me, was the past, not history'. So she records the 'outsiders' from the past, those left out of history. Her critical eye produces carefully crafted poetry which resonates with readers long after the poems have been read.

(830 words)

EXAMINER'S COMMENT

A confident personal response to the question, showing close engagement with Boland's poetry. Style is touched on slightly in paragraph 2. Good focused analysis in paragraphs 3–5 addresses all elements of the question (fascinating world, links to past and present, poet's controlled language). Accurate quotes and references are used effectively to support points throughout, although further development of the discussion in paragraphs 2 and 6 would have raised the standard.

GRADE: H2
P = 13/15
C = 12/15
L = 12/15
M = 5/5
Total = 42/50

Improving the answer

Paragraph 2 updated

2. In 'This Moment', Boland crafts an intense passing moment when she records a timeless, universal experience. It's a compelling glimpse of natural family love in an ordinary domestic setting. Short lines add to the hushed atmosphere and sense of anticipation – something important 'is getting ready to happen'. The poet presents us with an idyllic picture – the deep love between a mother and her child. Sibilant sound effects, 'Star and moths and rinds slanting around fruit', evoke the wonder of nature. Boland's precise sensuous imagery, 'One tree is black, One window is yellow as butter', paints the homely scene. The harmonious mood is captured in the present tense by carefully chosen verbs, 'Stars rise. Moths flutter. Apples sweeten in the dark'. This dramatic poem offers a welcome moment of relief and security in our tense modern world.

PROMPT!

- *Address all aspects of the question ('fascinating', 'past and present', 'language').*
- *Develop poem's central point using suitable reference and quotation.*
- *Vary expression by avoiding repetition.*

Class/Homework Exercise

1. Rewrite paragraph 6. (Aim for at least 130 words.)

PROMPT!

- *Focus on the full question in greater detail.*
- *Describe the doctor's harsh comments.*
- *Consider the similar tone used by the British ('their bones/ need toil').*
- *Contrast this with the poet's compassionate voice at the end.*

Revision Overview

'The War Horse'
Themes of violence, warfare, death, suburban domestic incident, memory.

'Child of Our Time'
Elegy, response to theme of random tragedy unleashed by lack of communication.

'The Famine Road'
Two parallel narratives explore themes of oppression and victimisation, the famine and the infertile woman.

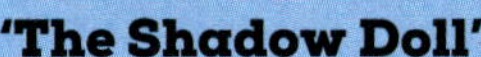

'The Shadow Doll'
Theme of women's oppression, emotions and sexuality suppressed.

'White Hawthorn in the West of Ireland'
Journey into West becomes reflection on thematic contrast between orderly suburbia and wild, mystical beauty of Irish landscape.

'Outside History'
Compelling examination of theme of the marginalised.

'The Black Lace Fan My Mother Gave Me'
Challenging alternative account of the theme of relationship between men and women.

'This Moment'
Reflection on theme of traditional role of women as mothers.

'The Pomegranate'
Reflective examination of themes of complex mother-daughter relationship and ageing process.

'Love'
Two narratives address theme of changes in relationships, personal story of young love and Aeneas's return to the underworld.

Last Words

'Eavan Boland's work continues to deepen in both humanity and complexity.'
Fiona Sampson

'Memory, change, loss, the irrecoverable past – such are the shared conditions of humankind, with which she scrupulously engages.'
Anne Stevenson

'Poets are those who ransack their perishing mind and find pattern and form.'
Eavan Boland

Paul Durcan
1944–

'That's what poetry is about: getting out of your miserable self and opening your eyes.'

Paul Durcan is one of modern Ireland's foremost and most prolific poets. He is known for his controversial, comic and deeply moving poems. An outspoken critic of his native country, he has traced its emergence from the repressions of the 1950s to the contradictions of the present day.

Born in Dublin in 1944, Durcan spent much of his childhood with relatives in County Mayo. In 1967, he met Nessa O'Neill. The couple later married and had two daughters. The marriage ended in 1984.

Among Durcan's many poetic influences are Eliot, Hopkins and Kavanagh. A variety of voices can be heard throughout Durcan's distinctive work, by turns hilarious, humane and heartbreaking. He uses many different forms, including dramatic monologues, ballads, mock news reports, songs and even prayers. His poetry can be surreal, mystical, passionate and ironic.

The subject matter of Paul Durcan's poems ranges widely, from explorations of cultural change in contemporary Ireland to intimate studies of family relationships. Many of the narrative poems he writes are autobiographical, often filled with black humour and satirical jibes. They seem to be carefully designed for oral appreciation.

Investigate Further

To find out more about Paul Durcan, or to hear readings of his poems not available in your eBook, you could do a search of some of the useful websites available such as YouTube, BBC Poetry, poetryfoundation.org and poetryarchive.org, or access additional material on this page of your eBook.

Prescribed Poems

○ **1 'Nessa'**
This deeply personal poem is centred around swimming, an extended metaphor conveying both the delights and dangers of falling in love. **Page 112**

○ **2 'The Girl with the Keys to Pearse's Cottage'**
This poem addresses aspects of Irish identity, belonging and the instability of place. **Page 116**

○ **3 'The Difficulty that is Marriage'**
In this short, introspective reflection, Durcan suggests that while true love is not free of problems, it can endure despite all the obstacles. **Page 120**

○ **4 'Wife Who Smashed Television Gets Jail' (OL)**
Durcan sometimes uses a mock journalistic style, particularly in his humorous critiques of Irish society. **Page 124**

○ **5 'Parents' (OL)**
This poem raises interesting questions about parent-child communication, a recurring theme in Paul Durcan's work. **Page 128**

○ **6 '"Windfall", 8 Parnell Hill, Cork'**
This long poem recounts both the happiness of family love and domesticity, and the bitter consequences of a marriage. **Page 132**

○ **7 'Six Nuns Die in Convent Inferno'**
In this lengthy narrative poem about a fire that destroyed a Dublin convent in 1986, Durcan characteristically transforms the details of the tragedy into an extended exercise in spiritual reflection. **Page 141**

○ **8 'Sport' (OL)**
Another painfully autobiographical poem in which Durcan recalls a football match from his youth and explores the troubled relationship he had with his father. **Page 150**

○ **9 'Father's Day, 21 June 1992'**
On a crucial train journey from Dublin to Cork, the poet confronts the erosive effects of time on his role as a husband and father. **Page 155**

○ **10 'The Arnolfini Marriage'**
This dramatic monologue was inspired by the famous Jan Van Eyck oil painting that is believed to represent a rich Italian merchant and his wife. **Page 160**

○ **11 'Rosie Joyce'**
Durcan has often used travel as a metaphor for reflection or soul-searching. In this upbeat poem celebrating the birth of his granddaughter, he remembers a car journey he took in May 2001 from Mayo to Dublin. **Page 165**

○ **12 'The MacBride Dynasty'**
This poem relates the time Durcan's mother made a personal journey back to her hometown to introduce her young son, 'the latest addition' to the family dynasty, to her uncle's famous wife, Maud Gonne. **Page 171**

○ **13 Three Short Poems: 'En Famille, 1979', 'Madman', 'Ireland 2002' Page 176**

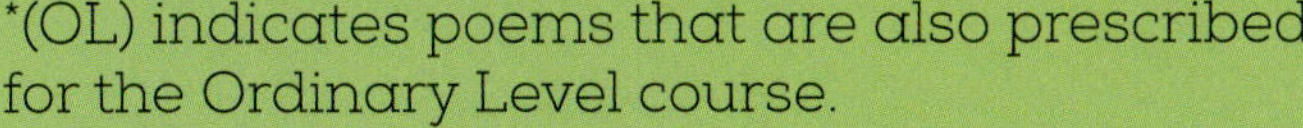

*(OL) indicates poems that are also prescribed for the Ordinary Level course.

POETRY FOCUS

1

Nessa

I met her on the first of August
In the Shangri-La Hotel,
She took me by the index finger
And dropped me in her well.
And that was a whirlpool, that was a whirlpool,
And I very nearly drowned.

Take off your pants, she said to me,
And I very nearly didn't;
Would you care to swim? she said to me,
And I hopped into the Irish Sea.
And that was a whirlpool, that was a whirlpool,
And I very nearly drowned.

On the way back I fell in the field
And she fell down beside me,
I'd have lain in the grass with her all my life
With Nessa:
She was a whirlpool, she was a whirlpool,
And I very nearly drowned.

O Nessa my dear, Nessa my dear,
Will you stay with me on the rocks?
Will you come for me into the Irish Sea
And for me let your red hair down?
And then we will ride into Dublin City
In a taxi-cab wrapped up in dust.
Oh you are a whirlpool, you are a whirlpool,
And I am very nearly drowned.

Shangri-La: legendary location often used in a similar context to the Garden of Eden to represent a hidden paradise. The Shangri-La Hotel was located in Dalkey, Co. Dublin.
index finger: forefinger, pointer finger, trigger finger; often used to make a warning gesture.
whirlpool: swirling body of water produced by the meeting of opposing currents.

on the rocks: a phrase describing a drink served with ice cubes; also refers to a disaster at sea.

'And that was a whirlpool'

Personal Response

1. What impression of Nessa do you get from reading the poem? Refer to the text in your answer.
2. Comment on the effectiveness of the poet's use of the whirlpool image.
3. Write your own personal response to the poem, highlighting the impact it made on you.

Critical Literacy

This well-known love poem comes from Paul Durcan's second collection, *O Westport in the Light of Asia Minor* (1975). The poet has said that he first met Nessa O'Neill in the bar of the Shangri-La Hotel in Dalkey when he was at a wedding reception there in August 1967. Soon afterwards, the couple moved to London and married. 'Nessa' includes elements of the aisling (dream vision) poetry tradition, which dates from late 17th-century Gaelic literature, when Ireland was often represented by an enchanting female figure. Durcan's poem is centred around swimming, an extended metaphor conveying both the delights and dangers of falling in love.

The poem's title and dramatic opening lines emphasise the significance of meeting Nessa 'on the first of August'. This date also marks the traditional Celtic harvest festival, a time for celebrations and arranging marriages. The Irish term *Lughnasa* even echoes Nessa's own name. From the outset, Durcan's first-person presentation associates the woman who was to be his soulmate with mythology. Their introduction 'In the Shangri-La Hotel' seems a suitably exotic setting, suggesting the close spiritual union the couple would share. However, line 3 foreshadows the uncertainty of romance as the poet recalls being led 'by the index finger'. Durcan uses the poem's central **metaphor of swimming to express exhilaration and risk-taking**. The lovers' intimacy is evoked in the erotic image of the wishing well, 'a whirlpool' in which he 'very nearly drowned'. The repetition and insistent rhythm of line 5 reflects the continuing fascination of this unforgettable turning point in the poet's life.

The tone is a mixture of colloquial intimacy and self-mocking incantation. From the outset, Durcan highlights Nessa's power to enchant. His **wry humour** is apparent in the self-deprecating comments about his initial nervousness: 'take off your pants, she said to me,/And I very nearly didn't'. The breathless enthusiasm of their first encounter is evident in lively phrasing: 'I hopped into the Irish Sea' (line 10). The poet's signature use of refrain forces the reader to appreciate the personal upheaval caused by his relationship with Nessa.

Line 13 marks a noticeable change of mood. Durcan focuses on the aftermath ('the way back') of that first swim when Nessa 'fell down beside me'. The **enduring remorse of knowing and losing love** is clear in the regretful line 'I'd have lain in the grass with her all my life'. The contrasting brevity and precise lyrical simplicity of line 16 ('With Nessa') is almost immediately undermined by the stark realisation of the whirlpool symbol as the poet faces the reality of love's impermanence. The poem's **richly textured final section** is particularly tender: 'O Nessa my dear, Nessa my dear' (line 19). Durcan delicately repeats his wife's name. Ironically, his plaintive desire for her to 'stay with me on the rocks' reveals a yearning for a marriage that was inevitably doomed. The poet's powerful vision of Nessa encompasses elements of both dreams and nightmares. Imagining her as an idealised heroic creature ('for me let your red hair down'), he wonders if she can still be with him in the sea. The heart-rending fantasy is abruptly replaced by a darker image of the couple journeying through Dublin 'In a taxi-cab wrapped up in dust' (line 24). An unmistakable sense of death – coupled with the acceptance of lost love – is tinged with the notion that their kindred spirits are united forever.

The hypnotic rhythm of the last two lines brings the poet's reflection of that special day when he met Nessa up to date. Using the present tense verb in the refrain, Durcan emphasises the ongoing and relentless hurt of the relationship breakdown: 'I am very nearly drowned.' Such **an honest expression of emotion and personal vulnerability** is characteristic of the poet. It has been said that the tragedy at the heart of Paul Durcan's writing is that he cannot accept tragedy. This is undoubtedly the case in 'Nessa', leaving readers with the lasting impression of a man who is still profoundly shocked by the enduring power of romantic love.

Writing About the Poem

'What often defines Paul Durcan's poetry is an underlying sense of failure in personal relationships.' Do you agree with this view? Give reasons for your response, referring to Durcan's poem 'Nessa'.

Sample Paragraph

While Durcan's poem, 'Nessa', is primarily a tribute to his ex-wife, it is also a warning that love doesn't always last. The idea of a relationship failing is suggested in the first stanza when Durcan describes their 'whirlpool' romance. This dramatic image indicates the wildness of their feelings and that they were taking a chance marrying. A whirlpool is exciting, but also dangerous. Durcan uses the refrain at the end of each stanza to reinforce the idea of being unsuccessful in love. Looking back on their marriage, he seems to be really criticising himself for his own carelessness. As though

he took love for granted when he 'hopped into the Irish Sea'. I think he blames the failure of the relationship on himself, as suggested by the phrase 'I fell'. Durcan's tone of longing – 'Will you stay with me on the rocks?' – is very well expressed in this tragic metaphor. Nessa is pictured as a beautiful and mysterious woman whose 'red hair' mesmerised the poet. The end really brings out the tragic disappointment of the couple's separation as Durcan makes it clear that the distress still exists – 'you are a whirlpool'. His tone is of anguish and disillusionment. The loss of true love will remain with him forever.

EXAMINER'S COMMENT

A focused personal response that addresses the question directly and traces the progress of thought in the poem. The critical discussion touches on several interesting aspects relating to the predominant sense of failure. Supportive quotes are integrated effectively into the answer. Impressive expression, overall, ensures that this is a top-grade response.

Class/Homework Exercises

1. 'Durcan's inventive poetry is filled with dramatic tension.' Discuss this statement in relation to 'Nessa'.
2. Paul Durcan's personal relationships have often been described as power struggles. Discuss this view with particular reference to the poem 'Nessa'.

Summary Points

- **Personal exploration of the intense experience of romantic love.**
- **Effective use of extended swimming/whirlpool metaphor.**
- **Dramatic atmosphere; varying tones – nostalgic, regretful.**
- **Hypnotic rhythm; emphatic refrain, memorable visual/cinematic effects.**

2 The Girl with the Keys to Pearse's Cottage

to John and Judith Meagher

When I was sixteen I met a dark girl;
Her dark hair was darker because her smile was so bright;
She was the girl with the keys to Pearse's Cottage;
And her name was Cáit Killann.

The cottage was built into the side of a hill;
I recall two windows and cosmic peace
Of bare brown rooms and on whitewashed walls
Photographs of the passionate and pale Pearse.

I recall wet thatch and peeling jambs
And how all was best seen from below in the field;
I used sit in the rushes with ledger-book and pencil
Compiling poems of passion for Cáit Killann.

Often she used linger on the sill of a window;
Hands by her side and brown legs akimbo;
In sun-red skirt and moon-black blazer;
Looking toward our strange world wide-eyed.

Our world was strange because it had no future;
She was America-bound at summer's end.
She had no choice but to leave her home –
The girl with the keys to Pearse's Cottage.

O Cáit Killann, O Cáit Killann,
You have gone with your keys from your own native place.
Yet here in this dark – El Greco eyes blaze back
From your Connemara postman's daughter's proudly mortal face.

Pearse's Cottage: Pádraic Pearse, Irish teacher and political activist who was one of the leaders of the 1916 Easter Rising, owned a small cottage in Rosmuc, Connemara. Pearse believed that the key to national identity and independence was knowledge of the language.
cosmic: endless, universal.

jambs: wooden doorframes.

rushes: marsh plants.
ledger-book: book used to keep records.

akimbo: standing confidently.

El Greco: Spanish Renaissance painter famous for his fantastical portraits.

Personal Response

1. Describe the atmosphere of country life that the poet creates in lines 5–10.
2. Select one image from the poem that you find particularly interesting. Briefly explain your choice.
3. Write a brief personal response to the poem, highlighting its impact on you.

Critical Literacy

'The Girl with the Keys to Pearse's Cottage' was published in Paul Durcan's first poetry collection, *O Westport in the Light of Asia Minor*, in 1975. Themes of identity, belonging and the instability of place are frequently addressed in Durcan's work. The concept of home is a recurring concern. In this case, the poet narrates a poem of love and loss which includes some elements of the traditional Irish ballad. The poetic voice incorporates both the experiences of the poet's 16-year-old self and his mature adult attitude to the painful legacy of emigration.

The poem's opening lines immediately bring the reader back to a bittersweet moment in Durcan's life: 'When I was sixteen I met a dark girl.' The **strong visual awareness and effective use of repetition** ('dark', 'dark hair', 'darker') suggest the native Irish colouring of the young girl. Her dazzling smile is captured in the long line that culminates with the monosyllabic adjective 'bright', perhaps mirroring sudden sunshine bursting from the clouds over the West of Ireland. We learn that the young woman held the 'keys to Pearse's Cottage'. Had she the means to unlock the secret of his house as well as enabling visitors to enter there? Reverently, the narrator reveals the identity of his lost love: 'And her name was Cáit Killann.'

The second stanza describes Pearse's cottage in remarkable detail: 'built into the side of a hill.' Durcan draws the reader into a romanticised place of 'cosmic peace'. He makes effective use of alliteration to emphasise the **simplicity and lack of ostentation** of the two-bedroomed house, with its 'bare brown rooms' and 'whitewashed walls'. In stark contrast to this are the photographs of the fiery nationalist politician himself, 'the passionate and pale Pearse'.

Stanza three delves further into the poet's memory ('I recall wet thatch and peeling jambs') as the ordinary scene opens up its secrets under the poet's observant gaze. This is a place that is past its best days, tired and weary. Is this how the people of the countryside regarded their environment? The **personal autobiographical detail** is conveyed in the picture of the young poet who sits 'in the rushes with ledger-book and pencil'. Instead of creating accounts, he compiles 'poems of passion' for the girl he loves. Again, alliteration suggests the copious number of poems the infatuated Durcan wrote. The naive awkwardness of expressing his feelings in a book dedicated to dry statistics reflects the engaging sincerity of youth.

In stanza four, Durcan lyrically recalls Cáit Killann's languid grace: 'she used linger on the sill of a window.' The slender vowel 'i' emphasises her confident, sensuous movements. Suddenly, the pen portrait erupts into colour – 'brown

legs', 'sun-red skirt', 'moon-black blazer'. These compound words indicate both her extraordinary effect on the poet and also **her effortless harmony with the native environment**. The beautiful Cáit belongs here. She gazes 'wide-eyed' and innocent 'toward our strange world'. Readers are left to wonder what she is about to discover.

The adult poet's answer in the penultimate stanza is that 'Our world was strange because it had no future'. His tone is suddenly bitter in response to the bleak realisation that emigration engulfs this crumbling place. 'She was America-bound at summer's end', almost as if she were a migratory bird. The stark political reality becomes a personal experience: 'she had no choice but to leave her home.' **Durcan has always addressed public issues** and he leaves us in no doubt of his own deep awareness that Irish life is lived in transit. Our young migrants become the diaspora scattered around the globe.

The final stanza is defined by a grief-stricken poetic voice lamenting the departure of someone who is loved. The poet repeats Cáit's name tenderly. **Plaintive assonant sounds** echo the traditional mourning or keening that was once found in the West of Ireland: 'O Cáit Killann, O Cáit Killann.' Now that she has left her 'own native place', it is as though a young plant was roughly torn from the Irish soil and transplanted elsewhere to bloom. The poet clearly regards Ireland as a 'dark' country, yet the memory of Cáit's vivid 'El Greco eyes' remains. In celebrating the alluring looks of the 'postman's daughter', Durcan has coloured the ordinariness of Connemara with the exotic fascination of international artistic beauty. El Greco, the Spanish painter, dared to view the world his way, sometimes representing it through exquisite portraits of intriguing women with shining eyes.

For Durcan, Cáit Killann also carried her own extraordinary light. The intensity of her gaze is conveyed in the explosive alliterative phrase 'blaze back' from her 'proudly mortal face'. Through his use of metaphor, Durcan has transformed this native Irish girl into a striking icon. In addition, he has brought the reader to a different vantage point from which to view **the tragedy of emigration**, which is such an intrinsically Irish experience. Is this realistic viewpoint similar to the perspective from which Pearse's cottage might be perceived: 'all was best seen from below in the field'? Does something have to be viewed from a distance in order to understand it? Have we been brought to a moment of epiphany as we contemplate the sombre reality of exile? At any rate, Cáit Killann remains a powerfully sad and realistic symbol of Irish emigration, an ironic reminder of what has become of Pearse's idealistic dreams.

Writing About the Poem

'In the poetry of Paul Durcan, reality is frequently shaped by the imagination.' Discuss this statement in relation to the poem, 'The Girl with the Keys to Pearse's Cottage'. Support your views with close reference to the text.

Sample Paragraph

Durcan's keen observation of mundane detail, 'wet thatch', 'bare brown rooms', 'whitewashed walls', etc., all root the poem firmly in the reality of rain-soaked Connemara. All is calm, 'cosmic peace', on the surface. Yet bubbling beneath this seeming ordinariness, strong feelings flow, portrayed vividly in the photographs of the 'passionate and pale Pearse' who once inhabited this place. The longing of a sixteen-year-old boy for the beautiful 'postman's daughter' can be sensed as he sat 'in the rushes' while 'Compiling poems of passion' for her. The girl of the 'sun-red skirt' is brought into another world through Durcan's inspired reference to her 'El Greco eyes'. The ordinary is opened up by his inventive metaphor. El Greco saw things in a unique way – exactly like Cáit, 'Looking toward our strange world wide-eyed'. She seems surprised at what she sees, perhaps because she is being forced to leave her native land, 'America-bound at summer's end'. Despite the sacrifice of the 1916 Rising, of which Pearse was a leader, this country is still unable to support its own people. But is the girl truly gone? I believe she exists only in the poet's memory. Suddenly the reality of this little place in the West of Ireland has been formed by the imagination of the poet to represent the tragedy of emigration.

EXAMINER'S COMMENT

A good personal response which engages well with the poem. Carefully considered terms, such as 'inventive' and 'inspired', indicate a sustained focus on addressing the question directly. Overall, the expression is very well managed, particularly the first sentence. Accurate quotations are effectively integrated into the critical discussion. A highly successful top-grade response.

Class/Homework Exercises

1. 'Paul Durcan's poetry is often concerned with the world of the Irish countryside that has now disappeared.' Discuss this statement in relation to 'The Girl with the Keys to Pearse's Cottage'. Support the points you make with reference to the text.
2. Durcan's poems address both personal and public themes. To what extent is this true of 'The Girl with the Keys to Pearse's Cottage'? Support your answer with reference to the text.

Summary Points

- **Prominent themes include idealism, national identity, home, exile, love and loss.**
- **Evocative images of Irish rural life and female beauty.**
- **Variety of tones – nostalgic, angry, sad.**
- **Effective use of autobiographical detail, symbolism, irony, repetition.**

3 The Difficulty that is Marriage

Difficulty: challenge, complication, problem.
Marriage: formal union of a couple; a close blend or mixture of two things.

We disagree to disagree, we divide, we differ;
Yet each night as I lie in bed beside you
And you are faraway curled up in sleep
I array the moonlit ceiling with a mosaic of question marks;
How was it I was so lucky to have ever met you?
I am no brave pagan proud of my mortality
Yet gladly on this changeling earth I should live for ever
If it were with you, my sleeping friend.
I have my troubles and I shall always have them
But I should rather live with you for ever
Than exchange my troubles for a changeless kingdom.
But I do not put you on a pedestal or throne;
You must have your faults but I do not see them.
If it were with you, I should live for ever.

array: adorn, arrange in an impressive way.
mosaic: pattern, montage.

pagan: unbeliever, atheist.
mortality: humanity, transience, death.
changeling: transient, secretly exchanged.

troubles: afflictions, difficulties.

exchange: swap, substitute.

pedestal: raised platform, exalted position.
faults: failings, weaknesses.

'a mosaic of question marks'

Personal Response

1. Why, in your opinion, would Paul Durcan regard marriage as a difficulty? Refer to the poem to support your response.
2. Choose one image from the poem that you thought was particularly effective and explain your choice.
3. Write a brief personal response to the poem, highlighting its impact on you.

Critical Literacy

Paul Durcan published 'The Difficulty that is Marriage' in his collection *Teresa's Bar* (1976). In considering his relationship with his wife, the poet's lyrical voice clearly reflects his intense feelings. He observes and explores a small everyday event, a married couple sharing a bed together, but who are estranged from each other. Reflecting on his upbringing, Durcan once said, 'We were educated to believe that women were, on the one hand, untouchable and pure and on the other hand, that they were the source of all evil ... women represent and embody freedom ... living in much closer harmony with their true selves.' The title of this very personal poem suggests that while true love is not immune from problems, it will endure despite such obstacles.

The opening line of this dramatic monologue is broken into abrupt staccato sections by its frequent punctuation marks and the alliterative letter 'd': 'We disagree to disagree, we divide, we differ.' Durcan cleverly pinpoints the destructive conflict in a marriage as two individuals try to live as a couple. In this case, they cannot even agree that they can disagree. After this turmoil of daily married life, three run-on lines smoothly convey, in unforced conversational tones, the stillness of the marriage bed: 'each night as I lie in bed beside you.' But while the couple are physically present in the one space, mentally and emotionally they are worlds apart. She is 'faraway curled up in sleep', content and at peace with herself. In contrast, the poet is lying awake, thinking, questioning. **Durcan's strong visual sensibility is evident** in the descriptive 'I array the moonlit ceiling with a mosaic of question marks'. The image has the immediacy of a snapshot coupled with surrealism as the reader views the ceiling patterned with the question marks of uncertainties: 'How was it I was so lucky to have ever met you?' Is the relationship broken into countless pieces by constant soul-searching and argument? Is the poet trying to reassemble the fragments into an ideal shape?

Durcan has always portrayed himself as an admirer of women, and has often cast his wife, Nessa, in her heroic role as someone to be admired, as the one person who provides stability in his insecure life. In line 6, he expresses the male pain of never doing well enough, criticising his own character: 'I am no brave pagan proud of my mortality'. He is not an audacious savage delighted

with his transient humanity. The self-deprecating tone changes to one of deep romanticism in his declaration that he would live forever 'on this changeling earth' if he could be 'with you, my sleeping friend'. There is a strong underlying sense that the poet feels uncomfortable in this world. In Irish folklore, a changeling refers to a child who has been secretly exchanged by the fairies for the parents' real child.

Line 9 reveals the dark side of Durcan's personality, 'I have my troubles', which is a common Irish euphemism for serious problems. Durcan has spoken of being committed by his family, against his will, to a range of psychiatric treatments, including electric convulsive therapy. He subsequently suffered from depression and has admitted, 'I think I came out of it with a kind of melancholia'. **Is the poet casting himself here in the role of sacrificial victim?** His father, with whom he had a difficult relationship, predicted that he would never be free of misfortune: 'Nemesis will follow you all the days of your life.' Is this why Durcan sees this earth as a 'changeling' place? Three words resonate: 'changeling', 'exchange' and 'changeless'. Is he willing to swap his longing for peace if he can always be with his beloved? 'But I should rather live with you for ever/Than exchange my troubles for a changeless kingdom.'

Paradoxically, while the poet denies that he exaggerates his feelings for his wife by exalting her 'on a pedestal or throne' (line 12) as if she were a saint or queen, at the same time he appears to worship her. He declares that 'You must have your faults', yet disarmingly admits, 'but I do not see them'. This short, introspective poem concludes with a statement of heightened emotion: 'If it were with you, I should live for ever.' The **reverential tone** suggests a strong sense of the spiritual fulfilment he receives from their relationship. Yet although this poem shows such high regard for his wife, Durcan remains the leading man throughout, demanding to be noticed despite all his charming self-criticism. Alternatively, it is possible to read the poem more generously in the light of another of the poet's statements: 'Heaven is other people: a house where there are no women and children is a very empty house.'

Writing About the Poem

'Paul Durcan has the gift of being able to make something out of nothing.' Discuss this statement with reference to his poem 'The Difficulty that is Marriage'. Support the points you make with reference to the text.

Sample Paragraph

'The Difficulty that is Marriage' explores the deep gulf between couples and the challenges they face. This is a common everyday reality that very many people can relate to. The obstacles to a successful relationship are vividly conveyed in the broken opening line, 'We disagree to disagree, we divide, we differ'. The woman's ability to be content with herself is evident in the simple phrase, 'faraway curled up in sleep'. In contrast, the man's anxiety is revealed in the cleverly constructed imaginative line, 'I array the moonlit ceiling with a mosaic of question marks'. Ironically, this married couple appear close, but really inhabit different universes. Durcan addresses the reality of complicated human relationships. Using the direct language of genuine emotion, the husband longs to be 'with you for ever'. We are left wondering if, instead of outlining differences, did the poet convey these feelings to his partner? I wonder did he ever tell her 'How was it I was so lucky to have ever met you'? Or did he just paint patterns on the ceiling? Perhaps this is the real difficulty of marriage, no one really knows for certain what the other is thinking or feeling. Durcan skilfully presents an ordinary occurrence, a married couple at night, one awake, one asleep, and creates a very important something out of a mundane nothing.

EXAMINER'S COMMENT

This is a competent response to a challenging question. There is a good personal approach throughout which shows engagement with the poem: 'We are left wondering if, instead of outlining differences, did the poet convey these feelings to his partner?' Among several interesting points is the focus on the complexity of relationships: 'no one really knows for certain what the other is thinking or feeling.' Effective use is made of accurate quotation. Expression is also clear and well controlled. A solid successful answer.

Class/Homework Exercises

1. 'Poetry has to be fundamentally cinematic, painterly and musical.' Discuss this view in relation to Durcan's poem 'The Difficulty that is Marriage'. Refer closely to the text in your answer.
2. In your opinion, what does Paul Durcan's poem reveal about his married relationship? Support the points you make with close reference to the text.

Summary Points

- **Explores the trials and triumphs of married relationships.**
- **Characteristically candid and emotional poetic voice.**
- **Tones vary – detached, personal, reflective, sardonic, reverential, loving.**
- **Dramatic monologue, contrast, exaggerated visual images.**

4 Wife Who Smashed Television Gets Jail

'She came home, my Lord, and smashed in the television;
Me and the kids were peaceably watching *Kojak*
When she marched into the living room and declared
That if I didn't turn off the television immediately
She'd put her boot through the screen;
I didn't turn it off, so instead she turned it off –
I remember the moment exactly because Kojak
After shooting a dame with the same name as my wife
Snarled at the corpse – Goodnight, Queen Maeve –
And then she took off her boots and smashed in the television;
I had to bring the kids round to my mother's place;
We got there just before the finish of *Kojak*;
(My mother has a fondness for *Kojak*, my Lord);
When I returned home my wife had deposited
What was left of the television into the dustbin,
Saying – I didn't get married to a television
And I don't see why my kids or anybody else's kids
Should have a television for a father or mother,
We'd be much better off all down in the pub talking
Or playing bar-billiards –
Whereupon she disappeared off back down again to the pub.'
Justice O'Brádaigh said wives who preferred bar-billiards to family television
Were a threat to the family which was the basic unit of society
As indeed the television itself could be said to be a basic unit of the family
And when as in this case wives expressed their preference in forms of violence
Jail was the only place for them. Leave to appeal was refused.

my Lord: official form of address to a judge in court.

Kojak: American TV crime drama starring Telly Savalas. The series was popular in Ireland during the mid-1970s.

Queen Maeve: legendary Irish queen with a colourful reputation.

bar-billiards: group table game in which short cues are used.

appeal: review to challenge a court sentence.

'peaceably watching *Kojak*'

Personal Response

1. In your opinion, what is the main point or message of this poem? Refer to the text in your response.
2. Comment on Durcan's use of irony throughout the poem, supporting the points you make with reference to the text.
3. Write a paragraph outlining your own feelings in response to this poem. Refer to the text in your answer.

Critical Literacy

In his hard-hitting critiques of Irish society, one of Paul Durcan's signatures is the poem written as pseudo-reportage, where an unlikely event is depicted in a seemingly journalistic style. Humour has always been an essential component of the distinctive Durcan style. This poem is divided into two sections: the first 21 lines in the voice of the husband and the final five-line report of the judge's opinion and verdict.

The news headline title and matter-of-fact simplicity of the opening lines increase their dramatic impact. There is an instantaneous quality to the initial evidence presented by the aggrieved husband who acts as a witness in the matter of his wife's prosecution, protesting that at the moment the act of violence occurred, 'Me and the kids were peaceably watching *Kojak*'. Unable to see the irony of viewing a violent TV drama, the man is immediately **ridiculed and mocked** by Durcan. His assertive wife is identified as 'Queen Maeve' solely because the husband describes Kojak as 'shooting a dame with the same name' (line 8). This instantly associates her with one of the great legendary symbols of female power – a queen of Connaught in the Ulster Cycle of Irish myths. However, in the real patriarchal world of Durcan's Ireland, the modern Maeve is merely seen as a deranged troublemaker.

The husband proceeds to condemn himself further by boasting that instead of taking his wife seriously, he has still not come to terms with the interruption to one of his favourite TV programmes. It is not altogether surprising to learn that he rushes off to seek comfort from his mother, who shares his 'fondness for *Kojak*' (line 13). However, aggressive as his wife's actions may be, it soon becomes clear that it is **her words and attitudes that serve to justify her condemnation**. As the story unfolds, Durcan slips effortlessly from the real to the surreal, often to inspired comic effect. When the distressed husband returns home, he discovers that his wife has dumped 'What was left of the television into the dustbin' (line 15).

In direct opposition to her uncommunicative husband and children, she boldly states: 'I don't see why my kids or anybody else's kids/Should have a television for a father or mother' (lines 17–18). **Durcan's bizarre humour is**

laced with unsmiling undertones. For him, TV violence and escapism compete with the less glamorous facts of real life. As a result, any interference with the illusions that television creates can now be treated as serious crimes. Our sympathy for the wife is further generated by exposing the delusions of the male judge.

In the poem's final lines, the satire becomes much more intense. Durcan undermines the astounding moral certainty in the arrogant speech delivered by 'Justice O'Brádaigh', who declares that 'the television itself could be said to be a basic unit of the family' (line 24). The unashamed verdict promotes the idea that **virtual violence has a rightful place at the heart of family life**, a reason for the judge to state that 'Jail was the only place' for transgressors such as Maeve, who will not be allowed to challenge her sentence since 'Leave to appeal was refused'. The snarling tone of such a dismissive ruling is in keeping with Justice O'Brádaigh's prevailing mindset of patronising self-delusion.

What sustains the tragicomic structure of this poem is Durcan's skilful depiction of the contrasting characters who are party to the scene: the precious husband, his frustrated wife and the condescending judge. Significantly, the wife herself is never directly heard. **Durcan is uncompromising in exposing negative attitudes towards voiceless women** – especially women who dare to resist rigid social expectations. His disapproval of the conventional pieties of Ireland's male-dominated society is characteristic of his poetry. However, a close reading of 'Wife Who Smashed Television Gets Jail' reveals that it is not the medium of television, but its abuse, that Durcan calls into question. As usual, in addressing such cultural issues, the poet entertains and gives readers time for thought.

Writing About the Poem

'Paul Durcan's deep sense of outrage is often evident in his poetry.' Discuss this view in relation to 'Wife Who Smashed Television Gets Jail', using references from the poem to support your answer.

Sample Paragraph

Paul Durcan has a reputation for what appear to be light-hearted poems, but his anger is never far from the surface. This is true of 'Wife Who Smashed Television Gets Jail' where he confronts society's hypocrisy. The idea of a wife being taken to court by a man who gives more attention to his TV seems ridiculous, but the real point is that women have very little power. I could easily imagine Durcan's anger at the man's superior tone – 'Me and the kids were peaceably watching *Kojak*'. Even his comment about the detective 'shooting a dame' is a reminder that it's a man's

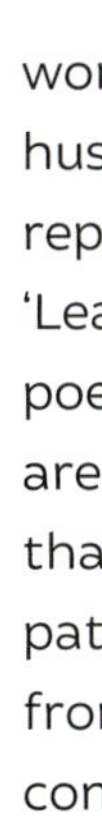

world. Durcan barely conceals his rage that men – the husband, the TV hero and the influential judge – all represent a macho world. I thought the last line – 'Leave to appeal was refused' – summed up the poet's appreciation of how women in Irish society are marginalised. The poet seems to be saying that it is nearly impossible not to be part of the patriarchal culture that prevents many women from expressing the view that emotions and communication are more important than escapist TV violence. The outrage was present throughout the poem especially during the comic scenes.

EXAMINER'S COMMENT

This is a clearly focused personal response showing good engagement with the poem. The focus on the dominance of male characters provided worthwhile support. Valuable use was also made of suitable references – particularly the Kojak quotation which was very effective. Expression was well controlled throughout. In-depth analysis guarantees a high grade.

Class/Homework Exercises

1. 'Humour and surrealism are Durcan's most powerful satirical weapons.' Discuss this statement with reference to the poem 'Wife Who Smashed Television Gets Jail'.
2. Durcan has been described as a 'feminist writer'. Based on your reading of this poem, do you agree or disagree with this view? Support your answer with reference to the text.

Summary Points

- **Durcan criticises aspects of Irish patriarchal society.**
- **Effective use of irony, surreal humour.**
- **Satirical exaggeration, comic journalistic writing style.**
- **Varying tones – ridicule, sympathy, outrage.**

POETRY FOCUS

5 Parents

A child's face is a drowned face:
Her parents stare down at her asleep
Estranged from her by a sea:
She is under the sea
And they are above the sea:
If she looked up she would see them
As if locked out of their own home,
Their mouths open,
Their foreheads furrowed –
Pursed-up orifices of fearful fish –
Their big ears are fins behind glass
And in her sleep she is calling out to them
    Father, Father
    Mother, Mother
But they cannot hear her:
She is inside the sea
And they are outside the sea.
Through the night, stranded, they stare
At the drowned, drowned face of their child.

Estranged: separated.

furrowed: wrinkled.

Pursed-up orifices: open-shaped mouths.

stranded: abandoned.

'And in her sleep she is calling out to them'

Personal Response

1. Write a paragraph giving your own immediate reaction to reading 'Parents'. Refer to the poem in your answer.
2. Select one image from the poem that you find particularly unsettling and briefly explain your choice.
3. Using reference to the text, comment on the poem's dramatic features.

Critical Literacy

'Parents' was published in Paul Durcan's 1978 collection, *Sam's Cross*. The poem raises interesting questions about parent–child communication, a recurring theme in Durcan's work. Characteristically, some of the poet's perceptions have a disturbing quality which convey shock as well as intensity.

The poem's opening metaphor – 'A child's face is a drowned face' – has a startling effect. The devastating image represents every parent's greatest fear and introduces an **overwhelmingly anxious mood** that will dominate the entire poem. Durcan develops the sea metaphor in lines 2–3, creating a desperate scene of helplessness, as the parents can only stare down at their precious child, 'Estranged from her by a sea'. The lack of intimate communication – symbolised by the impenetrable ocean – is a central theme. There is something unsettling about the parents' realisation that they are already detached from their newborn child and that they can never know her as much as they would wish.

Lines 4–5 reflect their sense of shock at the unfathomable gulf that exists between them and the child: 'She is under the sea/And they are above the sea.' The separate lines and contrasting prepositions emphasise the obstacle. Repetition and a deliberate rhythm further underline Durcan's sombre tone. For the first time in the poem, the child's perspective is presented when she imagines her parents being 'locked out of their own home' (line 7). Just as she is no longer within the security of the womb, they are also leading independent lives. Her growing understanding of the world is described in a series of increasingly distorted images. The 'furrowed' looks on her parents' foreheads are unnerving. The **surreal underwater sequence** becomes even more grotesque when Durcan compares the concerned adult expressions to 'Pursed-up orifices of fearful fish'. To the confused and frightened infant, the parents' ears are 'fins behind glass'.

Through lines 12–14, the developing drama of the parent–child exchange becomes all the more poignant. Durcan's dark vision of the child's distressed cry for attention ('Father, Father/Mother, Mother') transcends the moment and highlights the trauma of unfulfilled relationships between parents and children, lasting perhaps throughout entire lifetimes. For the poet, however, there is no denying the harsh fact of disconnection revealed in line 15: 'But

they cannot hear her'. An overpowering mood of desolation dominates the poem. The subdued tone and ironic alliteration echo **Durcan's sad acceptance that there will always be barriers between parents and children**. Throughout his writing career, the poet has explored his own troubled relationships, particularly with his father, who was a stern and distant figure.

There is a restrained **sense of resignation** in lines 16–19. Durcan repeats the stark truth about separation between individuals, contrasting the child 'inside the sea' with her parents, who are 'outside'. The final elegiac mood is achieved by the exaggerated illustration of the ever-watchful parents, who are left 'stranded', faced with the challenge of coming to terms with the 'drowned, drowned face of their child'. The repetition of 'drowned' in the long final line leaves readers thinking of the many questions raised in this short poem. As always, Durcan has addressed important issues, not just about how individual human beings interact, but about the mystery of life itself.

Writing About the Poem

'Paul Durcan writes well about detachment and isolation.' Discuss this view, with particular reference to 'Parents'. Refer closely to the text in your response.

Sample Paragraph

Durcan addresses interesting aspects of human experience in his poetry, and this is certainly the case in 'Parents'. The poem focuses on one set of unnamed parents and their young child, but takes a very negative view of the relationship. From the start, the parents are disconnected from their baby daughter, imagining that her sleeping face is 'a drowned face'. Their imagined fear of her death immediately suggests that her life is outside of their control. Durcan uses shocking sea images to show the lack of close contact with the child who appears to be 'under the sea'. This gap exists between them and they can never know her completely. Their panic is conveyed very effectively in nightmarish terms. The child sees them as alien, almost intimidating, like 'fearful fish'. She calls to them but 'they cannot hear her'. I felt this was a really heartbreaking moment, especially as the poet repeated her frantic words, 'Father, Father/Mother, Mother'. The separation they feel in never fully communicating is seen at the end of the poem where the parents are 'stranded' – another sea image

EXAMINER'S COMMENT

A successful response which tackles the question directly. Suitable references and quotations sustain the focused discussion of Durcan's treatment of isolation. There is some good personal engagement, particularly in the final sentence. The answer traces the development of thought in the poem very effectively, using the poet's succession of shocking images. Expression is varied and assured throughout, ensuring a top grade.

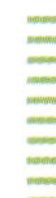

– 'Through the night'. This tragic insight into the distances between people is reinforced in the last line by the repetition of 'drowned' – a final reminder of detachment and alienation.

Class/Homework Exercises

1. 'Durcan's most compelling poems often raise significant questions about the complexity of human relationships.' To what extent is this true of 'Parents'? Support your answer with reference to the poem.
2. Durcan's poetic voice has been noted for its insistent, hypnotic rhythms. To what extent is this the case in 'Parents'? Support your answer with close reference to the text.

Summary Points

- **Durcan raises penetrating questions about parent–child relationships.**
- **Contrasting moods/tones – anxious, serious, intense, poignant, resigned.**
- **Striking and sustained visual imagery of the sea – distorted, unnerving.**
- **Effective use of powerful language and free rhythm.**

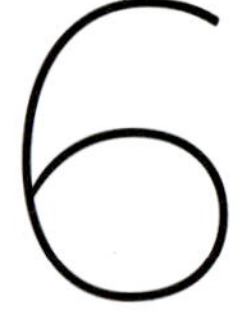

'Windfall', 8 Parnell Hill, Cork

Windfall: something good received unexpectedly; something the wind has blown down.

But, then, at the end of day I could always say –
Well, now, I am going home.
I felt elected, steeped, sovereign to be able to say –
I am going home.
When I was at home I liked to stay at home;
At home I stayed at home for weeks;
At home I used sit in a winged chair by the window
Overlooking the river and the factory chimneys,
The electricity power station and the car assembly works,
The fleets of trawlers and the pilot tugs,
Dreaming that life is a dream which is real,
The river a reflection of itself in its own waters,
Goya sketching Goya among the smoky mirrors.
The industrial vista was my Mont Sainte-Victoire.
While my children sat on my knees watching TV
Their mother, my wife, reclined on the couch
Knitting a bright-coloured scarf, drinking a cup of black coffee,
Smoking a cigarette – one of her own roll-ups.
I closed my eyes and breathed in and breathed out.

It is ecstasy to breathe if you are at home in the world.
What a windfall! A home of our own!
Our neighbours' houses had names like 'Con Amore',
'Sans Souci', 'Pacelli', 'Montini', 'Homesville'.
But we called our home 'Windfall'.
'Windfall', 8 Parnell Hill, Cork.
In the gut of my head coursed the leaf of tranquillity
Which I dreamed was known only to Buddhist Monks
In lotus monasteries high up in the Hindu Kush.
Down here in the dark depths of Ireland,
Below sea level in the city of Cork,
In a city as intimate and homicidal as a Little Marseilles,
In a country where all the children of the nation
Are not cherished equally
And where the best go homeless, while the worst
Erect block-house palaces – self-regardingly ugly –
Having a home of your own can give to a family
A chance in a lifetime to transcend death.

elected, steeped, sovereign: slang terms for being very lucky.

winged: high-backed chair; capable of flight.

life is a dream: play by the Spanish playwright Calderon, which deals with the problems of distinguishing between illusion and reality.

Goya: Spanish romantic painter whose works contain a subversive imaginative element.

smoky mirrors: a reference to a painting by Goya of a Spanish king with his family containing an image of Goya himself in a dark mirror looking out at the viewer. The message is one of underlying corruption and decay.

Mont Sainte-Victoire: beautiful French mountain often painted by Paul Cézanne.

Buddhist Monks: monks who live a simple meditative life. They believe that married couples should respect each other's beliefs and privacy.

lotus: sacred. The lotus refers to an exotic water lily and to a fruit that causes dreamy forgetfulness.

Hindu Kush: mountain range stretching from Afghanistan to Pakistan, meaning 'Kills the Hindu', a reference to the many Indian slaves who perished there from harsh weather conditions.

Marseilles: oldest city in France, a Mediterranean port that suffered many sieges and where 'La Marseillaise', the French national anthem, came from. It had a colony of famous artists and is now a gateway for immigrants from the African continent.

block-house palaces: a disparaging reference to new high-rise buildings that sprang up in modern Ireland.

At the high window, shipping from all over the world
Being borne up and down the busy, yet contemplative, river;
Skylines drifting in and out of skylines in the cloudy valley;
Firelight at dusk, and city lights;
Beyond them the control tower of the airport on the hill –
A lighthouse in the sky flashing green to white to green;
Our black-and-white cat snoozing in the corner of a chair;
Pastels and etchings on the four walls, and over the mantelpiece
'Van Gogh's Grave' and 'Lovers in Water';
A room wallpapered in books and family photograph albums
Chronicling the adventures and metamorphoses of family life:
In swaddling clothes in Mammy's arms on baptism day;
Being a baby of nine months and not remembering it;
Face-down in a pram, incarcerated in a high chair;
Everybody, including strangers, wearing shop-window smiles;
With Granny in Felixstowe, with Granny in Ballymaloe;
In a group photo in First Infants, on a bike at thirteen;
In the back garden in London, in the back garden in Cork;
Performing a headstand after First Holy Communion;
Getting a kiss from the Bishop on Confirmation Day;
Straw hats in the Bois de Boulougne, wearing wings at the seaside;

'Van Gogh's Grave': Vincent van Gogh (1853–90) was a famous Dutch post-Impressionist painter who suffered, like Durcan, from depression. He was a tortured soul who lived for his art.
'Lovers in Water': a reference to a painting by modern artist Francine Scialom Greenblatt that refers to a private place made public.
swaddling: strips of cloth wrapped around a newborn child to calm it; also a reference to how the infant Jesus is described in the gospel account.

Mammy and Daddy holding hands on the Normandy Beaches;
Mammy and Daddy at the wedding of Jeremiah and Margot;
Mammy and Daddy queuing up for *Last Tango in Paris*;
Boating on the Shannon, climbing mountains in Kerry;
Building sandcastles in Killala, camping in Barley Cove;
Picnicking in Moone, hide-and-go-seek in Clonmacnoise;
Riding horses, cantering, jumping fences;
Pushing out toy yachts in the pond in the Tuileries;
The Irish College revisited in the Rue des Irlandais;
Sipping an *orange pressé* through a straw on the roof of the Beaubourg;
Dancing in Père Lachaise, weeping at Auvers.
Year in, year out, I pored over these albums accumulating,
My children looking over my shoulder, exhilarated as I was,
Their mother presiding at our ritual from a distance –
The far side of the hearthrug, diffidently, proudly.
Schoolbooks on the floor and pyjamas on the couch –
Whose turn is it tonight to put the children to bed?

***Last Tango in Paris*:** romantic movie (1972) about a love affair that ends in tragedy.

Beaubourg: small, stylish hotel in Paris.
Père Lachaise: largest cemetery in Paris, containing the graves of many famous people.
Auvers: village where Van Gogh lived.

Our children swam about our home
As if it was their private sea,
Their own unique, symbiotic fluid
Of which their parents also partook.
Such is home – a sea of your own –
In which you hang upside down from the ceiling

symbiotic: safe, secure; similar to the natural pre-birth environment.

With equanimity, while postcards from Thailand on the mantelpiece
Are raising their eyebrow markings benignly:
Your hands dangling their prayers to the floorboards of your home,
Sifting the sands underneath the surfaces of conversations,
The marine insect life of the family psyche.
A home of your own – or a sea of your own –
In which climbing the walls is as natural
As making love on the stairs;
In which when the telephone rings
Husband and wife are metamorphosed into smiling accomplices,
Both declining to answer it;
Initiating, instead, a yet more subversive kiss –
A kiss they have perhaps never attempted before –
And might never have dreamed of attempting
Were it not for the telephone belling.
Through the bannisters or along the bannister rails
The pyjama-clad children solemnly watching
Their parents at play, jumping up and down in support,
Race back to bed, gesticulating wordlessly:
The most subversive unit in society is the human family.

We're almost home, pet, almost home ...
Our home is at ...
I'll be home ...
I have to go home now ...
I want to go home now ...
Are you feeling homesick?
Are you anxious to get home? ...
I can't wait to get home ...
Let's stay at home tonight and ...
What time will you be coming home at? ...
If I'm not home by six at the latest, I'll phone ...
We're nearly home, don't worry, we're nearly home ...

But then with good reason
I was put out of my home:
By a keen wind felled.
I find myself now without a home
Having to live homeless in the alien, foreign city of Dublin.
It is an eerie enough feeling to be homesick
Yet knowing you will be going home next week;
It is an eerie feeling beyond all ornithological analysis
To be homesick knowing that there is no home to go home to:
Day by day, creeping, crawling,
Moonlighting, escaping,
Bed-and-breakfast to bed-and-breakfast;
Hostels, centres, one-night hotels.

equanimity: composure, calmness.
benignly: compassionately, favourably.

psyche: consciousness; soul.

metamorphosed: changed.
accomplices: partners – usually in crime.

subversive: unsettling, rebellious.

gesticulating: gesturing dramatically.

keen: sharp, biting.

alien: unfamiliar, strange.

eerie: scary, unnatural.

ornithological: scientific study of birds.

Homeless in Dublin,
Blown about the suburban streets at evening,
Peering in the windows of other people's homes,
Wondering what it must feel like
To be sitting around a fire –
Apache or Cherokee or Bourgeoisie –
Beholding the firelit faces of your family,
Beholding their starry or their TV gaze:
Windfall to Windfall – can you hear me?
Windfall to Windfall ...
We're almost home, pet, don't worry anymore, we're almost home.

Apache: Native American tribe from Arizona.
Cherokee: Native American tribe from the southern United States.
Bourgeoisie: conservative middle class, chiefly concerned with wealth.

'Lovers in Water'

Personal Response

1. In your opinion, what is Durcan's central theme or point in this poem? Briefly explain your response.
2. The poet uses conversational language throughout the poem. What effect do you think this has on the reader?
3. Comment on the tone of the concluding line, 'We're almost home, pet, don't worry anymore, we're almost home'. Does the poet really believe this or is there a darker meaning?

Critical Literacy

'"Windfall", 8 Parnell Hill, Cork' was published in Paul Durcan's collection *The Berlin Wall Café* (1985). It chronicles not only the happy domesticity Durcan enjoyed in his marriage with his wife, Nessa, and their two daughters, but also the bitter consequences of the break-up of that marriage for the poet. The intensity of the pain of separation is searing as the ex-husband unflinchingly discloses the disintegration of his relationship. Paul Durcan has commented, 'Hardly a day goes by that I don't think about our marriage ... I put the breakdown of our marriage down to my stupidity'.

The opening line is written in the conditional tense and expresses a possibility for the future. The poet used to be able to say, 'Well, now, I am going home', as if all the ills of the world could be left outside when he retreated to his one safe place of contentment. Durcan explains how good he felt that he could make that statement: 'I felt elected, steeped, sovereign.' He felt chosen, 'steeped' in luck, free and dominant. But there is a note of regret here, clearly suggesting that he can no longer return home. The importance of **home is emphasised** by continual repetition: 'When I was at home I liked to stay at home;/At home I stayed at home for weeks'. From his privileged position in his 'winged chair', the poet could survey the familiar sights of the city port, 'the river and the factory chimneys'. He meditates, 'Dreaming that life is a dream which is real'. For Durcan, however, reality becomes uncertain, unfocused, 'The river a reflection of itself in its own waters'.

His mind turns to a painting by Goya where the painter has depicted himself in a 'smoky' mirror behind a group of people peering out at the viewer. The industrial cityscape of Cork seems every bit as important for the poet as Mont Sainte-Victoire was for another artist, Paul Cézanne. **A happy picture of domesticity** soon replaces the fluid, unsettling river images. We see Durcan and his family forming a secure, close-knit group: 'my children sat on my knees watching TV.' It is a picture of indolence. Their mother is described separately, as if not quite belonging to this unit. In contrast to the poet, she is much more engaged, 'Knitting', 'drinking', 'Smoking'. But Durcan is oblivious and blissfully happy in his comfortable habitat: 'I closed my eyes and breathed in and breathed out.'

Section two (line 20) conveys the heights of emotion, 'ecstasy', felt when an individual is at ease in the right place, 'at home in the world'. The poet describes this as a 'windfall', something good that has been received unexpectedly. The tone is complacent – almost cynical – when he recalls the names of his neighbours' homes: 'Con Amore' (with love), 'Sans Souci' (without worries), 'Homesville'. Some other houses are called after popes, suggesting the controlling religious influence on the local community. Durcan points out that he and his wife were above all that – 'But we called our home "Windfall"', as though nature itself had provided this haven for his family. Already there is an underlying suggestion that he took too much for granted. He **still feels a sense of deep serenity**, 'the leaf of tranquillity', known only to the monks who lived in Asia's remote mountain ranges.

The exotic image of 'lotus monasteries' evokes the **idealised state of wistful forgetfulness** enjoyed both by the monks and the poet himself. But this restful dreamscape is rudely torn apart by the shocking reality of bourgeois Ireland's 'dark depths'. Cork city is 'intimate', private and personal, but also 'homicidal', murderous, just like the subversive city of Marseilles, where the French Revolution started. Characteristically, Durcan makes a bitter reference to the Irish Constitution, which had not fulfilled its promises and instead produced 'a country where all the children of the nation/Are not cherished equally'. He ridicules the greed of the moneyed classes and their 'block-house palaces'. This section concludes (lines 36–37) that 'Having a home of your own' allows a family to 'transcend death'.

The dreamy sight of changing skies opens the poem's third section (line 38). Tall ships are 'drifting in and out of skylines in the cloudy valley'. **Family harmony appears to reign**: 'Our black-and-white cat snoozing in the corner of a chair.' The living room is filled with pictures and old photo albums that record in detail the changes in family life over two generations. But another disturbing note is struck as the poet describes early pictures of himself 'Face-down in a pram, incarcerated in a high chair'. Durcan was once regarded by his relations as the black sheep of the family and at one time he was even confined to a psychiatric hospital. As he studies the albums, he feels betrayed by the false expressions in the photographs: 'shop-window smiles.' The seemingly random collection of memories ranges widely over significant times and various places at home, at school and on holiday. The young Durcan is seen behaving wildly, 'Performing a headstand after First Holy Communion'. Yet he seems more regretful than bitter. Is the concluding image, 'wearing wings at the seaside', a reference to his innocence or his wish to escape?

The fourth section (line 59) continues with a hypnotic refrain, 'Mammy and Daddy'. Is the poet now openly sneering at the irony of these misleadingly happy photos? He has placed himself centre stage of two family units, as though watching himself growing from childhood to parenthood. For years, he

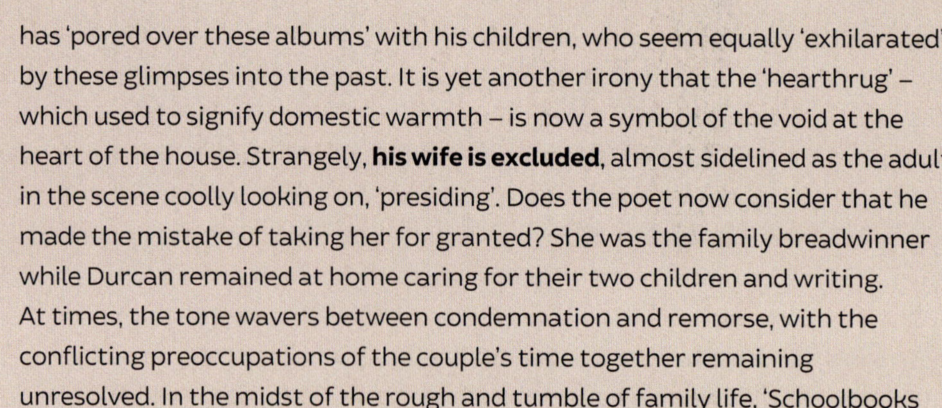

has 'pored over these albums' with his children, who seem equally 'exhilarated' by these glimpses into the past. It is yet another irony that the 'hearthrug' – which used to signify domestic warmth – is now a symbol of the void at the heart of the house. Strangely, **his wife is excluded**, almost sidelined as the adult in the scene coolly looking on, 'presiding'. Does the poet now consider that he made the mistake of taking her for granted? She was the family breadwinner while Durcan remained at home caring for their two children and writing. At times, the tone wavers between condemnation and remorse, with the conflicting preoccupations of the couple's time together remaining unresolved. In the midst of the rough and tumble of family life, 'Schoolbooks on the floor and pyjamas on the couch', her cool voice echoes, 'Whose turn is it tonight to put the children to bed?'

An allegorical **dream scene** reveals the spiritual and emotional aspects of family life in section five (line 76): 'Our children swam about our home/As if it was their private sea'. Their idyllic, unrestrained happiness is caught in the image of the 'symbiotic fluid' of which everyone 'partook'. Durcan believed that home was a place where one could be at liberty without consequences, even hanging 'upside down from the ceiling/With equanimity'. However, the sibilant line 'Sifting the sands underneath the surfaces of conversations' sounds a warning note. Is someone scrutinising, negatively reviewing? The couple are happy when they are partners in crime, 'smiling accomplices', preferring to continue kissing rather than answer the phone. There are signs that the poet could only relate to his wife when she was not behaving as a responsible adult. Meanwhile, the children watch their 'parents at play' sharing another 'subversive kiss' before running 'wordlessly' to bed. But from his intense study of the 'family psyche', Durcan has learned that **the challenges of an intimate relationship can be destructive**. His ringing assertion that 'The most subversive unit in society is the human family' abruptly contradicts any nostalgic homesickness he may have been experiencing.

In the sixth section (line 102), a reassuring parental voice is heard: 'We're almost home, pet, almost home'. The poet follows up with a litany of everyday phrases, some hanging unfinished, and all containing the word 'home'. It is as if this ubiquitous term – the crucial concept of 'home' and belonging – highlights **the overwhelming sense of security he associates with family life**: 'If I'm not home by six at the latest, I'll phone ...' The comforting tone concludes this short section as if Durcan himself and his family have almost made it 'home'. As always, the immediacy of his poetic voice resonates with readers, reinforcing the universal importance of close family relationships.

Inevitably, however, all the celebration of domesticity – whether real or imagined – is shattered in the penultimate section (line 114): 'But then with good reason/I was put out of my home.' The poet no longer refers to 'our home', as in the previous section, but to 'my home'. Does he think he has an

absolute right to be there? Durcan frankly admits that he was expelled 'with good reason'. But what was this reason – depression, alcoholism, a refusal to mature? Is he assuming the manipulative posture of the bad boy, disarmingly admitting his faults so that he will be immediately forgiven? There is more than a hint of **self-pity** in the claim that he was finally brought down 'By a keen wind'. Is this sharp, biting force really his wife?

Typically self-absorbed, the poet goes on to describe his experience of being without a home. He now has to live in the 'alien, foreign city of Dublin', a frightening, disorienting experience. He has discovered how strange it is to be 'homesick' and regards it as totally unnatural, 'beyond all ornithological analysis' if 'there is no home to go home to'. **Short lines effectively convey the aimless wanderings of a homeless man.** 'Day by day' he spends his time 'creeping, crawling,/Moonlighting, escaping'. What a contrast to his previous existence, when he was in control of his home in his 'winged chair', surveying his own 'Mont Sainte-Victoire' with his happy children on his knees. Now he moves restlessly from 'Bed-and-breakfast to bed-and breakfast;/Hostels, centres, one-night hotels'.

The poem's poignant final section (line 127) refers again to a 'Windfall', but now the word is said with **bitter irony**. It no longer refers to his comfortable home, but to himself as a rootless object 'Blown about the suburban streets at evening'. Longingly, he peers 'in the windows of other people's homes,/ Wondering what it must feel like/To be sitting around a fire'. This basic experience is enjoyed by all races and societies, 'Apache or Cherokee' or the socially advantaged 'Bourgeoisie'. They all have the privilege of looking at their families' faces illuminated by firelight, whether they gaze at the stars or the TV screen. The poet now resembles a distressed vessel that had been cast adrift. He is calling frantically for assistance: 'can you hear me?' At this point, the calming tones of a parent return, tenderly reassuring a distracted child: 'We're almost home, pet, don't worry anymore, we're almost home.' Is this longing so deeply ingrained in Durcan that he takes refuge in convincing himself that it is still a possibility? Or is the reality the awful truth that he can never again go back to '"Windfall", 8 Parnell Hill, Cork'?

Writing About the Poem

'Paul Durcan charms readers with his self-critical revelations while concealing his own self-centredness.' Discuss this statement in relation to the poem '"Windfall", 8 Parnell Hill, Cork'. Refer closely to the text in your response.

Sample Paragraph

In this poem, Durcan charms us by presenting memorable images of cosy family living, 'my children sat on my knees watching TV'. I did feel sympathy for him when I heard his graphic account of homelessness, 'creeping, crawling' as though he was unwanted, going from one place to another, 'Hostels, centres, one-night hotels'. He appears rootless, a windfall, belonging nowhere, 'Blown about the suburban streets'. But his admission of being 'put out' of his home 'with good reason' seems as if he is condemning himself just to get pity. His wife is busily 'Knitting'. She is 'presiding' while the poet and his children look at old pictures of him 'dancing'. She is the adult in the relationship, 'Whose turn is it tonight to put the children to bed?' I believe that his wife was becoming frustrated, 'Sifting the sands underneath the surfaces of conversations'. She refused to accept her husband's selfish behaviour. In my opinion, this poem is not really about Durcan's home, but about himself. He does attempt to hide his self-centred character. At the same time, I still feel sorry for him. He ends up a lonely man who has lost all, reduced to the pitiful state of peering into other people's homes and who can never say 'Well, now, I am going home'.

EXAMINER'S COMMENT

The paragraph touches on interesting aspects of how the poet appears to readers and there is a good attempt at addressing the crucial relationship between Durcan and his wife. Points are well illustrated with accurate quotation. There is some direct personal engagement: 'At the same time, I still feel sorry for him.' However, note-like commentary weakens the response: 'He ends up as a lonely man who has lost all.' Although the task is addressed, the quality of expression lowers the mark to a good middle grade.

Class/Homework Exercises

1. 'In many of his poems, Paul Durcan relishes conflict and self-analysis.' Discuss this statement in relation to '"Windfall", 8 Parnell Hill, Cork'. Support the points you make with suitable reference.
2. Based on your reading of this poem, describe Durcan's views on Irish family life. Support your answer with close reference to the text.

Summary Points

- **Key themes – domestic family happiness and the pain of broken relationships.**
- **Autobiographical/personal details; intense rhythms.**
- **Varying tones – reflective, ironic, celebratory, wistful, regretful, self-critical.**
- **Effective use of repetition, vivid images/metaphors.**

Six Nuns Die in Convent Inferno

PAUL DURCAN

To the
happy memory of six Loreto nuns
who died
between midnight and morning of
2 June 1986

I

We resided in a Loreto convent in the centre of Dublin city
On the east side of a public gardens, St Stephen's Green.
Grafton Street – the *paseo*
Where everybody *paseo*'d, including even ourselves –
Debouched on the north side, and at the top of Grafton Street,
Or round the base of the great patriotic pebble of O'Donovan Rossa,
Knelt tableaus of punk girls and punk boys.
When I used pass them – scurrying as I went –
Often as not to catch a mass in Clarendon Street,
The Carmelite Church in Clarendon Street
(Myself, I never used the Clarendon Street entrance,
I always slipped in by way of Johnson's Court,
Opposite the side entrance to Bewley's Oriental Café),
I could not help but smile, as I sucked on a Fox's mint,
That for all the half-shaven heads and the martial garb
And the dyed hair-dos and the nappy pins
They looked so conventional, really, and vulnerable,
Clinging to warpaint and to uniforms and to one another.
I knew it was myself who was the ultimate drop-out,
The delinquent, the recidivist, the vagabond,
The wild woman, the subversive, the original punk.
Yet, although I confess I was smiling, I was also afraid,
Appalled by my own nerve, my own fervour,
My apocalyptic enthusiasm, my other-worldly hubris:
To opt out of the world and to
Choose such exotic loneliness,
Such terrestrial abandonment,
A lifetime of bicycle lamps and bicycle pumps,
A lifetime of galoshes stowed under the stairs,
A lifetime of umbrellas drying out in the kitchens.

I was an old nun – an agèd beadswoman –
But I was no daw.
I knew what a weird bird I was, I knew that when we

Inferno: uncontrollable fire, conflagration.

***paseo*:** pedestrian area where people can take a leisurely stroll.

Debouched: emerged into the open.

O'Donovan Rossa: Jeremiah O'Donovan Rossa (1831–1915) was a prominent Irish Republican. Durcan refers to his large stone memorial as a 'pebble'.

tableaus: groups posing as though in a theatrical freeze.

martial garb: military-style clothes.

warpaint: heavy make-up.

recidivist: undesirable character.

apocalyptic: ruinous.

hubris: excessive pride or arrogance.

daw: jackdaw, noisy crow.

Went to bed we were as eerie an aviary as you'd find
In all the blown-off rooftops of the city:
Scuttling about our dorm, wheezing, shrieking, croaking,
In our yellowy corsets, wonky suspenders, strung-out garters,
A bony crew in the gods of the sleeping city.
Many's the night I lay awake in bed
Dreaming what would befall us if there were a fire:
No fire-escapes outside, no fire-extinguishers inside;
To coin a Dublin saying,
We'd not stand a snowball's chance in hell. Fancy that!
It seemed too good to be true:
Happy death vouchsafed only to the few.
Sleeping up there was like sleeping at the top of the mast
Of a nineteenth-century schooner, and in the daytime
We old nuns were the ones who crawled out on the yardarms
To stitch and sew the rigging and the canvas.
To be sure we were weird birds, oddballs, Christniks,
For we had done the weirdest thing a woman can do –
Surrendered the marvellous passions of girlhood,
The innocent dreams of childhood,
Not for a night or a weekend or even a Lent or a season,
But for a lifetime.
Never to know the love of a man or a woman;
Never to have children of our own;
Never to have a home of our own;
All for why and for what?
To follow a young man – would you believe it –
Who lived two thousand years ago in Palestine
And who died a common criminal strung up on a tree.

As we stood there in the disintegrating dormitory
Burning to death in the arms of Christ –
O Christ, Christ, come quickly, quickly –
Fluttering about in our tight, gold bodices,
Beating our wings in vain,
It reminded me of the snaps one of the sisters took
When we took a seaside holiday in 1956
(The year Cardinal Mindszenty went into hiding
In the US legation in Budapest.
He was a great hero of ours, Cardinal Mindszenty,
Any of us would have given our right arm
To have been his nun – darning his socks, cooking his meals,
Making his bed, doing his washing and ironing.)
Somebody – an affluent buddy of the bishop's repenting his affluence –
Loaned Mother Superior a secluded beach in Co. Waterford –
Ardmore, along the coast from Tramore –

aviary: enclosure or large cage for birds.

schooner: fast sailing ship.
yardarms: parts of a mast from which sails are hung.
rigging: ropes and other supports for sails.
Christniks: fans of Jesus; a pun on the word 'Beatniks'.

Lent: six-week period of penance leading up to Easter in Christian liturgy.

young man: a reference to Jesus.

snaps: photographs.

Cardinal Mindszenty: József Mindszenty (1892–1975), leader of the Catholic Church in Hungary. He was jailed for opposing communism.

affluence: wealth, privileged circumstances.

A cove with palm trees, no less, well off the main road.
There we were, fluttering up and down the beach,
Scampering hither and thither in our starched bathing-costumes.
Tonight, expiring in the fire, was quite much like that,
Only instead of scampering into the waves of the sea,
Now we were scampering into the flames of the fire.

That was one of the gayest days of my life,
The day the sisters went swimming.
Often in the silent darkness of the chapel after Benediction,
During the Exposition of the Blessed Sacrament,
I glimpsed the sea again as it was that day.
Praying – daydreaming really –
I became aware that Christ is the ocean
Forever rising and falling on the world's shore.
Now tonight in the convent Christ is the fire in whose waves
We are doomed but delighted to drown.
And, darting in and out of the flames of the dormitory,
Gabriel, with that extraordinary message of his on his boyish lips,
Frenetically pedalling his skybike.
He whispers into my ear what I must do
And I do it – and die.
Each of us in our own tiny, frail, furtive way
Was a Mother of God, mothering forth illegitimate Christs
In the street life of Dublin city.
God have mercy on our whirring souls –
Wild women were we all –
And on the misfortunate, poor fire-brigade men
Whose task it will be to shovel up our ashes and shovel
What is left of us into black plastic refuse sacks.
Fire-brigade men are the salt of the earth.

Isn't it a marvellous thing how your hour comes
When you least expect it? When you lose a thing,
Not to know about it until it actually happens?
How, in so many ways, losing things is such a refreshing experience,
Giving you a sense of freedom you've not often experienced?
How lucky I was to lose – I say, lose – lose my life.
It was a Sunday night, and after vespers
I skipped bathroom so that I could hop straight into bed
And get in a bit of a read before lights out:
Conor Cruise O'Brien's new book *The Siege*,
All about Israel and superlatively insightful
For a man who they say is reputedly an agnostic –
I got a loan of it from the brother-in-law's married niece –
But I was tired out and I fell asleep with the book open

Benediction: Catholic religious service of blessing.
Exposition of the Blessed Sacrament: prayerful part of Catholic devotion to the Blessed Sacrament (the consecrated bread and wine believed to be the real presence of Jesus Christ).

Gabriel: angel who served as God's messenger.
Frenetically: frantically, wildly.

Conor Cruise O'Brien: prominent Irish politician, writer and academic (1917–2008).
agnostic: religious sceptic.

Face down across my breast and I woke
To the racket of bellowing flame and snarling glass.
The first thing I thought was that the brother-in-law's married niece
Would never again get her Conor Cruise O'Brien back
And I had seen on the price-tag that it cost £23.00:
Small wonder that the custom of snipping off the price
As an exercise in social deportment has simply died out;
Indeed a book today is almost worth buying for its price,
Its price frequently being more remarkable than its contents.

The strange Eucharist of my death –
To be eaten alive by fire and smoke.
I clasped the dragon to my breast
And stroked his red-hot ears.
Strange! There we were, all sleeping molecules,
Suddenly all giving birth to our deaths,
All frantically in labour.
Doctors and midwives weaved in and out
In gowns of smoke and gloves of fire.
Christ, like an Orthodox patriarch in his dressing-gown,
Flew up and down the dormitory, splashing water on our souls:
Sister Eucharia; Sister Seraphia; Sister Rosario;
Sister Gonzaga; Sister Margaret; Sister Edith.
If you will remember us – six nuns burnt to death –
Remember us for the frisky girls that we were,
Now more than ever kittens in the sun.

Eucharist: Thanksgiving; refers to the Mass and Holy Communion (the consecrated bread and wine).
dragon: mythical creature representing fire.
molecules: body particles.

Orthodox patriarch: leader of the Eastern Orthodox Church, the second largest Christian Church in the world.

II

When Jesus heard these words at the top of Grafton Street
Uttered by a small, agèd, emaciated, female punk
Clad all in mourning black, and grieving like an alley cat,
He was annulled with astonishment, and turning round
He declared to the gangs of teenagers and dicemen following him:
'I tell you, not even in New York City
Have I found faith like this.'

That night in St Stephen's Green,
After the keepers had locked the gates,
And the courting couples had found cinemas themselves to die in,
The six nuns who had died in the convent inferno,
From the bandstand they'd been hiding under, crept out
And knelt together by the Fountain of the Three Fates,
Reciting the Agnus Dei: reciting it as if it were the torch song
Of all aid – Live Aid, Self Aid, AIDS, and All Aid –
Lord, I am not worthy
That thou should'st enter under my roof;
Say but the word and my soul shall be healed.

emaciated: skinny, skeletal.

dicemen: street performers, mime artists.

Fountain of the Three Fates: St Stephen's Green statue of the Three Fates or Graces controlling human destiny.
Agnus Dei: Lamb of God (Latin), referring to Christ, a contemplative prayer.
Live Aid, Self Aid: popular charities.
AIDS: acquired immune deficiency syndrome, a syndrome caused by human immunodeficiency virus (HIV).

Personal Response

1. Based on your reading of the poem, what is your impression of convent life in Ireland? Refer to the text in your answer.
2. Briefly describe Durcan's attitude to the nuns and their way of life. Is he always sympathetic to them? Explain your response.
3. Choose one short section of the poem that you consider particularly dramatic. Discuss the poet's language use, commenting on its effectiveness.

'six nuns burnt to death'

Critical Literacy

Paul Durcan has a reputation for being an incisive social commentator. His journalistic approach ranges widely over contemporary events, defining him as a poet of the present moment. But the poet is never content with mere reportage. This long narrative poem about a fire that destroyed a Dublin convent in 1986 characteristically transforms the details of the tragedy into an extended exercise in spiritual reflection. He focuses on one elderly nun who narrates the story of this disaster and reveals the personal choices she had made and her memories of happier times.

Durcan's poems are primarily narrative in form, but they often combine incidents, impressions and flights of fancy. In this case, the title contrasts the dramatic newspaper heading, 'Six Nuns Die in Convent Inferno', with the poignant memorial celebrating the women who dedicated their lives to Christ. What is most evident in the opening lines of Part I is **the spirited voice of the nun** who provides a short history of the Loreto convent where she 'resided'. The gentle, self-deprecating humour of the sisters joining the Grafton Street crowds and 'scurrying' past punks who 'Knelt' indicates a lively sense of irony.

The narrator is particularly amused by the displays of youthful rebelliousness she notices: 'the half-shaven heads' and 'dyed hair-dos' (lines 15–16). She is also convinced that **her 'subversive' choice of vocation** makes her 'the ultimate drop-out'. In retrospect, she is still shocked by her decision to 'opt out of the world' and follow the religious life in all its 'exotic loneliness'. But despite the long 'lifetime' of 'bicycle pumps' and 'umbrellas drying out', she always understood the significance of her alternative calling as a nun: 'I knew what a weird bird I was' (line 33). From her 'agèd beadswoman' perspective, stooped and dressed in black, she is able to imagine how she must appear to outsiders, who might compare her eccentric appearance in full religious habit to 'a daw' – not that any criticism dampens her enthusiasm. Durcan develops the bird metaphor – 'we were as eerie an aviary as you'd find', suggesting the enclosed convent environment.

The speaker's **reflections become increasingly surreal** when she recalls occasional fears ('what would befall us if there were a fire') and the accompanying prospect of a 'Happy death'. Durcan uses a dramatic sailing image to bring to mind the thought of being accidentally killed while 'sleeping at the top of the mast/Of a nineteenth-century schooner'. His attitude to the nuns, encompassing both admiration and astonishment, shows how closely he himself identifies with these unusual women who have 'Surrendered the marvellous passions of girlhood'. He also acknowledges the contribution made by the Loreto nuns in Ireland to providing spiritual guidance and education. Their essential work is compared to the sailors who 'stitch and sew the rigging and the canvas'. The poet's trademark repetition

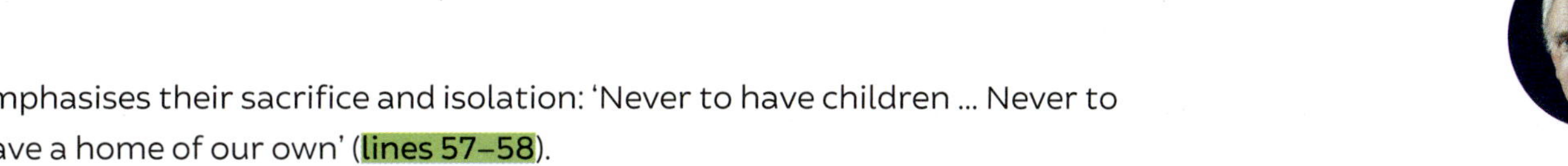

emphasises their sacrifice and isolation: 'Never to have children ... Never to have a home of our own' (lines 57–58).

Many of Durcan's more loosely structured poems are composed by 'cutting' and 'reassembling' various narrative scenes. In line 63, the speaker remembers the 'disintegrating dormitory' and the terrifying ecstasy of 'Burning to death in the arms of Christ'. Amid the chaos – accentuated by exclamatory language – there is **the unsettling sense of souls desperate to emerge as angels**: 'Beating our wings in vain.' In another sudden change of space and time, the narrator associates this crucial moment with an earlier experience when the nuns 'took a seaside holiday in 1956'. The nostalgia for a simpler, old-fashioned era is apparent in the innocent hero-worship of Cardinal Mindszenty and the youthful pleasures of carefree times, 'scampering into the waves'. However, the fond memory is short-lived and the secluded beach abruptly becomes the raging fire that consumed the sisters: 'Now we were scampering into the flames.'

Nevertheless, the elation experienced by the speaker during moments of devout prayer is expressed in terms of the 'day the sisters went swimming'. Durcan uses the nun's elegiac recollection to emphasise the central importance of unconditional Christian faith. Her **visionary account** equates Christ with all of the natural world, including 'the fire in whose waves/We are doomed but delighted to drown' (lines 93–94). A touch of surreal humour is added to her portrait when she imagines the 'boyish' angel Gabriel, 'Frenetically pedalling his skybike'. Her childlike sincerity is also obvious when she worries about the 'poor fire-brigade men' and the loss of a book she borrowed from her niece – 'it cost £23.00'.

Throughout the poem, Durcan promotes the radical Christian values of charity, piety and the achievement of sanctity through suffering, all virtues epitomised in Christ's own life on earth. The nun who narrates this tragic story readily accepts her fate as God's will: 'The strange Eucharist of my death' (line 132). In trying to make sense of the horrific event, the poet interweaves an ingenious series of random insights ('all sleeping molecules') and nightmarish images ('I clasped the dragon to my breast'). The inferno itself is personified, dramatising this central moment of Christian renewal – the paradoxical transition into the spiritual afterlife from earthly existence, 'giving birth to our deaths'. But we are never allowed to forget that at the heart of this sacrifice is the reality of human loss: 'six nuns burnt to death.' As the individual names are recorded precisely, readers can share **Durcan's tender and sad compassion**. The narrator's modest request – to be remembered as 'the frisky girls that we were' (line 146) – is particularly moving. Characteristically playful to the end, she chooses a universal image of childhood innocence to describe her vision of eternal happiness: 'Now more than ever kittens in the sun.'

The 18 lines that make up Part II of the poem are told as third person narrative. The didactic tone echoes countless gospel stories. Durcan imagines the aftermath of the tragedy, with Jesus relocated to Grafton Street, where he is humbled by the story of the grieving nun, now in the persona of 'a small, agèd, emaciated, female punk' (line 149). His shocked reaction ('annulled with astonishment') reflects the poet's well-documented objections to current Catholic teaching on aspects of marriage breakdown. Within this framework, linking the nuns' deaths to the vulnerability of some women today, **Durcan achieves a bizarre satirical effect**. But while he mocks Ireland's conservative Catholic lawmakers, he shows the highest regard for the unshakable faith of individuals, such as the victims of the convent fire.

The poem ends as it began, back in St Stephen's Green, where a final dramatic scenario is played out under cover of darkness. Trance-like, the dead nuns kneel 'by the Fountain of the Three Fates' happily chanting the Agnus Dei (line 161) 'as if it were the torch song' at an outdoor music festival. **The words of this Communion prayer are spoken in preparation for the Divine encounter** – sentiments that are entirely in keeping with the faith of the six Loreto sisters. Durcan's tone of conviction and use of italics reflect the significance of recognising human unworthiness and the acceptance of divine healing love.

From the outset, the poet has venerated the nuns who lost their lives, articulating their religious impulses in particular. The poem's surreal and theatrical elements broaden our understanding of Durcan's subject matter, increasing the clarity of **his imaginative vision**. In blending psychological and physical impressions, he has managed to translate the sensational newspaper story of the inferno into an incisive exploration of individual religious experience.

Writing About the Poem

'Durcan's unique poetic voice is particularly evident in his elegies for victims.' Discuss this view based on your reading of 'Six Nuns Die in Convent Inferno', supporting the points you make with reference to the poem.

Sample Paragraph

Paul Durcan's poetry is always accessible and his distinctive voice is evident in 'Six Nuns Die in Convent Inferno'. This elegy shows his sympathy for the victims of the fire, but also shows their deaths in the true religious sense. The nuns are now with God. The rambling style is typical of Durcan. His narrator is one of the nuns who died, a jolly person,

still childish and mischievous. She sees herself as a comic character and refers to the O'Donovan Rossa memorial as 'the patriotic pebble'. She saw death – even the terrible inferno – as a 'very strange Eucharist', a release. The poem wandered in and out of times in her life, mixing the fire scene with her walks around Stephen's Green and memories of a holiday in Tramore. Durcan uses names to create a sense of place. His respect for the nuns was obvious in his use of prayers. The whole poem paid tribute to the nuns' deep faith, suggesting that they are obsessed with religion. Durcan's conclusion was dreamlike, showing the spirits of the nuns celebrating their entry to Heaven through a vibrant image of dancing in the dark. I thought the tribute was sincere without being sentimental, another feature of Durcan's poems.

EXAMINER'S COMMENT

This fresh response shows clear personal engagement with the poem: 'I liked the way her character was gradually revealed.' The answer touches on several interesting points – focusing particularly well on characteristics of Durcan's style, for example his anecdotal approach and use of place names. The expression is satisfactory, but more use could be made of supportive quotations (and some are slightly inaccurate). Falls just below the top grade.

Class/Homework Exercises

1. 'Durcan makes good use of surreal effects in addressing religious themes.' Discuss this statement based on your reading of 'Six Nuns Die in Convent Inferno'. Support the points you make with reference to the poem.
2. 'Vivid imagery is often a feature of Paul Durcan's most compelling poems.' To what extent is this the case in 'Six Nuns Die in Convent Inferno'? Support your answer with reference to the text.

Summary Points

- **Narrative of the fire tragedy becomes an extended spiritual reflection.**
- **Key themes include personal choices, sacrifice, faith, the religious life.**
- **Fragmented, theatrical structure; striking images – realistic, surreal.**
- **Varying tones – ironic, compassionate, satirical, critical.**

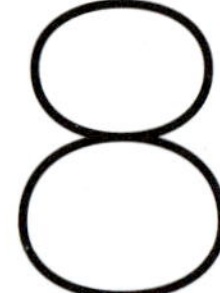

8 Sport

Sport: an activity involving effort and skill in which an individual or team compete; also refers to a person who behaves in a good way in response to teasing or defeat.

There were not many fields
In which you had hopes for me
But sport was one of them.
On my twenty-first birthday
I was selected to play
For Grangegorman Mental Hospital
In an away game
Against Mullingar Mental Hospital.
I was a patient
In B Wing.
You drove all the way down,
Fifty miles,
To Mullingar to stand
On the sidelines and observe me.

I was fearful I would let down
Not only my team but you.
It was Gaelic football.
I was selected as goalkeeper.
There were big country men
On the Mullingar Mental Hospital team,
Men with gapped teeth, red faces,
Oily, frizzy hair, bushy eyebrows.
Their full forward line
Were over six foot tall
Fifteen stone in weight.
All three of them, I was informed,
Cases of schizophrenia.

There was a rumour
That their centre-half forward
Was an alcoholic solicitor
Who, in a lounge bar misunderstanding,
Had castrated his best friend
But that he had no memory of it.
He had meant well – it was said.
His best friend had had to emigrate
To Nigeria.

fields: pitches, areas, disciplines.

away game: played at an opponent's place, seen as an advantage to the opposing team.

observe: examine, consider, scrutinise.

schizophrenia: long-term mental disorder with symptoms including emotional instability, detachment from reality and withdrawal into self.

castrated: removed testicles; deprived of power, made docile.

To my surprise,
I did not flinch in the goals.
I made three or four spectacular saves,
Diving full stretch to turn
A certain goal around the corner,
Leaping high to tip another certain goal
Over the bar for a point.
It was my knowing
That you were standing on the sideline
That gave me the necessary motivation –
That will to die
That is as essential to sportsmen as to artists.
More than anybody it was you
I wanted to mesmerise, and after the game –
Grangegorman Mental Hospital
Having defeated Mullingar Mental Hospital
By 14 goals and 38 points to 3 goals and 10 points –
Sniffing your approval, you shook hands with me.
'Well played, son.'

I may not have been mesmeric
But I had not been mediocre.
In your eyes I had achieved something at last.
On my twenty-first birthday I had played on a winning team
The Grangegorman Mental Hospital team.
Seldom if ever again in your eyes
Was I to rise to these heights.

flinch: cower, dodge, shy away.

motivation: reasons to act and be enthusiastic.

mesmerise: fascinate, captivate.

Sniffing: snorting, showing contempt for.

mesmeric: brilliant, hypnotic.
mediocre: only average, amateurish, ordinary.

'I had achieved something'

Personal Response

1. Based on an initial reading of the poem, what is your impression of Paul Durcan's father? Refer closely to the text in your response.
2. Trace the changing tones of voice as the poem progresses. Support your answer with appropriate reference.
3. Are you sympathetic or not to the character of Durcan himself that emerges from the poem? Refer to the text to support the points you make.

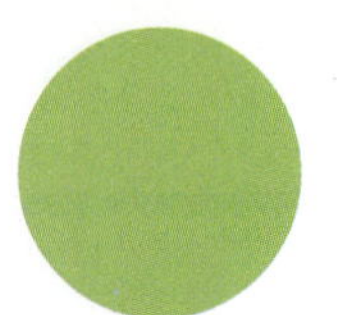

Critical Literacy

'Sport' is from Paul Durcan's collection *Daddy, Daddy*, for which he was awarded the Whitbread Prize (1990). This poem is painfully autobiographical, as he not only recalls a difficult time in his youth, but also explores the troubled relationship he had with his father. Durcan has remarked: 'My father would say, "Paul is a sissy. Come on, be a man." I was aware of his deep disappointment.'

The poet's father was a judge in the circuit court. He was an introverted man, apparently ill-suited to the legal profession. Nevertheless, Durcan shared 'many rich moments' with him in early childhood. But in the mid-1950s, 'the picture darkened' when the young Durcan was about 10. Paul began to receive beatings and there was pressure about exam performance. He contracted a serious bone disease at 13, which ended his athletic career. Because of difficulties with his behaviour in his late teens, members of his wider family had him committed to a psychiatric hospital.

The poem opens candidly, with Durcan addressing his father directly. He immediately registers an acute awareness of his father's disappointment with him in many areas: 'there were not many fields/In which you had hopes for me/But sport was one of them.' Sometimes, when men find it hard to communicate, they can relate through sport. They can express their emotions as they discuss the winning or losing of a match without being considered odd. The Gaelic football game Durcan recalls was played on his 21st birthday, the day he becomes a man. In line 6, **the chilling context of this occasion** is revealed. It was an 'away game' between the inmates of 'Grangegorman Mental Hospital' and 'Mullingar Mental Hospital'. Durcan is 'a patient/In B Wing', a vulnerable individual. He acknowledges his father's efforts to attend the match, driving 'Fifty miles,/To Mullingar to stand/On the sidelines'. The inference is that the father was never really involved in the poet's life. Durcan also suggests his father's disapproving character when he is described as coming to 'observe me'. It is almost as if his son was a laboratory specimen. The curt tone clearly indicates that **his father's attendance was far from supportive**.

Nevertheless, there is no denying the son's extreme anxiety to impress: 'I was fearful I would let down/Not only my team but you' (lines 15–16). The young man was obviously keen to please his father in this unlikely Gaelic match, where he had been 'selected as goalkeeper'. Durcan's fondness for dark humour is evident in his exaggerated description of the opposition players. The Mullingar team had 'gapped teeth, red faces,/Oily, frizzy hair, bushy eyebrows'. They scarcely seemed human. **Odd details reflect the poet's visual alertness.** The opposing team consisted of 'big country men' whose 'full forward line/Were over six foot tall/Fifteen stone in weight'. These three suffered from schizophrenia, a withdrawal from reality into fantasy. As if the situation was not surreal enough already, Durcan recounts the 'rumour'

(line 28) about another member of the Mullingar team, 'an alcoholic solicitor' who had mindlessly 'castrated his best friend'. Readers are left with an uneasy sense of absurd comedy based on uncontrollable male violence.

As for the game itself, the poet is amazed by his own performance: 'To my surprise,/I did not flinch in the goals.' The dramatic jargon of sports writing is used, perhaps self-mockingly, to describe his exploits on the field of play, making 'spectacular saves' that were at 'full stretch'. Action-packed verbs convey his tremendous agility – 'Diving', 'Leaping' – and all for the approval of his father, 'knowing/That you were standing on the sideline'. Durcan makes a revealing comment in line 47 that **both artists, such as himself, and sportsmen must have absolute motivation** – 'That will to die'. They will give their all and risk everything in their desire to succeed.

The young man's need to make an impact on his father accelerates: 'it was you/I wanted to mesmerise.' Characteristically, the overwhelmingly decisive triumph of Durcan's team is recorded with **mock-heroic pride**: '14 goals and 38 points to 3 goals and 10 points.' Despite this great triumph, however, the father's minimal response, his monosyllabic ruling, is less than enthusiastic: 'Well played, son.' There is no embrace. Instead, a formal handshake takes place. The disappointment of the young man contrasts with the emotionally stilted father 'Sniffing ... approval'. Is he suggesting that his son is merely satisfactory, damning him with faint praise? Of course, we see everything from the son's perspective. During the early 1960s, a father's function in Irish society was to provide for his family. Obvious displays of affection were not common between parents and children, especially sons. Is Durcan's forensic examination of the father–son relationship almost as unhealthy as his father's scrutiny of him? Are both tragically locked into damaging behavioural attitudes?

In the poem's concluding section, Durcan ruefully admits, 'I may not have been mesmeric' (line 56). Yet he also asserts 'But I had not been mediocre' and had indeed 'achieved something at last'. The phrase 'at last' forcefully expresses how intensely aware the poet is of his father's lack of confidence in him. After all, he had accomplished something, playing on a 'winning team'. It was, however, a mental hospital patients' team. Does this matter greatly to the father – and to the son? **The poem ends on a poignant note**: 'seldom if ever again in your eyes/Was I to rise to these heights.' Dark shadows of family relationships were cast by the father's continuing disappointment. The son is still devastated about what it means to be a man and always to feel not quite good enough.

Writing About the Poem

'Durcan's poetry is not just revealing, it also has a shockingly frank quality.' Discuss this statement in relation to the poem 'Sport'. Refer closely to the text in your answer.

Sample Paragraph

The highly personal poem 'Sport' comes from Durcan's collection *Daddy, Daddy*, whose title is a reference to the American poet Sylvia Plath's cry to her father, 'Daddy, daddy, you bastard, I'm through'. I think the lines in 'Sport' are almost as shocking. They convey, in a frank manner, the longing of the son for his father's approval. Durcan reveals his lack of confidence in lines such as, 'I was fearful I would let down/Not only my team but you'. Like most young men, he desperately wanted to 'mesmerise' his uncommunicative father. The urgent tone seems to suggest the spellbinding effect he wishes to make on him. I thought the father's lukewarm response was hurtful, especially the cold words 'Well played, son'. The poet does not shy away from disclosing that just as his father stood on 'the sidelines' to 'observe' him, he now appears obsessed with studying his father. I believe he feels just as let down by his father's behaviour as his father is by his: 'But I had not been mediocre.' His continuing disappointment mirrors his father's feelings towards him as he notes in the concluding lines, 'Seldom if ever again in your eyes/ Was I to rise to these heights'. Durcan is quite brave to detail the awkward relationship he had with his father with such devastating honesty.

EXAMINER'S COMMENT

A well-written paragraph that uses suitable reference to outline the poet's central theme, the difficult father-son relationship. The use of pertinent descriptive terms, such as 'uncommunicative', 'lukewarm' and 'devastating', helps to define their strained relationship. There is clear evidence throughout of close engagement with the poem: 'I believe he feels just as let down by his father's behaviour as his father is by his.' A highly successful response which merits the top grade.

Class/Homework Exercises

1. 'Paul Durcan blends fact, fiction and fantasy to create a realistic view of the world.' Discuss this viewpoint in relation to the poem, 'Sport'. Support your opinions with close reference to the text.
2. In your opinion, what kind of relationship did the poet have with his father? Support your answer with close reference to the poem, 'Sport'.

Summary Points

- **Characteristically personal exploration of a complex father–son relationship.**
- **Effective use of tragicomedy, mock-heroism and irony.**
- **Tone varies – casual, sad, comic, self-mocking.**
- **Revealing narrative/descriptive details, lively verbs.**

PAUL DURCAN

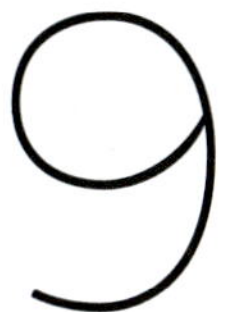

Father's Day, 21 June 1992

Father's Day: an important family occasion in honour of male parenting, traditionally celebrated on the third Sunday of June.

Just as I was dashing to catch the Dublin–Cork train,
Dashing up and down the stairs, searching my pockets,
She told me that her sister in Cork wanted a loan of the axe;
It was late June and
The buddleia tree in the backyard
Had grown out of control.
The taxi was ticking over outside in the street,
All the neighbours noticing it.
'You mean that you want me to bring her down the axe?'
'Yes, if you wouldn't mind, that is –'
'A simple saw would do the job, surely to God
She could borrow a simple saw.'
'She said that she'd like the axe.'
'OK. There is a Blue Cabs taxi ticking over outside
And the whole world inspecting it,
I'll bring her down the axe.'
The axe – all four-and-a-half feet of it –
Was leaning up against the wall behind the settee –
The fold-up settee that doubles as a bed.
She handed the axe to me just as it was,
As neat as a newborn babe,
All in the bare buff.
You'd think she'd have swaddled it up
In something – if not a blanket, an old newspaper,
But no, not even a token hanky
Tied in a bow round its head.
I decided not to argue the toss. I kissed her goodbye.

The whole long way down to Cork
I felt uneasy. Guilt feelings.
It's a killer, this guilt.
I always feel bad leaving her
But this time it was the worst.
I could see that she was glad
To see me go away for a while,
Glad at the prospect of being
Two weeks on her own,
Two weeks of having the bed to herself,
Two weeks of not having to be pestered
By my coarse advances,

buddleia tree: colourful flowering shrub; butterfly bush.

swaddled: wrapped.

token: symbolic, nominal.

argue the toss: dispute the issue.

prospect: expectation.

pestered: bothered.

coarse advances: unrefined sexual demands.

Two weeks of not having to look up from her plate
And behold me eating spaghetti with a knife and fork.
Our daughters are all grown up and gone away.
Once when she was sitting pregnant on the settee
It snapped shut with herself inside it,
But not a bother on her. I nearly died.

As the train slowed down approaching Portarlington
I overheard myself say to the passenger sitting opposite me:
'I am feeling guilty because she does not love me
As much as she used to, can you explain that?'
The passenger's eyes were on the axe on the seat beside me.
'Her sister wants a loan of the axe ...'
As the train threaded itself into Portarlington
I nodded to the passenger 'Cúl an tSúdaire!'
The passenger stood up, lifted down a case from the rack,
Walked out of the coach, but did not get off the train.
For the remainder of the journey, we sat alone,
The axe and I,
All the green fields running away from us,
All our daughters grown up and gone away.

Cúl an tSúdaire: Irish name for Portarlington (literally 'back of the tanner', referring to the tannery once located there). Durcan might well be making a snide comment about the town's humble origins.

'the train threaded itself into Portarlington'

Personal Response

1. In your opinion, what does the poem's first stanza reveal about the relationship between the poet and his wife? Refer closely to the text in your answer.
2. Select one image (or line) that has a surreal or bizarre impact in the poem. Briefly explain your choice.
3. Comment on the significance of the poem's final line: 'All our daughters grown up and gone away.'

Critical Literacy

Because so much of his poetry has been autobiographical, Durcan's insecure relationships are already widely known. 'Father's Day, 21 June 1992' is taken from *A Snail in my Prime* (1993) and recounts a crucial train journey when the poet confronts the adverse effects of time on his role as a husband and father. Typically, the poem alternates between tragicomedy, surreal scenes and devastating self-awareness. The abrupt changes of tone and mood are likely to be disconcerting for readers, who can never be entirely sure about the poet's true feelings.

In the anecdotal opening lines, Durcan assumes the persona of a slightly confused figure 'dashing' about the house. From the outset, there are suggestions of marriage difficulties, particularly in his impatient account of his wife's attitude: 'She told me that her sister in Cork wanted a loan of the axe.' Everyone involved in this uneasy family drama seems slightly eccentric. **Durcan often finds grim humour in the most unexpected circumstances.** Is he suggesting that his sister-in-law is dangerously deranged? The poet's mention of the garden shrub that is now 'out of control' adds to the unstable atmosphere. Could this be a reference to his domineering wife and her sister? Or is the marriage itself veering close to crisis? Meanwhile, the waiting taxi is 'ticking over', another possible symbol of the explosive domestic situation.

The strained exchange between the couple (lines 9–16) illustrates their barely concealed frustration with each other. Although the poet is reluctant to bring an axe on public transport, his wife is politely insistent: 'if you wouldn't mind.' She seems to be a strangely disembodied presence, reflecting the considerable lack of communication in the marriage. In choosing to do as he is asked on this occasion – 'I decided not to argue the toss' – Durcan indicates a history of marital disagreements. Almost as a defence mechanism to block out the truth about a relationship under threat, **Durcan's description of the scene becomes increasingly trance-like**. He exaggerates the importance of the axe – 'all-four-and-a-half feet of it' – comparing it to 'a newborn babe' (line 21). The simile has a poignant association with happier times, when his infant children represented what

was truly meaningful about Father's Day. In a blurred state of distorted memories and nostalgic self-pity, the poet personifies the axe and wonders why it could not have been 'swaddled' or at least gift-wrapped with 'a bow round its head'.

Durcan's small domestic narrative develops in the poem's second stanza. On the train journey from Dublin to Cork, his tone is much more reflective as he laments his guilty mood: 'I always feel bad leaving her.' Acknowledging that his wife is 'glad' to be alone, he indulges in mock-serious self-criticism. Not only will she welcome a fortnight's break from his 'coarse advances', but she will no longer have to endure his irritating table manners, 'eating spaghetti with a knife and fork' (line 41). Whether such overstated self-accusation is totally sincere is, of course, open to question. At any rate, whatever humour that exists is soon replaced with **the stark reality of loss** that is at the core of the poet's unhappiness: 'Our daughters are all grown up.' This heartbreaking admission, enhanced by broad assonant effects, provides a momentary explanation for the couple's failing marriage. However, in a sudden change in tone, the poet recalls a comic occasion when his wife was pregnant and almost got trapped in the fold-up settee. Ironically, the memory does not lessen his deep sense of disappointment.

The third stanza is set at Portarlington Station, where Durcan seems overwhelmed by profound feelings of sorrow. However, his situation quickly turns into an anarchic event. In a dreamlike sequence, the poet imagines confiding in another passenger about his guilt 'because she does not love me/As much as she used to'. **The surreal sense of disorientation grows** when the encounter is viewed from the perspective of the stranger, whose 'eyes were on the axe on the seat beside me'. Needless to say, when Durcan calls out the station name in Irish, 'Cúl an tSúdaire', the frightened passenger leaves the coach as quickly as possible. Again, the farcical episode is underpinned with underlying heartbreak.

In the final lines, we see a broken human being abandoned in a bizarre world of utter isolation: 'we sat alone,/The axe and I.' The ending is particularly lyrical, evoking the sadness of innocent times gone forever: 'All the green fields running away from us.' Durcan often uses the metaphor of travel to express significant changes in his life. The train journey to Cork is a remarkably sombre one, depicting a forlorn man still struggling to come to terms with the effects of time and the devastating fact that 'All our daughters' are 'grown up and gone away'. The concluding mood is one of estrangement and desolation. Durcan is painfully aware that he no longer has a reason to celebrate Father's Day.

Writing About the Poem

'Father's Day, 21 June 1992' is one of Paul Durcan's most personal and revealing poems. What aspects of the poem affected you most?

Sample Paragraph

After studying 'Father's Day, 21 June 1992', I had mixed feelings. In some ways, the poem is a desperately sad memory of the time when Durcan realised his marriage was ending. The couple seemed like strangers – 'I decided not to argue the toss'. The mood in the family home is awkward. The discussion about bringing an axe on the train seems ludicrous, but it's difficult not to have sympathy for both the poet and his wife. There is a distance between them, evident in the ironic comment, 'I kissed her goodbye'. For me, the most moving part of the poem is Durcan's acknowledgement 'Our daughters are all grown up and gone away'. The serious tone and slow rhythm of this long thoughtful line, filled with mournful assonance, emphasises the poet's essential depression. He now accepts that there is nothing to keep his marriage alive and the poem's concluding lines left me genuinely sympathetic. Father's Day has lost all meaning for Durcan. The image of 'All our green fields running away from us' is very appropriate. As he looks out of the train window, the beauty of the Irish countryside is out of reach for the ageing poet. I thought this was a very moving symbol of his empty life – and I felt it was in keeping with the elegiac mood.

EXAMINER'S COMMENT

A very good personal response, showing true engagement with the poem: 'the poem's concluding lines left me genuinely sympathetic.' The focus throughout is on the emotional interaction with the poet's experience of failure and loss. Effective use is made of supportive quotes. Expression is also clear and varied: 'The serious tone and the slow rhythm of this long thoughtful line, filled with mournful assonance, emphasises the poet's essential depression.' In-depth analysis merits the top grade.

Class/Homework Exercises

1. 'The use of humour in Paul Durcan's poems provides revealing insights into his complex personal relationships.' Discuss this view, with particular reference to 'Father's Day, 21 June 1992'.
2. Trace the changing tones in the poem, 'Father's Day, 21 June 1992'. Support your answer with close reference to the text.

Summary Points

- **Durcan considers the destructive impact of time on his role as husband and father.**
- **Dislocated dreamlike atmosphere, heightened drama, edgy dialogue.**
- **Effective use of travel metaphor, irony, surreal scenes.**
- **Contrasting tones of discomfort, dark humour, reflection and resignation.**

10 The Arnolfini Marriage

after Jan Van Eyck

We are the Arnolfinis.
Do not think you may invade
Our privacy because you may not.

We are standing to our portrait,
The most erotic portrait ever made,
Because we have faith in the artist

To do justice to the plurality,
Fertility, domesticity, barefootedness
Of a man and a woman saying 'we':

To do justice to our bed
As being our most necessary furniture;
To do justice to our life as a reflection.

Our brains spill out upon the floor
And the terrier at our feet sniffs
The minutiae of our magnitude.

The most relaxing word in our vocabulary is 'we'.
Imagine being able to say 'we'.
Most people are in no position to say 'we'.

Are you? Who eat alone? Sleep alone?
And at dawn cycle to work
With an Alsatian shepherd dog tied to your handlebars?

We will pause now for the Angelus.
Here you have it:
The two halves of the coconut.

The Arnolfini Marriage: painted by the Dutch artist Jan Van Eyck in 1434 and regarded as a masterpiece, it has become a well-known symbol of marriage yet it retains its mystery.

Arnolfinis: generally believed to represent the Italian merchant Giovanni and his wife Constanza, possibly in their home in the Flemish city of Bruges, perhaps undertaking a civil marriage ceremony. It was commissioned a year after Constanza died.
invade: infringe, violate, intrude on.
privacy: undisturbed time, secrecy.
erotic: sensual, suggestive.
faith: complete trust.

To do justice: to be fair and reasonable.
plurality: range, various meanings, truth.
barefootedness: in 15th-century Flanders, it was traditional to remove shoes for a wedding ceremony. This emphasised the marriage rite's blessedness and inviolability.

reflection: light thrown back from a surface; image formed by a reflection; a serious thought.

minutiae: small, precise details.
magnitude: greatness, importance.

Angelus: Christian devotional prayers commemorating the announcement to Mary that she was going to give birth to Jesus, the son of God.
coconut: fruit of the coconut palm, consisting of a hard fibrous husk and white inner core.

'We are the Arnolfinis'

Personal Response

1. Based on your reading of the poem, do you think that the speakers are trying to shock or discomfort the reader? Briefly explain your views.
2. What, in your opinion, is Durcan's attitude towards the Arnolfinis? Refer to the poem in your answer.
3. Select one image from the poem that you found particularly interesting. Comment on its effectiveness.

Critical Literacy

Paul Durcan's collection *Give Me Your Hand* (1994) was inspired by paintings in London's National Gallery. He has taken some of the most famous paintings in the world and interpreted them with his own distinctive poetic voice. We see the artwork 'through the prism of his imagination' as he projects himself into the famous characters of the paintings, slipping in and out of the pictures and 'sending us on flights of our own'. 'The Arnolfini Marriage' was inspired by the Jan Van Eyck oil painting, which is believed to represent a rich Italian merchant and his wife. It was painted in Bruges in 1434, 'in its own way new and revolutionary ... For the first time in history, the artist became the perfect eye-witness'.

The opening line of this dramatic monologue simply states, 'We are the Arnolfinis', a confident declaration by an assured, well-to-do couple. Durcan assumes their personas and viewpoint. The regular form of the poem – eight three-line stanzas – mirrors the orderly composition of the portrait. The speakers issue a stern warning to the reader: 'Do not think you may invade/Our privacy because you may not'. The formal tone contains more than a suggestion that Durcan is casting a satirical eye on the prim couple. Although this painting has become a famous symbol of marriage, representing the Arnolfinis in the intimate environment of their home, it conceals as much as it reveals. It is, however, an utterly convincing picture of a room as well as the people who inhabit it. Argument rages over the original painting, but the most recent view suggests that the couple are Giovanni and Constanza Arnolfini. Some critics maintain that the woman is simply holding up her full-skirted dress in the contemporary fashion. Although the wife looks pregnant, there are no recorded children for this couple. In the painting, the man's hand is raised as if taking an oath. Is it a record of a marriage contract in the form of a painting? **Durcan is clearly fascinated – both by the questions raised and by the answers we will never know**, since we cannot 'invade' the couple's 'privacy'.

The announcement at the start of the second stanza is also intriguing: 'We are standing to our portrait'. It is as if they are taking up position in readiness for military action. Is the poet suggesting that marriage can also have its share of conflict? Nonetheless, the speakers describe the painting as the 'most erotic portrait ever made'. It is certainly a sensual, stimulating picture celebrating the couple's sexual relationship as well as the sanctity of marriage. Throughout stanza three, Durcan emphasises the faith the Arnolfinis have in the artist's ability 'to do justice to the plurality' of their married lives. **There are many aspects to a man and woman saying 'we'.** A chance of having children, 'Fertility', is now possible. The challenge of living together as man and wife, 'domesticity', must now be faced. The removal of shoes, 'barefootedness', could suggest the vulnerability of laying bare one's soul to another in an intimate relationship. Going barefoot also means landing on the forefoot, the centre of gravity. This guarantees optimum balance and increased stability – but is this true for every marriage?

In stanza four, the Arnolfinis assert that they want the artist to 'do justice' and be objective in his depiction of their 'bed/As being our most necessary furniture'. It is central to their marriage. They hope the artist will execute a work of integrity, 'to our life as a reflection'. They want a true likeness. **Durcan's fondness for the surreal** becomes evident in the fifth stanza with the introduction of a more disturbing image: 'Our brains spill out upon the floor.' Does this suggest the suppressed aggression within the relationship? Meanwhile, the little dog, usually a symbol of loyalty, is sniffing 'the minutiae of our magnitude', the small details that reveal the couple's sense of their importance. In the sixth stanza, the repetition of 'we' shows the complacency of the couple now that they are man and wife: 'The most relaxing word in our vocabulary is "we".' They luxuriate in their ability to say it: 'imagine being able to say "we".' Then they realise that most people are not so fortunate – 'are in no position to say "we".' Durcan has used the process of repetition to develop this thought. But is he also thinking about his own marriage and that he never expected it to fail?

The tone of the seventh stanza sharply challenges us with the uncomfortable question: 'Are you?' The solitary state of the reader is highlighted by the emphatic 'Who eat alone? Sleep alone?' Durcan sketches some of the mundane routines of modern life for people who 'at dawn cycle to work'. **What a contrast to the opulence of the Arnolfinis.** He uses another surreal image ('an Alsatian shepherd dog tied to your handlebars') to perhaps exaggerate the insecurity of our contemporary world.

In the last stanza, the couple 'pause now for the Angelus'. This Christian act of devotion commemorates the occasion when the angel Gabriel declared to Mary that she was to conceive the son of God: 'blessed is the fruit of thy womb, Jesus.' Here is the good news, the possibility of redemption. A final dreamlike image is presented when the two figures in the portrait are seen as 'The two halves of the coconut'. Is Durcan laughing at the Arnolfinis? Or does this naive metaphor refer to the Hindu custom of breaking a coconut at a wedding ceremony to ensure the blessing of the gods? In some other societies, the coconut is regarded as the tree that provides all the necessities of life. As always, the poem (like the Van Eyck painting) shows and conceals equally. Once again, **boundaries are blurred** and the reader is challenged to view the accepted norms relating to married life in a different way.

Writing About the Poem

'Durcan's poetry celebrates plurality of perspective.' Discuss this statement in relation to the poem 'The Arnolfini Marriage'. Refer closely to the text in your response.

Sample Paragraph

In 'The Arnolfini Marriage', Durcan clearly demonstrates the important role the artist adopts in showing how necessary it is to hold more than one view on things, 'we have faith in the artist/To do justice to the plurality'. Durcan wants us to consider this portrait of the Arnolfinis as a symbol of marriage and all it entails. Is it a battlefield, 'We are standing to our portrait'? Is it a contented, cosy state, 'The most relaxing word in our vocabulary is "we"'? This poem reminds me of the cult of celebrity in our times. We see someone's image and we feel we know this person intimately. Durcan warns us of this one-sided view, 'Do not think you may invade/Our privacy'. Although we see these people in the most intimate of settings, beside a bed, we do not know the real purpose of the painting. The poet recognises a number of meanings in the picture: a record of a civil marriage, a wish for a fertile marriage or a memorial to a dead wife. A surreal image concludes the poem, 'two halves of the coconut'. Is it a reference to a blessing of a wedding? As usual, Durcan has succeeded in showing us that there are many ways to view someone or something. He has challenged our fixed notions of the way things are. After all, who goes to work with 'an Alsatian shepherd dog tied' to a bicycle? The puzzles in the poem show the complexity of human behaviour.

EXAMINER'S COMMENT

Overall, a well-focused response that addresses a demanding question. There is effective use of quotation throughout and some good personal engagement with the poem. Apart from an over-reliance on questions, the paragraph offers several interesting discussion points about Durcan's perspective. The focus on addressing the task ('He has challenged our fixed notions of the way things are.') in the question merits the top grade.

Class/Homework Exercises

1. 'Durcan does verbally what painting does visually.' Discuss this view, using suitable reference to the poem 'The Arnolfini Marriage'.
2. Some of Durcan's poems are known for their strange, dreamlike quality. To what extent is this true of 'The Arnolfini Marriage'? Support your response with close reference to the text.

Summary Points

- **Dramatic monologue where Durcan assumes the personas of the rich married couple.**
- **Effective use of repetition, questions, suggestion.**
- **Characteristic fondness for distorted/surreal description.**
- **Contrasting tones – formal, reflective, challenging.**

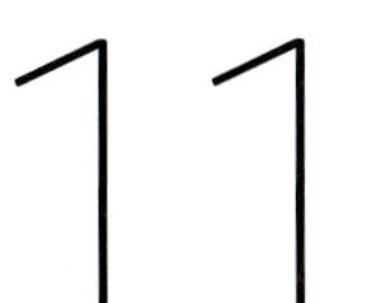

Rosie Joyce

PAUL DURCAN

I

That was that Sunday afternoon in May
When a hot sun pushed through the clouds
And you were born!

I was driving the two hundred miles from west to east,
The sky blue-and-white china in the fields
In impromptu picnics of tartan rugs;

When neither words nor I
Could have known that you had been named already
And that your name was Rosie –

Rosie Joyce! May you some day in May
Fifty-six years from today be as lucky
As I was when you were born that Sunday:

To drive such side-roads, such main roads, such ramps, such roundabouts,
To cross such bridges, to by-pass such villages, such towns
As I did on your Incarnation Day.

By-passing Swinford – Croagh Patrick in my rear-view mirror –
My mobile phone rang and, stopping on the hard edge of P. Flynn's highway,
I heard Mark your father say:

'A baby girl was born at 3.33 p.m.
Weighing 7 and a 1/2 lbs in Holles Street.
Tough work, all well.'

II

That Sunday in May before daybreak
Night had pushed up through the slopes of Achill
Yellow forefingers of Arum Lily – the first of the year;

Down at the Sound the first rhododendrons
Purpling the golden camps of whins;
The first hawthorns powdering white the mainland;

impromptu: spontaneous, spur-of-the-moment.

Incarnation Day: Rosie's day of birth, seen by Durcan as blessed.
Croagh Patrick: Co. Mayo mountain and place of religious pilgrimage.
P. Flynn's highway: satirical reference to an impressive new road in the constituency of a former government minister, Padraig Flynn.

Holles Street: Dublin maternity hospital.

Arum Lily: colourful flower.

the Sound: the small village of Achill Sound on Achill Island.
rhododendrons: vivid shrubs that flower in springtime.
whins: gorse; wild bushes with yellow flowers.
hawthorns: thorny hedgerow bushes that usually have white flowers.

The first yellow irises flagging roadside streams;
Quills of bog-cotton skimming the bogs;
Burrishoole cemetery shin-deep in forget-me-nots;

The first sea pinks speckling the seashore;
Cliffs of London Pride, groves of bluebell,
First fuchsia, Queen Anne's Lace, primrose.

I drove the Old Turlough Road, past Walter Durcan's Farm,
Umbrella'd in the joined handwriting of its ash trees;
I drove Tulsk, Kilmainham, the Grand Canal.

Never before had I felt so fortunate
To be driving back into Dublin city;
Each canal bridge an old pewter brooch.

I rode the waters and the roads of Ireland,
Rosie, to be with you, seashell at my ear!
How I laughed when I cradled you in my hand.

Only at Tarmonbarry did I slow down,
As in my father's Ford Anglia half a century ago
He slowed down also, as across the River Shannon

We crashed, rattled, bounced on a Bailey bridge;
Daddy relishing his role as Moses,
Enunciating the name of the Great Divide

Between the East and the West!
We are the people of the West,
Our fate to go East.

No such thing, Rosie, as a Uniform Ireland
And please God there never will be;
There is only the River Shannon and all her sister rivers

And all her brother mountains and their family prospects.
There are higher powers than politics
And these we call wildflowers or, geologically, people.

Rosie Joyce – that Sunday in May
Not alone did you make my day, my week, my year
To the prescription of Jonathan Philbin Bowman –

Quills of bog-cotton: stems of sedge plants with flower heads resembling tufts of cotton.

sea pinks: grass-like stalks with pink flowers.
London Pride: long-stemmed evergreen plant that flowers in pale pink clusters.
fuchsia: widely cultivated bush with brilliant deep purplish-reddish colours.
Queen Anne's Lace: tall plant with fern leaves and bright white flowers.

pewter: dark grey-coloured metal.

Ford Anglia: brand of family car.

Bailey bridge: small temporary bridge.
relishing: delighting in, appreciating.
Moses: Biblical figure and religious prophet chosen by God to lead the Jewish people out of slavery.

geologically: geographically, in natural history.

Jonathan Philbin Bowman: journalist and broadcaster.

Daymaker!
Daymaker!
Daymaker!

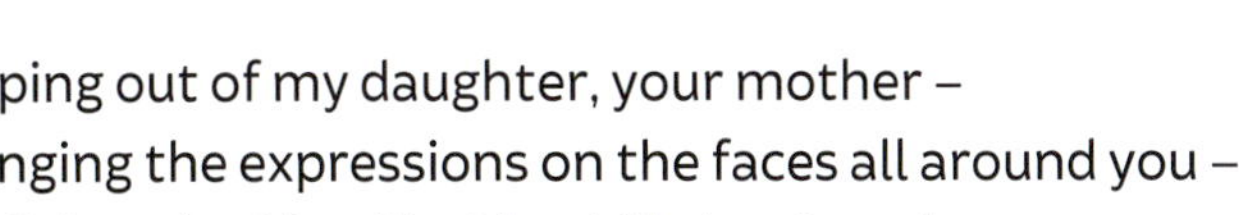

Popping out of my daughter, your mother –
Changing the expressions on the faces all around you –
All of them looking like blue hills in a heat haze –

But you saved my life. For three years
I had been subsisting in the slums of despair,
Unable to distinguish one day from the next.

III

On the return journey from Dublin to Mayo
In Charlestown on Main Street
I meet John Normanly, organic farmer from Curry.

He is driving home to his wife Caroline
From a Mountbellew meeting of the Western Development Commission
Of Dillon House in Ballaghadereen.

He crouches in his car, I waver in the street,
As we exchange lullabies of expectancy;
We wet our foreheads in John Moriarty's autobiography.

The following Sunday is the Feast of the Ascension
Of Our Lord into Heaven:
Thank You, O Lord, for the Descent of Rosie onto Earth.

Daymaker: Durcan repeats a comment used by Philbin Bowman about people who made him feel more cheerful.

subsisting: struggling to live.

wet our foreheads: colloquial expression for having a celebratory drink (based on baptising a newborn child).
John Moriarty: Irish philosopher and mystic.
Feast of the Ascension: important Christian day commemorating the bodily ascension of Jesus into heaven.

'There is only the River Shannon'

Personal Response

1. Based on your reading of Section I of the poem, describe Paul Durcan's mood as he drives to Dublin. Support your answer with reference to the text.
2. What does Durcan reveal about his attitude to Ireland in Section II? In your response, use suitable reference to the poem.
3. Vivid imagery is a recurring feature of this poem. Select one image that you consider particularly striking and comment briefly on your choice.

Critical Literacy

'Rosie Joyce' (taken from Paul Durcan's 2004 collection, *The Art of Life*) celebrates the birth of the poet's granddaughter. Her arrival into the world represents a wonderful new beginning in the poet's life. He has frequently used the metaphor of travel to signify self-renewal, opportunities to reflect on change and emotional development. In this case, Durcan recalls a car journey he took in May 2001 from County Mayo to Dublin. Along the way, images of landscape and movement reveal his newfound sense of optimism.

The casual, narrative opening of Section I is typical of so many of Durcan's autobiographical poems. There is a nostalgic quality to the description of that golden Sunday afternoon: 'a hot sun pushed through the clouds' (line 2). Rosie's birth is immediately symbolised through images drawn from the world of nature. **The idyllic setting reflects Durcan's euphoric tone** perfectly. Breathless exclamatory phrasing ('And you were born!') and the repetition of the child's name convey the poet's immense joy. Run-on lines underpin the insistent rhythm. It is Rosie's 'Incarnation Day' (line 15), a special occasion on which the poet feels truly blessed.

Driving 'two hundred miles from west to east', Durcan is intensely aware of the newness of nature that is reflected all around him. Seeing the world through a child's eyes, he takes great delight in listing everything he notices: 'such side-roads, such main roads, such ramps, such roundabouts.' His deeply satisfying sense of freedom to travel through the country at large is obvious. By persistently naming local places ('By-passing Swinford – Croagh Patrick in my rear-view mirror'), **Durcan acknowledges their equally distinctive importance**. He recounts the crucial details of the telephone message alerting him of Rosie's birth. The simple facts recording the baby's weight and time of birth – 'A baby girl was born at 3.33 p.m.' (line 19) – contrast sharply with Durcan's highly emotional response.

Section II focuses on the Irish landscape in summertime. Durcan highlights the colourful diversity and energy of an island in bloom: 'Yellow forefingers of Arum Lily – the first of the year' (line 24). **The sense of regeneration is everywhere**: 'the first rhododendrons', 'first hawthorns', ' first yellow irises'. Repetition suggests the widespread growth and the careful choice of

forceful verbs ('powdering', 'skimming', 'speckling') adds to our understanding of the vivid power of nature at its height. Everywhere he looks, Durcan sees the shrubs and flowers celebrating Rosie's birth – even the graveyard at Burrishoole is 'shin-deep in forget-me-nots' (line 30). The poet mentions more of the place-names on his cross-country route: 'the Old Turlough Road, past Walter Durcan's Farm.' The intimacies of setting and the poet's enthusiastic voice carry into reflections of his excitement: 'Never before had I felt so fortunate' (line 37). Indeed, his great desire to be with Rosie seems almost biblical: 'I rode the waters and the roads of Ireland.'

The poet's careful observation of rural villages reminds him of a journey he once took 'half a century ago'. During that earlier drive, he remembers his father 'relishing his role as Moses' as he named the River Shannon 'the Great Divide/Between the East and the West' (lines 48–49). Durcan takes the opportunity of his granddaughter's birth to present his own view: 'No such thing, Rosie, as a Uniform Ireland.' The poet develops his plea for tolerance and acceptance by emphasising the diversity of the country's geography: 'There is only the River Shannon and all her sister rivers/And all her brother mountains.' With simple clarity ('There are higher powers than politics'), **the poet dismisses the boundaries of class, religion and gender that have often divided Irish people**. After emphatically expressing devotion to his '*Daymaker*' granddaughter, Durcan acknowledges Rosie as his personal saviour in a tone that is manifestly reverential: 'you saved my life. For three years/I had been subsisting in the slums of despair' (lines 67–68).

In Section III, the mood is much more subdued as the poet recounts details of his 'return journey from Dublin to Mayo'. The daily social routines that mark small communities are illustrated by the chance meeting in Charlestown between Durcan and an old friend, an 'organic farmer from Curry'. Somewhat typically of Irish people's behaviour, their encounter is not without its awkward nuances: 'He crouches in his car, I waver in the street' (line 76). Before long, however, the two men share a drink in honour of the new baby. They discuss the life of Co. Kerry poet and philosopher, John Moriarty. This seemingly mundane moment represents what is best about Ireland's cultural and communal identity. **Rosie Joyce has now been accepted into her new natural and spiritual environment.** The cycle of life and death continues. In the poem's final lines, Durcan returns to his earlier religious mood with a formal offering of thanksgiving for his granddaughter's life. The tone becomes deliberately whimsical and prayer-like, building to a climax: 'Thank you, O Lord, for the Descent of Rosie onto Earth.'

Writing About the Poem

'Paul Durcan frequently uses journeys as a metaphor for reflection or soul-searching.' Discuss this statement with particular reference to 'Rosie Joyce'.

Sample Paragraph

Durcan's love of travel is evident in 'Rosie Joyce'. Journeys are often metaphors for new insights into life. His car journey from Mayo to visit his infant granddaughter in Dublin gives him the perfect opportunity. He begins to think deeply about what it means to be Irish. Everything on the route fills him with joy – and his upbeat tone is emphatic as he drives past 'such villages, such towns'. He is particularly excited by the colourful vegetation – 'Purpling the golden camps of whins'. The variety and energy of nature thrills him. But the journey also reminds him of his youth when his father would tell him how the River Shannon was the 'Great Divide/ Between the East and the West'. However, Durcan no longer agrees and his message is a resounding: 'No such thing, Rosie, as a Uniform Ireland.' The trip has given the poet a chance to clarify his views on the diverse Ireland that Rosie will know. I thought Durcan's description of the island as a place of great scenic variety was central to the poem – 'There is only the River Shannon and all her sister rivers'. He is welcoming the child into a pluralist Ireland – where he accepts cultural diversity. For Durcan, the physical and spiritual journey – one of great happiness and discovery – is a glimpse of how the first Christians felt when they celebrated the birth of Jesus.

EXAMINER'S COMMENT

This clearly written response focuses effectively on the significance of the poet's journey – both on a personal and cultural level. Useful quotations support key discussion points and the expression is generally well handled (although dashes are overused). There is also some good engagement with the poem, especially when discussing Durcan's varied tones, e.g. 'his upbeat tone is emphatic'. A top-grade response.

Class/Homework Exercises

1. 'Durcan's poems can be challenging at times, but they provide a singularly refreshing view of Ireland.' Discuss this view with particular reference to 'Rosie Joyce'. Support the points you make with reference to the poem.
2. Paul Durcan's poems have been described as diary entries which reveal the poet's private life. Discuss this view with particular reference to the poem, 'Rosie Joyce'.

Summary Points

- **Characteristically introspective exploration of regeneration.**
- **Effective use of the extended travel metaphor.**
- **Detailed description, recurring images of movement, landscape, birth.**
- **Contrasting moods and tones of delight, reflection and resignation.**

12 The MacBride Dynasty

PAUL DURCAN

What young mother is not a vengeful goddess
Spitting dynastic as well as motherly pride?
In 1949 in the black Ford Anglia,
Now that I had become a walking, talking little boy,
Mummy drove me out to visit my grand-aunt Maud Gonne
In Roebuck House in the countryside near Dublin,
To show off to the servant of the Queen
The latest addition to the extended family.
Although the eighty-year-old Cathleen Ni Houlihan had taken to her bed
She was keen as ever to receive admirers,
Especially the children of the family.
Only the previous week the actor MacLiammóir
Had been kneeling at her bedside reciting Yeats to her,
His hand on his heart, clutching a red rose.
Cousin Séan and his wife Kid led the way up the stairs,
Séan opening the door and announcing my mother.
Mummy lifted me up in her arms as she approached the bed
And Maud leaned forward, sticking out her claws
To embrace me, her lizards of eyes darting about
In the rubble of the ruins of her beautiful face.
Terrified, I recoiled from her embrace
And, fleeing her bedroom, ran down the stairs
Out onto the wrought-iron balcony
Until Séan caught up with me and quieted me
And took me for a walk in the walled orchard.
Mummy was a little but not totally mortified:
She had never liked Maud Gonne because of Maud's
Betrayal of her husband, Mummy's Uncle John,
Major John, most ordinary of men, most
Humorous, courageous of soldiers,
The pride of our family,
Whose memory always brought laughter
To my grandmother Eileen's lips. 'John,'
She used cry, 'John was such a gay man.'
Mummy set great store by loyalty; loyalty
In Mummy's eyes was the cardinal virtue.
Maud Gonne was a disloyal wife
And, therefore, not worthy of Mummy's love.
For dynastic reasons we would tolerate Maud,
But we would always see through her.

vengeful: vindictive.
goddess: deity, powerful creature.
Spitting: hissing.
dynastic: old established family superiority.

Maud Gonne: English-born Irish revolutionary who had a stormy relationship with W. B. Yeats. She married Major John MacBride, with whom she had one son.

Cathleen Ni Houlihan: Cathleen is an old woman of Ireland who mourns the loss of her four provinces, which have been taken by the English. Maud Gonne played her in Yeats's famous play.
MacLiammóir: Micheál MacLiammóir, a flamboyant English-born Irish actor.
Yeats: famous Irish poet who celebrated Maud Gonne in his poetry throughout his life.
Cousin Séan: Séan MacBride was Maud and Major John's only son. He went on to win a Nobel Peace Prize.
lizards: reptiles with rough, prickly skin.
recoiled: jumped back, flinched.

wrought-iron: tough form of iron fashioned into swirling shapes.
mortified: embarrassed, uncomfortable.

Uncle John: Major John MacBride was the uncle of Paul Durcan's mother. He was executed by the British for his part in the 1916 Rising.

cardinal: greatest, essential.
disloyal: treacherous, unfaithful.

tolerate: endure, accept.
see through: see the reality, realise the truth about.

'the ruins of her beautiful face'

Personal Response

1. From your reading of the poem, briefly describe Durcan's attitude to Maud Gonne when he was taken to meet her.
2. Surreal imagery is a feature of Paul Durcan's poetry. Choose one surreal image from the poem that made an impact on you and discuss its effectiveness.
3. Comment on Durcan's use of repetition in this poem. Support your answer with reference to the text.

Critical Literacy

'The MacBride Dynasty' was published in Paul Durcan's 2007 collection, *The Laughter of Mothers*. These poignant poems commemorate his mother, Sheila MacBride Durcan. They contrast sharply with the many withering poems about his father, Judge John Durcan. The poet's mother was the niece of one of the renowned martyrs of 1916, Major John MacBride, the husband of Maud Gonne. This poem relates the time Durcan's mother made a personal journey back to her hometown to introduce her young son ('the latest addition' to the family dynasty), to her uncle's famous wife.

The opening lines dramatically pose an intriguing question with mock solemnity: 'What young mother is not a vengeful goddess/Spitting dynastic as well as motherly pride?' The epic reference suggests the angry response to a slur on the family name. **The MacBrides regarded themselves as a family of significance** in the Mayo region, as can be seen from the poem's title. They were a dynasty, a prominent and powerful family who retained their power and influence through several generations. If an injustice is perceived to have been done to one of the family, the other members close ranks against the outsider. The onomatopoeic verb 'Spitting' graphically depicts the mythical outrage of the young mother. Precise details root the visit to 'grand-aunt Maud' firmly in reality: 'In 1949 in the black Ford Anglia.' At that time, most people in Ireland could not afford to own a car. Broad-vowelled assonance ('walking, talking') mimics the babbling of the five-year-old Durcan as the proud mother drives to Roebuck House to show off her young son to Maud.

The lengthy run-on line 9 describes how the 80-year-old Maud had 'taken to her bed'. Is there a suggestion that she is a self-indulgent woman? She is referred to as the mythical character she played in Yeats's drama. In this personal narrative, **Durcan seems to be slowly dismantling the popular image of Maud Gonne** as a beautiful young woman, the feminist Irish activist loved by Yeats. Her vanity is obvious: 'She was keen as ever to receive admirers.' The rarefied, overly dramatic world she existed in is cleverly demonstrated by the intimate anecdote showing the famous Irish actor MacLiammóir on his knees at her bedside, 'clutching a red rose' while reciting the poetry of Yeats to her. Is the tone slightly disapproving?

The formal, almost regal atmosphere of the house is captured in the description of how 'Cousin Séan and his wife Kid led the way up the stairs' as the door was opened and the arrival of Durcan's mother was announced. But the young Durcan is no MacLiammóir. He does not pay court, but runs away, terrified at this monster 'sticking out her claws' and whose 'lizards of eyes' flitted quickly about. With this bizarre image, the leading lady of nationalistic politics is reduced to a crumbling wreck as the devastation of her beauty by the cruel hand of time is laid bare: 'In the rubble of the ruins of

her beautiful face' (line 20). The alliteration stresses the **poignancy of this devastating portrait**.

Maud Gonne's relationship with the MacBrides was intricate. She had turned down Yeats's offers of marriage and had married Major John in Paris in 1903. When the marriage ended, she made allegations of domestic violence. She raised her son in Paris until MacBride's execution and then returned to Ireland. The run-on lines (lines 21–25) convey the alarm of a little boy terrified out of his wits until his cousin calms him down with a 'walk in the walled orchard'. The long vowel 'a' and the gentle 'w' alliteration produce a soothing effect. Line 26 carefully records his mother's subtle reaction to his behaviour: 'a little but not totally mortified.' **Was she secretly glad that her little son had not behaved well to a woman she did not respect?** The poet candidly reveals the source of his mother's distaste for Gonne: her 'Betrayal of her husband'. In contrast, a much more favourable picture is painted of Major John, not only through the poet's voice, but also his mother's. He is the 'pride of our family'. His light-heartedness is also noted: he 'always brought laughter/To my grandmother Eileen's lips'.

Durcan's ability to capture Irish speech is shown in line 35: 'Mummy set great store by loyalty.' The admirable characteristic is repeated: 'loyalty/In Mummy's eyes was the cardinal virtue.' But Maud had committed the cardinal sin of being 'a disloyal wife', for which there is no forgiveness. The repetition of the word 'Mummy' – delivered in a highly sarcastic tone – shows how the poet is influenced by his mother's judgement that Maud was 'not worthy of Mummy's love'. **Is Durcan also critical of his intolerant mother**, who adopts a superior attitude to the infamous Maud? Once again, the underlying MacBride tensions are exposed. The family ('we') would accept her grudgingly, but only 'For dynastic reasons'.

The chilling qualification is in the final line: 'But we would always see through her.' History might well be fooled by Maud's mythical status, but the family knew what she truly was. Has Durcan succeeded in debunking another official state myth? No person or thing is immune to criticism or satirical comment. As **a challenging poetic voice**, he has always 'seen through' falseness. He believes language in Ireland has been abused 'by poets as much as by gunmen and churchmen'. Is he also criticising Yeats?

Writing About the Poem

'Durcan's confessional poetry often blends private and public aspects of family life.' Discuss this statement with reference to 'The MacBride Dynasty'.

Sample Paragraph

From the title of the poem to the slyly humorous last line, Durcan captures what others miss. He does not shy away from questioning widely accepted beliefs. In this poem, he exposes not only the power struggles within a self-important family, the 'MacBride Dynasty', but also he reveals the real Maud Gonne as she is in her later years, 'She was keen as ever to receive admirers'. The poet publicly deals with private matters and personally comments on some famous Irish public figures. The one-sided stance adopted by the MacBride family is clear for all to see in the flattering portrait of 'Uncle John'. His mother's critical attitude to the 'disloyal' Maud is revealed. She would 'tolerate' this woman, but only for 'dynastic reasons'. The poet reveals the elderly Maud Gonne to the public gaze, 'In the rubble of the ruins of her beautiful face'. Her power to influence has disappeared. In a way, she is a pathetic figure. She is now seen as a reptile with 'claws'. The absurdity between reality and image is being exposed through this fantasy. She is no longer the woman Yeats worshipped. A great myth has been exposed to the public.

EXAMINER'S COMMENT

This is a very good attempt at addressing a challenging question. There is close engagement with the poem: 'The absurdity between reality and image is being exposed through this fantasy', and a clear thematic response. Overall, points are effectively supported by useful reference and quotation. Ideas are expressed fluently throughout: 'The poet deals publicly with private matters.' A very high standard which deserves the top grade.

Class/Homework Exercises

1. 'Poetry is a form of entertainment, but it is not cheap.' Discuss this statement made by Durcan in relation to the poem 'The MacBride Dynasty'. Support your views with suitable reference to the text.
2. Durcan's poetic voice often goes beyond critical comment and can even become cruel on occasion. Discuss this view, supporting your answer with particular reference to 'The MacBride Dynasty'.

Summary Points

- **Autobiographical/anecdotal poem commemorating the poet's family.**
- **Dramatic opening, bizarre scenes, dark humour.**
- **Effective use of authentic speech patterns.**
- **Use of photographic imagery, run-on lines, assonance, repetition.**
- **Contrasting tones – critical, sardonic, reflective, sarcastic.**

13 Three Short Poems

Paul Durcan's enigmatic two-line poems are sharp and epigrammatic. They are also characteristic of his richly textured work in accommodating his contradictory responses to Ireland and to personal relationships.

En Famille, 1979

Bring me back to the dark school – to the dark school of childhood:
To where tiny is tiny, and massive is massive.

'En Famille, 1979' almost appears to be a cry for help, as though the poet has never come to terms with the traumatic effects of his earliest experiences. The 'dark school' presents **a disturbing metaphor of his boyhood** and the force of his most intimate hopes and fears. Repetition and the exaggerated extremes of 'tiny' and 'massive' suggest childhood innocence. Durcan's use of the French title phrase (meaning 'with one's family' or 'at home') is heartbreakingly poignant.

Madman

Every child has a madman on their street:
The only trouble about *our* madman is that he's our father.

'Madman' offers further evidence that Paul Durcan's **poetry can encompass nightmares as well as dreams**. Despite this poem's humorous whimsy and surface levity, there is something harrowing about the admission. Terms such as 'madman' are often used casually. Within the immediate family context, however, the word takes on a much greater personal significance.

Ireland 2002

Do you ever take a holiday abroad?
No, we always go to America.

'Ireland 2002' is typical of those small 'nutshell poems' that aim to encapsulate a given period of recent history or define Irish contemporary life. The piece is usually read as a **trenchantly satirical criticism of the country's moneyed classes**, for whom America isn't considered 'abroad'. It could also refer to Ireland's history of emigration to the United States and that our diaspora no longer seems foreign. The poem is a reminder of how Ireland has become so culturally influenced by US fashions and attitudes over recent times. Durcan's glib tone echoes the self-absorbed nature of complacent Celtic Tiger Ireland at its height.

Sample Leaving Cert Questions on Durcan's Poetry

1. **'Paul Durcan tells bittersweet stories, often examining themes that are relevant to contemporary Ireland, in a style that is both accessible and entertaining.' To what extent do you agree or disagree with this statement? Support your answer with reference to the poetry of Paul Durcan on your course.**
2. **From your study of the poetry of Paul Durcan on your course, select the poems that, in your opinion, best show his effective use of bleak and satirical humour to convey a sense of frustration and personal failure. Justify your response by discussing Durcan's effective use of bleak and satirical humour to convey a sense of frustration and personal failure.**
3. **'Durcan makes effective use of a range of stylistic features to communicate compelling insights into both the delights and disappointments of human experience.' To what extent do you agree or disagree with this statement? Support your answer with reference to the poetry of Paul Durcan on your course.**

Understanding the Prescribed Poetry Question

Marks are awarded using the PCLM Marking Scheme: P = 15; C = 15; L = 15; M = 5 Total = 50

- **P** (Purpose = 15 marks) refers to the set question and is the launch pad for the answer. This involves engaging with all aspects of the question. Both theme and language must be addressed, although not necessarily equally.
- **C** (Coherence = 15 marks) refers to the organisation of the developed response and the use of accurate, relevant quotation. Paragraphing is essential.
- **L** (Language = 15 marks) refers to the student's skill in controlling language throughout the answer.
- **M** (Mechanics = 5 marks) refers to spelling and grammar.
- Although no specific number of poems is required, students usually discuss at least 3 or 4 in their written responses.
- Aim for at least 800 words, to be completed within 45–50 minutes.

How do I organise my answer?

(Sample question 1)

'Paul Durcan tells bittersweet stories, often examining themes that are relevant to contemporary Ireland, in a style that is both accessible and entertaining.' To what extent do you agree or disagree with this statement? Support you answer with reference to the poetry of Paul Durcan on your course.

Sample Plan 1

Intro: (*Stance: agree with viewpoint in the question*) Durcan examines love/loss, troubled relationships, human rights, estrangement and regeneration – themes relevant to modern Ireland explored through poignant stories. He effectively uses imagery, repetition, dialogue, autobiographical detail, dramatic monologue and dark humour to reach and entertain his reader.

Point 1: (*Love/Loss – Symbol/Repetition*) 'The Girl with the Keys to Pearse's Cottage' – bittersweet tale conveys the harmony of setting and girl through descriptive detail and repetition ('bare brown rooms', 'brown legs akimbo'). The girl becomes the tragic symbol of what has become of Pearse's vision. She is 'gone' – another victim of emigration.

NOTE

In keeping with the PCLM approach, the student has to take a stance by agreeing and/or disagreeing that Durcan's bittersweet stories examine:

- **bittersweet stories** (poignant personal experiences of love and loss, dramatic episodes, tender anecdotes, compelling accounts of Irish history and everyday life)
- **themes relevant to contemporary Ireland** (family life, love, marriage, Irish identity, exile, patriarchy, parent/child relationships, transience, history, death, regeneration, etc.)

... told:

- **in a style that is both accessible and entertaining** (engaging personal memories, intimate monologues, satirical humour and irony, clear details, surreal elements, varying tones, provoking questions, diverting dreamlike atmosphere, candid poetic voice, etc.)

Point 2: (*Parent/Child – Autobiography/Dialogue*) 'Sport' frankly explores a complex father/son relationship. Poignant anecdote using candid details ('Well played, son') and dry humour (the team consisted of three 'cases of schizophrenia') contrast effectively, making the poem both entertaining and distressing.

Point 3: (*Estrangement – Dramatic Monologue/Symbol*) 'The Difficulty that is Marriage' – unsettling narrative account of the conflict between two warring partners. Alliterative repetition conveys the endless quarrels ('We disagree to disagree'). Issue of modern marriage explored. Variety of tones – detached, reflective, sardonic, loving – create an intriguing dramatic monologue.

Point 4: (*Regeneration – Metaphor/Autobiography*) 'Rosie Joyce' celebrates the poet's tender memory of his granddaughter's birth. Using a journey as a metaphor for his spiritual awakening, he details the lush renewal in the Irish countryside through repetition ('first rhododendrons', 'first yellow irises'). Humour in concluding lines. Reversed Irish prayer entertains ('Thank you, O Lord, for the Descent of Rosie onto Earth').

Conclusion: Different personas and narratives set in distinctive worlds are used to explore the faults and failings of contemporary Ireland. Range of stylistic features used to create interesting, understandable and touching poetic stories.

Sample Paragraph: Point 2

A heartbreaking moment in the uneasy relationship between father and son is explored in the autobiographical poem 'Sport'. Durcan, committed to a psychiatric hospital, plays for its team under the father's critical gaze. I could sympathise with the poet who felt like a laboratory specimen. The poem does not shirk from detailing the intense pressure of the parent/child relationship. Durcan feels the need to perform, to 'mesmerise' his father. Yet he could not impress him. His account of his heroic efforts are met with 'Sniffing' approval as they 'shook hands' formally. It's clear that Durcan hoped for something more than his father's brief comment, 'Well played, son'. Each is paralysed in traditional Irish culture – they are unable to express their feelings. The father's continuing disappointments plainly stated in the poem's concluding lines, 'Seldom if ever again in your eyes/Was I to rise to these heights'. The surreal descriptive detail of the psychiatric hospital's team, 'Men with gapped teeth, red faces', adds a distressing but comic context to the young poet's experience. Overall, 'Sport' includes some humour, but I thought it was a very moving example of Durcan's unhappy family life.

EXAMINER'S COMMENT

Insightful personal response that tackles the three elements of the question (bittersweet narratives, contemporary themes and appealing style). Close engagement with the text is evident in the references to key images, backed up by apt quotations. Impressive comments on monosyllabic language and surreal aspects. Varied, fluent expression adds to the top-grade quality.

(Sample question 2)

From your study of the poetry of Paul Durcan on your course, select the poems that, in your opinion, best show his effective use of bleak and satirical humour to convey a sense of frustration and personal failure. Justify your response by discussing Durcan's effective use of bleak and satirical humour to convey a sense of frustration and personal failure.

Sample Plan 2

Intro: (*Stance: agree with viewpoint in the question*) Durcan reveals a deep sense of disappointment and personal inadequacy, particularly in the realm of relationships, in his poetry through his skilful use of stark, satirical humour.

Point 1: (*Romantic love – self-mockery*) 'Nessa' details his experience of the danger and delight of falling in love. A self-mocking refrain ('And I very nearly drowned') and self-deprecating humour ('take off your pants, she said to me,/And I very nearly didn't') convey how the poet feels overwhelmed.

Point 2: (*Parent/child – distorted imagery*) 'Parents' raises uncomfortable questions about the true nature of parent/child relationships. Through two startling perspectives the poet shows the shocking disconnect. Parents are onlookers ('Estranged from her by a sea'), while the frightened child regards their concerned expressions as 'Pursed up orifices of fearful fish'.

Point 3: (*Marital breakdown – bitter irony*) '"Windfall", 8 Parnell Hill, Cork' is a poignant chronicle of the depressing consequences of personal marital breakdown. Sharp irony ('Windfall') and disturbing images show him as a rootless object ('Blown about the suburban streets at evening').

Point 4: (*Negative effect of time – tragicomedy*) 'Father's Day, 21 June 1992' reflects on the negative effect of time on the poet's role as husband and father ('Our daughters are all grown up'). Edgy dialogue establishes the disconnect between husband and wife ('She said that she'd like the axe'). A bizarre train journey is a metaphor for self-discovery – his marriage is coming to an end. The unsettling atmosphere is increased through surreal simile (the axe is 'As neat as a new born babe').

Conclusion: Poet adopts the persona of 'bittersweet clowning' to reveal his anguished dismay and personal feelings of inadequacy in his relationships. Dark, self-mocking humour successfully conveys his deep disappointment.

NOTE

In keeping with the PCLM approach, the student has to take a stance by justifying his/her selection of Durcan's poems which best demonstrate the poet's:

- **effective use of bleak and satirical humour** (self-mockery, bizarre imagery, surreal/distorted dream sequences, bitter irony, caustic repetition, grim humour, edgy dialogue, etc.)

... to convey:

- **a sense of frustration and personal failure** (intense experience of love, anxiety in parent/child relationship, destructive consequences of relationship breakdown, time's negative effect, gap between reality and ideal, loneliness, personal inadequacy, etc.)

Sample Paragraph: Point 3

'"Windfall", 8 Parnell Hill, Cork' poignantly reveals Durcan's sadness at feeling discarded after his marriage ended. He describes himself as a 'windfall' in deeply ironic tones, since his family's house had been named this. But now he is out of his cosy home, and compares himself to the fallen leaves, 'Blown about the suburban streets'. Yet even in this comfortless state, his dark humour is evident, when he reflects on what it means to belong, 'Apache, Cherokee' or middle-class 'Bourgeoisie'. Durcan wonders about what others experience at home, 'Beholding the fire-lit faces' of their loved ones. The peaceful image is ironic. He feels cut off from family warmth and is like an abandoned ship putting out distress calls, 'Windfall to Windfall – can you hear me?' This surreal call is agonising because the tragic reality is that he is never going home again. He candidly admits that he was 'with good reason ... put out of my home' and that he only related to his wife when they were 'smiling accomplices'. The poet's earlier humour is replaced with the realisation that he had taken things for granted, 'closed my eyes and breathed in and breathed out'. In this emotive poem, Durcan conveys his personal failure through heartbreaking irony and gloomy self-criticism.

EXAMINER'S COMMENT

Clear points focusing on both elements of the question (dark humour and self-reproach). Good engagement with the text, with some insightful discussion of irony. Comments are presented in a considered and assured manner, using supportive quotes that are skilfully interwoven throughout. Expression is also well-controlled in this top-grade response.

Leaving Cert Sample Essay

From your study of the poetry of Paul Durcan on your course, select the poems that, in your opinion, best show how the poet reveals the darker aspects of his poetic vision through his skilful use of poetic narrative and dramatic scenes. Justify your selection by showing how Paul Durcan reveals the darker aspects of his poetic vision through his skilful use of poetic narrative and dramatic scenes in the poems you have selected.

Sample Essay

(Durcan reveals darker vision through use of narrative and dramatic scenes)

INDICATIVE MATERIAL

Durcan's skilful use of narrative and dramatic scenes:

- inventive use of illustrative anecdotes, surreal situations, autobiographical narratives, animated characters, real and imaginary scenes, moments of conflict, use of symbols, vivid conversational speech, etc.

... reveals:

- the darker aspects of his poetic vision
- personal regrets, unhappy memories, breakdown of relationships, failures of materialistic society, critical views of Ireland's religious life, patriarchy, history, etc.

1. Paul Durcan's poems are known for their emotional subjects, satirical humour and surreal narratives. He often returns to important moments in his own life to explore themes, such as marriage and family relationships. Examples are 'Nessa' and 'Sport'. At other times, he recreates dramatic scenes from real life. These are often exaggerated, as in 'Wife Who Smashed Television Gets Jail' where the poet comments on aspects of Irish society that he feels strongly about. I find Durcan's poetry interesting because it shows the reality of everyday life. I would agree, however, that many of the poems on the course reflect his critical views and reveal Durcan's pessimistic vision.

2. 'Nessa' reflects on the poet's personal relationship with his wife through the extended metaphor of a whirlpool. Durcan presents an intense scene that is both exciting and treacherous. Nessa is described as if she were a young enchantress in an Irish fable. She leads the hopelessly devoted lover away, 'She took me by the index finger'. Her powerful attraction is emphasised in the poet's hypnotic phrase, 'She was a whirlpool, she was a whirlpool'. His skilful use of the central comparison makes it a compelling symbol that combines the highs and lows of romantic love. Although there is the thrill of Nessa seducing him, he focuses on love's darker side. Durcan feels like his life is spinning dangerously out of control. He is aware that falling in love has left him vulnerable – 'I very nearly drowned'. This is most evident in the poignant concluding scene where he seems gripped with fear and uncertainty about the future of their relationship – 'Will you stay with me on the rocks?'

3. The stress of family life is a recurring theme in Durcan's poetry. In 'Sport', he remembers the uneasy relationship he had with his father. His memory is of playing as a young man in a GAA football match. The sports setting is very cleverly used to illustrate his competitive urge to play well – but the son's real aim was to impress his father who was watching the match. The situation seems like a cat-and-mouse game between two characters. Despite the surreal moments on the pitch, the whole episode is almost entirely filled with regret. This is seen in the bleak admission, 'I was fearful I would let you down'. Although Durcan remembers playing well and being complimented by his father, the memory is seen as an exceptional moment that only highlighted their failed relationship – 'Seldom if ever again in your eyes was I to rise to these heights'. The football anecdote demonstrates the unhappiness of the poet's youth and his longing to be respected and loved. The poem is typical of Durcan's downbeat view of real life where emotions are often hidden.

4. Durcan sometimes takes a critical view of Irish society. 'Wife Who Smashed Television Gets Jail' explores this – the theme of modern family life. It highlights the negative impact TV and social media can have on family life. Without us knowing, television has come to substitute both friends and family. Durcan sets the dramatic scene in a courtroom where this ridiculous case is being heard. It's funny and serious at the same time. The husband is taking a case against his wife. She feels so ignored and marginalised that she's provoked into the action of getting rid of the family television. However, she is given a jail sentence for banning the TV. Once again, beneath the humour and irony, Durcan is pointing out the dark side of society. Marriage breakdown is common now because people have too many distractions.

5. Not all of Durcan's poems reveal a negative side. He uses memories and anecdotes to reflect on the more positive parts of life as well. In 'Rosie Joyce', he recalls a happy car journey across Ireland to visit his newborn granddaughter. The journey is highly symbolic and the poet's tone is upbeat throughout as he celebrates the joy he feels – 'you make my day, my week, my year'. While I found it a little sentimental, it shows a balance to the usual depressed viewpoint and that was very welcome. There is a dramatic quality as well, with Durcan using repetition to emphasise his delight – 'Daymaker! Daymaker! Daymaker!' The intensity of his emotions is also seen in his sense of being close to nature with all its renewed spring colours. It's as if the whole world is celebrating – 'first hawthorns powdering white the mainland'.

6. However, many of Durcan's poems focus on his own disappointments and the more disturbing aspects of modern-day life. There is plenty of dark humour as he reveals his private thoughts. Yet at the heart of his poetry is a man who struggled to deal with the break-up of his marriage and who struggles to keep his mind away from a distant past he prefers to forget. Durcan probes dark, bitter themes of contemporary Irish life, loneliness and strained relationships. His reflective stories challenge the accepted views on Irish life as he observes real life and drifts into surreal situations to examine his personal experiences.

(840 words)

EXAMINER'S COMMENT

Thoughtful response which addresses both elements of the question with a high level of insight. Some solid critical commentary on 'Nessa' and 'Sport', backed by apt reference highlighting the dramatic and narrative qualities used in the poems. However, closer analysis would have improved paragraph 4 which is note-like and lacks development. Paragraph 5 challenges the main thrust of the question effectively. Overall, expression is generally impressive.

GRADE: H1
P = 14/15
C = 13/15
L = 13/15
M = 5/5
Total = 45/50

 Revision Overview

'Nessa'
Dramatic anecdotal presentation of theme of romantic adventure, giddy experience of falling in love.

'The Girl with the Keys to Pearse's Cottage'
Narrative exploration of themes of teenage infatuation, loss, identity.

'The Difficulty that is Marriage'
Critical dramatic monologue probes themes of marital fragility and conflict.

'Wife Who Smashed Television Gets Jail'
Humorous mock journalistic report on theme of modern family life.

'Parents'
Unsettling dramatic study of themes of death and the afterlife, surreal moments, use of contrast and symbols add to feeling of helplessness.

'"Windfall", 8 Parnell Hill, Cork'
Intimate chronicle of themes of personal domestic bliss and bitter consequences of the break-up of a relationship.

'Six Nuns Die in Convent Inferno'
Reflective analysis of nuns' religious philosophy through first-person narrative of elderly nun.

'Sport'
Candid investigation of troubled relationship between father and son.

'Father's Day, 21 June 1992'
Train journey becomes occasion for reflection on adverse effect of time on poet's role as husband and father.

'The Arnolfini Marriage'
Challenging dramatic monologue scrutinising marriage and good fortune.

'Rosie Joyce'
Newfound enthusiastic celebration of birth of poet's granddaughter.

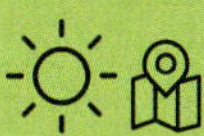

'The MacBride Dynasty'
Anecdotal family journey. Thematic questioning of accepted beliefs of the self-important. Exposure of distance between reality and fantasy.

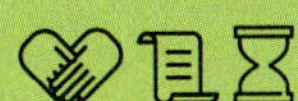

Last Words

'His songs celebrate our small mercies and tender decencies in a world that favours the corrupt.'
Paula Meehan

'He makes particularly engaging poems out of passing conversations – "You're looking great – are you going to a wedding?"/"Oh God no – I'm coming back from a wake"'.
Deirdre Collins

'Like all first-class comedians, he is deadly serious.'
Terry Eagleton

LOVE

RELATIONSHIPS

SUFFERING

HISTORY/MEMORY

TRAVEL/JOURNEYS

RELIGION/SPIRITUALITY

TIME

JOY/HOPE

Robert Frost
1874–1963

'A poem begins in delight and ends in wisdom.'

One of the great 20th-century poets, Robert Frost is highly regarded for his realistic depictions of rural life and his command of American colloquial speech. His work frequently explores themes from early 1900s country life in New England, often using the setting to examine complex social and philosophical ideas. Nature is central to his writing. While his poems seem simple at first, they often transcend the boundaries of time and place with metaphysical significance and a deeper appreciation of human nature in all its beauty and contradictions. Despite many personal tragedies, Frost had a very successful public life. It is ironic that such a calm, stoical voice emerged from his difficult background. At times bittersweet, sometimes ironic, or often marvelling at his surroundings, Robert Frost continues to be a popular and often-quoted poet. He was honoured frequently during his lifetime, receiving four Pulitzer Prizes.

Investigate Further

To find out more about Robert Frost, or to hear readings of his poems, you could do a search of some of the useful websites available such as YouTube, BBC Poetry, poetryfoundation.org and poetryarchive.org, or access additional material on this page of your eBook.

Prescribed Poems

Note that Frost uses American spellings and punctuation in his work.

○ **1 'The Tuft of Flowers' (OL)**
One of Frost's best-loved works, this poem describes how a simple clump of wild flowers succeeds in uniting two separate people.
Page 186

○ **2 'Mending Wall' (OL)**
Repairing a damaged wall between his neighbour and himself, Frost considers the theme of community and fellowship, and wonders if 'Good fences make good neighbors'. **Page 190**

○ **3 'After Apple-Picking'**
Set on his New England farm at the end of the apple harvest, Frost meditates on the nature of work, creativity and of what makes a fulfilled life. **Page 195**

○ **4 'The Road Not Taken'**
Another of Frost's most popular poems. Using the symbol of a remote country crossroads, the poet dramatises the decisions people face in life – and the consequences of their choices.
Page 199

○ **5 'Birches'**
The sight of some forest birches excites Frost's imagination to associate childhood games of swinging on the trees with the process of writing poetry.
Page 203

○ **6 '"Out, Out–"' (OL)**
This affecting poem is based on an actual story of a serious chainsaw accident. Despite the tragedy, Frost leaves readers in no doubt about life's grim reality: 'It goes on'. **Page 207**

○ **7 'Spring Pools'**
In this captivating lyric poem, the fragile beauty and transience of the pools give Frost an acute awareness of the natural cycle of growth, decay and renewal.
Page 211

○ **8 'Acquainted with the Night'**
This short lyric depicts the dark, alienating side of urban life.
Page 214

○ **9 'Design'**
Frost's sonnet, depicting nature as volatile and terrifying, addresses the possibility of an underlying plan or design for the universe.
Page 218

○ **10 'Provide, Provide'**
Another poem that deals with some of Frost's favourite themes – time, old age and independence.
Page 221

*(OL) indicates poems that are also prescribed for the Ordinary Level course.

POETRY FOCUS

1 The Tuft of Flowers

Tuft: cluster, bunch.

I went to turn the grass once after one
Who mowed it in the dew before the sun.

turn: upturn; toss grass to dry it out.

The dew was gone that made his blade so keen
Before I came to view the levelled scene.

keen: sharp; effective.

I looked for him behind an isle of trees;
I listened for his whetstone on the breeze.

whetstone: stone used for sharpening scythes.

But he had gone his way, the grass all mown,
And I must be, as he had been—alone,

'As all must be,' I said within my heart,
'Whether they work together or apart.'

But as I said it, swift there passed me by
On noiseless wing a bewildered butterfly,

Seeking with memories grown dim o'er night
Some resting flower of yesterday's delight.

And once I marked his flight go round and round,
As where some flower lay withering on the ground.

And then he flew as far as eye could see,
And then on tremulous wing came back to me.

tremulous: trembling or nervous.

I thought of questions that have no reply,
And would have turned to toss the grass to dry;

But he turned first, and led my eye to look
At a tall tuft of flowers beside a brook,

brook: stream.

A leaping tongue of bloom the scythe had spared
Beside a reedy brook the scythe had bared.

scythe: implement used for cutting grass or hay.

The mower in the dew had loved them thus,
By leaving them to flourish, not for us,

Nor yet to draw one thought of ours to him,
But from sheer morning gladness at the brim.

The butterfly and I had lit upon,
Nevertheless, a message from the dawn,

That made me hear the wakening birds around,
And hear his long scythe whispering to the ground,

And feel a spirit kindred to my own;
So that henceforth I worked no more alone;

But glad with him, I worked as with his aid,
And weary, sought at noon with him the shade;

And dreaming, as it were, held brotherly speech
With one whose thought I had not hoped to reach.

'Men work together,' I told him from the heart,
'Whether they work together or apart.'

lit upon: discovered.

kindred: closely related to.

'A leaping tongue of bloom'

Personal Response

1. Describe the dominant mood in lines 1–10 of the poem.
2. Choose two images from the poem that you found particularly interesting and effective. Briefly explain your choice in both cases.
3. Would you describe the poem as uplifting? Give reasons for your answer.

Critical Literacy

The poem describes how a simple, uncut clump of wild flowers can unite two separate people. It is one of Frost's best-loved works and typifies his technique of bringing readers through an everyday rustic experience to reveal a universal truth – in this case about alienation, friendship and communication. The poem consists of 20 rhymed couplets written in strict verse. Frost once remarked that 'writing without structure is like playing tennis without a net'.

The narrative voice in the opening section of the poem is relaxed, in keeping with the unhurried rhythm. Frost's initial tone is low-key and non-committal. The speaker has gone out to turn the grass so that it can dry. Someone else had mowed it earlier 'in the dew before the sun'. Lines 5–6 reveal the speaker's sense of solitude and isolation; the unnamed mower has 'gone his way'. This leads him to consider **the loneliness of the scene and of human experience**. The introspective mood becomes more depressed as the poet searches for his fellow worker. Figurative descriptions of the 'levelled scene' and 'an isle of trees' add to the atmosphere of pessimism as the speaker implies that he must also be 'alone'. For Frost, this is the essential human experience for all, 'Whether they work together or apart'.

The poem's middle section is marked by the sudden appearance of a 'bewildered butterfly'. After fluttering 'round and round' looking for the 'resting flower' that gave it such delight the day before, it then flies close to the speaker: 'on tremulous wing came back to me.' The adjective 'tremulous' suggests fragility and a **new sense of excited anticipation in the air**. The butterfly seems to reflect the speaker's 'questions that have no reply'. Perhaps they have both enjoyed great happiness in the past. The butterfly eventually turns and leads the speaker to a 'tall tuft of flowers beside a brook' that have escaped the mower's scythe – not by accident, but because 'he had loved them' and left them to flourish out of 'sheer morning gladness'.

The significance of the meadow flowers and the brook cannot be overlooked, because here the **mood suddenly changes to optimism**. The presence of the mysterious butterfly establishes communication between the early morning mower and the narrator. Frost suggests this connection with his vivid description of the spared flowers as 'A leaping tongue of bloom'. In the final section, the speaker and the butterfly 'lit upon,/ Nevertheless, a message from the dawn'. With images such as the 'wakening birds around' and a 'spirit kindred to my own', we might assume that this 'message' could indeed be about human friendship and communal love.

The ending is paradoxical: 'Men work together ... Whether they work together or apart'. However, **Frost believed in spiritual presence and was inspired by an overwhelming sense of fellowship and community**. Although apart, the speaker and the absent mower are working with a shared appreciation of nature's beauty and a common commitment to a better world. The poem could also be interpreted biographically, since Frost had lost several of his loved ones and may well have written it as an emotional outlet. Even though his family

members were deceased, he remains close to them in spirit. Whatever the poet's intention, readers can draw their own conclusions from the poem.

Writing About the Poem

In your view, is 'The Tuft of Flowers' a dramatic poem? Refer closely to the text in your answer.

Sample Paragraph

'The Tuft of Flowers' has been described as a lyrical soliloquy. The narrative element is there from the start. The first mower seems a mysterious character. The central character (poet) is obviously close to nature as he goes about his work. His inner drama interests me most, as his attitude changes from loneliness at the beginning to happiness and companionship. The two moods contrast dramatically. First, the sadness of 'I listened for his whetstone' and 'brotherly speech' and then the more sociable 'Men work together'. The vivid imagery is also dramatic, especially the butterfly's flight – 'On noiseless wing' – and the description of the small outcrop of flowers – 'A leaping tongue of bloom'. Frost sets his poems in the secluded New England landscape and this provides a beautiful location for what are deep meditations about the important questions in life – 'questions that have no reply'. The rhythm of the poem quickens in the final lines as the poet expresses his positive view of life – 'Men work together'. I thought this was the ideal way to round off this quietly dramatic poem.

EXAMINER'S COMMENT

A very well controlled answer focusing on some key dramatic elements, such as the use of the character's 'inner drama' and 'lyrical soliloquy'. Good personal interaction and commentary. References were handled effectively and points were clearly presented: 'The rhythm of the poem quickens in the final lines as the poet expresses his positive view of life – "Men work together".' A highly successful top-grade response.

Class/Homework Exercises

1. In your opinion, what is Frost's main theme or message in 'The Tuft of Flowers'? Refer closely to the text of the poem in your answer.
2. 'The poetry of Robert Frost is known for its simple, everyday language.' To what extent is this evident in 'The Tuft of Flowers'? Support your answer with reference to the poem.

Summary Points

- **Typically narrative style – from the poet's own personal experience.**
- **Human fellowship and how humans can learn from nature are central themes.**
- **Contrasting moods – pessimism changes to optimism.**
- **Rhyming couplets create unity and help in expressing the poet's ideas.**
- **Effective use of onomatopoeia, rich imagery and symbolism.**

2 Mending Wall

Something there is that doesn't love a wall,
That sends the frozen-ground-swell under it,
And spills the upper boulders in the sun;
And makes gaps even two can pass abreast.
The work of hunters is another thing:
I have come after them and made repair
Where they have left not one stone on a stone,
But they would have the rabbit out of hiding,
To please the yelping dogs. The gaps I mean,
No one has seen them made or heard them made,
But at spring mending-time we find them there.
I let my neighbor know beyond the hill;
And on a day we meet to walk the line
And set the wall between us once again.
We keep the wall between us as we go.
To each the boulders that have fallen to each.
And some are loaves and some so nearly balls
We have to use a spell to make them balance:
'Stay where you are until our backs are turned!'
We wear our fingers rough with handling them.
Oh, just another kind of out-door game,
One on a side. It comes to little more:
There where it is we do not need the wall:
He is all pine and I am apple orchard.
My apple trees will never get across
And eat the cones under his pines, I tell him.
He only says, 'Good fences make good neighbors.'
Spring is the mischief in me, and I wonder
If I could put a notion in his head:
'Why do they make good neighbors? Isn't it
Where there are cows? But here there are no cows.
Before I built a wall I'd ask to know
What I was walling in or walling out,
And to whom I was like to give offense.
Something there is that doesn't love a wall,
That wants it down.' I could say 'Elves' to him,
But it's not elves exactly, and I'd rather
He said it for himself. I see him there
Bringing a stone grasped firmly by the top
In each hand, like an old-stone savage armed.

Something there is that doesn't love a wall: ice and frost often erode walls.

abreast: side by side.

Good fences make good neighbors: one reading is that a strong fence protects by keeping people apart.

Elves: small supernatural beings, often malevolent.

He moves in darkness as it seems to me,
Not of woods only and the shade of trees.
He will not go behind his father's saying,
And he likes having thought of it so well
He says again, 'Good fences make good neighbors.'

'No one has seen them made'

Personal Response

1. In your opinion, who or what is it that doesn't love a wall? Support your answer with reference to the poem.
2. There are two speakers in the poem. Which one is the wiser, in your view? Refer to the text in your answer.
3. Point out two examples of humour in the poem and comment on how effective they are in adding to the message of 'Mending Wall'.

Critical Literacy

This popular poem of Robert Frost's was written in 1913 and appeared first in his collection, *North of Boston.* When the land was being cleared for agriculture, the stones gathered were made into walls. Frost once said this poem 'contrasts two types of people'. President John F. Kennedy asked the poet to read this poem to Khrushchev, Russia's leader at the time of the Cuban Missile Crisis, when there was a possibility of another world war.

'Mending Wall' was responsible for creating a public image of Frost as an ordinary New England farmer who wrote about normal events and recognisable settings in simple language. Line 1 is mysterious: 'Something there is that doesn't love a wall.' **A force is at work to pull down the barriers** people insist on erecting. The speaker repairs the holes in the wall left by hunters: 'I have come after them and made repair.' But there are other holes in the wall, though 'No one has seen them made or heard them made'. In a yearly ritual, 'at spring mending-time', the poet and his neighbour meet to carry out repairs. Each looks after his own property as they walk along: 'To each the boulders that have fallen to each.' But a tone of coldness creeps into the poem amid this neighbourly task, with the repetition of how the wall has separated them at all times: 'set the wall between us', 'keep the wall between us'.

It is a difficult task, as the stones fall off as quickly as they are placed: 'Stay where you are until our backs are turned!' The **good-humoured banter** of the workers comes alive in the remark, and readers feel as if they are there in New England watching the wall being repaired. The light-hearted mood is continued in line 21 when the poet describes the activity as an 'out-door game'. Then he comments that they don't even really need the wall where it is: 'He is all pine and I am apple orchard.' The poet jokes that his apple trees cannot go over and eat his neighbour's pine cones. His neighbour then says: 'Good fences make good neighbors.' He comes across as a serious type, quoting old sayings, in **contrast** to the poet: 'Spring is the mischief in me.' Frost is associating himself with the turbulent force that is pushing through the land, creating growth and pulling down walls. The neighbour is shown as one who has accepted what has been said without question, one who upholds the status quo.

In line 30, the poet poses questions to himself and wishes he could say to his neighbour, 'Why do they make good neighbours?' **He begins to consider what a wall is keeping in and keeping out.** He also wonders what is pulling down the wall. He mockingly suggests 'Elves', then discounts that. Frost depicts his rather uncommunicative neighbour in a series of unflattering images: 'an old-stone savage armed', 'He moves in darkness'. Is the poet saying that we must question received wisdom and not blindly follow what we are told? The neighbour, who accepts, is presented as a figure of repression who 'moves in darkness'. He just repeats 'Good fences make good neighbors' like a mantra. Is the poet suggesting that there are some people who derive comfort from just remaining the same, who do not welcome change ('He will not go behind his father's saying')?

The tone of the poem changes as the easy, neighbourly sociability of a shared task is replaced by a **feeling of tension**, first in the effort to keep the tumbling wall upright, and then in the opposite attitudes of the two neighbours – the mischievous, questioning poet and the taciturn, unquestioning neighbour. The desire for human co-operation is often stopped, not by outside circumstances, but by a lack of desire on the part of the people involved. This is the poet commenting on human dilemmas. The easy-going, almost philosophical tone of someone musing to himself is written in unrhymed blank verse. The colloquial conversational phrases are all tightly controlled throughout this thought-provoking poem.

Writing About the Poem

'Frost's deceptively simple poems explore profound truths about life.' Discuss this statement in relation to the poem 'Mending Wall'.

Sample Paragraph

Frost has very successfully given us a picture of two opposite personalities in this poem. The moody neighbour who doggedly walks on his side of the wall, 'We keep the wall between us both as we go', is vividly described. Here is a person who accepts what was told to him without question 'Good fences can make good neighbours'. It is as if he is reciting the two-times tables. This is fact. He is comfortable in his traditional mindset. 'He will not go behind his father's saying.' The poet describes him in unflattering terms, referring to him as 'an old stone-armed savage'. He also states that he moved 'in darkness'. Frost does not agree with this unquestioning attitude. It is not only a wall which divides these two, there is a completely different mindset. The poet has a lively personality, 'Stay where you are until our backs have turned', regarding the work as a game. However, he asks the fundamental question about any boundary, 'I'd ask to know/What I was walling in or out'. He also asks the sensitive question about who he was likely to give offence to, with his wall. We are left wondering, are walls natural or necessary? Must we break down barriers to live as good neighbours? What if we are over-run?

EXAMINER'S COMMENT

A solid response exploring the distance between contrasting personalities, a traditionalist and a maverick. Points are well developed through a fluent use of language, 'It is as if he is reciting the two-times tables. This is fact'. The questions towards the end show a lively engagement with the poem. However, the response is slightly weakened by inaccurate quoting: 'an old stone-armed savage', 'walling in or out'. This prevents the answer achieving the highest grade.

Class/Homework Exercises

1. Comment on Frost's use of imagery in 'Mending Wall'. Do you find it effective? Refer closely to the text in your answer.
2. 'Frost's poems often have a universal significance and raise interesting questions about human relations.' To what extent do you agree or disagree with this view? Support your answer with reference to 'Mending Wall'.

Summary Points

- **Key themes include community, fellowship, boundaries and borders.**
- **Characteristic use of accessible, everyday language and humorous touches.**
- **Effective use of symbolism, slow-moving rhythm and unrhymed blank verse.**
- **Variety of tones: narrative, relaxed, interrogative, apprehensive and reflective.**

After Apple-Picking

ROBERT FROST

My long two-pointed ladder's sticking through a tree
Toward heaven still,
And there's a barrel that I didn't fill
Beside it, and there may be two or three
Apples I didn't pick upon some bough.
But I am done with apple-picking now.
Essence of winter sleep is on the night,
The scent of apples: I am drowsing off.
I cannot rub the strangeness from my sight
I got from looking through a pane of glass
I skimmed this morning from the drinking trough
And held against the world of hoary grass.
It melted, and I let it fall and break.
But I was well
Upon my way to sleep before it fell,
And I could tell
What form my dreaming was about to take.
Magnified apples appear and disappear,
Stem end and blossom end,
And every fleck of russet showing clear.
My instep arch not only keeps the ache,
It keeps the pressure of a ladder-round.
I feel the ladder sway as the boughs bend.
And I keep hearing from the cellar bin
The rumbling sound
Of load on load of apples coming in.
For I have had too much
Of apple-picking: I am overtired
Of the great harvest I myself desired.
There were ten thousand thousand fruit to touch,
Cherish in hand, lift down, and not let fall.
For all
That struck the earth,
No matter if not bruised or spiked with stubble,
Went surely to the cider-apple heap
As of no worth.
One can see what will trouble
This sleep of mine, whatever sleep it is.
Were he not gone,
The woodchuck could say whether it's like his
Long sleep, as I describe its coming on,
Or just some human sleep.

Essence: scent.

glass: ice.

hoary: covered in frost.

russet: reddish-brown.

ladder-round: a rung or support on a ladder.

stubble: remnant stalks left after harvesting.

woodchuck: groundhog, a native American burrowing animal.

Personal Response

1. Select one image that evokes the hard, physical work of apple-picking. Comment on its effectiveness.
2. What do you understand lines 27–29 to mean?
3. Write a short personal response to this poem.

Critical Literacy

The poem is a lyrical evocation of apple harvesting in New England. Frost takes an ordinary experience and transforms it into a meditative moment. Harvesting fruit soon becomes a consideration of how life has been experienced fully but with some regrets and mistakes. Frost chose not to experiment but to use a traditional writing style, or as he said, he preferred 'the old-fashioned way to be new'. 'After Apple-Picking' is not free verse, but it is among Frost's least formal works, containing 42 lines varying in length, a rhyme scheme that is also highly irregular and no stanza breaks.

'Toward heaven still'

The speaker in the poem (either Frost himself or the farmer persona he often adopted) feels himself drifting off to sleep with the scent of apples in the air. He thinks of the ladder he has left in the orchard still pointing to 'heaven'. Is the poet suggesting that his work has brought him closer to God? The slow-moving rhythm and broad vowel sounds ('two-pointed', 'bough', 'drowsing') in the opening lines reflect his **lethargic mood**. Although he seems close to exhaustion, he is pleased that the harvest is complete: 'But I am done with apple-picking now.' Ironically, his mind is filled with random thoughts about the day's work. The drowsy atmosphere is effectively communicated by the poet's mesmerising description: 'Essence of winter sleep is on the night.'

This dreamlike state releases Frost's imagination and he remembers the odd sensation he felt while looking through a sheet of ice he had removed earlier from a drinking trough. While the memory is rooted in reality, it appears that he has experienced the world differently: 'I cannot rub the strangeness from my sight.' As he is falling asleep, he is conscious that his dreaming will be associated with **exaggerated images of harvesting**: 'Magnified apples appear and disappear' (line 18). The poet emphasises the sensuousness of what is happening. The vivid apples display 'every fleck of russet' and he can feel the pressure of the 'ladder-round' against his foot. He hears the 'rumbling sound' of the fruit being unloaded. The images suggest abundance: 'load on load of apples', 'ten thousand thousand'. Frost's use of repetition, both of evocative sounds and key words, is a prominent feature of the poem that enhances our appreciation of his intense dream.

Physically and mentally tired, the poet also relives the anxiety he had felt about the need to save the crop from being 'bruised or spiked with stubble', and not to lose them to 'the cider-apple heap'. In the poem's closing lines, which seem deliberately vague and distorted, Frost wonders again about the nature of consciousness: 'This sleep of mine, whatever sleep it is.' Like so many of his statements, the line is rich in possible interpretations. For some critics, the poem appears to be exploring the art and craft of writing. Others take a broader view, seeing it as **a metaphor for how human beings live their lives**. The poet's own final thoughts are of the woodchuck's winter retreat, before he eventually surrenders to his own mysterious 'sleep'.

'After Apple-Picking' is typical of Frost's work. Despite the apparent cheerfulness of much of the writing, it has **undertones of a more sober vision of life**. As always, there is a thoughtful quality to the poem. The reference to the approach of winter hints at the constant presence of mortality. Frost's question about what kind of sleep to anticipate suggests untroubled oblivion or possibly some kind of renewal, just as the woodchuck reawakens in the springtime after its long hibernation.

Writing About the Poem

'Frost's work has a surface cheerfulness which conceals a more serious vision of life.' Discuss this statement in relation to the poem, 'After Apple-Picking'. Support your answer with reference to the poem.

Sample Paragraph

In 'After Apple-Picking', Robert Frost creates a mood of otherworldliness. At the start, his accurate description of the orchard is realistic. But some of the poem seems symbolic – such as the ladder pointing to heaven which might suggest Frost's religious feelings. The setting is calm and the poet feels tired but satisfied after his demanding physical work – 'there's a barrel that I didn't fill'. But his tiredness soon makes his mood more dreamy – 'Essence of winter sleep is on the night'. The sibilance and slender vowels add to this languid atmosphere. I could trace a growing surreal quality to the poem as Frost drifts in and out of consciousness, remembering flashes of his work – 'The scent of apples: I am drowsing off'. He mentions 'sleep' repeatedly, reflecting his weariness. The rhythm is slow and irregular, just like his confused thoughts. By the end of the poem, he is in a dreamlike state, equally obsessed with apple-picking and his own need for sleep. He even wonders about 'whatever sleep it is'. As he drifts off, he thinks of animals that sleep through winter and compares himself to the woodchuck. The whimsical mood reflects his deep interest in nature and is a characteristic of this great American poet.

EXAMINER'S COMMENT

This is a very well written and accomplished answer that ranges widely and shows some close personal engagement: 'I could trace a growing surreal quality to the poem as Frost drifts in and out of consciousness, remembering flashes of his work.' There is an assured sense of the central mood and this is supported with apt quotations. Interesting references to Frost's style ensure the highest grade.

Class/Homework Exercises

1. Comment on the effectiveness of the poem's imagery in appealing to the senses. Refer closely to the text in your answer.
2. 'Many of Frost's poems appear simple, but often have layers of underlying meanings.' Discuss this view, with particular reference to 'After Apple-Picking'.

Summary Points

- **Subject matter considers creativity, human achievement and the cycle of life.**
- **Dreamlike atmosphere and contrasting tones – peaceful, nostalgic, regretful.**
- **Rich sensory imagery and symbolism convey underlying themes.**
- **Effective use of repetition, sibilance and assonance throughout.**

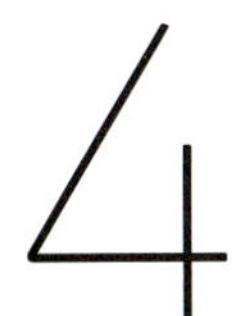

The Road Not Taken

ROBERT FROST

Two roads diverged in a yellow wood,
And sorry I could not travel both
And be one traveler, long I stood
And looked down one as far as I could
To where it bent in the undergrowth;

Then took the other, as just as fair,
And having perhaps the better claim,
Because it was grassy and wanted wear;
Though as for that, the passing there
Had worn them really about the same,

And both that morning equally lay
In leaves no step had trodden black.
Oh, I kept the first for another day!
Yet knowing how way leads on to way,
I doubted if I should ever come back.

I shall be telling this with a sigh
Somewhere ages and ages hence:
Two roads diverged in a wood, and I—
I took the one less traveled by,
And that has made all the difference.

diverged: separate and go in different directions.

undergrowth: small trees and bushes growing beneath larger trees in a wood.

claim: attraction, entitlement.

'where it bent in the undergrowth'

Personal Response

1. In your opinion, is this a simple poem or does it have a more profound meaning? Outline your views, supporting them with relevant quotation.
2. Select one image from the poem that you consider particularly effective or interesting. Briefly justify your choice.
3. Frost has been described as someone who 'broods and comments on familiar country things ... catching a truth in it'. In your view, what is the tone of this poem? Does it change or remain the same?

Critical Literacy

One of Frost's most popular poems, it was the first published in the collection *Mountain Interval* (1916). It was inspired by his friend, the poet Edward Thomas. Frost told Thomas, 'No matter which road you take, you'll always sigh, and wish you'd taken another'. Frost also said he was influenced by an event which happened to him at a crossroads after a winter snowstorm in 1912. He met a figure, 'my own image', who passed silently by him. Frost wondered at 'this other self'. The poem dramatises the choices we make in life and their consequences.

Huge themes are summarised in this simple narrative. In the first stanza, the speaker stands in a wood where two roads run off in different directions. He has to make a decision – which one will he take? The roads are 'about the same', so the emphasis is not on the decision, but on the **process of decision-making and its consequences**. The speaker decides that he cannot see where the first road is leading ('it bent in the undergrowth'), so he chooses the other one, though it is unclear why. The reference to the 'yellow wood' suggests that the poet is mature enough to realise the consequences of his decision. He won't have this opportunity again: 'I doubted if I should ever come back.' The beautiful image of the 'yellow wood' conjures up a picture of autumn in New England, but it also has a deeper meaning and is tinged with regret. A person can't do everything in life; choice is part of the human condition.

Frost has said, 'I'm not a nature poet. There's always something else in my poetry'. Here, in this simple act, he **explores what it means to be human** and dramatises the decision-making process. There is the human desire to avoid making a decision ('sorry I could not travel both') and the consideration of the possible choices ('long I stood/And looked down one as far as I could'). The regular rhyme scheme mirrors the poet looking this way and that as he tries to decide which to choose *(abaab, cdccd, efeef, ghggh)*. This unusual rhyme also underlines the curious choice made. Frost felt that 'the most important thing about a poem ... is how wilfully, gracefully, naturally entertainingly and beautifully its rhymes are'.

In stanza two, **he makes the decision**: he 'took the other one'. Why? Was it because it 'was grassy and wanted wear'? Is this someone who is individualistic and likes to do something different to the crowd? Does this suggest a desire for adventure? Then the poet becomes increasingly mischievous. After pointing out the difference between the two roads, he now declares that they were not so different: 'the passing there/Had worn them really about the same.'

In the third stanza, he continues to **point out the similarity of the two roads**, which 'equally lay'. So is the idea that if you choose the less conventional route in life, you may not end up having adventures? The reader is now as confused as the poet was when trying to decide what to do. A second great truth is then revealed: no matter what we get, we always want what we don't have. The regret is evident in the emphatic 'Oh, I kept the first for another day!' But, of course, there won't be another day, because time marches on and we cannot return to the past; we can only go on, as 'way leads on to way'.

At the start of stanza four, the poet realises in **hindsight** that he will tell of this day in the future, 'ages and ages hence', but it will be 'with a sigh'. Has his choice resulted in suffering? Frost's own personal life was littered with tragedy. Does the repetition of 'I' and the inclusion of the dash suggest that the poet is asserting his maverick individuality as he resolutely declares: 'I took the one less traveled by,/And that has made all the difference'? Do you think he feels he made the right choice for himself?

This common experience of choice and decision-making is caught succinctly in Frost's simple narrative. It seems like a person thinking aloud; the language seems ordinary. Yet upon closer examination, we become aware of the **musical sound effects**. The repeated 'e', coupled with the sibilant 's' ('it was grassy') and alliteration ('wanted wear') convey a calm, deliberating voice. This poem is inclusive rather than exclusive, as it invites us to share in the poet's decision-making.

Writing About the Poem

'Frost uses traditional form not in an experimental way, but adapted to his purpose.' Discuss this statement with reference to 'The Road Not Taken'. Refer to the poem in your answer.

Sample Paragraph

Frost forms his poems not in an experimental way, but in a deliberate way which suits his purpose. He uses iambic pentameter, a traditional metre used by Shakespeare and it is an ironic, sceptical voice, 'yet knowing how way leads on to way', which resonates in 'The Road Not Taken'. The structure of the poem mirrors the deliberating process, as first the speaker tries to avoid making a choice, then considers the alternatives, 'long I stood'. The decision is made and almost immediately there is a sense of regret: 'Oh, I kept the first for another day.' The rhyme scheme of the first stanza is *abaab*. This mirrors the unusual choice the poet made. Frost believed in the 'sound of sense', not necessarily the meaning of words. This is illustrated in the line, 'Because it was grassy and wanted wear'. The alliteration and sibilance suggest an almost idyllic wilderness. So Frost structures the form of his poems for a purpose. In this poem the rhyme scheme mimics the glancing this way and that as the speaker tries to decide what route to take. These are some of the ways Frost uses form for a purpose, rather than experimenting just for its own sake.

EXAMINER'S COMMENT

This thoroughly developed answer shows a deep sense of engagement, particularly the discussion on the poetic voice: 'an ironic, sceptical voice, "Yet knowing how way leads on to way".' Points on style range widely and clearly demonstrate an understanding of Frost's skill in using structure, rhyme and sound effects. Expression is also excellent throughout. The well-sustained focus and integrated quoting ensure that the standard reached the highest grade.

Class/Homework Exercises

1. Frost's ambition was to 'write a few poems it will be hard to get rid of'. To what extent is this true of 'The Road Not Taken'?
2. 'The ending of "The Road Not Taken" has often been described as ambiguous and inconclusive.' Discuss this view, with particular reference to the poem.

Summary Points

- **Key themes – the natural world and the consequences of making choices in life.**
- **The autumnal setting provides a suitable context for this simple narrative.**
- **Reflective tone and characteristically simple language throughout.**
- **Effective use of the extended metaphor, emphatic rhyme and appealing musical effects.**

Birches

ROBERT FROST

When I see birches bend to left and right
Across the lines of straighter darker trees,
I like to think some boy's been swinging them.
But swinging doesn't bend them down to stay.
Ice-storms do that. Often you must have seen them
Loaded with ice a sunny winter morning
After a rain. They click upon themselves
As the breeze rises, and turn many-colored
As the stir cracks and crazes their enamel.
Soon the sun's warmth makes them shed crystal shells
Shattering and avalanching on the snow-crust—
Such heaps of broken glass to sweep away
You'd think the inner dome of heaven had fallen.
They are dragged to the withered bracken by the load,
And they seem not to break; though once they are bowed
So low for long, they never right themselves:
You may see their trunks arching in the woods
Years afterwards, trailing their leaves on the ground
Like girls on hands and knees that throw their hair
Before them over their heads to dry in the sun.
But I was going to say when Truth broke in
With all her matter-of-fact about the ice-storm
I should prefer to have some boy bend them
As he went out and in to fetch the cows—
Some boy too far from town to learn baseball,
Whose only play was what he found himself,
Summer or winter, and could play alone.
One by one he subdued his father's trees
By riding them down over and over again
Until he took the stiffness out of them,
And not one but hung limp, not one was left
For him to conquer. He learned all there was
To learn about not launching out too soon
And so not carrying the tree away
Clear to the ground. He always kept his poise
To the top branches, climbing carefully
With the same pains you use to fill a cup
Up to the brim, and even above the brim.

birches: deciduous trees with smooth, white bark.

click: tapping sound made by the branches when they touch.

crazes their enamel: cracks the ice on the trees.
crystal shells: drops of melting ice on branches.
avalanching: collapsing.

bracken: fern leaves.

limp: loose; wilted.

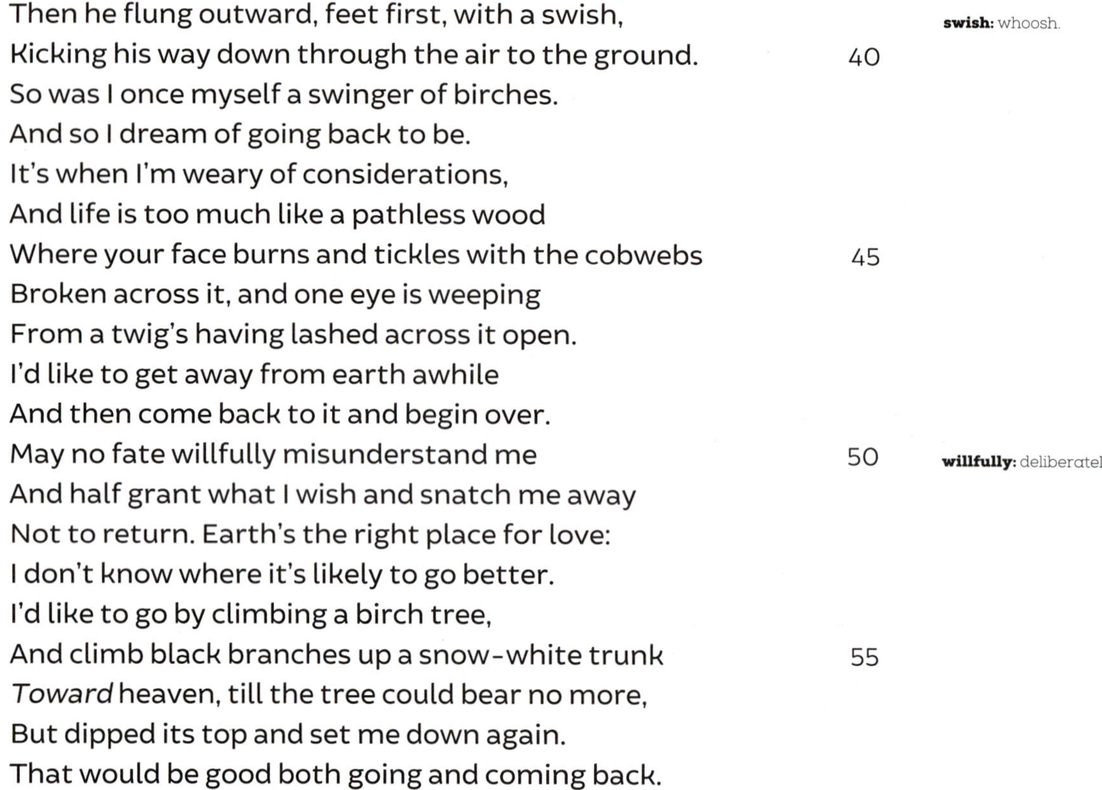

Then he flung outward, feet first, with a swish,
Kicking his way down through the air to the ground.
So was I once myself a swinger of birches.
And so I dream of going back to be.
It's when I'm weary of considerations,
And life is too much like a pathless wood
Where your face burns and tickles with the cobwebs
Broken across it, and one eye is weeping
From a twig's having lashed across it open.
I'd like to get away from earth awhile
And then come back to it and begin over.
May no fate willfully misunderstand me
And half grant what I wish and snatch me away
Not to return. Earth's the right place for love:
I don't know where it's likely to go better.
I'd like to go by climbing a birch tree,
And climb black branches up a snow-white trunk
Toward heaven, till the tree could bear no more,
But dipped its top and set me down again.
That would be good both going and coming back.
One could do worse than be a swinger of birches.

swish: whoosh.

willfully: deliberately.

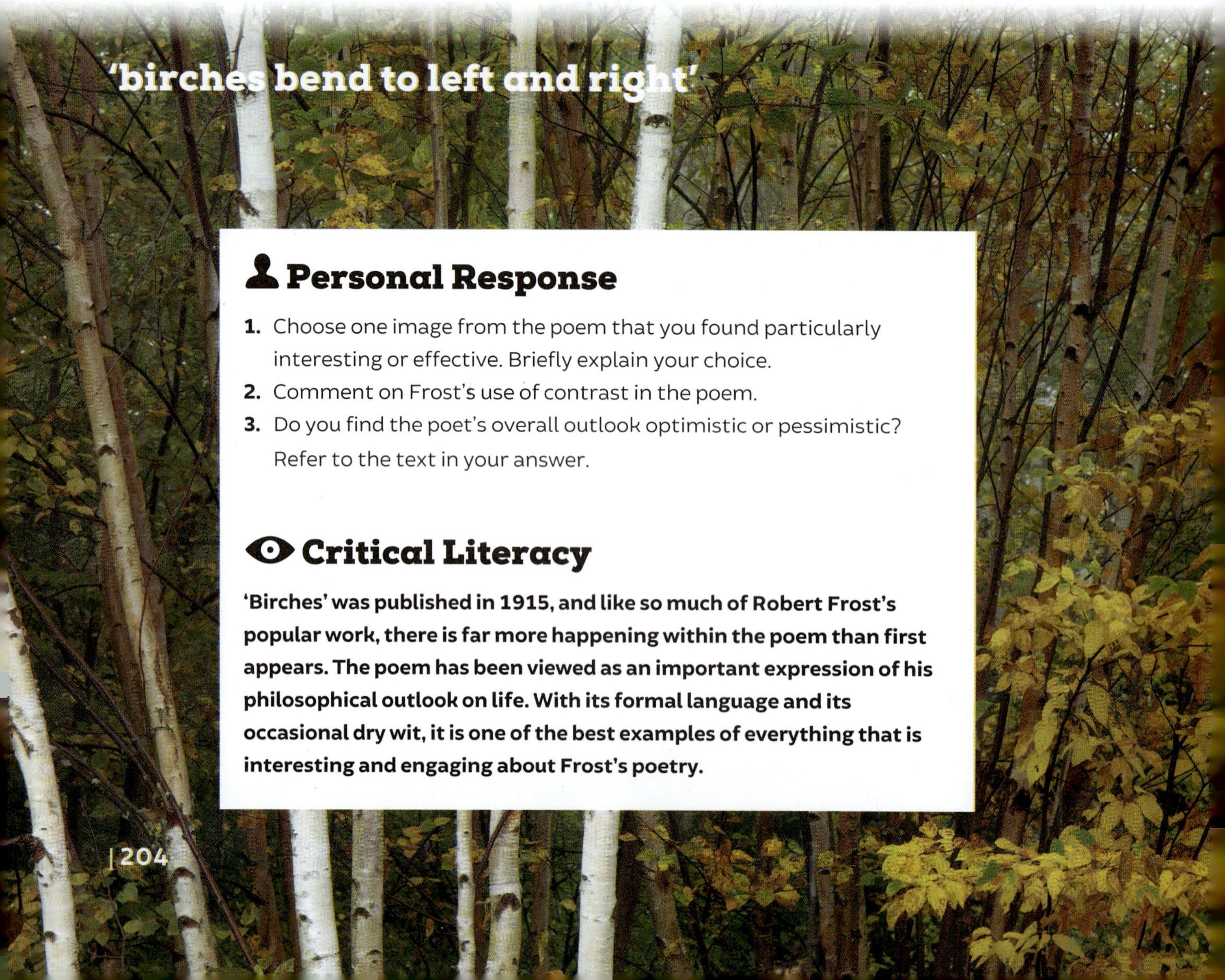

'birches bend to left and right'

Personal Response

1. Choose one image from the poem that you found particularly interesting or effective. Briefly explain your choice.
2. Comment on Frost's use of contrast in the poem.
3. Do you find the poet's overall outlook optimistic or pessimistic? Refer to the text in your answer.

Critical Literacy

'Birches' was published in 1915, and like so much of Robert Frost's popular work, there is far more happening within the poem than first appears. The poem has been viewed as an important expression of his philosophical outlook on life. With its formal language and its occasional dry wit, it is one of the best examples of everything that is interesting and engaging about Frost's poetry.

The opening description of the leaning birches is interesting, as Frost compares them to the 'straighter darker trees'. The scene immediately brings him back to his childhood and he likes to think that 'some boy's been swinging them'. This tension between what has actually happened and what the poet would like to have happened – between the real world and the world of the imagination – runs through much of the poem. Throughout lines 1–20, he wonders why the birches are bent 'to left and right'. He accepts that the true reason is because of the ice weighing them down. The poet's **precise, onomatopoeic language** – particularly the sharp 'c' effect in 'cracks and crazes their enamel' – echoes the tapping sound of the frozen branches. Vivid, sensual imagery brings the wintry scene to life: 'crystal shells', 'snow crust', 'withered bracken'. Frost's conversational tone is engaging: 'You'd think the inner dome of heaven had fallen.' Characteristically, he adds a beautiful simile, comparing the bent branches 'trailing their leaves on the ground' to girls who are drying their cascading hair in the sunshine.

In the poem's second section (lines 21–40), Frost resists the accurate explanation ('Truth') for the bent trees, preferring to interpret the scene imaginatively. He visualises a lonely boy ('too far from town to learn baseball') who has learned to amuse himself among the forest birches. In simple, factual terms, the poet describes the boy as he 'subdued his father's trees'. We are given a sense of his youthful determination to 'conquer' them all until 'not one was left'. His persistence teaches him valuable lessons for later life. Swinging skilfully on the trees, the boy learns 'about not launching out too soon'. Readers are left in no doubt about the rich **metaphorical significance of the birches**. In highlighting the importance of 'poise' and 'climbing carefully', Frost reveals his belief in discipline and artistry as the important elements of a successful life ('to fill a cup/Up to the brim'). Such symbolism is a common feature of his poetry.

Lines 41–59 are more nostalgic in tone. Frost recalls that he himself was once 'a swinger of birches' and extends the metaphor of retreating into the world of imagination and poetry. The similarities between climbing birches and writing poems become more explicit: 'I'd like to get away from earth.' However, he stresses that he does not wish for a permanent escape because 'Earth's the right place for love'. Is this what poets do when they withdraw into their imaginations and reflect on reality in an attempt to explore the beauty and mystery of life? They are dreamers, idealists. The birch trees are similarly grounded, but they also reach '*Toward* heaven'. The emphatic image (the italics are Frost's) suggests his continuing aspiration for **spiritual fulfilment through the poetic imagination**: 'That would be good both going and coming back.' Frost ends his poem by stating his satisfaction with overcoming challenges and benefiting from the desire to achieve by writing: 'One could do worse than be a swinger of birches.'

Writing About the Poem

'Frost's search for spiritual fulfilment is effectively captured through detailed description.' Discuss this statement in relation to the poem, 'Birches'. Support your answer with reference to the text.

Sample Paragraph

Frost's simple images create a connection between the poet and his readers. I liked the closely observed descriptions of the ice-covered branches: 'the sun's warmth makes them shed crystal shells.' The sibilance here adds to the beauty of the language. Using onomatopoeia, Frost captures the sounds of the forest in the bitter weather. The trees 'click upon themselves'. The poet loved nature and had a keen eye for its beauty. I also liked his comparison of the trail of leaves to the 'girls on hands and knees that throw their hair'. It was dramatic and unusual. The boy's movement playing on the trees is dynamic: 'Then he flung outward, feet first.' Near the end of the poem, Frost describes a harsher side of the forest when 'your face burns and tickles with the cobwebs'. As someone who spent my childhood in the country, I could relate to this tactile image. Frost is a wonderful writer whose poems give a clear sense of the New England landscape. 'Birches' is a very successful piece of description, mainly due to the poet's precise choice of words and the vivid imagery.

EXAMINER'S COMMENT

This paragraph showed a good knowledge of the text and a clear personal appreciation of Frost's writing skills: 'The sibilance here adds to the beauty of the language.' However, the response does not fully address the task and there is no reference to the 'search for spiritual fulfilment'. This weakens the answer, which deserves a middle grade.

Class/Homework Exercises

1. In your opinion, what is the central theme or message in 'Birches'? Support your answer with reference to the text.
2. 'While Frost's poetry contains elements of suffering, there are also moments of comfort and joy in his work.' To what extent is this true of 'Birches'? Support your answer with reference to the poem.

Summary Points

- **Central themes include childhood, creativity, imagination and escapism.**
- **Motion of swinging can be seen as a metaphor for transcending harsh realities.**
- **Recurring contrasts: light/darkness, love/pain, life/death, Heaven/Earth.**
- **Effective use of descriptive details, striking images, sibilance and assonance.**
- **Tones vary: reflective, nostalgic, philosophical.**

ROBERT FROST

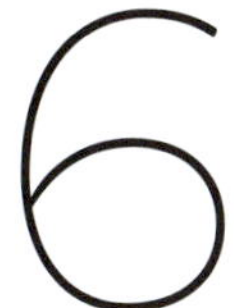

"Out, Out—"

"Out, Out–": phrase from a speech which Macbeth, King of Scotland, made on hearing of the death of his wife and when he was surrounded by enemies. He was commenting on the fragility of life: 'Out, out brief candle. Life's but a walking shadow' (Shakespeare).

The buzz-saw snarled and rattled in the yard
And made dust and dropped stove-length sticks of wood,
Sweet-scented stuff when the breeze drew across it.
And from there those that lifted eyes could count
Five mountain ranges one behind the other
Under the sunset far into Vermont.
And the saw snarled and rattled, snarled and rattled,
As it ran light, or had to bear a load.
And nothing happened: day was all but done.
Call it a day, I wish they might have said
To please the boy by giving him the half hour
That a boy counts so much when saved from work.
His sister stood beside them in her apron
To tell them 'Supper.' At the word, the saw,
As if to prove saws knew what supper meant,
Leaped out at the boy's hand, or seemed to leap—
He must have given the hand. However it was,
Neither refused the meeting. But the hand!
The boy's first outcry was a rueful laugh,
As he swung toward them holding up the hand
Half in appeal, but half as if to keep
The life from spilling. Then the boy saw all—
Since he was old enough to know, big boy
Doing a man's work, though a child at heart—
He saw all spoiled. 'Don't let him cut my hand off—
The doctor, when he comes. Don't let him, sister!'
So. But the hand was gone already.
The doctor put him in the dark of ether.
He lay and puffed his lips out with his breath.
And then—the watcher at his pulse took fright.
No one believed. They listened at his heart.
Little—less—nothing!—and that ended it.
No more to build on there. And they, since they
Were not the one dead, turned to their affairs.

lifted eyes: reference to Psalm 21 – 'I will lift up mine eyes unto the hills' – but the people here don't. The sunset is ignored.

Vermont: a state in New England, USA.

ether: form of anaesthetic.

Personal Response

1. What kind of world is shown in the poem? Consider the roles of adults and children. Refer to the text in your response.
2. Choose one image from the poem that you find particularly vivid and dramatic. Briefly explain your choice.
3. In your opinion, what is the central theme or message of '"Out, Out—"'? Refer closely to the poem in your response.

Critical Literacy

Based on an actual event that occurred in 1910, the poem refers to a tragic accident when the son of a neighbour of Frost's was killed on his father's farm. By chance, he had hit the loose pulley of the sawing machine and his hand was badly cut. He died from heart failure due to shock. The event was reported in a local paper.

This **horrifying subject matter**, the early violent death of a young boy, was, in Frost's opinion, 'too cruel' to include in his poetry readings. The title, which is a reference to a speech from Shakespeare's *Macbeth*, is a telling comment on how tenuous our hold on life is. The scene is set in a busy timber yard: a world of actual buzz saw, snarling action. In line 1, Frost's rasping onomatopoeic sounds give a vivid sense of the noisy, dangerous yard. The **long, flowing, descriptive lines** paint a picture of a place full of menace where work has to be done. But there is beauty in the midst of this raw power: 'Sweet-scented stuff when the breeze drew across it.' The soft sibilant 's', the assonance of the long 'e' and the compound word 'Sweet-scented' all go to show the surprising beauty to be found in the midst of the practical 'stove-length sticks of wood'.

The **surroundings are also beautiful**, if only the people would look up. But they, unlike the poet, are unaware of 'Five mountain ranges one behind the other/Under the sunset far into Vermont', as their focus is on the work. Repetition of the verbs 'snarled and rattled' mimics the action of the repeated sawing. The detail 'As it ran light, or had to bear a load' shows how the saw pushed through the wood, then lightly ran back through the cut. Line 9 tells us that the day was 'all but done'. A foreshadowing of the impending tragedy is given in 'I wish they might have said'. This is the only time in the whole poem when the personal pronoun 'I' is used. The poet's compassionate understanding for the young boy is evident as he explains how much it matters to a boy to be given precious time off from such hard work: 'That a boy counts so much.' The colloquial language in line 10, 'Call it a day', brings the reader right into this rural scene, rooting the poem in ordinary day-to-day life. Tragic irony is embedded in the line, for soon there will be no more days for the boy.

A domestic detail adds to the reality of this scene as the boy's sister appears 'in her apron/To tell them "Supper"'. In this central episode in line 14, the saw suddenly becomes personified, as if it too 'knew what supper meant'. The fragmented language, 'Leaped out at the boy's hand, or seemed to leap—', reminds us of the fragmented teeth of the saw as it seeks its prey. The mystifying accident is referenced in 'seemed to'. How could it have happened? The helplessness of the victim, the boy, is shown: 'Neither refused the meeting.' We are reminded of someone almost paralysed into inaction at the split second of a horrific accident. Was this destiny? Is the poet adversely commenting on the mechanisation of farming, or on the practice of getting a boy to do a man's job? **All the attention is now focused on the shocking injury**: 'But the hand!' The pity of the event is palpable in this climactic phrase.

The boy's reaction is chilling and poignant. He holds up the hand, 'spilling' its life blood. He pathetically asks for help, begging his sister not to let the doctor amputate his hand: 'Don't let him.' Now the poet interjects: 'So.' What more is to be said? It is like a dramatic drawn-out breath after the tension of the awful accident. The harsh reality is there for all to see: 'the hand was gone already.' The boy realised this when he 'saw all'. Without the use of his hands, there would be no man's work for him any more: 'He saw all spoiled.'

The closing section in lines 28–31 shows the details of the medical help: the 'dark of ether', the boy's breath 'puffed'. Now the lines break up into fragments as the terrible final act of the tragedy unfolds: 'No one believed.' The heartbeats ebbed away: 'Little—less—nothing!' The **sober reality hits home**: 'and that ended it.' There is now no future for the boy: 'No more to build on.' Frost has said that the reality of life is that 'it goes on'. And so the people there, because they were not the one dead, 'turned to their affairs'. Neither the people nor the poet are being callous and unfeeling. Seamus Heaney refers to this as the 'grim accuracy' of the poem's conclusion.

The tone in this narrative poem ranges from the anger and menace of the saw, to the calm of the beautiful rural countryside, to the wistful reflections of the poet and on to the horror of the accident. In the end, Frost's ironic tone gives way to the cold fear of the finality of death, when all is changed forever.

Writing About the Poem

In writing about Frost, Seamus Heaney commented, 'Here was a poet who touched things as they are, somehow'. Discuss this statement with reference to the poem, '"Out, Out—"'.

Sample Paragraph

'"Out, Out–"' is one of Frost's most unsettling poems. The tragic story of a young boy who suffers a terrible accident while working in a saw-mill is a shocking reminder of how fragile life can be. I think it was very brave of the poet to just say things as they are, rather than pretending that life is not dark sometimes. I also felt as if I were actually in the timber yard as the saw 'snarled and rattled' in Vermont. The detail of sound and smell, 'Sweet-scented stuff', brought me there. Frost, it seems to me, is also commenting negatively on the practice of having a young boy perform a man's job. The wistful 'I wish they might have said' condemns those who insisted on getting the job finished at the expense of the boy. It was too much to ask of a 'big boy', a 'child at heart'. The reality of the boy's life fading away was vividly captured by the poet in the line 'Little—less—nothing!' The punctuation adds to the effect of the heartbeat becoming weaker and finally stopping. Frost dared to say what life is like. He 'touched things as they are'. He achieved this by his craftsmanship as a poet, and his compassionate eye as a human being.

EXAMINER'S COMMENT

A thoughtful, personal exploration of the poem, using quotations that are carefully integrated into the answer, all of which results in a well-deserved high grade. Contemporary references illustrate the continuing relevance of Frost as a realistic voice. The point regarding Frost's skilful use of punctuation is well developed: 'The punctuation adds to the effect of the heartbeat becoming weaker and finally stopping.'

Class/Homework Exercises

1. It has been said that Frost's poems are 'little voyages of discovery'. Write a personal response to this poem, using quotations from the poem to support your answer.
2. 'Frost's poems are filled with disturbing reminders of life's harsh realities.' Discuss this view, with particular reference to '"Out, Out–"'.

Summary Points

- **Key themes – life's unfairness and unpredictability of human existence.**
- **Highly dramatic poem, with characters facing a crisis in a particular setting.**
- **Powerful onomatopoeic effects: alliteration and assonance.**
- **Contrasting images – beautiful landscape, dangerous sawmill.**

7 Spring Pools

ROBERT FROST

These pools that, though in forests, still reflect
The total sky almost without defect,
And like the flowers beside them, chill and shiver,
Will like the flowers beside them soon be gone,
And yet not out by any brook or river,
But up by roots to bring dark foliage on.

The trees that have it in their pent-up buds
To darken nature and be summer woods—
Let them think twice before they use their powers
To blot out and drink up and sweep away
These flowery waters and these watery flowers
From snow that melted only yesterday.

defect: blemish; flaw.

brook: small stream.

foliage: plants; undergrowth.

'darken nature'

Personal Response

1. What aspects of the spring pools are conveyed in the first stanza? Refer to the text in your answer.
2. Choose one image from the poem that you found particularly striking. Briefly explain your choice.
3. Write your own personal response to the poem.

Critical Literacy

'Spring Pools' captures a moment at the end of winter during which the poet reflects on the natural cycle of growth, decay and renewal. Rain falls from the sky, settles in pools and is then drawn up into the trees. In recalling the origins of this beautiful lyric poem, Frost commented, 'One night I sat alone by my open fireplace and wrote "Spring Pools". It was a very pleasant experience, and I remember it clearly, although I don't remember the writing of many of my other poems.'

The poem's title seems to celebrate new growth and regeneration. Ironically, stanza one focuses mainly on the fragility of nature. As always, Frost's **close observation of the natural world is evident** from the start. The clear pool water mirrors the overhead sky 'almost without defect'. While the simple images of the forest and flowers are peaceful, there is no escaping the underlying severity of 'chill and shiver'. The entire stanza of six lines is one long sentence. Its slow-moving pace, repetition and assonant vowels ('pools', 'brook', 'roots') enhance the sombre mood. Pool water will be absorbed by the tree roots to enrich the leaves and create 'dark foliage'. Then water and flowers will all 'soon be gone'. Frost pays most attention to the interdependence within the natural world and the transience of the beauty around him.

In stanza two, the poet addresses the trees directly, warning them to 'think twice before they use their powers'. He personifies them as an intimidating presence, associating them with dark destructiveness and 'pent-up' energy to 'blot out and drink up and sweep away'. Such forceful language combines with a resurgent rhythm to emphasise the power of the trees. The tone **becomes increasingly regretful** in the final lines. We are left with another evocative image of how nature's beauty is subject to constant change: 'snow that melted only yesterday.'

Frost's **poem is typically thought-provoking**, touching on familiar themes regarding the mysteries of nature and the passing of time. Some critics interpret 'Spring Pools' as a metaphor for the creative process – water has long been a symbol of inspiration. Frost's own writing is wonderfully controlled, in keeping with the sense of order within the natural world that he describes. Both stanzas mirror each other perfectly and the regular rhyme scheme completes the fluency of the lines.

Writing About the Poem

'Reflective consideration of nature is central in Frost's thought-provoking poetry.' Discuss this statement in relation to the poem, 'Spring Pools'. Refer closely to the text in your response.

Sample Paragraph

There is a sense of loss going through much of 'Spring Pools'. It struck me first in the negative language of the opening stanza. Frost refers to the perfect sky 'without defect', implying that something might soon destroy the perfection. The peaceful setting of the winter flowers is also spoiled when the poet points out that they 'chill and shiver'. The mood is downbeat – everything will end and 'soon be gone'. The image of the trees ('dark foliage') adds to my sense of this depressing feeling. In the second part of the poem, Frost points out the irony of springtime as a season of decay just as much as of growth. To some degree, I think this is a realistic view, but it does take away from the joy of spring. The mood deteriorates as the poem continues. The trees are seen as destructive, drying up the water and removing the flowers. They 'darken nature' – a dramatic way of summing up the overall mood of this poem.

EXAMINER'S COMMENT

This focused paragraph uses quotations effectively to communicate the central mood of the poem, 'Frost refers to the perfect sky "without defect", implying that something might soon destroy the perfection'. Some further discussion of style, particularly tone and rhythm, would have added to the answer which just fails to achieve the top grade.

Class/Homework Exercises

1. In your view, what is the central theme or message of 'Spring Pools'? Refer closely to the poem in your answer.
2. 'One of Frost's great skills is the craftsmanship he displays in using sounds to convey meaning.' Discuss this statement, with particular reference to 'Spring Pools'.

Summary Points

- **Central themes include time itself and the cycle of life, death and renewal.**
- **Contrasting moods – serious, sombre, pensive and regretful.**
- **Rich, musical effects: assonance, sibilance and emphatic end-rhyme.**
- **Characteristic use of simple, accessible language and sensuous imagery.**

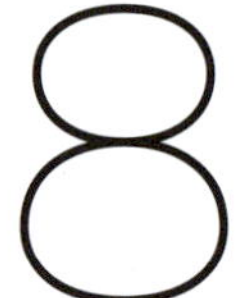

8 Acquainted with the Night

I have been one acquainted with the night.
I have walked out in rain—and back in rain.
I have outwalked the furthest city light.

I have looked down the saddest city lane.
I have passed by the watchman on his beat
And dropped my eyes, unwilling to explain.

I have stood still and stopped the sound of feet
When far away an interrupted cry
Came over houses from another street,

But not to call me back or say good-bye;
And further still at an unearthly height,
One luminary clock against the sky

Proclaimed the time was neither wrong nor right.
I have been one acquainted with the night.

luminary clock: moon; a real clock shining with reflected light; simply passing time.
Proclaimed: announced.

Personal Response

1. In your opinion, what is the central theme or message of this poem? Refer to the text in your answer.
2. Is there a sense of drama in this poem? Refer to the text in your answer.
3. Write your own personal response to the poem.

Critical Literacy

'Acquainted with the Night' is a sonnet from Robert Frost's collection, *West-Ring Brook* (1928). Unusually, it is set in a bleak city rather than the countryside. This is one of Frost's darkest poems and portrays an isolated figure filled with despair. It is reminiscent of the Modernist poets, such as T. S. Eliot, or the American artist Edward Hopper, whose paintings frequently showed solitary individuals.

The 20th century was a time of huge social upheaval and warfare, and was primarily focused on material progress rather than spiritual awareness. Many people became alienated, lonely and confused. Frost's poem begins with a declaration: 'I have been one acquainted with the night.' It is a frank statement, rather like the admissions made at an AA (Alcoholics Anonymous) meeting. It is also reminiscent of the Old Testament reference to **one who was despised and rejected by men**, a man of sorrows 'acquainted with grief'. The second line in this first stanza shows the direction that the poem will take. There are two journeys: the body travels outwards towards the edge of the city ('I have walked out in rain') while the mind travels inwards to the edge of the psyche ('and back in rain').

This **alienation is echoed in the form of the poem**, which is not a conventional 14-line sonnet (either three quatrains and a rhyming couplet, or an octet and sestet); here there is a terza rima format. The poet uses a three-line rhyming stanza, concluding with a rhyming couplet. The terza rima was used by the great Italian poet Dante in his famous poem 'The Divine Comedy' to describe the descent into hell. Is Frost using this structure in his poem because he is describing his descent into his own private hell? (His life had included many family tragedies.) This is a highly personal poem, as it uses 'I' at the beginning of seven of its fourteen lines. The rhythm imitates a slow walking movement: 'I have outwalked the furthest city light.' The poet has now gone beyond the last visible sign of civilisation. The use of iambic pentameter is the metre closest to the speaking voice in English, and the measured flow underlines the poet's melancholy mood.

The **sombre mood** of overwhelming anxiety is shown in the long vowel sounds of the second stanza: 'I have looked down the saddest city lane.' The broad vowels 'a' and 'o' lengthen the line and show the world-weariness of one who has seen and experienced too much. Although it is set at night, the traditional time for romance and lovers, we are presented with never-ending rain and gloom. A listless mood is created by the repetition of 'I have'. The run-on line suggests the relentless trudging of this weary man who is too caught up in his own dark thoughts to even bother communicating with the 'watchman'. He is 'unwilling to explain' and is jealously guarding his privacy. Is this walk symptomatic of his inner state? Can nothing penetrate this extreme loneliness?

The run-on line continues in the third stanza. Frost comes to an abrupt stop on his journey as an 'interrupted cry' rings out across the **desolate urban landscape**. Who cried? Why? And why was the cry 'interrupted'? Is something awful happening to someone? Can anything be done about it? It seems not. The poet merely remarks in the next stanza that it has nothing to do with him, 'not to call me back or say good-bye'. This is the chilling aspect of living in a big city: the sense of just being another person nobody cares about. These others have no substance, being reduced to the 'sound of feet' or a 'cry'.

In the fourth stanza, the poet speaks of a 'luminary clock'. This could be the moon or a real clock that is reflecting light. Is it symbolic of time passing incessantly? Why is it at an 'unearthly height'? Is it because time rules the human world and nothing can change this? The final couplet proclaims that the 'time was neither wrong nor right'. We are left wondering what the time was neither right nor wrong for – what was supposed to happen? There is a **sense of confusion** here, and echoes of Hamlet's declaration that 'the time is out of joint'. The poem ends as it begins: 'I have been one acquainted with the night'. We have come full circle, though **nothing has been achieved**. There is no sense of comfort or guidance, only the realisation of spiritual emptiness and a hostile world.

Writing About the Poem

'Robert Frost writes dramatic lyrics of homelessness.' Discuss this statement in relation to the poem 'Acquainted with the Night'. Refer closely to the text in your response.

Sample Paragraph

The sense of homelessness is central to this sonnet. The individual in the poem seems to be always on his own, not connected either with family, friend or acquaintance, a loner in a big anonymous city. There is no network to comfort this man, no community to offer help and encouragement. The hero does not want to engage, 'And dropped my eyes'. The poem is like a mini drama as the main character plays out his exterior action: 'I have walked out in rain', and his interior journey, 'unwilling to explain'. The setting is vividly realised as the bleak urban landscape is drawn with its endless rain and strange noises. So there is character, action, setting and mood. The music of this lyrical poem is the rhythm of a slow walk as the steady iambic pentameter tempo steps out a hypnotic beat: 'I have outwalked the furthest city light.' The broad vowels add to this downbeat atmosphere as the poem grinds on relentlessly: 'I have looked down the saddest city lane.' This is indeed dark mood music, as the drawn-out vowel sounds 'lane', 'explain', 'beat' and 'feet' echo the despair of this lonely man.

EXAMINER'S COMMENT

This paragraph addresses the three elements of the question ('homelessness', 'dramatic' and 'lyric'). The response shows a real appreciation of poetic technique, as the terms are not only explained, but are examined well in relation to the poem: 'The music of this lyrical poem is the rhythm of a slow walk as the steady iambic pentameter tempo steps out a hypnotic beat.' Assured expression throughout. A highly successful top-grade answer.

Class/Homework Exercises

1. Seamus Heaney describes this poem as 'dark'. What type of darkness is there? Is it literal or metaphorical or both? Refer to the text in your answer.
2. 'The personal narrative voice in Frost's poems can give readers an added sense of realism.' Discuss this view, with particular reference to 'Acquainted with the Night'.

Summary Points

- **Time, loneliness and the breakdown of communication are key themes.**
- **Powerful evocation of the anonymous urban atmosphere.**
- **The darkness symbolises a pervading sense of spiritual emptiness.**
- **Effective use of simple language, repetition, assonance and end-rhyme.**

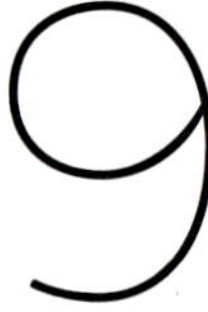

Design

Title: the poem's title refers to the argument that the natural design of the universe is proof of God's existence.

I found a dimpled spider, fat and white,
On a white heal-all, holding up a moth
Like a white piece of rigid satin cloth—
Assorted characters of death and blight
Mixed ready to begin the morning right,
Like the ingredients of a witches' broth—
A snow-drop spider, a flower like froth,
And dead wings carried like a paper kite.

What had that flower to do with being white,
The wayside blue and innocent heal-all?
What brought the kindred spider to that height,
Then steered the white moth thither in the night?
What but design of darkness to appall?—
If design govern in a thing so small.

dimpled: indented.

heal-all: plant (once used as a medicine).

blight: disease in plants; evil influence.

witches' broth: revolting recipes used to cast spells.

thither: to there, to that place.

appall: horrify (to make pale, literally).

'a dimpled spider, fat and white'

Personal Response

1. How important a part does the colour white play in this poem? Refer to the text in your answer.
2. Select one comparison from the poem that you consider particularly effective. Briefly explain your choice.
3. Write a short personal response to the poem, highlighting the impact it made on you.

Critical Literacy

'Design' explores our attempts to see order in the universe – and our failure to recognise the order that is present in nature. Frost's sonnet raises several profound questions. Is there a design to life? Is there an explanation for the evil in the world? The poet was fascinated by nature from a philosophical point of view. His choice of the traditional sonnet form allows him to address such an important theme in a controlled way.

In the opening line, Frost describes how he finds a 'dimpled spider, fat and white' on a flower, 'holding up a moth' it has captured. The adjective 'dimpled' usually has harmless connotations, but in this context, and combined with the word 'fat', it suggests an unattractive image of venomous engorgement. The colour white (used four more times in this short poem) also tends to have positive overtones of innocence and goodness. But most spiders are brown or black, and purity here quickly gives way to pale ghastliness. Indeed, the **tone becomes increasingly menacing** as the octave proceeds. The unwary moth has been lured to its grizzly death on the 'white heal-all' flower, which makes the situation even more deceitful.

Frost's similes reflect the deathly atmosphere. The hapless moth is held 'Like a white piece of rigid satin cloth'. The 'characters of death' in this grim drama are compared to the 'ingredients of a witches' broth'. Lines 7–8 are particularly ironic. Frost revises his view of the grotesque scene, seeing the **tragic coincidence** involving the 'snow-drop spider' and 'a flower like a froth'. While the images might appear attractive, there is a lingering suggestion of gloom and ferocity.

The focus changes in the sestet as the tone grows passionately angry. Frost uses a series of **rhetorical questions demanding an explanation** for what he has witnessed: 'What had that flower to do with being white'? Is this implying that nature isn't so innocent after all? He re-runs the sequence of events and wonders what 'steered the white moth thither in the night'. The possibility that such a catastrophic event might be part of a great 'design of darkness' appalls the poet. However, the poem's final line ('If design govern in a thing so small') is the most intriguing of all. The word 'if' leaves the possibility that there is no grand plan for the universe, that it is all accidental. Whether predestination or chance is the more terrifying reality is left for readers to consider.

Writing About the Poem

'Frost presents contrasting views on nature in his thought-provoking poetry.' Discuss this statement in relation to the poem, 'Design'. Refer closely to the text in your answer.

Sample Paragraph

In 'Design', Frost takes an ironic approach to nature. Unlike other poems (e.g. 'The Tuft of Flowers'), where he ends up being reassured by the beauty of his natural environment, 'Design' is disquieting. The first few lines describe a repulsive side of nature's basic law – kill or be killed. I found the image of the spider quite revolting: 'fat and white'. The poet conveys a sense of violence when nature begins 'the morning right'. Dead moths are routine – often in beautiful settings. Nature is full of such contradictions. The image of the moth like a 'white piece of rigid satin cloth' suggested the lining of a coffin and reminded me that we see signs of mortality all around us. At the same time, Frost seems to be realistic about nature. Even in violent situations, there are beautiful creatures. The 'dead wings' are compared to a graceful 'paper kite'. Overall, the poet probably shows a less attractive side to nature in the poem, but it is not totally bleak. I liked the way he managed simple language to raise deep and disturbing questions about our natural world.

EXAMINER'S COMMENT

A balanced response, demonstrating a good understanding of the poem. References and quotations were carefully chosen and used effectively. Genuine engagement, e.g. 'The image of the moth like a "white piece of rigid satin cloth" suggested the lining of a coffin and reminded me that we see signs of our own mortality all around us'. Varied, confident expression underpins the top-grade standard.

Class/Homework Exercises

1. Sonnets frequently move from description to reflection ('sight to insight'). To what extent is this true of 'Design'? Refer closely to the poem in your answer.
2. 'Robert Frost often expresses complex ideas by using starkly contrasting images.' Discuss this statement, with particular reference to Frost's poem, 'Design'.

Summary Points

- **Sonnet form used to explore the dark unpredictability of nature.**
- **The poet challenges the belief of a divine design for the world.**
- **Variety of tones – ironic, disturbing, confrontational.**
- **Effective use of vivid imagery, startling contrasts and descriptive details.**

Provide, Provide

ROBERT FROST

The witch that came (the withered hag)
To wash the steps with pail and rag
Was once the beauty Abishag,

The picture pride of Hollywood.
Too many fall from great and good
For you to doubt the likelihood.

Die early and avoid the fate.
Or if predestined to die late,
Make up your mind to die in state.

Make the whole stock exchange your own!
If need be occupy a throne,
Where nobody can call *you* crone.

Some have relied on what they knew;
Others on being simply true.
What worked for them might work for you.

No memory of having starred
Atones for later disregard,
Or keeps the end from being hard.

Better to go down dignified
With boughten friendship at your side
Than none at all. Provide, provide!

Abishag: beautiful young woman who comforted King David in his old age.

crone: witchlike; old, withered woman.

Atones: makes amends (for sin or wrongdoing).

boughten: bought.

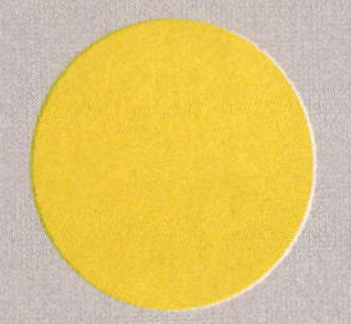

Personal Response

1. Is the advice given in the poem to be taken seriously or humorously, or a mixture of both? Discuss, using reference from the poem to support your answer.
2. What elements in the poem resemble a fairy tale or fable? Are they upbeat and reassuring or dark and disturbing? Briefly explain your answer.
3. What conclusion, if any, does the poem come to? Refer to the text to support your view.

Critical Literacy

'Provide, Provide' appeared at the height of Frost's fame, in a collection entitled *A Further Rage* (1936). It was based on a real person he had seen cleaning steps. The poem contrasts with most of Frost's work, as the tone is bitter and the emphasis is on material success. The Great Depression, a time of mass unemployment in America, was taking place. Is Frost suggesting that self-sufficiency is the answer?

The first stanza advises us to **plan for the future**. Why? A cold, bleak scene of a withered old woman doing a menial job of washing steps is given as a salutary picture of not providing. This is what happened to Abishag. The reference to the biblical character adds a timeless element – this is a truth for all generations. In this poem, old age equals diminishing beauty and success.

In stanza two, the destructive element of time is stressed as the poem comes to the present, 'Hollywood'. Even in the dream factory, beauty does not last. The tone of the poem is one of **addressing a public audience**, as if at an evangelical rally: 'For you to doubt the likelihood.' Fortune is fickle and undependable, as most people know.

The poem now offers **mock advice: the only solution is to die young** ('Die early'). In the third stanza, **the only other solution is to become wealthy** and 'die in state'. The implication is that to achieve this end, one has to work hard and acquire wealth. An imperative verb, 'Make', in the fourth stanza encourages us to grab material success: 'Make the whole stock exchange your own!' The exclamation mark captures the tone of persuasion that pervades this unusual poem. The quaint image of the throne adds to the timeless element, as it is a universal symbol of power and importance. Only political power, privilege and riches provide protection against the harsh reality of ageing. If 'you' don't want the same fate as Abishag, 'you' must be alert. Stanza five reminds us that there are always choices in life. Some people succeed on knowledge and ability, others on being honest and genuine.

Independence was very important to Frost. Now, in stanza six, the poem cautions us that even if our early lives were wonderful, 'having starred', that memory is not a safeguard against the misfortune that might happen later in life. Dark humour in the final stanza suggests, with wry, unsentimental honesty, that it is better to **buy friendship** ('boughten') than suffer loneliness at the end of life. Is this cynical view that bought friends are better than none realistic? The poem concludes with great urgency: 'Provide, provide!' Frost did not believe in a benevolent God ruling the universe, but rather takes the view that there is an indifferent God and we are subject to random darkness. This is by no means an affirmative poem.

Frost favoured **traditional poetic structures**, declaring that he was 'one of the notable craftsmen of this time'. Here the full rhyme of *aaa, bbb, ccc, ddd,* etc. does not seem strained. We hardly notice it in such a carefully crafted poem of seven three-line stanzas. Rhythmic blank verse, set against colloquial speech, gives this poem its energy. The use of the imperative verbs, especially 'Provide, provide', demands that we take the poet's message on board. Frost presents **painful ideas** – in this instance a cynical view of fame and success – **in a controlled form**. He has said, 'The poems I make are little bits of order.'

Writing About the Poem

'Poetry is a momentary stay against confusion.' Discuss this statement in relation to the poem, 'Provide, Provide'. Use references from the text to support your views.

Sample Paragraph

The bleak situation painted by Frost is very different from his other poems where a quiet voice alerts us to the beauties of nature. In 'Provide, Provide', the focus is on 'look out for your old age, as no one is going to want you'. I wonder if Frost was uncomfortable about being famous. The poem is stating that change is the only certainty and encourages us to get ourselves in order if we don't want to have a miserable time when looks and youth are gone. I like the mock serious tone in which this message is delivered: 'If need be occupy a throne,/ Where nobody can call you crone.' I think this dry, cynical tone appeals especially to today's reader who is saturated with this 'fame' issue. I also think that humour is very effective in delivering a message, particularly one as unappealing as this. The airbrushed perfection of the groomed Hollywood stars is captured perfectly in the alliterative phrase: 'The picture pride of Hollywood.' But the poet knew that this is not how it is – 'the end' is 'hard'.

EXAMINER'S COMMENT

This lively, personal approach to a very challenging question effectively explores Frost's own personal circumstances, his views on poetry and life. In-depth discussion of Frost's style is satisfying – 'The airbrushed perfection of the groomed Hollywood stars is captured perfectly in the alliterative phrase: "the picture pride of Hollywood".' Impressive vocabulary and confident expression throughout. A high-grade answer.

Class/Homework Exercises

1. 'A poem begins in delight and ends in wisdom.' Is this a valid statement in relation to the poem 'Provide, Provide'? Use quotation from the poem in your explorations.
2. 'In many of his poems, Robert Frost reveals himself as neither an optimist nor a pessimist, but as a realist.' To what extent is this true of 'Provide, Provide'? Support your answer with reference to the poem.

Summary Points

- **Central themes – time's erosive power, transience and endurance.**
- **Characteristically simple, accessible language and colloquial speech.**
- **Range of tones: serious, light-hearted, mocking, ironic, cynical.**
- **Effective use of contrasting images, repetition.**

Sample Leaving Cert Questions on Frost's Poetry

1. **'Frost makes skilful use of a variety of stylistic features to tell dramatic stories that often have a universal significance.' To what extent do you agree or disagree with this statement? Support your answer with reference to the poetry of Robert Frost on your course.**
2. **From your study of the poetry of Robert Frost on your course, select the poems that, in your opinion, best show his effective use of specific places to communicate a sense of alienation and the barriers that exist between people. Justify your selection by showing how Frost's effective use of specific places communicates a sense of alienation and the barriers that exist between people.**
3. **'Robert Frost's reflective poetry is defined largely by conversational language, descriptive detail and underlying compassion.' Discuss this view, supporting your answer with reference to both the thematic concerns and poetic style in the poetry of Robert Frost on your course.**

Understanding the Prescribed Poetry Question

Marks are awarded using the PCLM Marking Scheme:
P = 15; C = 15; L = 15; M = 5
Total = 50

- **P** (Purpose = 15 marks) refers to the set question and is the launch pad for the answer. This involves engaging with all aspects of the question. Both theme and language must be addressed, although not necessarily equally.
- **C** (Coherence = 15 marks) refers to the organisation of the developed response and the use of accurate, relevant quotation. Paragraphing is essential.
- **L** (Language = 15 marks) refers to the student's skill in controlling language throughout the answer.
- **M** (Mechanics = 5 marks) refers to spelling and grammar.
- Although no specific number of poems is required, students usually discuss at least 3 or 4 in their written responses.
- Aim for at least 800 words, to be completed within 45–50 minutes.

How do I organise my answer?

(Sample question 1)

'Frost makes skilful use of a variety of stylistic features to tell dramatic stories that often have a universal significance.' To what extent do you agree or disagree with this statement? Support your answer with reference to the poetry of Robert Frost on your course.

Sample Plan 1

Intro: (*Stance: agree with viewpoint in the question*) Despite experiencing personal tragedy, Frost believed in endurance, 'life – it goes on'. Through dramatic stories of universal relevance, he delights and shocks in poems that include vivid imagery, powerful sound effects, dynamic personification and the innovative use of traditional poetic forms.

Point 1: (*Randomness of life – imagery, onomatopoeia*) '"Out, Out—"' stoically portrays unfairness and unpredictability of human experience. Dramatic account of a tragic accident. Onomatopoeic verbs ('snarled', 'rattled') convey dangerous working conditions in yard. In contrast, beauty of landscape is depicted through serene imagery.

NOTE

In keeping with the PCLM approach, the student has to take a stance by agreeing and/or disagreeing that Frost makes skilful use of:

- **a variety of stylistic features** (vivid imagery, symbols and metaphors, striking onomatopoeia, personification, repetition, contrast, direct dialogue, colloquialisms, traditional poetic forms, formal rhyme, variety of tones and atmospheres, etc.)

... to tell:

- **dramatic stories with universal significance** (reflections on randomness and unfairness of life, isolation and cruelty of human existence, beauty of nature, creativity, order, transience, endurance, acceptance, etc.)

Point 2: (*Isolation – sonnet form*) 'Acquainted with the Night' addresses the global collapse of human communication in a hostile urban setting. Breaks with traditional sonnet form to describe the descent into hell. Concluding rhyming couplet offers no comfort ('time was neither wrong nor right'). The speaker's lonely story illustrates the hostility of a nightmarish world.

Point 3: (*Boundaries – personification, direct speech*) 'Mending Wall' explores the function of borders ('walling in or walling out'). Anecdote of Frost and his neighbour highlights a general truth ('Good fences make good neighbors'). Colloquial speech brings the scene to life. Personification creates nature's dynamic force which abhors boundaries ('sends the frozen-ground-swell under it').

Point 4: (*Order – imagery, tone*) 'Design' challenges human attempts to see order in the universe. Anecdote leads to intense reflection about our world. Revolting imagery ('spider, fat and white') and a menacing tone ('dead wings carried') shows a disturbing environment. Rhetorical questions demand an explanation for this random cruelty.

Conclusion: Effective use of stylistic devices convey Frost's dramatic stories of universal significance, creating poetry which 'begins in delight and ends in wisdom'.

Sample Paragraph: Point 1

'"Out, Out—"' is a chilling account that recreates a true-life tale, in which a boy loses his hand in an saw-mill accident. The poem focuses on how this isolated incident signifies the random nature of everyday life. Frost often writes about the isolation of the individual and the mystery of human existence. The tragic accident is outlined in a series of graphic images. The menacing buzz-saw 'snarled and rattled' repeatedly, like a predator circling. The dramatic event is made more shocking by being played out against the serene background of a beautiful rural landscape, conveyed in flowing run-on lines: 'Five mountain ranges one behind the other/Under the sunset far into Vermont'. The poet presents us with the painful universal truth of the finality of death. The little boy died, 'that ended it'. This is the sober realisation of the awful reality of death, 'No more to build on'. Frost concludes with the unsettling fact that despite terrible tragedy, life goes on regardless. This shocking story effectively uses poetic devices to relate the universal experience of the continuation of life in spite of tremendous suffering and grief.

EXAMINER'S COMMENT

There is a clear sense of engagement with the poem's themes in this well-written high-grade response. While both elements of the question are addressed, some consideration might have been given to setting, characters and sound effects. Expression is excellent throughout and there is some good discussion on graphic imagery. Textual support is good and the point about the contrasting 'serene background' is impressive.

(Sample question 2)

'From your study of the poetry of Robert Frost on your course, select the poems that, in your opinion, best show his effective use of specific places to communicate a sense of alienation and the barriers that exist between people. Justify your selection by showing how Frost's effective use of specific places communicates a sense of alienation and the barriers that exist between people.

Sample Plan 2

Intro: (*Stance: agree with viewpoint in the question*) Frost uses detailed description of various locations to explore themes of loneliness, powerlessness, transience and ageing through simple colloquial language, vibrant imagery, symbols and onomatopoeia.

Point 1: (*New England farm – sound effects*) 'After Apple-Picking' explores the surreal moment between consciousness and unconsciousness ('I am drowsing off') using irregular rhythm ('For all/That struck the earth') and sibilance ('Essence of winter's sleep'). This dramatic sense of alienation is rooted in a specific place and time, at the end of the harvest on a New England farm.

Point 2: (*Autumnal wood – simple language*) 'The Road Not Taken' highlights the moment when a person stands alone, separated from all others, trying to make a decision ('Then took'). It is set in a precise place, a forked road in an autumn wood ('a yellow wood'). Frost affirms individuality. Simple language conveys the deep philosophical analysis.

Point 3: (*Birch wood in winter – metaphor, onomatopoeia*) 'Birches' uses the metaphor of a child swinging on the trees as a metaphor to transcend the harsh realities of life ('I'd like to get away from earth awhile'). The particular place is evoked through onomatopoeia ('cracks and crazes their enamel') to link the thoughtful exploration to reality.

Point 4: (*Pools in winter – assonance, monosyllables*) 'Spring Pools' lyrically addresses nature's destructive capabilities, loss and transience through slender assonance ('chill and shiver'). Loss is effectively conveyed through monosyllabic verbs ('blot', 'sweep'). This insightful exploration on isolation is set in a very real location.

NOTE

In keeping with the PCLM approach, the student has to agree or disagree that Frost's poems best show:

- **effective use of specific places** (rural locations provide the backdrop for personal reflection and decision-making, natural settings associated with self-discovery, birch woods evoke childhood, work-places universalise human experiences, alienated urban scenes reflect modern life through haunting atmospheres, sensory imagery, repetition, simple language, sound effects, etc.)

... to communicate:

- **a sense of alienation and the barriers that exist between people** (loss, loneliness, decay, separateness, sleep/ consciousness, insights, transcendence, etc.)

Conclusion: Poet roots his deeply thoughtful poetry exploring alienation and isolation by placing them in realistically detailed settings, a New England landscape, a forked road in an autumnal wood, climbing ice-laden birch trees and reflective pools at the close of winter.

Sample Paragraph: Point 2

Frost sets 'The Road Not Taken' in a specific place, a remote country wood, 'Two roads diverged in a yellow wood'. He examines the moment every human dreads, standing alone making a decision, 'Then took'. All humans want to have everything, 'sorry I could not travel both', but there is an overwhelming barrier to this in human life. When a decision is made there is no going back, 'I doubted if I should ever come back'. The poet praises, not human community, but human individualism, 'I took the one less traveled by and that has made all the difference'. Frost uses simple language to convey deep philosophical reflection on decision-making, 'both that morning equally lay in leaves no step had trodden black'. The poem highlights the loneliness of modern life where individuals are constantly faced with tough decisions.

EXAMINER'S COMMENT

This middle-grade response includes some worthwhile commentary on the theme of decision-making. This is supported well with relevant quotation. A more developed discussion would have focused in greater detail on the poet's use of symbolism, contrasting tones and the effectiveness of simple language. Frost uses all of these features to universalise his views about alienation.

Leaving Cert Sample Essay

'Frost's evocative portrayal of the world of nature is conveyed through simple language, sensuous imagery and vivid symbolism.' To what extent do you agree or disagree with this view? Support your answer with reference to Frost's subject matter and writing style in his prescribed poems.

Sample Essay

1. Many of Frost's poems are closely connected with nature – often in rural New England settings. He usually begins by observing nature and then proceeds to finding some connection to the experience of humans. For Frost, the natural world is not just beautiful, but is also an inspiration. At times, nature seems to become a central character in his poetry rather than merely a background. Frost's poetic style is generally simple and direct. Yet there are often layers of meaning in poems such as 'After Apple-Picking', 'Mending Wall' and 'Spring Pools'. His writing is subtle as well, filled with rich symbolism and sensuous imagery.

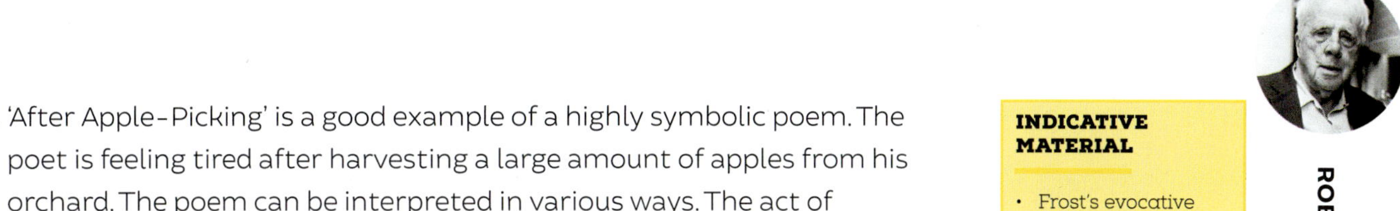

2. 'After Apple-Picking' is a good example of a highly symbolic poem. The poet is feeling tired after harvesting a large amount of apples from his orchard. The poem can be interpreted in various ways. The act of harvesting can be seen as a symbol for the daily work in life. In Frost's case, this might refer to his own creative ability to write poetry. The poem is sometimes seen as an acceptance of ageing. Frost is in the autumn of his life and is now prepared for death – 'toward heaven still'. Although he has regrets – 'there's a barrel that I didn't fill' – he is easing gently from this earthly life, 'Essence of winter sleep is on the night … I am drowsing off'. The sensual language suggests he is caught between reality and otherworldliness. This is emphasised by the gentle sibilant 's' sounds.

3. The description throughout the poem is simple, with some everyday conversational expressions and easy natural rhythms – 'I keep hearing from the cellar bin the rumbling sound of apples coming in'. Frost's writing is rich and vivid. The poem conveys a strange sense of exhaustion and disorientation which affects his senses. His outlook is compared to looking at the world through a thin sheet of ice – 'I skimmed this morning from the drinking trough'. In this trance-like state, everything is slightly distorted, especially the colourful magnified apples which reveal all their small marks close up – 'every fleck of russet showing clear'. The poem ends uncertainly – but still set in the world of nature. Frost drifts off to sleep – 'whatever sleep it is'. One suggestion is that he is saying that all of life and death is mysterious – as symbolised by the cycle of nature.

4. Other poems by Frost use rural landscapes and homely farmers to illustrate ordinary day-to-day living. 'Mending Wall' tells a simple story of Frost and his neighbour. The two men meet in friendship every year to re-build a stone wall that forms the border between their farms. The poet seems to depict nature as a negative force. He suggests, half playfully, that there is a mysterious force that 'does not love a wall'. Presumably, this is nature personified. While he himself sees no real need for a barrier, his neighbour is convinced that 'Good fences make good neighbors'. There are many examples of powerful images – the two men build with their bare hands and are tired from lifting boulders – 'We wear our fingers rough with handling them'. The vowel sounds give a strong sense of their coarse texture. Other memorable images are of the ground swelling under the wall, the farmers using a 'spell' to keep the rocks balanced. Nature provides a setting for this small drama. At one stage, the neighbour raises a rock that makes Frost imagine him as 'an old-stone savage armed'. The poet sees him as a possible threat – 'He moves on darkness'. Once again, Frost finds symbolic meaning in a small-scale natural ritual.

INDICATIVE MATERIAL

- Frost's evocative portrayal of nature (poet's close personal affinity with the natural world, nature is beautiful, dark and mysterious, often used as a background metaphor to explore the poet's views on life, realistic attitude to the natural cycle, clarifies humanity's place in the world, etc.)

.... is conveyed through:

- simple language, sensuous imagery and vivid symbolism (colloquial language, direct speech, natural speech rhythms, striking images, vibrant symbols and metaphors, suggestive sounds, etc.)

5. In 'The Tuft of Flowers', he observes a field that another man has cut. His mood is shown by the image of the butterfly searching for the flower that's been cut down. As usual, Frost finds hidden meanings about life's loneliness. But as he admires the flowers, he engages with the world around him. His eyes are opened to the beauty. He celebrates the beauty of the natural world. In one vivid image, he describes the flower's colours as being like flames leaping – 'A leaping tongue of bloom'. By contrast, 'Spring Pools' takes a disturbing approach to nature. Frost describes trees soaking up the spring pools. They are soon covered in leaves. They 'blot out' forest flowers. Everything is changed – and beauty destroyed – in the natural cycle. The water reflects 'the total sky'. But there is a sense of a dark side to nature. Both these poems show Frost's broad view of nature.

6. In conclusion, nature plays a key role in Frost's poetry – often providing a basis for insights about the mystery of life. His poems use plain, everyday language, but also include startling symbols and vivid sensuous language. New England settings are used as the background of numerous poems where Frost gives a vivid portrayal of nature's fragile beauty.

(805 words)

EXAMINER'S COMMENT

Good overall response that tackles all the main aspects of the question. Some close analysis of style – particularly sound – in paragraph 4. Impressive phrasing (e.g. 'a strange sense of exhaustion and disorientation', 'a small-scale natural ritual'). Focused critical commentary supported by accurate quotation ranges widely over several key poems. Impressive expression up to paragraph 4 – but occasional lapses in language control towards the end. Paragraph 5 was repetitive and note-like. Succinct conclusion rounded off the essay effectively.

GRADE: H2
P = 14/15
C = 13/15
L = 12/15
M = 5/5
Total = 44/50

 Revision Overview

'The Tuft of Flowers'
Lyrical soliloquy meditating on themes of loneliness and methods of communication.

'Mending Wall'
Dramatic monologue addresses two contrasting perspectives (narrator/neighbour).

'After Apple-Picking'
Thought-provoking monologue inspired by the annual harvest leads to contemplation of creative process.

'The Road Not Taken'
Simple narrative exploring themes of individualism, personal choice and the consequences of making decisions.

'Birches'
Detailed descriptive nature poem reveals poet's philosophy on life.

'"Out, Out–"'
Dramatic narrative poem about a shocking fatal accident, widening to meditation on the brevity of human existence and nature's indifference.

'Spring Pools'
Lyrical poem presents nature's destructive capabilities – blight, darkness, death. The natural world can renew itself, yet time dominates creation.

'Acquainted with the Night'
Dark meditative sonnet. Lyrical exploration of isolation and difficulties of communication through dramatic presentation of lonely figure in alien cityscape.

'Design'
Stimulating sonnet challenges accepted belief in ordered universe and benign creator.

'Provide, Provide'
Wry illustration of time's ravages and consequences. Contrasting images of youth/age, beauty/ugliness, wealth/poverty.

Last Words

'Like a piece of ice on a hot stove, the poem must ride on its own melting.'
Robert Frost

'Robert Frost: the icon of the Yankee values, the smell of wood smoke, the sparkle of dew, the reality of farm-house dung, the jocular honesty of an uncle.'
Derek Walcott

'I'll say that again, in case you missed it first time round.'
Robert Frost

RELATIONSHIPS

NATURE

MEANING OF LIFE

TIME

TRAVEL/ JOURNEYS

SUFFERING

Seamus Heaney 1939–2013

'Walk on air against your better judgement.'

Seamus Heaney was born in 1939 in Co. Derry, the eldest of nine children. He was accepted into Queen's University, Belfast in 1957 to study English Language and Literature. Heaney's poetry first came to public attention in the 1960s, when he and a number of other poets, including Michael Longley and Derek Mahon, came to prominence. They all shared the same fate of being born into a society that was deeply divided along religious grounds and was to become immersed in violence, intimidation and sectarianism. In 1966, Heaney's first poetry collection, *Death of a Naturalist*, was published. Throughout the 1970s, he was publishing prolifically and giving public readings. He has also written several volumes of criticism. Widely regarded as the finest poet of his generation, he was awarded the Nobel Prize for Literature in 1995 'for works of lyrical beauty and ethical depth, which exalt everyday miracles and the living past'. In accepting the award, Heaney stated that his life had been 'a journey into the wideness of language, a journey where each point of arrival ... turned out to be a stepping stone rather than a destination'.

Investigate Further

To find out more about Seamus Heaney, or to hear readings of his poems not already available in your eBook, you could search some useful websites, such as YouTube, BBC Poetry, poetryfoundation.org and poetryarchive.org, or access additional material on this page of your eBook.

Prescribed Poems

○ **1 'The Forge'**
At one level, the poem celebrates a traditional craft. However, its central focus is on the mystery and beauty of the creative process itself. **Page 234**

○ **2 'Bogland'**
The poet contrasts the expansive North American grasslands with the narrowly bounded landscape of Ireland's boglands. **Page 238**

○ **3 'The Tollund Man'**
Photographs of the preserved body of an Iron Age man found in the bogs of Denmark, prompted Heaney to trace parallels between the imagined circumstances of the Tollund Man's death and more recent violence in the North of Ireland. **Page 242**

○ **4 'Mossbawn: Sunlight'**
This wonderfully atmospheric poem is a nostalgic celebration of the poet's childhood on the family farm in Co. Derry and his close relationship with his aunt. **Page 247**

○ **5 'A Constable Calls' (OL)**
Based on another memory from his boyhood, the poet describes an uneasy encounter when his father was questioned by a local policeman. **Page 251**

○ **6 'The Skunk'**
Sensuous language and an edgy, romantic atmosphere enhance this unusual and playful love poem. **Page 256**

○ **7 'The Harvest Bow'**
A tightly wrought personal poem based on the central image of a decorative 'throwaway love-knot'. The straw bow provides a physical link between Heaney and his father, the present and the past, nature and art. **Page 260**

○ **8 'The Underground' (OL)**
Based on a memory from their honeymoon, the poem explores the enduring love between Heaney and his wife. **Page 264**

○ **9 'Postscript'**
In this short lyric, the poet succeeds in conveying the extraordinary through an everyday experience – the memory of a vivid journey westward to the Co. Clare coastline. **Page 268**

○ **10 'A Call' (OL)**
Another poem dealing with two of Heaney's favourite themes: the father–son relationship and the passing of time. **Page 271**

○ **11 'Tate's Avenue'**
In this beautifully discreet and understated love poem, Heaney recalls three car rugs that mark important stages in the changing relationship between himself and his wife. **Page 275**

○ **12 'The Pitchfork'**
Another typical Heaney poem, celebrating traditional rural life. The poet makes 'a journey back into the heartland of the ordinary', where he is both observer and visionary. **Page 279**

○ **13 'Lightenings viii'**
In his short account of how a mysterious floating air-ship appeared above the monks' oratory at Clonmacnoise monastery, Heaney blurs the lines between reality and illusion and challenges our ideas about life. **Page 283**

*(OL) indicates poems that are also prescribed for the Ordinary Level course.

1 The Forge

Title: the forge refers to a blacksmith's workshop, where iron implements are made and mended. (In the poem, a smith is shaping horseshoes.)

All I know is a door into the dark.
Outside, old axles and iron hoops rusting;
Inside, the hammered anvil's short-pitched ring,
The unpredictable fantail of sparks
Or hiss when a new shoe toughens in water.
The anvil must be somewhere in the centre,
Horned as a unicorn, at one end square,
Set there immoveable: an altar
Where he expends himself in shape and music.
Sometimes, leather-aproned, hairs in his nose,
He leans out on the jamb, recalls a clatter
Of hoofs where traffic is flashing in rows;
Then grunts and goes in, with a slam and a flick
To beat real iron out, to work the bellows.

axles: bars or shafts on which wheels rotate.
anvil: iron block that the smith uses as a work surface.

unicorn: mythical animal (usually a white horse) with a spiralled horn growing from its forehead.
expends: burns up, expresses.

jamb: upright door support.

bellows: instrument for drawing air into a fire.

'The unpredictable fantail of sparks'

Personal Response

1. Describe the poet's attitude to the forge. Is he fascinated or fearful, or both? Support your answer with reference to the poem.
2. Based on your study of the poem, what is your impression of the blacksmith?
3. Comment on the effectiveness of the phrase 'The unpredictable fantail of sparks'.

Critical Literacy

'The Forge' comes from Seamus Heaney's second collection, *Door into the Dark*, which was published in 1969. The sonnet form has a clear division of an octave (the first eight lines) and a sestet (the final six lines). While the octave, apart from its initial reference to the narrator, focuses on the inanimate objects and occurrences inside and outside the forge, the sestet describes the blacksmith and his work.

The poem's opening line ('All I know is a door into the dark') is both modest and assured. There is also a **mystical undertone** (a sense of otherworldliness) as Heaney revisits his childhood and his fascination with a local forge. The image, with its negative and mysterious connotations, incites our curiosity and invites us to find out what answers lie beyond. The poet recalls unwanted objects strewn outside, 'old axles and iron hoops rusting'. The irregular rhythm in line 2 suggests the disorder of what has been discarded. He **contrasts** the lifeless exterior scene with the vigorous atmosphere ('the hammered anvil's short-pitched ring') inside the forge. The world outside is decrepit and old, a wasteland, whereas the noisy forge is a place of brilliant sparks where iron is beaten out and renewed.

Heaney's visual and aural images are characteristically striking. His vivid metaphor of 'The unpredictable fantail of sparks' (line 4) lets us see the glorious flurry of erratic flashing light and hear the twang of reverberating iron.

Onomatopoeic effects add to our sense of the physical activity taking place as the blacksmith works on a new horseshoe. Suddenly, the incandescent metal begins to 'hiss when a new shoe toughens in water'. The **tone is sympathetic** and attentive as the poet reimagines the smells, sounds and tactile impressions of the blacksmith's workshop.

Lines 6–9 contain the sonnet's central image of the smith's anvil: 'an altar/ Where he expends himself in shape and music'. Interestingly, the transition from the octave to the sestet is a run-on (or enjambment) based around this key metaphor. One effect of this is to enable us to experience the anvil as a **sacred or magical point of transition** between the material and

immovable world of everyday life and the fluid, imaginative world of human consciousness. Heaney stresses the **mystery of the creative process**, associating it with the mythical creature of medieval fiction, 'Horned as a unicorn'. Although the simile seems somewhat strained, the comparison with a legendary beast still serves to highlight the mysterious qualities ('shape and music') of poetry.

The final lines focus on the blacksmith's physical characteristics. **Heaney leaves us with a down-to-earth image of a gruff, hardworking man**, 'leather-aproned, hairs in his nose'. Is the poet suggesting that art – and poetry in particular – is independent of education and social class? Seemingly wary of the world at large, the smith remembers an earlier era of horse-drawn carriages, when his skills were fully appreciated. Contrasting images of 'a clatter/Of hoofs' and modern traffic 'flashing in rows' reflect the changes he has lived through. In the end, he grudgingly accepts that he must return 'into the dark' and resume doing what he does best: 'To beat real iron out, to work the bellows'.

Heaney's poem can immediately be read as an elegy to the past and a lament for the lost tradition of the blacksmith. Readers can also interpret the anvil as a metaphor of an unreachable heritage, a traditional craft made redundant by modernisation. Many critics have seen the blacksmith figure as a **symbol or construction of the role of the poet**, one who opens the 'door into the dark', the creative artist who ritually 'expends himself in shape and music' and who 'grunts' and flicks words and language, forging his poems. As with so much of Heaney's work, the poem shows his ability to subtly evoke resonance by making us wonder.

Writing About the Poem

'Seamus Heaney's descriptive powers often endow portraits of local people with mythic qualities.' Discuss this statement with reference to 'The Forge'.

Sample Paragraph

In Heaney's elegy to the past, the disappearing tradition of the local blacksmith is brought vividly to life. Through dynamic sound effects ('ring', 'hiss') combined with the use of the compound word 'short-pitched', Heaney presents us with the imposing portrait of a powerful craftsman turning metal into useful farming tools. This unassuming blacksmith who 'grunts and goes in' is given another persona, one of epic quality. He becomes a High Priest at his 'altar', the anvil. We get a sense of legendary times, suggested by the image of the anvil shape, 'Horned as a unicorn'. The poet envisions the surly craftsman in a mythical role,

changing one everyday substance into something special. Like Heaney himself, the priest is involved in the mysterious creative process. Yet the description of the anvil's shape is firmly rooted in physical reality – one end is shaped like a horn. The blacksmith too is exactly described, 'warts and all'. He stands, 'leather-aproned, hairs in his nose', but he has the ability to control the constructive power of fire. Monosyllabic sounds highlight his magical skills, 'with a slam and a flick/To beat real iron out'. Reality and legend blend seamlessly.

EXAMINER'S COMMENT

This mature top-grade response focuses well on Heaney's powers of description – particularly his use of aural effects. The more challenging aspect of 'mythic qualities' is handled successfully, with clear points linking the anvil and altar. Expression is carefully controlled, using varied sentence lengths and a wide-ranging vocabulary (e.g. 'dynamic', 'persona', envisions'). Apt quotations are also used throughout.

Class/Homework Exercises

1. 'Heaney's visual and aural imagery depict a harsh, rural life with lyrical beauty.' Discuss this statement in relation to 'The Forge'.
2. 'Many of Heaney's carefully crafted poems are populated with characters who have made a deep impression on him.' Discuss this view with reference to 'The Forge'.

Summary Points

- **Lament for and preservation of a traditional craft and rural life.**
- **Interesting experimental use of structure and rhyme scheme of sonnet form.**
- **Clever contrasts – exterior/interior, past/present, reality/legend.**
- **Striking sound effects – onomatopoeia, assonance, sibilant 's'.**
- **Sensuous visual images and symbols create a powerful sense of time and place.**

2 Bogland

for T.P. Flanagan

We have no prairies
To slice a big sun at evening –
Everywhere the eye concedes to
Encroaching horizon,

Is wooed into the cyclops' eye
Of a tarn. Our unfenced country
Is bog that keeps crusting
Between the sights of the sun.

They've taken the skeleton
Of the Great Irish Elk
Out of the peat, set it up
An astounding crate full of air.

Butter sunk under
More than a hundred years
Was recovered salty and white.
The ground itself is kind, black butter

Melting and opening underfoot,
Missing its last definition
By millions of years.
They'll never dig coal here,

Only the waterlogged trunks
Of great firs, soft as pulp.
Our pioneers keep striking
Inwards and downwards,

Every layer they strip
Seems camped on before.
The bogholes might be Atlantic seepage.
The wet centre is bottomless.

prairies: a large open area of grassland (in North America).

concedes: gives way to; admits defeat.

Encroaching: advancing gradually beyond acceptable limits.

wooed: courted, enticed.

cyclops' eye: in Greek mythology, a race of one-eyed giants.

tarn: small mountain lake.

Great Irish Elk: large northern deer found preserved in Irish bogland.

definition: transformation (into coal).

pioneers: adventurers, explorers.

seepage: the slow escape of liquid through a material.

Personal Response

1. In your opinion, what is Heaney's central theme or point in this poem? Briefly explain your response.
2. How does Heaney employ the senses to allow the reader to share in his experience of the bogland? Refer closely to the poem in your answer.
3. Trace the poet's tone throughout the poem. Comment on where, how and why, in your opinion, the tone changes. Support your views with reference to the text.

Critical Literacy

'Bogland' (1969) is the result of a Halloween holiday Heaney spent with T.P. Flanagan (the artist to whom this poem is dedicated). Flanagan recalls that 'the bogland was burnt the colour of marmalade'. Heaney felt it was 'one of the most important poems' he had written because 'it was something like a symbol. I felt the poem was a promise of something else ... it represented a free place for me'. He thought the bogland was a 'landscape that remembered everything that happened in and to it'. Heaney recalled when they were children that they were told 'not to go near the bog because there was no bottom to it'.

In the opening stanza, a **comparison** is drawn between the American prairies ('We have no prairies') and Ireland's bogs. Heaney said, 'At that time, I had ...

'Encroaching horizon,/Is wooed into the cyclops' eye/Of a tarn'

been reading about the frontier and the west as an important myth in the American consciousness, so I set up – or rather, laid down – the bog as an answering Irish myth'. The prairie in America represents the vastness of the country, **its unfenced expanse a metaphor for the freedom of its people** to pursue their dreams and express their beliefs. At first, Ireland's bog represents opposite values. It seems narrow, constricting and inward looking: 'the eye concedes', 'Encroaching horizon', 'cyclops' eye'. In America, the pioneers moved across the country. In Ireland, the pioneers looked 'Inwards and downwards', remembering, almost wallowing in, the past. Is the poet suggesting that Ireland is defined by the layers of its difficult history? Or is each set of pioneers on an adventure, one set discovering new places, the other set rediscovering forgotten places?

Stanza two captures the **bog's fluidity** in the onomatopoeic phrase 'keeps crusting/Between the sights of the sun'. Heaney draws the changing face of the bog, its element of mystery and danger, as it did not always remain exactly the same, but subtly fluctuates. The poet's sense of awe at this place is expressed in stanza three as he recounts the discovery of the Great Irish Elk as 'An astounding crate full of air'. Here the poet is referring to another aspect of the bog – its **ability to preserve the past**.

In stanza four, the bog's capacity to hold and preserve is emphasised when 'Butter sunk under/More than a hundred years' was recovered fit for use, 'salty and white'. This place is 'kind'. Stanza four runs into stanza five in a parallel reference to the bog's fluidity. The bog never becomes hard; 'its last definition' is 'Missing', so it will never yield coal. The squidgy nature of the bog is conveyed in stanza six in the phrase 'soft as pulp'. The phrases of the poem are opening and melting into each other in imitation of the bog. Is this in stark contrast to the hardening prejudices of the two communities in the North of Ireland? **The Irish explore their past**; to them, history is important as they 'keep striking/Inwards and downwards'.

Heaney leaves us with an **open-ended conclusion** in stanza seven. He remembers that the bog 'seemed to have some kind of wind blowing through it that could carry on'. The boglands are feminine, nurturing, welcoming: 'The wet centre is bottomless'. The poet is aware of the depth and complexity of the national consciousness. Should we, like the bog, embrace all aspects of our national identity? Is this how we should carry on? Is there a final truth? Is it unreachable? The poem is written in seven spare, unrhymed stanzas and uses casual, almost colloquial language.

Writing About the Poem

'Through the rich musicality of his poetry, Seamus Heaney evokes the difficulty of establishing a national identity.' Discuss this statement with reference to 'Bogland'.

Sample Paragraph

A collective pronoun, 'We', opens 'Bogland'. However, the poet suggests that the Irish define themselves negatively in comparison to the vast open expanse of America, 'We have no prairies'. While their pioneers move forward in their exploration of new territories, ours dig 'Inwards and downwards'. We seem to be in danger of being seduced, almost deformed by our concern with history, 'wooed into the cyclops' eye/Of a tarn'. Yet, through his visual and aural description of the bog, Heaney succeeds in creating a proud symbol of nationhood and belonging. The bog – just like our history – preserves, becoming a repository of treasures, both natural ('the Great Irish Elk') and manmade ('Butter ... recovered salty and white'). We, the Irish, are an accumulation of many narratives, 'Every layer they strip/Seems camped on before'. The bog symbolises a nation in a perpetual state of change. Hard 'k' and 'c' sounds ('keeps crusting') capture the thin surface which breaks to reveal the soft interior of the bog, 'kind black butter'. Run-on lines echo the ever-changing nature of the bog and history, 'soft as pulp'. History continues forever.

EXAMINER'S COMMENT

A close sensitive analysis of the poem, engaging with the subtle connections between its musical language and the theme of identity. Very good range of informed and incisive points on symbolism, sound effects and run-on lines. Expression is varied and controlled. Excellent use of reference and quotation throughout add to the quality of the discussion in this top-grade response.

Class/Homework Exercises

1. 'Heaney's sensuous imagery often evokes a haunting and dramatic sense of place.' To what extent is this true of 'Bogland'? Support your answer with reference to the poem.
2. 'Through his succinct and exact use of language, Seamus Heaney enables us to make sense of the world and ourselves.' Discuss this view with reference to 'Bogland'.

Summary Points

- **Importance of history and identity expressed through the central symbol of bogland.**
- **Free verse, lack of rhyme and rhythm mimic the fluid nature of the bog.**
- **Contrasting tones of insecurity, awe and amazement turn to quiet reflection.**
- **Use of striking sound effects, visual imagery, personification and allusions to myth.**
- **Structure of poem imitates activity of digging – short lines drill down the page, while stacked stanzas reflect the layered nature of the bog.**

3 The Tollund Man

The Tollund Man: a reference to the well-preserved body found in 1950 by two turfcutters in Tollund, Denmark. The man had been hanged over 2,000 years earlier. One theory suggested that his death had been part of a ritualistic fertility sacrifice. The Tollund Man's head was put on display in a museum at Aarhus.

I

Some day I will go to Aarhus
To see his peat-brown head,
The mild pods of his eye-lids,
His pointed skin cap.

In the flat country near by
Where they dug him out,
His last gruel of winter seeds
Caked in his stomach,

Naked except for
The cap, noose and girdle,
I will stand a long time.
Bridegroom to the goddess,

She tightened her torc on him
And opened her fen,
Those dark juices working
Him to a saint's kept body,

Trove of the turfcutters'
Honeycombed workings.
Now his stained face
Reposes at Aarhus.

II

I could risk blasphemy,
Consecrate the cauldron bog
Our holy ground and pray
Him to make germinate

The scattered, ambushed
Flesh of labourers,
Stockinged corpses
Laid out in the farmyards,

Aarhus: a city in Jutland, Denmark.

pods: dry seeds.

gruel: thin porridge.

girdle: belt.

torc: decorative metal collar.

fen: marsh or wet area.

kept: preserved.

Trove: valuable find.

Honeycombed workings: patterns made by the turfcutters on the peat.

blasphemy: irreverence.

Consecrate: declare sacred.

cauldron bog: basin-shaped bogland (some of which was associated with pagan rituals).

germinate: give new life to.

Tell-tale skin and teeth
Flecking the sleepers
Of four young brothers, trailed
For miles along the lines.

III

Something of his sad freedom
As he rode the tumbril
Should come to me, driving,
Saying the names

Tollund, Grauballe, Nebelgard,

Watching the pointing hands
Of country people,
Not knowing their tongue.

Out there in Jutland
In the old man-killing parishes
I will feel lost,
Unhappy and at home.

sleepers: wooden beams underneath railway lines.
four young brothers: refers to an infamous atrocity in the 1920s when four Catholic brothers were killed by the police.

tumbril: two-wheeled cart used to carry a condemned person to execution.

Tollund, Grauballe, Nebelgard: places in Jutland.

'Something of his sad freedom'

Personal Response

1. Comment on Heaney's tone in the first three stanzas of the poem.
2. Select one image from the poem that you find startling or disturbing and explain its effectiveness.
3. What is your understanding of the poem's final stanza? Refer closely to the text in your answer.

Critical Literacy

Seamus Heaney was attracted to a book by P.V. Glob, *The Bog People*, which dealt with preserved Iron Age bodies of people who had been ritually killed. It offered him a particular frame of reference or set of symbols he could employ to engage with Ireland's historical conflict. The martyr image of the Tollund Man blended in the poet's mind with photographs of other atrocities, past and present, in the long rites of Irish political struggles. This elegiac poem comes from Heaney's third collection, *Wintering Out* (1972).

Part I opens quietly with the **promise of a pilgrimage**: 'Some day I will go to Aarhus'. The tone is expectant, determined. Yet there is also an element of detachment that is reinforced by the Danish place name, 'Aarhus'. Heaney's placid, almost reverential mood is matched by his economic use of language, dominated by simple monosyllables. The evocative description of the Tollund Man's 'peat-brown head' and 'The mild pods of his eye-lids' conveys a sense of gentleness and passivity.

Lines 5–11 focus on the dead man's final hours in a much more realistic way. Heaney suggests that the Tollund Man's own journey begins when 'they dug him out', destroyed and elevated at the same time. The poet's meticulous observations ('His last gruel of winter seeds/Caked in his stomach') emphasise the dead man's **innocent vulnerability**. In the aftermath of a ritualistic hanging, we see him abandoned: 'Naked except for/The cap, noose and girdle'. While the poet identifies himself closely with the victim and makes a respectful promise to 'stand a long time', the action itself is passive.

Heaney imagines the natural boglands as the body of a fertility goddess. The revelation that the sacrificial victim was 'Bridegroom to the goddess' (line 12) conveys a more **ominous, forceful tone** as the bleak bog itself is also equated with Ireland, female and overwhelming: 'She tightened her torc on him'. Sensuous and energetic images in lines 13–16 suggest the physical intimacy of the couple's deadly embrace. The Tollund Man becomes 'a saint's kept body', almost a surrogate Christ, buried underground so that new life would spring up. He is left to chance, 'Trove of the turfcutters', and finally resurrected so that 'his stained face/Reposes at Aarhus'. The delicate blend of sibilance and broad vowel sounds suggest tranquillity and a final peace.

Part II suddenly becomes more emphatic and is filled with references to religion. Heaney addresses the spirit of the Tollund Man, invoking him 'to make germinate' (line 24) and give life back to the casualties of more recent violence in Northern Ireland. He acknowledges his own discomfort ('I could risk blasphemy') for suggesting that we should search for an alternative deity or religious symbol to unite people. But although it appears to be in contrast with the earlier violence, the poet's restrained style actually accentuates the horror of one infamous sectarian slaughter ('Of four young brothers'). The callous nature of their deaths – 'trailed/For miles along the lines' – is associated with the repulsive rituals in ancient Jutland. Heaney's **nightmarish images** ('Stockinged corpses') are powerful and create a surreal effect. However, the paradoxical 'survival' and repose of the Tollund Man should, the poet implies, give him the power to raise others.

Part III returns to the mellow beginning, but instead of anticipation, there is sorrow and a sense of isolation. Heaney hopes that the 'sad freedom' (line 33) of the Tollund Man 'Should come to me'. Along with religion and a sense of history and myth, evocative language is central to Heaney's poetry,

and here the idea of isolation is brought sharply to the reader through the sense of being 'lost' in a foreign land. Yet ultimately the paradoxical nature of exile is realised: the poet feels at home in a state of homelessness, and welcomes the feeling of not belonging to society which he shares with the Tollund Man, who is no longer tied to religious forces. This estrangement from society is emphasised by the list of foreign names ('Tollund, Grauballe, Nebelgard'). **The poem ends on a note of pessimistic resignation** that describes both the familiar sense of isolation and hopelessness Heaney experiences: 'I will feel lost,/Unhappy and at home'.

Heaney's imaginary pilgrimage to Aarhus has led to a **kind of revelation**. By comparing modern Ulster to the 'old man-killing parishes' (line 42) of remote Jutland, the poet places the Northern Irish conflict in a timeless, mythological context. It is as though the only way Heaney can fully express the horrific scenes he has seen in Ireland is to associate them with the exhumed bodies of ancient bog corpses.

Writing About the Poem

'Heaney often addresses the ugliness of human cruelty in subtle poems that are rich in imagery and language use.' Discuss this statement with reference to 'The Tollund Man'.

Sample Paragraph

Throughout 'The Tollund Man', Heaney reflects on the universal experience of human cruelty. He links the ritually murdered body of the Iron Age victim sacrificed to the unnamed 'goddess' to the executions of 'four young brothers' in the Northern Ireland Troubles. A statement of quiet determination opens the poem, 'Some day I will go to Aarhus', its subtle monosyllables emphasising the poet's resolve. The vulnerability of the victim of Jutland's 'man-killing parishes' is shown in the gentle assonance of the vivid visual image, 'The mild pods of his eye-lids'. The pathetic fate of the victims who were dragged 'miles along lines' is also conveyed through slender assonance of the letter 'i'. Harsh 't' and 'ck' sounds suggest the suffering of the young men, 'Tell-tale skin and teeth/Flecking the sleepers'. The barbarity of the Tollund Man's hanging is also conveyed through abrupt sounds. The terrifying goddess 'tightened her torc' around her 'Bridegroom'. Through the meticulous observation of a detached observer, Heaney succeeds in engaging our sympathy for these victims. His use of powerful images and musical language increases our sense of their tragic lives.

EXAMINER'S COMMENT

This is a first-rate response that shows a very close appreciation of both the poem's subject matter and style. Points are clear, succinct and successfully supported with accurate quotations. The two central elements of the question are addressed, with some particularly incisive commentary on subtle sound effects (e.g. 'subtle monosyllables' and 'gentle assonance'). Expression is also impressive ('the meticulous observation of a detached observer').

Class/Homework Exercises

1. 'Heaney explores the unpalatable truth of cyclical violence and complicit acceptance through a lyrical examination of the living past.' Discuss this view, supporting your answer with reference to 'The Tollund Man'.
2. 'There is a haunting dreamlike quality to Seamus Heaney's fascination with history and mythology.' Discuss this statement, supporting your answer with reference to 'The Tollund Man'.

Summary Points

- **Examination of cyclical human violence, vulnerable victims and foreignness.**
- **Varying tones – resolve, reverence, detachment, uncertainty, despair, empathy.**
- **Use of similarity and contrast – Tollund Man/four young brothers; colloquial sound patterns/stately British rhetoric; individual human experience/universal experience.**
- **Lyrical and musical qualities; onomatopoeia, assonance, harsh cacophonous sounds.**
- **Short lines and fragmented rhythm convey the disturbing reality of death.**
- **List of foreign place names has intriguing, unsettling effect.**

4 Mossbawn: Sunlight

for Mary Heaney

There was a sunlit absence.
The helmeted pump in the yard
heated its iron,
water honeyed

in the slung bucket
and the sun stood
like a griddle cooling
against the wall

of each long afternoon.
So, her hands scuffled
over the bakeboard,
the reddening stove

sent its plaque of heat
against her where she stood
in a floury apron
by the window.

Now she dusts the board
with a goose's wing,
now sits, broad-lapped,
with whitened nails

and measling shins:
here is a space
again, the scone rising
to the tick of two clocks.

And here is love
like a tinsmith's scoop
sunk past its gleam
in the meal-bin.

Title: Mossbawn was Heaney's birthplace. 'Bawn' refers to the name the English planters gave to their fortified farmhouses. 'Bán' is Gaelic for 'white'. Heaney wonders if the name could be 'white moss' and has commented, 'In the syllables of my home, I see a metaphor of the split culture of Ulster.'

Dedication: the poem is dedicated to the poet's aunt, Mary Heaney, who lived with the family throughout Heaney's childhood. He shared a special relationship with her, 'a woman with a huge well of affection and a very experienced, dry-eyed sense of the world'.

griddle: circular iron plate used for cooking food.

scuffled: moving quickly, making a scraping noise.

plaque: area of intense heat, originally a hot plate.

measling: red spots on legs made by standing close to heat.

the tick of two clocks: the two time sequences in the poem, past and present.

tinsmith: person who made pots and pans from tin.

meal-bin: a container used to hold flour, etc.

'to the tick of two clocks'

Personal Response

1. Describe the atmosphere in the poem 'Mossbawn', with particular reference to Heaney's treatment of time.
2. What image of Mary Heaney, the aunt, is drawn? Do you find the picture appealing or unappealing? Quote from the poem in support of your views.
3. Choose one image or phrase from the poem that you found particularly effective, and briefly explain why you found it so.

Critical Literacy

'Sunlight' appeared in the collection *North* (1975) and was the first of two poems under the title 'Mossbawn', the name of Heaney's family home. To the poet, this farm was 'the first place', an idyllic Garden of Eden, full of sunlight and feminine grace, a contrast to the reality of the outside world. At this time, terrible atrocities were being committed in the sectarian struggle taking place in the North of Ireland.

This poem opens with a **vivid, atmospheric portrayal of the silent sunlit yard**, a beautiful, tranquil scene from Heaney's boyhood in the 1940s. The pump marked the centre of this private world, which was untroubled by the activities outside. American soldiers had bases in Northern Ireland during the Second World War. For the impressionable Heaney growing up, the water pump was a symbol of purity and life. This guardian of domestic life is described as 'helmeted', a sentry soldier on duty, ready to protect. The phrase 'water honeyed' (line 4) emphasises this slender iron idol as an image of deep and hidden goodness, the centre of another world. The poet creates a nostalgic picture of a timeless zone of domestic ritual and human warmth. These were childhood days of golden innocence and security. The repetition of 'h' (in 'helmeted', 'heated' and 'honeyed') portrays the heating process as the reader exhales breath. The sun is described in the striking simile 'like a

griddle cooling/against the wall'. This homely image of the iron dish of the home-baked flat cake evokes a view of a serene place.

Line 10 moves readers from the place to the person. 'So' introduces us to a **warm, tender portrait of Heaney's beloved Aunt Mary at work.** She is a symbol of the old secure way of life, when a sense of community was firm and traditional rural values were held in high esteem. We are shown the unspectacular routine of work; she 'dusts the board' for baking. We see her domestic skill, her hands 'scuffled' as she kneads the dough. Visual detail paints this picture as if it were a Dutch still life from the artist Vermeer: 'floury apron', 'whitened nails'. The simplicity of this special atmosphere is evident as Heaney acknowledges: 'here is love'. The people in this scene are not glamorous. Realistic details remind us of their ordinariness: 'broad-lapped', 'measling shins'.

The **closing simile** in lines 26–8, 'like a tinsmith's scoop/sunk past its gleam/ in the meal-bin', **shows how the ordinary is transformed into the extraordinary** by the power of love. The two time zones of passing time and a timeless moment are held in the alliterative phrase 'the tick of two clocks'. We are invited to listen to the steady rhythm of the repetitive 't'. As the life-giving water lies unseen beneath the cold earth, the aunt's love is hidden, but constant, like the water in the pump. The radiant glow of love is hidden like a buried light. The change of tenses at the word 'Now' brings the moment closer as the abstract becomes concrete, and the outside becomes inside. The short four-line stanzas run on, achieving their own momentum of contained energy in this still scene, which reaches its climax in the poignant final stanza.

Writing About the Poem

'Seamus Heaney often uses childhood memories to shape sensuous poetry.' Discuss this statement with reference to 'Mossbawn: Sunlight'.

Sample Paragraph

Using a tight structure of seven quatrains, Heaney re-creates his childhood experience through the details of his home life. In recalling his family's farm-yard, the 'helmeted pump' stands as guardian in this idyllic place. It represents the hidden energies of this special setting and the people Heaney remembers. Everything Heaney writes appeals to our senses. The steady repetitive rhythm, run-on lines and assonance ('slung bucket') create a still exterior painting of a quiet landscape. Personification ('the sun stood') adds to the magic. The cinematic quality zooms to an interior shot of his aunt baking in the kitchen. Gentle

onomatopoeic sounds ('scuffled', 'dusts') barely ruffle the surface silence. The poet changes the tense from past to present ('There was', 'here is') while he re-creates the living memory of Mossbawn, which resonates to the sound of the 'tick of two clocks', then and now. Love, in the person of his aunt, resides in this timeless place, concealed but present, conveyed in the beautiful simile of the final lines, like the 'tinsmith's scoop/sunk past its gleam/in the meal-bin'.

EXAMINER'S COMMENT

Succinct top-grade standard that focuses on the effectiveness of Heaney's sensual language. Confidently written and aptly supported by quotations.

Class/Homework Exercises

1. Seamus Heaney's Nobel Prize for Literature was awarded for 'lyrical beauty ... which brings out the miracles of the ordinary day and the living past'. Discuss this statement using reference to both the content and style of 'Mossbawn: Sunlight'.
2. 'Heaney presents readers with small domestic dramas that explore recurring themes of love and longing in his poems.' Discuss this view with particular reference to 'Mossbawn: Sunlight'.

Summary Points

- **Recurring themes of love and yearning.**
- **Slow-moving rhythm complements poignant childhood memories.**
- **Evocative tones of fondness, longing and nostalgia.**
- **Exterior scene contrasted with gentle domestic activity within.**
- **Simple language, warm, homely images.**
- **Striking use of personification, simile and evocative sound effects.**

SEAMUS HEANEY

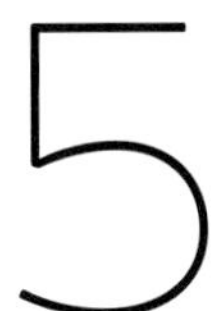

A Constable Calls

His bicycle stood at the window-sill,
The rubber cowl of a mud-splasher
Skirting the front mudguard,
Its fat black handlegrips

Heating in sunlight, the 'spud'
Of the dynamo gleaming and cocked back,
The pedal treads hanging relieved
Of the boot of the law.

His cap was upside down
On the floor, next his chair.
The line of its pressure ran like a bevel
In his slightly sweating hair.

He had unstrapped
The heavy ledger, and my father
Was making tillage returns
In acres, roods, and perches.

Arithmetic and fear.
I sat staring at the polished holster
With its buttoned flap, the braid cord
Looped into the revolver butt.

'Any other root crops?
Mangolds? Marrowstems? Anything like that?'
'No.' But was there not a line
Of turnips where the seed ran out

In the potato field? I assumed
Small guilts and sat
Imagining the black hole in the barracks.
He stood up, shifted the baton-case

Further round on his belt,
Closed the domesday book,
Fitted his cap back with two hands,
And looked at me as he said goodbye.

cowl: covering shaped like a hood.

'spud': potato-like shape.

the boot of the law: heavy footwear of policemen, suggesting power and oppression.

bevel: marked line on policeman's forehead made by his cap.

ledger: book containing records of farm accounts.
tillage returns: amount harvested from cultivated land.

braid: threads woven into a decorative band.

Mangolds: beets grown for animal feed.
Marrowstems: long, green vegetables.

black hole: small cell in the police station.

domesday book: William the Conqueror, the English king, had ordered a survey to be carried out of all the land and its value in England; also refers to Judgement Day, when all will be brought to account.

A shadow bobbed in the window.
He was snapping the carrier spring
Over the ledger. His boot pushed off
And the bicycle ticked, ticked, ticked.

bobbed: moved up and down.
carrier spring: spiral metal coil on the back of a bike used to secure a bag, etc.

'the boot of the law'

Personal Response

1. How does the poet create an atmosphere of tension in this poem? Support your response with reference to the text.
2. What type of relationship do you think the young boy has with his father? Refer closely to the text in your response.
3. Critics disagree about the ending of the poem. Some find it 'false', others 'stunning'. How would you describe the ending? Give reasons for your response.

Critical Literacy

'A Constable Calls' was written in 1975 and forms the second part of the poem sequence 'Singing School'. The Heaneys were a Catholic family. The constable would have been a member of the Royal Ulster Constabulary and probably a Protestant. This poem was written when the tensions between the two communities in Northern Ireland were at their height. Heaney's 'country of community ... was a place of division'.

'A Constable Calls' is written from the **viewpoint of a young boy** caught in the epicentre of the Troubles, a time of recent sectarian violence in Northern Ireland. The poem explores fear and power from the perspective of the Nationalist community. Catholics did not trust the RUC (Royal Ulster Constabulary). In the opening stanzas, crude strength, power and violence are all inherent in the cold, precise language used to describe the constable's bicycle. The 'handlegrips' suggest handcuffs, while the 'cocked back' dynamo hints at a gun ready to explode, its trigger ready for action. It also signifies confidence and cockiness. The oppression of the local authorities is highlighted in the phrase 'the boot of the law'. Heaney personifies the bicycle, which he describes as being 'relieved' of the pressure of the weight of the constable. This poem was written during the civil rights protest marches, when Nationalists were sometimes treated very severely by the RUC. This is evoked in the assonance of the broad vowels in 'fat black' and the harsh-sounding repetition of 'ck' in the phrase 'cocked back'. Here are the observations of the child of a divided community. The character (and symbolic significance) of the constable is implicit in the description of his bicycle.

In stanzas three to five, Heaney gives us an explicit **description of the constable**. His uniform and equipment are all symbols of power, which the young boy notes in detail: 'the polished holster/With its buttoned flap, the braid cord/Looped into the revolver butt'. This is no friendly community police officer. The repetition of 'his' tells us that the possession of power belongs to him and what he represents. He is not a welcome visitor. His hat lies on the ground. He is not offered refreshment, although he is presumably thirsty from his work. Even the one human detail ('slightly sweating hair')

revolts us. Is he as tense as the Catholic family in this time of sectarian conflict? The print of his great authority is stamped on him like a 'bevel', but does his power weigh heavily on him?

The policeman's function was to oblige the boy's father to give an account of his farm crop returns. Their terse exchange underlines the **tension in this troubled community**. The interrogation by the constable consists of four questions: 'Any other root crops?/Mangolds? Marrowstems? Anything like that?' This is met by the father's short, clipped, monosyllabic reply: 'No'. The encounter is summed up succinctly in the line 'Arithmetic and fear'. In the seventh stanza, the young boy becomes alarmed as he realises that his father has omitted to account for 'a line/Of turnips'. He 'assumed/Small guilts'. His perceived Catholic inferiority is graphically shown in the reference to the 'domesday book', or 'ledger', belonging to the constable. The child imagines a day of reckoning, almost like Judgement Day, when God calls every individual to account for past sins. He imagines the immediate punishment of 'the black hole in the barracks', the notorious police cell where offenders were held. This terror of being incarcerated by the law ran deep in the Catholic psyche throughout the Troubles.

In the end, the constable takes his leave (stanzas seven and eight), formally fitting 'his cap back with two hands'. We can empathise with the boy as he 'looked at me'. In the final stanza, the oppressive presence of the visitor ('A shadow') is wryly described as 'bobbed', an ironic reference to the friendly English bobby – which this particular constable was not. The verbs in this stanza continue the underlying ominous mood: 'snapping', 'pushed off'. The **poem concludes** with an intimidating reference to the sound of the departing bicycle as a slowly ticking time bomb: 'And the bicycle ticked, ticked, ticked'. Does this suggest that the tension in this divided community was always on the verge of exploding? Do you consider this an effective image or do you think the symbolism is too obvious?

Writing About the Poem

'Seamus Heaney often presents moments of epiphany using autobiographical experience.' Discuss this statement in relation to 'A Constable Calls'.

Sample Paragraph

In his poem, 'A Constable Calls', a young Seamus Heaney recalls a tense incident from his childhood days in Northern Ireland during the 1950s. A local policeman calls to interview the boy's father about the taxes that are due to be paid on his farm crops. Through the attentive observant eye of the small boy, the divisions within the community are dramatised.

The focus is immediately placed on the constable's bicycle which 'stood at the window-sill' and then zooms to a close-up of the 'rubber cowl of a mud-splasher' and the 'dynamo gleaming and cocked back'. This strikingly vivid description suggests the repressive power felt by the Catholic Nationalists. The crude metaphor, 'the boot of the law', reinforces this impression. After a tense interrogation between the officer and the boy's father ('Any other root crops? ... No'), the young boy is filled with guilt at his father's lie and fears that there might be consequences. Although he is not fully aware of the significance of the encounter, the youthful Heaney experiences a coming-of-age sense of the sectarian world around him. The menacing final line describing the spokes of the constable's bicycle wheels as they 'ticked, ticked, ticked' predicts the terrible violence of bombs and explosions that will define Northern Ireland during the so-called Troubles of the 1970s and 80s.

EXAMINER'S COMMENT

A top-grade response, successfully describing the setting for this dramatic confrontation between the constable and Heaney's father. There is a clear explanation of the uneasy atmosphere in which the poet gains an early awareness of sectarian conflict. Supporting quotations are integrated effectively into the commentary and the expression is excellent. The impressive final sentence succinctly sums up the poem's narrative very well.

Class/Homework Exercises

1. 'The question of identity looms large in Seamus Heaney's precisely controlled poetry.' Discuss this statement with reference to 'A Constable Calls'.
2. 'Heaney frequently writes evocative poems that explore the harsh reality of ordinary life.' Discuss this view, referring both to the content and style of 'A Constable Calls'.

Summary Points

- **Key themes include conflict, repressive authority and the loss of innocence.**
- **Engaging use of first-person narrative and closely observed detail.**
- **Tension between divided community results in child's discomfort.**
- **Compelling psychological drama (threat, interrogation, lies, guilt, danger recedes).**
- **Dynamic cinematic movement (zooms, pans, slow motion, close-up).**
- **Short snappy lines juxtaposed with flowing lines and run-on quatrains.**
- **Ominous conclusion.**

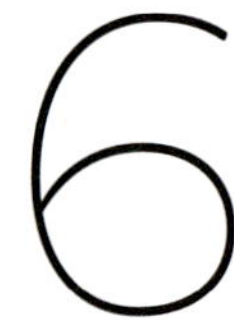

The Skunk

Up, black, striped and damasked like the chasuble
At a funeral mass, the skunk's tail
Paraded the skunk. Night after night
I expected her like a visitor.

The refrigerator whinnied into silence.
My desk light softened beyond the verandah.
Small oranges loomed in the orange tree.
I began to be tense as a voyeur.

After eleven years I was composing
Love-letters again, broaching the word 'wife'
Like a stored cask, as if its slender vowel
Had mutated into the night earth and air

Of California. The beautiful, useless
Tang of eucalyptus spelt your absence.
The aftermath of a mouthful of wine
Was like inhaling you off a cold pillow.

And there she was, the intent and glamorous,
Ordinary, mysterious skunk,
Mythologized, demythologized,
Snuffing the boards five feet beyond me.

It all came back to me last night, stirred
By the sootfall of your things at bedtime,
Your head-down, tail-up hunt in a bottom drawer
For the black plunge-line nightdress.

damasked: patterned; rich, heavy damask fabric.
chasuble: garment worn by a priest saying Mass.

whinnied: sound a horse makes.
verandah: roofed platform along the outside of a house.

voyeur: a person who watches others when they are being intimate.

broaching: raising a subject for discussion.

mutated: changed shape or form.

eucalyptus: common tree with scented leaves found in California.
aftermath: consequences of an unpleasant event.

Mythologized: related to or found in myth.

sootfall: soft sound (like soot falling from a chimney).

plunge-line: low-cut.

Personal Response

1. In your opinion, how effective is Heaney in creating the particular sense of place in this poem? Refer closely to the text in your answer.
2. The poet compares his wife to a skunk. Does this image work, in your view? Quote from the poem in support of your response.
3. Comment on the poem's dramatic qualities. Refer to setting, characters, action and sense of tension/climax, particularly in the first and last stanzas.

Critical Literacy

'The Skunk' comes from Heaney's 1979 collection, *Field Work*. The poet called it a 'marriage poem'. While spending an academic year (1971–2) teaching in the USA, he had been reading the work of Robert Lowell, an American poet. Lowell's poem, 'Skunk Hour', describes how isolation drives a man to become a voyeur of lovers in cars. Heaney's reaction to his own loneliness is very different; he rediscovers the art of writing love letters to his wife, who is living 6,000 miles away in Ireland. This separation culminated in an intimate, humorous, erotic love poem which speaks volumes for the deep love and trust between husband and wife.

In the opening stanza, we are presented with four words describing the skunk's tail, 'Up, black, striped and damasked'. The punctuation separates the different aspects of the animal's tail for the reader's observation. An unusual simile occurs in line 1. In a **playfully irreverent tone**, Heaney likens the skunk's tail to the black and white vestments worn by a priest at a funeral. He then gives us an almost cartoon-like visual image of the animal's tail leading the skunk. The self-importance of the little animal is effectively captured in the verb 'Paraded'. All the ceremony of marching is evoked. The poet eagerly awaits his nightly visitor: 'Night after night/I expected her'. Skunks are small black-and-white striped American mammals, capable of spraying foul-smelling liquid on attackers.

In stanza two, the poet's senses are heightened. The verbs 'whinnied', 'softened' and 'loomed' vividly capture the **atmosphere of the soft, exotic California night**. The bright colours of orange and green are synonymous with the Golden State. The anticipation of stanza one now sharpens: 'I began to be tense'. He regards himself as a 'voyeur', but here there is no sense of violation. He is staring into darkness, getting ready to communicate with his wife. In stanza three, the poet, after a break of 11 years, is penning love letters again. In this separation period, he realises how much he misses her. His wife's presence, although she is absent, fills his consciousness. He is totally preoccupied with her. He uses the simile 'Like a stored cask' to show how he values her as something precious. The word 'wife' is savoured like fine wine and his affection is shown in his appreciation of 'its slender vowel',

which reminds him of her feminine grace. She is present to him in the air he breathes, 'mutated into the night earth and air/Of California'.

Heaney's depth of longing is captured in the **sensuous language** of stanza four. The smell of the eucalyptus 'spelt your absence'. The word 'Tang' precisely notes the penetrating sensation of loneliness. Even a drink of wine, 'a mouthful of wine', does not dull this ache. Instead it intensifies his desire, 'like inhaling you off a cold pillow'. Now, the skunk, long awaited, appears. It is full of contradictions: 'glamorous', 'Ordinary'. We hear in stanza five the sound the little animal makes in the onomatopoeic phrase 'Snuffing the boards'. Only in stanza six is the comparison between the wife and the skunk finally drawn: 'It all came back to me last night'. Heaney imagines himself back home. His wife is rummaging in the bottom drawer for a nightdress. She adopts a slightly comic pose, 'head-down, tail-up', reminding him of the skunk as she 'hunt[s]'. The sibilance of the line 'stirred/By the sootfall of your things' suggests the tender intimacy between the married couple. The word 'sootfall' conveys the gentle rustle of clothes falling. The reader's reaction is also 'stirred' to amused surprise as the realisation dawns that the adjectives 'intent and glamorous,/Ordinary, mysterious ... Mythologized, demythologized' also apply to his wife. A **mature, trusting relationship** exists between the couple.

Longer lines suggest ease. The poet is relaxed and playful, his language conversational and sensuous. All our senses are 'stirred'. The light is romantic ('softened') and the colour black is alluring. The touch of the 'cold pillow' will now be replaced by the warm, shared bed. The sounds of California and the couple's bedroom echo: 'Snuffing', 'sootfall'. The 'aftermath of a mouthful of wine' lingers on the tongue. This is something of a rarity, a **successful love poem about marriage**, tender but not cosy, personal but not embarrassingly self-revealing.

Writing About the Poem

'Seamus Heaney makes use of a wide range of striking images to explore experiences of people, places and events.' Discuss this statement in relation to 'The Skunk'.

Sample Paragraph

Heaney's poems are filled with memorable images. He writes about subjects that are sometimes tinged with loneliness and often filled with love, as in 'The Skunk'. Through the innovative image of the little nocturnal animal, the skunk, whose tail paraded ... 'Up, black, striped and damasked', he conveys the beauty and wonder of married love. It is both

mundane and mysterious. This dramatic poem appeals to our senses. Evocative personification is used along with powerful aural imagery, 'The refrigerator whinnied'. Heaney uses vivid visual detail, 'Small oranges loomed in the orange tree'. The Californian setting, with its exotic 'Tang of eucalyptus', is conjured up effectively. The lonely poet is separated from his wife and wistfully recalls her presence, 'The aftermath of a mouthful of wine/ Was like inhaling you off a cold pillow'. Detailed images connect her to the skunk moving around in the yard outside the house where the poet is staying. He observes the animal's posture, 'head-down, tail-up' and the sultry lonely atmosphere is suddenly replaced by the soft, sensuous 'sootfall of your things'. The close intimacy of the married couple is highlighted in the detail of the 'black plunge-line nightdress'. By closely linking people, places and events together, Heaney presents a mysterious moment of insight about romantic love.

EXAMINER'S COMMENT

A close analysis of the poem, addressing the question with great confidence. Informed and focused discussion – particularly of how the poet uses sensual imagery. Expression is varied ('innovative', 'mundane and mysterious', 'close intimacy') and well controlled. Excellent use of reference and quotation throughout add to the quality of the discussion in this top-grade response.

Class/Homework Exercises

1. 'Relationships, personal or otherwise, lie at the heart of Heaney's most accessible poems.' Discuss this view with reference to the poem, 'The Skunk'.
2. 'Throughout his lyrical poems, Seamus Heaney conjures up a sense of the universal, even when focusing on distinct personal experiences.' Discuss this statement with reference to both the content and style of 'The Skunk'.

Summary Points

- **Unusual, playful, intimate love poem.**
- **Range of tones – irreverent, reflective, wistful, emotive.**
- **Striking visual, aural, tactile imagery.**
- **Personification and onomatopoeia evoke atmosphere, people and places.**
- **Disconcerting juxtaposition of past/present, animal/person, loss/love, ordinary/mysterious.**
- **Contrasting line lengths (brief end-stopped lines, flowing run-on lines and stanzas) create urgency, tension and longing.**

7 The Harvest Bow

Title: the harvest bow, an emblem of traditional rural crafts, was made from straw and often worn in the lapel to celebrate the end of harvesting. Sometimes it was given as a love-token or kept in the farmhouse until the next year's harvest.

As you plaited the harvest bow
You implicated the mellowed silence in you
In wheat that does not rust
But brightens as it tightens twist by twist
Into a knowable corona,
A throwaway love-knot of straw.

Hands that aged round ashplants and cane sticks
And lapped the spurs on a lifetime of game cocks
Harked to their gift and worked with fine intent
Until your fingers moved somnambulant:
I tell and finger it like braille,
Gleaning the unsaid off the palpable,

And if I spy into its golden loops
I see us walk between the railway slopes
Into an evening of long grass and midges,
Blue smoke straight up, old beds and ploughs in hedges,
An auction notice on an outhouse wall –
You with a harvest bow in your lapel,

Me with the fishing rod, already homesick
For the big lift of these evenings, as your stick
Whacking the tips off weeds and bushes
Beats out of time, and beats, but flushes
Nothing: that original townland
Still tongue-tied in the straw tied by your hand.

The end of art is peace
Could be the motto of this frail device
That I have pinned up on our deal dresser –
Like a drawn snare
Slipped lately by the spirit of the corn
Yet burnished by its passage, and still warm.

implicated: intertwined; revealed indirectly.
mellowed: matured, placid.

corona: circle of light, halo.

lapped the spurs: tied the back claws of fighting birds.
gamecocks: male fowl reared to take part in cock-fighting.
Harked: listened, attuned.
somnambulant: automatically, as if sleepwalking.
braille: system of reading and writing by touching raised dots.
Gleaning: gathering, grasping; understanding.
palpable: what can be handled or understood.

midges: small biting insects that usually swarm near water.

flushes: rouses, reveals.

The end of art is peace: art brings contentment (a quotation from the English poet Coventry Patmore, 1823–96). It was also used by W.B. Yeats.
device: object, artefact.
deal: pine wood.
snare: trap.

burnished: shining.

'A throwaway love-knot of straw'

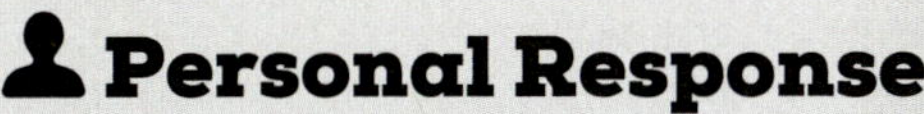

Personal Response

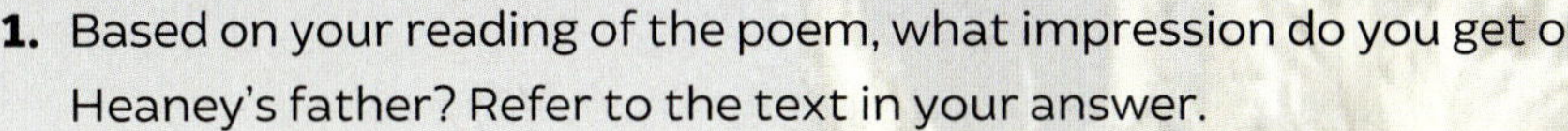

1. Based on your reading of the poem, what impression do you get of Heaney's father? Refer to the text in your answer.
2. In your view, is the harvest bow a symbol of love? Give reasons for your answer, using reference to the poem.
3. What do you understand by the line 'The end of art is peace'? Briefly explain your answer.

Critical Literacy

'The Harvest Bow' (from the 1972 collection *Field Work*) is an elegiac poem in which Heaney pays tribute to his father and the work he did with his hands, weaving a traditional harvest emblem out of stalks of wheat. Remembering his boyhood, watching his father create the corn-dolly, he already knew that the moment could not last. The recognition of his father's artistic talents leads the poet to a consideration of his own creative work.

The poem begins with a measured description of Heaney's reticent father as he twists stalks of wheat into decorative love-knots. The delicate phrasing in stanza one ('You implicated the mellowed silence in you') reflects the poet's awareness of how the **harvest bow symbolised the intricate bond between father and son**. The poet conveys a subdued but satisfied mood as another farm year draws to a close. Autumnal images ('wheat that does not rust') add to the sense of accomplishment. Heaney highlights the practised techniques involved in creating this 'throwaway love-knot of straw'. The harvest bow 'brightens as it tightens twist by twist'. Emphatic alliteration and internal rhyme enliven the image, almost becoming a metaphor for the father's expertise. The bow is likened to 'a knowable corona', a reassuring light circle representing the year's natural cycle.

In stanza two, the intricate beauty of the straw knot prompts Heaney to recall some of the other manual skills his father once demonstrated 'round ashplants and cane sticks'. He acknowledges the older man's 'gift' of concentration and 'fine intent' as he fashioned the harvest bow ('your fingers moved somnambulant') **without conscious effort towards artistic achievement**. Is Heaney also suggesting that poets should work that way? Carefully handling the bow 'like braille', the poet clearly values it as an expression of undeclared love: 'Gleaning the unsaid off the palpable'.

The pleasurable sentiments of Heaney's childhood memories are realised by the strength of detailed imagery in stanza three: 'I see us walk between the railway slopes'. Such **ordinary scenes are enhanced by sensuous details** of 1940s rural life: 'Blue smoke straight up, old beds and ploughs in hedges'. Many of the sounds have a plaintive, musical quality ('loops', 'slopes', 'midges', 'hedges'). The poet seems haunted by his father's ghost, and the

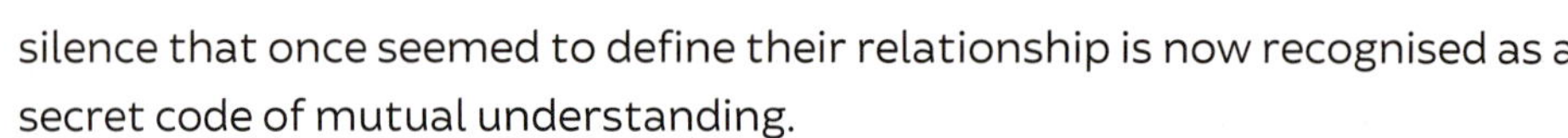

silence that once seemed to define their relationship is now recognised as a secret code of mutual understanding.

Stanza four focuses on the relentless passing of time. The **tone is particularly elegiac** as Heaney recalls his father 'Whacking the tips off weeds' with his stick. In retrospect, he seems to interpret such pointless actions as evidence of how every individual 'Beats out of time' – but to no avail. The poet extends this notion of time's mystery by suggesting that it is through art alone ('the straw tied by your hand') that 'tongue-tied' communities can explore life's wonder.

At the start of stanza five, Heaney tries to make sense of the corn-dolly, now a treasured part of his own household 'on our deal dresser'. It mellows in its new setting and gives out heat. While 'the spirit of the corn' may have disappeared from the knot, the power of the poet's imagination can still recreate it there. So rather than being merely a nostalgic recollection of childhood, the poem takes on universal meaning in the intertwining of artistic forces. We are left with a deep sense of lost rural heritage, the unspoken joy of a shared relationship and the rich potential of the poet's art. For Heaney, **artistic achievements produce warm feelings of lasting contentment**. Whatever 'frail device' is created, be it a harvest bow or a formal elegy, '*The end of art is peace*'.

Writing About the Poem

'Heaney makes effective use of striking imagery to explore universal themes of love and loss.' Discuss this statement with reference to 'The Harvest Bow'.

Sample Paragraph

Heaney's nostalgic poem, 'The Harvest Bow', is a powerful elegy for his father. Its finely crafted imagery and sound effects describe the traditional home-made straw bow which celebrates the end of the farming year. The poet recalls that his father worked with 'fine intent' to fashion the 'love-knot' from the fresh wheat 'that does not rust' because it has been transformed into a work of art. Remembering this 'frail device' allows Heaney to go back in time like a 'drawn snare', enabling him to 'spy into its golden loops' and re-experience treasured moments. Strong aural images, broad vowels and enjambment evoke the serene mood, 'I see us walk between the railway slopes/Into an evening of long grass and midges'. Poignant memories of childhood are universal and almost everyone has special moments that symbolise family

EXAMINER'S COMMENT

This is a sustained high-grade response that shows close engagement with the poem. All the elements of the question (imagery, love and loss, universal significance) are addressed. Relevant quotations – referring to a range of imagery patterns – are used to support discussion points. Expression is well controlled and the critical vocabulary is very impressive.

love. Heaney's father 'Beats out of time' with his stick, an image that lives forever in his memory. The phrase suggests the close bond shared by father and son, but also hints at the cruelty of time and sense of loss. For Heaney, the harvest bow is a trap which entangles his memory, yet the presence of his father escapes and lives again in the adult poet's heart, 'still warm'.

Class/Homework Exercises

1. 'Seamus Heaney frequently uses detailed observation and a lyrical style to explore close family relationships.' Discuss this view with reference to 'The Harvest Bow'.
2. 'Heaney's carefully judged language enables readers to relate to recurring themes that are often grounded in the past.' Discuss this statement with reference to both the subject matter and style of 'The Harvest Bow'.

Summary Points

- **Elegy directly addresses the poet's father.**
- **Warm, emotional tone, consoling perfection of the past.**
- **Similarity drawn between intricate artistry of the bow maker and poet.**
- **Contrasting aspects of his father – tough, practical, silent, tender, skilled.**
- **Multiple word meanings, e.g. 'implicate' = 'show', 'entrap', 'include'.**
- **Clever aural word-play imitates the complexity of the harvest bow.**
- **Concluding reassuring motto – art confronts every destructive life experience and creates order.**

8 The Underground

There we were in the vaulted tunnel running,
You in your going-away coat speeding ahead
And me, me then like a fleet god gaining
Upon you before you turned to a reed

Or some new white flower japped with crimson
As the coat flapped wild and button after button
Sprang off and fell in a trail
Between the Underground and the Albert Hall.

Honeymooning, mooning around, late for the Proms,
Our echoes die in that corridor and now
I come as Hansel came on the moonlit stones
Retracing the path back, lifting the buttons

To end up in a draughty lamplit station
After the trains have gone, the wet track
Bared and tensed as I am, all attention
For your step following and damned if I look back.

vaulted: domed, arched.

going-away coat: new coat worn by the bride leaving on honeymoon.
fleet: fast; momentary.
reed: slender plant; part of a musical instrument.

japped: tinged, layered.

the Albert Hall: famous London landmark and concert venue.

the Proms: short for promenade concerts, a summer season of classical music.
Hansel: fairytale character who, along with his sister Gretel, retraced his way home using a trail of white pebbles.

'Our echoes die in that corridor'

Note: in Greek mythology, Eurydice, the beloved wife of Orpheus, was killed by a venomous snake. Orpheus travelled to the Underworld (Hades) to retrieve her. It was granted that Eurydice could return to the world of the living, but on condition that Orpheus should walk in front of her and not look back until he had reached the upper world. In his anxiety, he broke his promise, and Eurydice vanished again – but this time forever.

Personal Response

1. Comment on the atmosphere created in the first two stanzas. Refer to the text in your answer.
2. From your reading of this poem, what do you learn about the relationship between the poet and his wife? Refer to the text in your answer.
3. Write a short personal response to 'The Underground', highlighting the impact it made on you.

Critical Literacy

'The Underground' is the first poem in *Station Island* (1984). It recounts a memory from Heaney's honeymoon when he and his wife (like a modern Orpheus and Eurydice) were rushing through a London Underground Tube station on their way to a BBC Promenade Concert in the Albert Hall. In Dennis O'Driscoll's book, *Stepping Stones*, Heaney has said, 'In this version of the story, Eurydice and much else gets saved by the sheer cussedness of the poet up ahead just keeping going.'

The poem's title is filled with a sense of threat. Underground journeys are shadowed with a certain menace. Not only is there a mythical association with crossing into the land of the dead, but there is also the actuality of accidents and terrorist outrages. The first stanza of Heaney's personal narrative uses everyday colloquial speech ('There we were in the vaulted tunnel running') to introduce his **dramatic account**. The oppressively 'vaulted' setting and urgent verbs ('speeding', 'gaining') increase this sense of disquiet. For the poet, it is a psychic and mythic underground where he imagines his own heroic quest ('like a fleet god'). What he seems to dread most is the possibility of change and that, like a latter-day Orpheus, he might somehow lose his soulmate.

Cinematic images and run-on lines propel the second stanza forward. This **fast-paced rhythm is in keeping with the restless diction** – 'the coat flapped wild'. The poet's wife is wearing her going-away wedding outfit and in the course of her sprint, the buttons start popping off. Internal rhyme adds to the tension; 'japped' and 'flapped' play into each other, giving the impression that whatever is occurring is happening with great intensity.

The poem changes at the beginning of the third stanza and this is evident in the language, which is much more playful, reflecting Heaney's assessment of the occasion in hindsight. He now recognises the youthful insecurity of the time: 'Honeymooning, mooning around'. The reference to the fictional Hansel and Gretel hints at the immaturity of their relationship as newlyweds and emphasises the couple's initial fretfulness. But recalling how he carefully gathered up the buttons, like Hansel returning from the

wilderness, **Heaney appears to have now come to terms with his uneasy past**: 'Our echoes die in that corridor'.

This new-found confidence underscores the poet's recollections in the fourth stanza. The action and speed have now ceased. After the uncertainty of the 'draughty lamplit station', he has learned to trust his wife and his own destiny. Unlike Orpheus, the tragic Greek hero, Heaney has emerged from his personal descent into Hades, 'Bared and tense'. Although **he can never forget the desolation of being threatened with loss**, the poet has been well served by the experience, having realised that it will always be him – and not his wife – who will be damned if he dares to look back.

The ending of the poem is characteristically compelling. Commenting on it in *Stepping Stones*, Heaney has said, 'But in the end, the "damned if I look back" line takes us well beyond the honeymoon.' Although some critics feel that the final outlook is more regretful, it is difficult to miss the sheer determination that is present in the poem's last line. The **poet's stubborn tone leaves us with overwhelming evidence of his enduring devotion to love**, an emotional commitment which seems to be even more precious with the passing of time.

Writing About the Poem

'Heaney's poetry operates successfully across several levels, dramatically observing and quietly reflecting.' Discuss this statement with reference to 'The Underground'.

Sample Paragraph

EXAMINER'S COMMENT

An intelligent top-grade response that addresses both elements of this challenging question. Some focused commentary on dramatic aspects ('frantic dash', 'reality and nightmare', 'cinematic detail '). Apt quotations are successfully integrated into the discussion. Assured vocabulary ('interweaves', 'subterranean', 'alternative') is also impressive.

'The Underground' is another of Heaney's autobiographical poems in which he gives a dramatic account of a frantic dash by his young wife and himself through London's Underground train station. What is interesting is how he interweaves past and present into reality and nightmare throughout the poem. Urgent verbs ('speeding', 'gaining') and run-on lines further suggest the headlong rush. Heaney's close observations lead to deep reflection. He is aware of the carefree quality of young love – 'Honeymooning, mooning around'. The poet introduces Greek mythology into the poem – the Orpheus and Eurydice tale of tragic loss in the Underworld. Suddenly, the personal has become a universal experience. The hunting and chasing aspects of love have always existed throughout human history. Another cinematic detail – the falling buttons – is associated with the 'moonlit stones' from the fairytale of Hansel and Gretel. Heaney, like Hansel, goes back, 'retracing the path', to find a way

forward. The poem's striking final phrase, 'damned if I look back', also works on two levels. Heaney is determined to keep going and put real effort into the couple's relationship. The alternative is loss of love – a kind of damnation that he fears. Unlike the tragic myths mentioned earlier in the poem, his relationship is based on trust and will survive.

Class/Homework Exercises

1. 'Heaney frequently invokes a vivid range of memories and mythological echoes to reveal intense feelings in his poetry.' Discuss this view with reference to 'The Underground'.
2. 'Heaney's love poems celebrate his subjects warmly, yet realistically, through the use of precise visual imagery and aural detail.' Discuss this statement with reference to both the subject matter and style of 'The Underground'.

Summary Points

- **Nostalgic love poem of a specific event infused with Greek myth and fairy story.**
- **Personal narrative using colloquial speech and engaging imagery.**
- **Dramatic atmosphere, pacy rhythm, dynamic verbs, run-on lines.**
- **Aural music of internal rhyme and assonance.**
- **Fear of loss contrasted with the poet's determined commitment to his wife.**

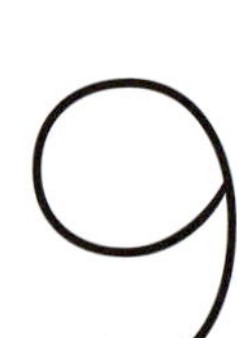

9 Postscript

And some time make the time to drive out west
Into County Clare, along the Flaggy Shore,
In September or October, when the wind
And the light are working off each other
So that the ocean on one side is wild
With foam and glitter, and inland among stones
The surface of a slate-grey lake is lit
By the earthed lightning of a flock of swans,
Their feathers roughed and ruffling, white on white,
Their fully grown headstrong-looking heads
Tucked or cresting or busy underwater.
Useless to think you'll park and capture it
More thoroughly. You are neither here nor there,
A hurry through which known and strange things pass
As big soft buffetings come at the car sideways
And catch the heart off guard and blow it open.

the Flaggy Shore: stretch of coastal limestone slabs in the Burren, Co. Clare.

working off: playing against.

cresting: stretching, posing.

buffetings: vibrations, shudderings.

Personal Response

1. Choose one image from the poem that you find particularly effective. Briefly explain your choice.
2. What is your understanding of the poem's final line?
3. In your opinion, is the advice given by Heaney in 'Postscript' relevant to our modern world? Give reasons to support your response.

'along the Flaggy Shore'

Critical Literacy

This beautiful pastoral lyric comes at the end of Seamus Heaney's 1996 collection, *The Spirit Level.* The title suggests an afterthought, something that was missed out earlier. As so often in his poetry, Heaney succeeds in conveying the extraordinary by way of an everyday experience – in this case, the vivid memory of a journey westwards. The poem resonates with readers, particularly those who have also shared moments when life caught them by surprise.

Line 1 is relaxed and conversational. The poet invites others (or promises himself, perhaps) to 'make the time to drive out west'. The phrase 'out west' has connotations both of adventurous opportunity and dismal failure. By placing 'And' at the start of the poem, Heaney indicates a link with something earlier, some unfinished business. **Keen to ensure that the journey will be worthwhile**, he recommends a definite destination ('the Flaggy Shore') and time ('September or October').

The untamed beauty of the Co. Clare coastline is described in some detail: 'when the wind/And the light are working off each other' (lines 3–4). The phrase 'working off' is especially striking in conveying the **tension and balance between two of nature's greatest complementary forces: wind and light**. Together, they create an effect that neither could produce singly.

Close awareness of place is a familiar feature of the poet's writing, but in this instance he includes another dimension – the notion of in-betweeness. The road Heaney describes runs between the ocean and an inland lake. Carefully chosen images **contrast** the unruly beauty of the open sea's 'foam and glitter' with the still 'slate-grey lake' (line 7). In both descriptions, the sounds of the words echo their sense precisely.

The introduction of the swans in line 8 brings unexpected drama. Heaney captures their seemingly effortless movement between air and water. The poet's **vigorous skill with language** can be seen in his appreciation of the swans' transforming presence, which he highlights in the extraordinary image of 'earthed lightning'. His expertly crafted sketches are both tactile ('feathers roughed and ruffling') and visual ('white on white'). Tossed by the wind, their neck feathers resemble ruffled collars. To Heaney, these exquisite birds signify an otherworldly force that is rarely earthed or restrained. In response, he is momentarily absorbed by the swans' purposeful gestures and powerful flight.

In line 12, the poet cautiously accepts that such elemental beauty can never be fully grasped: 'Useless to think you'll park and capture it'. Because we are 'neither here nor there', we can only occasionally glimpse 'known and strange things'. Despite this, the poem concludes on a redemptive note, acknowledging those special times when we edge close to the miraculous. These **experiences transcend our mundane lives** and we are shaken by revelation, just as unexpected gusts of winds ('soft buffetings') can rock a car.

Heaney's journey has been both **physical and mystical**. It is brought to a crescendo in line 16, where it ends in the articulation of an important truth. He has found meaning between the tangible and intangible. The startling possibility of discovering the ephemeral quality of spiritual awareness is unnerving enough to 'catch the heart off guard and blow it open'. The seemingly contradictory elements of comfort and danger add to the intensity of this final image. Heaney has spoken about the illumination he felt during his visit to the Flaggy Shore as a 'glorious exultation of air and sea and swans'. For him, the experience was obviously inspirational, and the poem that it produced might well provide a similar opportunity for readers to experience life beyond the ordinary material world.

Writing About the Poem

'Heaney's work often addresses the wonder of poetic inspiration through the use of carefully chosen images.' Discuss this statement in relation to 'Postscript'.

Sample Paragraph

'Postscript' starts with a casual invitation, 'And some time make the time', building to a crescendo and concluding with a highly charged insight. The poem evokes the creative process of making and reading poetry, the ability of language to transport a person to a magical place ('when the wind/And the light are working off each other') which is just beneath the material world ('You are neither here nor there'). Heaney focuses on the excitement of inspiration. The unexpected satisfaction of creativity is caught in the interaction of wind, light, ocean, lake and swans. Heaney focuses on nuances of colour ('white on white') and texture ('roughed and ruffling') to capture the enchanting moment. The less attractive aspects of the swans are also carefully noted – their arrogance ('headstrong-looking heads') and their paddling feet ('busy underwater'). Quietly, the poet cautions readers to appreciate and fully experience this moment, 'Useless to think you'll park and capture it'. The final line explodes with the emotion of being truly alive in the moment. The wind, like the poem itself, triggers uncontrollable emotion. Both come like 'big soft buffetings' to 'catch the heart off guard and blow it open'.

EXAMINER'S COMMENT

An insightful response to the question. Informed discussion points focused throughout on the theme of the creative process and Heaney's use of language. Good choice of accurate quotations integrated effectively into the commentary. Expression is impressive also: varied sentence length, wide-ranging vocabulary ('crescendo', 'nuances', 'triggers uncontrollable emotion') and good control of syntax. A high-grade standard.

Class/Homework Exercises

1. 'Seamus Heaney's poems are capable of capturing moments of insight in a strikingly memorable fashion.' Discuss this statement with reference to 'Postscript'.
2. 'Heaney evokes the beauty and mystery of Ireland's natural landscape through the precision of his language.' Discuss this view with reference to both the subject matter and style of 'Postscript'.

Summary Points

- **Conversational description of a car drive 'out west' into Co. Clare.**
- **The poem pays tribute to the sheer power of perception.**
- **Resonance of memory, contrasting joy at visual experience with sadness at realisation of its transience.**
- **Vivid visual imagery and subtle sound effects used to convey the scene.**
- **Cautious, reflective tone contrasts with exhilarating description.**

SEAMUS HEANEY

10 A Call

'Hold on,' she said, 'I'll just run out and get him.
The weather here's so good he took the chance
To do a bit of weeding.'
So I saw him
Down on his hands and knees beside the leek rig,
Touching, inspecting, separating one
Stalk from the other, gently pulling up
Everything not tapered, frail and leafless,
Pleased to feel each little weed-root break,
But rueful also ...
Then found myself listening to
The amplified grave ticking of hall clocks
Where the phone lay unattended in a calm
Of mirror glass and sunstruck pendulums ...

And found myself then thinking: if it were nowadays,
This is how Death would summon Everyman.

Next thing he spoke and I nearly said I loved him.

tapered: slender; reducing in thickness towards the end.
frail: weak.

rueful: expressing regret.

amplified: increased the strength of the sound.

pendulums: weights that hang from a fixed point and swing freely, used to regulate the mechanism of a clock.

Everyman: character in fifteenth-century morality plays.

'Pleased to feel each little weed-root break'

Personal Response

1. How does Heaney dramatise this event? Refer to setting, mood, dialogue, action and climax in your response.
2. Describe the mood of 'A Call'. Does it change during the course of the poem? Support your answer with suitable quotations.
3. One literary critic said that the 'celebration of people and relationships in Heaney's poetry is characterised by honesty and tenderness'. To what extent do you agree or disagree with this view? Refer to the text in your response.

Critical Literacy

'A Call' comes from Heaney's collection *The Spirit Level* (1996) and deals with two of the poet's recurring themes: the father–son relationship and the passing of time. The setting is a routine domestic scene of a mother talking, a father weeding, a son calling. *The Spirit Level* refers to balance, getting the level right, measuring. It also suggests poetry, which is on another plane, free-floating above the confines of the earth. Heaney spoke about this in his Nobel Prize speech, saying 'I am permitting myself the luxury of walking on air'.

This personal narrative opens with a conversational directness, as Heaney is told to 'Hold on'. Heaney has phoned his parents' home and his mother is responding to her son's request to speak with his father. When she puts the receiver down (these were the days of the land line), the poet has time to imagine the old man at work in his garden: 'The weather here's so good, he took the chance/To do a bit of weeding'. The rhythm of colloquial dialogue is realistically caught by the use of everyday expressions and a **simple scene of domesticity is established**. In line 4, the poet becomes the engrossed spectator on the fringes of the scene: 'So I saw him'. The detail of 'Down on his hands and knees beside the leek rig' invites the reader to observe for themselves.

Fragmented description shows the care and skill of the gardener's activity, 'Touching, inspecting, separating', as the father tends his vegetable patch. All farming tradition is associated with decay and growth, and the weakest is usually discarded, 'gently pulling up/Everything not tapered'. The onomatopoeia of the word 'break', with its sharp 'k' sound, suggests the snap of the root as it is pulled from the soil. The father takes pleasure ('Pleased to feel') in his work ('each little weed-root break') but he is, perhaps, regretful too ('rueful') that a form of life is ending, snapped from the nurturing earth.

In line 11, the **visual imagery is replaced by aural effects**. The mood in the deserted hallway indicates a significant change in the tone of the poem. Sounds are 'amplified' due to the subdued atmosphere of the location and Heaney's long wait to hear his father's voice. Time is passing, not just for the

weeds but also for the man, measured by the 'grave ticking of hall clocks'. Here the poem begins to move between earthbound-reality and airiness. The image of ticking clocks in a sea ('calm') of 'mirror glass and sunstruck pendulums' is almost surreal. Broad vowel sounds create an air of serenity and otherworldliness. The word 'amplified' vividly conveys the echo of the clocks and we can imagine their loud ticking as the sound increases in intensity. The inclusion of the word 'grave' is an obvious reminder that death is edging closer – and not just for the poet's father.

In line 15, Heaney moves from observation to meditation, walking on air, 'And found myself then thinking'. Death is depicted as a personal communication, like a phone call from a loved one. The poet is pushing at the boundaries of what is real. His father, like the weeds, will be uprooted, spirited away to some afterlife. Here Heaney is 'seeing things'; he is mediating between states of awareness. **A keen sense of mortality informs the poem**. The last line stands apart, as Heaney is jolted out of his daydreaming: 'Next thing he spoke'. Family love is an important theme throughout Heaney's poetry. In this case, he considers the deep-rooted closeness of the father–son relationship and we witness the frustrating attempts at communication between them, 'and I nearly said I loved him'. Was it an awareness of his father's mortality which prompted this reaction from the poet? The careful phrasing, relaxed and casual, reflects the powerful love between these silent men and the heart-breaking tension of the impossibility of articulating their feelings. In the poem's poignant conclusion ('Next thing he spoke and I nearly said I loved him'), father and son are both united and separated at the same time.

The title of this poem is intriguing. Apart from referring to a telephone call, it also signals the final summons that 'Everyman' will receive from Death. While the dominant tone of 'A Call' celebrates the poet's father and his regard for nature, there is an underlying elegiac quality that reveals Heaney's deep awareness of mortality and loss.

Writing About the Poem

'Seamus Heaney's poetry engages the reader through his use of striking imagery and thought-provoking themes.' Discuss this statement with reference to 'A Call'.

Sample Paragraph

The poem, 'A Call', engages readers from the closely observed domestic scene to the dreamlike imagery depicting mortality and the tender admission of emotion, 'I nearly said I loved him'. We hear Heaney's mother's natural speaking voice, 'Hold on', while she rushes to get his

father. We also imagine the father working quietly in his garden through a carefully punctuated list of verbs, 'Touching, inspecting, separating'. Heaney also depicts a surreal scene of passing time through the broad vowels of the 'sunstruck pendulums' which beat relentlessly. His dark humour continues through the image of Death using the modern means of communication, the telephone, to call human beings to the next world. The tender domestic scene then gives way to serious reflections on transience. As often happens in Heaney's poems, he celebrates life while accepting the reality of death. Through his multi-layered images of the telephone and the weed, Heaney teaches his readers about the significance of ordinary experiences.

EXAMINER'S COMMENT

An insightful, well-informed response. Engagement with both Heaney's imagery and themes is evident throughout. Perceptive discussion of the poet's recognition of life and death is well supported by apt, accurate quotations. Expression is excellent ('carefully punctuated', 'serious reflections on transience'). A confident top-grade answer that shows close interaction with the poem.

Class/Homework Exercises

1. 'Seamus Heaney's reflective poetry often reveals moments of sensitivity that can enrich our experience of life.' Discuss this statement with reference to 'A Call'.
2. 'Heaney's lyrical poems go beyond description to disclose rich insights into universal themes.' Discuss this view with reference to both the subject matter and style of 'A Call'.

Summary Points

- **Autobiographical poem expands into profound meditation.**
- **Colloquial, direct speech is engaging.**
- **Effective use of carefully observed visual detail.**
- **Assonance, internal rhyme and alliteration heighten the musicality of the poem.**
- **Personification adds an ominous note.**
- **Unusual line breaks highlight the poem's focus on transience.**
- **Final line poignantly evokes both the communication and the lack of communication between father and son.**

Tate's Avenue

Title: Tate's Avenue is located in South Belfast, a popular student area. Heaney's girlfriend (later his wife) lived there in the late 1960s.

Not the brown and fawn car rug, that first one
Spread on sand by the sea but breathing land-breaths,
Its vestal folds unfolded, its comfort zone
Edged with a fringe of sepia-coloured wool tails.

Not the one scraggy with crusts and eggshells
And olive stones and cheese and salami rinds
Laid out by the torrents of the Guadalquivir
Where we got drunk before the corrida.

Instead, again, it's locked-park Sunday Belfast,
A walled back yard, the dust-bins high and silent
As a page is turned, a finger twirls warm hair
And nothing gives on the rug or the ground beneath it.

I lay at my length and felt the lumpy earth,
Keen-sensed more than ever through discomfort,
But never shifted off the plaid square once.
When we moved I had your measure and you had mine.

vestal: innocent, untouched (Heaney is comparing the crumpled rug to the modest dresses of vestal virgins in ancient Rome).
sepia-coloured: faded brownish colour; old looking.

Guadalquivir: river in Andalusia, Spain.
corrida: bullfight.

locked-park: Belfast's public parks were closed on Sundays in the 1960s.

plaid: checked, tartan.

'As a page is turned, a finger twirls warm hair'

Personal Response

1. Comment on the poet's use of sound effects in the first two stanzas.
2. 'I had your measure and you had mine.' Briefly explain what you think Heaney means by this statement.
3. Write your own personal response to the poem.

Critical Literacy

'Tate's Avenue' (from the 2006 collection *District and Circle*) is another celebration of Heaney's love for Marie Devlin. They married in 1965 and lived off Tate's Avenue in South Belfast during the late 1960s. Here, the poet reviews their relationship by linking three separate occasions involving a collection of car rugs spread on the ground by the couple over the years.

Stanza one invites us to eavesdrop on a seemingly mundane scene of everyday domesticity. It appears that the poet and his wife have been reminiscing – presumably about their love life over the years. Although the negative opening tone is emphatic ('Not the brown and fawn car rug'), we are left guessing about the exact nature of the couple's discussion. A few tantalising details are given about 'that first' rug, connecting it with an early seaside visit. Heaney can still recall the tension of a time when the couple **were caught between their own desire and strong social restrictions**. He describes the rug in terms of its texture and colours: 'Its vestal folds unfolded' (suggesting their youthful sexuality) contrasting with the 'sepia-coloured wool tails' (symbolising caution and old fashioned inhibitions). As usual, Heaney's tone is edged with irony as he recalls the 'comfort zone' between himself and Marie.

The repetition of 'Not' at the start of stanza two clearly indicates that the second rug is also rejected, even though it can be traced back to a more exotic Spanish holiday location. Sharp onomatopoeic effects ('scraggy with crusts and eggshells') and the list of Mediterranean foods ('olive stones and cheese and salami rinds') convey **a sense of freedom and indulgence**. Although the couple's hedonistic life is communicated in obviously excessive terms ('Laid out by the torrents of the Guadalquivir'), Heaney's tone is somewhat dismissive. Is he suggesting that their relationship was mostly sensual back then?

'Instead' – the first word in stanza three – signals a turning point in the poet's thinking. Back in his familiar home surroundings, he recalls the rug that mattered most and should answer whatever doubts he had about the past. He has measured the development of their relationship in stages associated with special moments he and Marie shared. The line 'it's locked-park Sunday Belfast' conjures up memories of their early married life in the Tate's Avenue district. The sectarian 1960s are marked by dour

Protestant domination, a time when weekend pleasures were frowned upon and even the public parks were closed. Despite such routine repression and the unromantic setting ('A walled back yard, the dust-bins high and silent'), **the atmosphere is sexually charged**.

Heaney is aware of the scene's **underlying drama**; the seconds tick by 'As a page is turned, a finger twirls warm hair'. The unfaltering nature of the couple's intimacy is evident in the resounding declaration: 'nothing gives on the rug or the ground beneath it'.

This notion of confidence in their relationship is carried through into stanza four and accentuated by the alliterative 'I lay at my length and felt the lumpy earth'. The resolute rhythm is strengthened by the robust adjectival phrase 'Keen-sensed' and the insistent statement: 'But never shifted off the plaid square once'. Heaney builds to a discreet and understated climax in the finely balanced last line: 'When we moved I had your measure and you had mine'. While there are erotic undertones throughout, the poet presents us with restrained realism in place of excessive sensuality. 'Tate's Avenue' is a **beautiful, unembarrassed poem of romantic and sexual love within a committed relationship**. Characteristically, when Heaney touches on personal relationships, he produces the most tender and passionate emotions.

Writing About the Poem

'Seamus Heaney's poetry frequently explores intense relationships in a style that is fresh and innovative.' Discuss this statement with reference to 'Tate's Avenue'.

Sample Paragraph

'Tate's Avenue' is one of Heaney's most romantic poems. The poet traces the progress of his relationship with his wife through the unusual approach of recalling three rugs that mark stages in their lives together. The tentative, breathless nature of early courtship is revealed in both the colour ('sepia-coloured', reminiscent of an old photo) and texture ('vestal folds unfolded') of the first rug. Yet the strong physical attraction is revealed through sibilance and personification, 'Spread on sand by the sea but breathing land-breaths'. An emphatic 'Not' adds to the drama of the poem as the first two rugs are rejected. The adverb 'Instead' signals the decision to choose a 'plaid square' to truly sum up their deep feelings for each other. The focus zooms in on the sensuous detail, 'a finger twirls warm hair'.

EXAMINER'S COMMENT

An excellent top-grade response that shows a very good understanding of this unusual love poem. Detailed examination of language use (dramatic settings, contrasting atmospheres, energetic imagery and aural effects) is supported by apt and accurate quotations. Expression is also skilfully controlled and the paragraph is well rounded off in the concise final sentence.

The verb conveys the enticing allure of their mutual attraction. Yet no relationship runs smoothly all of the time. The 'lumpy earth' and 'discomfort' of the final stanza vividly conveys this reality to the reader. But this determined couple did not give up and the poem concludes in a wonderful moment of unity between the lovers, 'I had your measure and you had mine'. In this inventive study of important times in their relationship, Heaney conveys the drama and immediacy of their love. Overall, restrained, sensuous tension is presented in this lively study of intimacy.

Class/Homework Exercises

1. 'Heaney's poetry realistically depicts people and places through carefully chosen language and imagery.' Discuss this view with reference to 'Tate's Avenue'.
2. 'Seamus Heaney's poems are often filled with vivid sensuousness and evocative description.' Discuss this statement with reference to 'Tate's Avenue'.

Summary Points

- **Tender, compelling poem celebrates love in a committed relationship.**
- **Precise, vibrant details illustrate the various scenes.**
- **The headlong rush of young love is conveyed in the enjambment of the second quatrain.**
- **In contrast, the more measured pace of mature love is found in the final stanza.**
- **Compound words, onomatopoeia, alliteration and assonance create a rich aural texture.**
- **Compact four-quatrain structure adds to the understated quality of the poem.**

12 The Pitchfork

SEAMUS HEANEY

Of all implements, the pitchfork was the one
That came near to an imagined perfection:
When he tightened his raised hand and aimed with it,
It felt like a javelin, accurate and light.

So whether he played the warrior or the athlete
Or worked in earnest in the chaff and sweat,
He loved its grain of tapering, dark-flecked ash
Grown satiny from its own natural polish.

Riveted steel, turned timber, burnish, grain,
Smoothness, straightness, roundness, length and sheen.
Sweat-cured, sharpened, balanced, tested, fitted.
The springiness, the clip and dart of it.

And then when he thought of probes that reached the farthest,
He would see the shaft of a pitchfork sailing past
Evenly, imperturbably through space,
Its prongs starlit and absolutely soundless –

But has learned at last to follow that simple lead
Past its own aim, out to an other side
Where perfection – or nearness to it – is imagined
Not in the aiming but the opening hand.

javelin: long spear thrown in a competitive sport, also used as a weapon.

chaff: husks of grain separated from the seed.
grain: wheat.
tapering: reducing in thickness towards one end.

Riveted: fastened.
burnish: the shine on a polished surface.

clip: clasp; smack (colloquial).
dart: follow-on movement; small pointed missile thrown as a weapon.
probes: unmanned, exploratory spacecraft; a small measuring or testing device.
imperturbably: calmly, smoothly; unable to be upset.
prongs: two or more projecting points on a fork.

'When he tightened his raised hand and aimed with it'

Personal Response

1. What is the tone of this poem? Does it change or not? Refer closely to the text in your response.
2. Select one image (or one line) that you find particularly interesting. Briefly explain your choice.
3. What do you think about the ending of this poem? Do you consider it visionary or far-fetched? Give reasons for your answer.

Critical Literacy

'The Pitchfork' was published in Heaney's 1991 collection, *Seeing Things*. These poems turn to the earlier concerns of the poet. Craft and natural skill, the innate ability to make art out of work, is seen in many of his poems, such as 'The Forge'. Heaney is going back, making 'a journey back into the heartland of the ordinary'. The poet is now both observer and visionary.

In stanza one, Heaney describes a pitchfork, an ordinary farming 'implement'. Through **looking at an ordinary object with intense concentration**, the result is a fresh 'seeing', where the ordinary and mundane become marvellous, 'imagined perfection'. For Heaney, the creative impulse was held in the hand, in the skill of the labourer ('tightened his raised hand and aimed with it'). This skill was similar to the skill of the poet. They both practise and refine their particular ability. The pitchfork is now transformed into a sporting piece of equipment, 'a javelin'. The heaviness of physical work falls away as it becomes 'accurate and light' due to the practised capability of the worker. This is similar to the lightness of being and the **freeing of the poet's spirit** that Heaney allows himself to experience in this collection of poetry.

The worker is described as sometimes playing 'the warrior or the athlete' (stanza two). **Both professions command respect** and both occupations require courage and skill. But the worker's work is also described realistically, 'worked in earnest in the chaff and sweat'. This is heavy manual labour, and Heaney does not shirk from its unpleasant side. However, the worker is not ground down by it because he 'loved' the beauty of the pitchfork. Here we see both the poet and the worker dazzled, as the intent observation of the humble pitchfork unleashes its beauty, its slender 'dark-flecked ash'. The shine of the handle is conveyed in the word 'satiny'. Such tactile language allows the reader to feel the smooth, polished wooden handle. Now three pairs of eyes (the worker's, the poet's and our own) observe the pitchfork.

Close scrutiny of the pitchfork in stanza three continues with a virtuoso display of description, as **each detail is lovingly depicted**, almost like a slow sequence of close-ups in a film. The meeting of the handle and fork is caught

in the phrase 'Riveted steel'. The beauty of the wood is evoked in the alliteration of 'turned timber'. The marvellous qualities of the wood are itemised with growing wonder: its shine ('burnish'), its pattern ('grain'). It is as if the worker and the poet are twirling the pitchfork round as they exclaim over its 'Smoothness, straightness, roundness, length and sheen'. This is more like the description one would give to a work of art or a thoroughbred animal than to a farm implement. The skill that went into the making of the pitchfork is now explored in a list of verbs beginning with the compound word 'Sweat-cured'. This **graphically shows the sheer physical exertion that went into making this instrument**, as it was 'sharpened, balanced, tested, fitted'. The tactile quality of the pitchfork is praised: 'The springiness, the clip and dart of it'. The worker, just like the athlete or warrior, tests his equipment.

In stanza four, the labourer imagines space 'probes' searching the galaxy, 'reached the farthest'. **The long line stretches out in imitation of space**, which pushes out to infinity. The pitchfork now becomes transformed into a spaceship, 'sailing past/Evenly, imperturbably through space'. This ordinary pitchfork now shines like the metal casing of a spaceship, 'starlit', and moves, like the spacecraft, through the vastness of outer space, 'absolutely soundless'.

Stanza five shows the poet becoming a mediator between different states, actual and imagined, ordinary and fantastical. He stands on a threshold, philosophising about the nature of his observation as a familiar thing grows stranger. Together (poet, worker and reader), all follow the line of the pitchfork to 'an other side', a place where 'perfection' is 'imagined'. Perfection does not exist in our world. But it is not the 'tightened' hand, which was 'aiming' at the beginning of the poem, which will achieve this ideal state, but the 'opening hand' of the last stanza. Is the poet suggesting we must be open and ready to receive in order to achieve 'perfection'? Heaney states: '**look at the familiar things you know. Look at them with ... a quality of concentration ... you will be rewarded with insights and visions**.'

Writing About the Poem

'In celebrating traditional rural crafts in his poetry, Heaney reveals his own skills as a master craftsman of the written word.' Discuss this view with reference to 'The Pitchfork'.

Sample Paragraph

'The Pitchfork' is based on a treasured memory of his father who spent his life working on the family farm in Co. Derry. The poet has often written about farming implements in poems that celebrate traditional skills. 'The Pitchfork' begins with a dynamic image as Heaney remembers his father in an ideal way, holding the fork 'like a javelin'. In his innocent eyes, his father was god-like – 'imagined perfection'. The poet lovingly describes the pitchfork in great detail: 'Riveted steel, turned timber'. Hard 't' sounds suggest the father's strength in handling the pitchfork with confidence. The sense of deep respect for the traditional work of the farm as well as for his father is found in the tone of admiration when Heaney imagines the older man playing 'the warrior or the athlete'. He is clearly saying that his father is an expert craftsman. The poet moves from describing the everyday activity of gathering in the hay to a visionary level as the fork hangs in the air, 'starlit and absolutely soundless'. The poet himself transforms the implement into a mysterious spacecraft. In his imagination, he has returned to childhood and is watching the fork moving 'imperturbably through space'. Through his own precise language skills, Heaney celebrates the working life of the father he idealised.

EXAMINER'S COMMENT

Clear, high-grade response tackling all elements of the question and showing a good understanding of the poem. Impressive awareness of Heaney's expertise with language (particularly imagery, tone and sound effects). Focused quotations are used effectively to support key points and the expression is varied and well controlled.

Class/Homework Exercises

1. 'Seamus Heaney's poetry addresses thought-provoking themes in language that is both realistic and mystical.' Discuss this view with reference to 'The Pitchfork'.
2. 'In Heaney's most compelling poems, ordinary objects are lovingly and exactly described.' Discuss this statement with particular reference to 'The Pitchfork'.

Summary Points

- **Exploration of commitment, craft and creativity.**
- **Focus on physical details in the first four stanzas.**
- **Impact of cinematic imagery and energetic rhythm.**
- **Sudden change of pace and mood in the last stanza.**
- **Compelling ending reinforces poet's devotion to generosity and acceptance.**

13 Lightenings viii

Lightenings: insights, transcendent experiences.

SEAMUS HEANEY

The annals say: when the monks of Clonmacnoise
Were all at prayers inside the oratory
A ship appeared above them in the air.

The anchor dragged along behind so deep
It hooked itself into the altar rails
And then, as the big hull rocked to a standstill,

A crewman shinned and grappled down the rope
And struggled to release it. But in vain.
'This man can't bear our life here and will drown,'

The abbot said, 'unless we help him.' So
They did, the freed ship sailed, and the man climbed back
Out of the marvellous as he had known it.

annals: monastic records.
Clonmacnoise: established in the sixth century, the monastery at Clonmacnoise was renowned as a centre of scholarship and spirituality.
oratory: place of prayer, small chapel.

shinned: climbed down, clambered.

abbot: head of the monastery.

'Out of the marvellous'

Personal Response

1. How is the surreal atmosphere conveyed in this poem? Quote in support of your response.
2. Choose one striking image from the poem and comment on its effectiveness.
3. In your view, what does the air-ship symbolise? Refer to the text in your answer.

Critical Literacy

Written in four tercets (three-line stanzas), 'Lightenings viii' (from Seamus Heaney's 1991 collection, *Seeing Things*), tells a legendary story of a miraculous air-ship which once appeared to the monks at Clonmacnoise, Co. Offaly. Heaney has said: 'I was devoted to this poem because the crewman who appears is situated where every poet should be situated: between the ground of everyday experience and the airier realm of an imagined world.'

Heaney's matter-of-fact approach at the start of stanza one leads readers to expect a straightforward retelling of an incident recorded in the 'annals' of the monastery. The story's apparently scholarly source seems highly reliable. While they were at prayers, the monks looked up: 'A ship appeared above them in the air'. We assume that the oratory is open to the sky. The simplicity of the colloquial language, restrained tone and run-through lines all ease us into a **dreamlike world** where anything can happen. But as with all good narratives, the magic ship's sudden appearance raises many questions: Why is it there? Where has it come from? Is this strange story all a dream?

Then out of the air-ship came a massive anchor, which 'dragged along behind so deep' (stanza two) before lodging itself in the altar rails. The poet makes **effective choices in syntax (word order) and punctuation**, e.g. placing 'so deep' at the end of the line helps to emphasise the meaning. The moment when the ship shudders to a halt is skilfully caught in a carefully wrought image: 'as the big hull rocked to a standstill'.

A crewman clambered down the rope to try to release the anchor, but he is unsuccessful. Heaney chooses his words carefully: 'shinned', 'grappled', 'struggled' (stanza three) are all powerful verbs, helping to create a clear picture of the sailor's physical effort. The phrase 'But in vain' is separated from the rest of the line to emphasise the man's hopelessness. The contrasting worlds of magic and reality seem incompatible. Ironically, the story's turning point is the abbot's instant recognition that the **human, earthly atmosphere will be fatal to the visitor**: 'This man can't bear our life here and will drown'.

But a solution is at hand: 'unless we help him' (stanza four). The unconditional generosity of the monks comes naturally to them: 'So/They did'. The word 'So' creates a pause and uncertainty before the prompt, brief opening of the next line: 'They did'. When the anchor is eventually disentangled and 'the freed ship sailed', **the crewman will surely tell his travel companions about the strange beings he encountered** after he 'climbed back out of the marvellous as he had known it'. This last line is somewhat surprising and leaves the reader wondering – marvelling, even.

Heaney's poem certainly raises interesting questions, blurring the lines between reality and illusion, and challenging our ideas about human consciousness. **The story itself can be widely interpreted**. Is the ship a symbol of inspiration while the monks represent commitment and dedication? Presumably, as chroniclers of the annals (preserving texts on paper for posterity), they were not aware of the miracle of their own labours – crossing the barrier from the oral tradition to written records – which was to astonish the world in the forthcoming centuries and help spread human knowledge.

'Lightenings viii' is a beautiful poem that highlights the fact that **the ordinary and the miraculous are categories defined only by human perception**. For many readers, the boat serves as an abstract mirror image, reversing our usual way of seeing things. In Heaney's rich text, we discover that from the outsider's perspective, the truly marvellous consists not of the visionary or mystical experience, but of the seemingly ordinary experience.

Writing About the Poem

'Heaney's evocative language often makes room for everyday miracles and otherworldly wisdom.' Discuss this statement with reference to 'Lightenings viii'.

Sample Paragraph

Heaney's poem 'Lightenings viii' is an account of a surreal experience when the Clonmacnoise monks imagined they saw a ship appearing above them in the sky. We all think of miracles as things that are beyond explanation – and this story illustrates the power and mystery of imagination. Heaney's tone is dreamlike – particularly the wistful narrative style. The long lines and broad vowel sounds suggest an unhurried atmosphere where anything can happen – 'as the big hull rocked to a standstill'. I found the poem to have several meanings. The monks who are 'all at prayers' believe

EXAMINER'S COMMENT

This focused paragraph addresses the question effectively and shows close engagement with the poet's possible themes and language use. Discussion points are clearly expressed and aptly supported. The comments on Heaney's style (dreamlike tone, narrative approach, assonant effects,) are particularly impressive. Expression throughout this high-grade response is very well controlled.

that the mysterious sailors have come out 'of the marvellous' – but the stranded sailors see the safe, earthbound monks in the same way. Indeed, their rescue is arranged by the concerned abbot. The poet seems to be saying that everything in life can be viewed as a wonder – it all depends on a person's perspective. The abbot chooses to save the desperate crewman – 'This man can't bear our life here and will drown'. For me, this is the poet's central lesson – we should help others when we can. If we do, then our lives will be filled with everyday miracles which we can transform into wise behaviour.

Class/Homework Exercises

1. 'Heaney's poetic world is one of wonder and mystery that is matched by the energy of his language.' Discuss this view with reference to 'Lightenings viii'.
2. 'Many of Seamus Heaney's poems communicate intense observations through thought-provoking images and symbolism.' Discuss this statement with reference to both the subject matter and style of 'Lightenings viii'.

Summary Points

- **Characteristic narrative style and use of colloquial language.**
- **Dramatic qualities – characters, setting, tension, dialogue, resolution.**
- **The poem is concerned with visionary experiences, yet rooted in the physical world.**
- **Effective use of vivid imagery, assonance, powerful verbs.**
- **Contrasting worlds – mundane monks and magical sailors.**

Sample Leaving Cert Questions on Heaney's Poetry

1. **From your study of the poetry of Seamus Heaney on your course, select the poems that, in your opinion, best show his effective use of landscape and specific locations to communicate a sense of longing and loss. Justify your selection by showing how Heaney's effective use of landscape and specific locations communicates a sense of longing and loss.**
2. **'Seamus Heaney's poems are often grounded in personal memories conveyed through language that is deeply sensuous and rich in imagery.' To what extent do you agree or disagree with this statement? Support your answer with reference to the poetry of Seamus Heaney on your course.**
3. **'Heaney's carefully crafted poems often explore the significance of love – in its various forms – without ever lapsing into sentimentality.' Discuss this view, supporting your answer with reference to both the thematic concerns and poetic style of the poetry of Seamus Heaney on your course.**

How do I organise my answer?

(Sample question 1)

From your study of the poetry of Seamus Heaney on your course, select the poems that, in your opinion, best show his effective use of landscape and specific locations to communicate a sense of longing and loss. Justify your selection by showing how Heaney's effective use of landscape and specific locations to communicate a sense of longing and loss.

Sample Plan 1

Intro: (*Stance: agree with viewpoint in the question*) Heaney's sense of place is central in much of his poetry in his compassionate examination of ordinary family life, evolving relationships and cultural memory. His deep feelings of loss are effectively communicated through descriptive detail, evocative aural effects and nostalgic tone.

Point 1: (*Farm – love/longing*) 'Mossbawn' recreates the rural childhood idyll of Heaney's childhood home using effective similes (the sun stood/ like a griddle/cooling'), onomatopoeia ('scuffled'). Unusual contrasts link past and present ('tick of two clocks'). Mixed tenses and a warm nostalgic tone indicate his yearning ('here is love/like a tinsmith's scoop').

Understanding the Prescribed Poetry Question

Marks are awarded using the PCLM Marking Scheme: P = 15; C = 15; L = 15; M = 5 Total = 50

- **P** (Purpose = 15 marks) refers to the set question and is the launch pad for the answer. This involves engaging with all aspects of the question. Both theme and language must be addressed, although not necessarily equally.
- **C** (Coherence = 15 marks) refers to the organisation of the developed response and the use of accurate, relevant quotation. Paragraphing is essential.
- **L** (Language = 15 marks) refers to the student's skill in controlling language throughout the answer.
- **M** (Mechanics = 5 marks) refers to spelling and grammar.
- Although no specific number of poems is required, students usually discuss at least 3 or 4 in their written responses.
- Aim for at least 800 words, to be completed within 45–50 minutes.

NOTE

In keeping with the PCLM approach, the student has to take a stance – agreeing, disagreeing or partially agreeing – with the statement that:

- **Heaney's effective use of landscape and specific locations** (real and imaginary locations, Irish landscapes, domestic settings, bogland, cities, the natural world, 'other worlds', etc.)

... communicates:

- **a sense of longing and loss** (through evocative, nostalgic tones, visual/ aural imagery, personification, mythical allusion, striking comparisons, etc.)

Point 2: (*London tube station – love/loss*) 'The Underground' uses the myth of Orpheus and Eurydice to add universal interest to the mad dash of two lovers to a concert. Dramatic language ('speeding', 'gaining') intensify the memory. The terror of lost love is depicted in the monosyllabic verb, 'damned'.

Point 3: (*Spain, Belfast – longing*) 'Tate's Avenue' explores an evolving love and longing. Young hedonistic love in an exotic location is shown in the list 'olive stones and cheese and salami rinds', while reserved love is recalled in the dour description of a Sunday afternoon in Belfast ('walled back yard, the dustbins high and alert').

Point 4: (*Irish bog – lost memory*) 'Bogland' shows how landscape can offer a tender image of history ('the Great Irish Elk'). Run-on lines evoke fluid nature of bog, emphasising the poet's sense of lost time. Importance of history to Irish conveyed in 'striking/Inwards and downwards'.

Conclusion: Poems reveal Heaney's sense of longing and loss in his evocative descriptions of places which are suffused with loving memories. The poet's skilful language closely links particular places and fond memories.

Sample Paragraph: Point 4

'Bogland' explores the strong link between place and Ireland's communal past. Heaney states that Irish bogs record natural history – 'the Great Irish Elk' – and long forgotten Celtic traditions – 'Butter sunk under ... salty and white'. With a sense of yearning, he details this mysterious remote landscape which is continually changing. Soft 'm' and 's' sounds suggest the oozing nature of the bog ('Melting', 'Missing', 'seepage'). Heaney uses a combination of harsh consonants and gentle sibilance to capture its identity, 'crusting between the sights of the sun'. Lost history is preserved in the bogland, 'Every layer they strip seems camped on before'. The poem's structure cleverly mirrors the act of digging. Short lines and stacked stanzas reflect the neat piles of turf on the bogland, a poignant reminder of a lost age. Throughout the poem, Heaney reflects on the importance of history to Irish people. The peat boglands both conceal and reveal previous times. The poet's tone of longing is particularly evident in the final line, 'The wet centre is bottomless', suggesting that the search for the past is endless.

EXAMINER'S COMMENT

An insightful response that tackles the question directly and shows excellent understanding of the poem. Discussion of Heaney's skilful use of sound and structure to locate feelings of loss are very well developed. Impressive expression throughout. Quotations are carefully integrated into the answer, all of which results in a well-deserved top grade.

(Sample question 2)

'Seamus Heaney's poems are often grounded in personal memories conveyed through language that is deeply sensuous and rich in imagery.' To what extent do you agree or disagree with this statement? Support your answer with reference to the poetry of Seamus Heaney on your course.

Sample Plan 2

Intro: (*Stance: agree with viewpoint in the question*) Heaney's autobiographical poems spring from vivid memories of people and events. Using visual and aural imagery, he blends the past into the present, enabling readers to see, hear, smell and taste these memories.

Point 1: (*Childhood memory – imagery/cinematic detail*) 'A Constable Calls' re-creates a tense meeting between the poet's father and an RUC policeman – reflecting the troubled relationship between the two Northern Ireland cultures. Terse dialogue ('any other root crops?') and juxtaposed lines convey the oppressively powerful presence of the law.

Point 2: (*Adult memory – image/edgy humour*) 'The Skunk' is a playful love poem using the irreverent image of the little animal ('damasked like the chasuble/At a funeral Mass'). Sensuous language conjures up the lonely existence of the poet longing for the presence of his absent wife ('whinnied', 'useless/Tang of eucalyptus').

Point 3: (*Childhood memory – image/sound effects*) 'The Harvest Bow' uses the decorative 'throwaway love-knot of straw' to symbolise the intricate bond between son and father. Sound effects convey age-old skill used in creation of the bow ('brightens as it tightens twist by twist'). Onomatopoeic verbs capture the actions of the father ('Whacking', 'Beats out').

Point 4: (*Adult memory – image/dark humour*) 'A Call' details a personal narrative of a telephone call home. Ominous onomatopoeia recalls the fragility of man's hold on life ('break'). Rich vowels recreate the passage of time ('amplified grave ticking of hall clocks'). Final frank admission of failure to speak openly ('I nearly said I loved him').

Conclusion: Heaney offers sharp, vigorous re-enactments of cherished memories with rare exactness. Finely crafted poems contain striking visual and aural imagery, vibrant cinematic details and dramatic dialogue.

NOTE

In keeping with the PCLM approach, the student has to take a stance by agreeing and/or disagreeing that Heaney's poetry is:

- **grounded in personal memories** (childhood, farm life, places and people, politics, cultural tensions in Northern Ireland, etc.)

... conveyed through:

- **language that is deeply sensuous and rich in imagery** (vivid details, sensuous imagery, striking metaphors, energetic sound effects, dramatic encounters, cinematic detail, engaging conversational language, dark humour, nostalgic, reverential tones, etc.)

In 'The Harvest Bow', Heaney creates a precise description of his father, a reserved man. The poet illustrates the subtlety of their intricate relationship, full of 'mellowed silence'. The harvest bow is not just an emblem of Irish rural life, but a rich metaphor of enduring love between son and father. Their undeclared love is signified in the decorative harvest bow emblem, 'I tell and finger it like braille, Gleaming the unsaid off the palpable'. The crafted straw bow is a 'frail device'. It conjures up heartfelt memories for Heaney of long shared walks in the quiet countryside, 'evenings of long grass and midges' – the sensuous sibilant sounds suggesting the bittersweet sense of past times. The final stanza of this deeply personal and poignant poem returns to the present through the treasured emblem 'pinned up on the deal dresser'. The dramatic simile 'Like a drawn snare' not only reminds that the corn is trapped in the bow, but that it has now died as well. Heaney's father may be gone, but his memory lives in the harvest bow and the son's lyrical tribute, 'still warm'.

EXAMINER'S COMMENT

A successful top-grade paragraph that focuses on both parts of the question (personal memories and rich language). The response shows a real appreciation of Heaney's poetic techniques, particularly his use of metaphorical language and sound effects. Apt quotes are used effectively to support discussion points and there is assured expression throughout.

INDICATIVE MATERIAL

Heaney's controlled use of evocative language:

- vivid sensuous images, aural music, clever use of contrasts, personal narratives, conversational speech, variety of tones (elegiac, nostalgic, inspirational), etc.

... addresses:

- aspects of identity and belonging
- autobiographical focus, individuality, distinctiveness, fitting in, national/cultural identity, use of real people, places and placenames in Ireland and abroad, etc.

Leaving Cert Sample Essay

From your study of the poetry of Seamus Heaney on your course, select the poems that, in your opinion, best demonstrate his controlled use of evocative language to address aspects of identity and belonging. Justify your selection by demonstrating Heaney's controlled use of evocative language to address aspects of identity and belonging in the poems you have chosen.

Sample Essay

1. Growing up in Co. Derry, Seamus Heaney inherited a divided identity as both British and Irish. He addresses aspects of his unsettled background in poems such as 'A Constable Calls' and 'The Tollund Man'. The connections with his past help him to explore his sense of belonging. Heaney's personal poems are influenced greatly by his rural Irish upbringing and he writes about childhood experiences with genuine affection in 'The Forge' and 'Mossbawn: Sunlight'. In addition, he often considers his adult identity as a poet. Heaney uses colloquial language, suggestive imagery, haunting sound effects, dynamic verbs and contrasting tones to reveal various aspects of identity and belonging.

2. 'The Forge' is a traditional sonnet nostalgically recreating a scene from the poet's boyhood. Heaney conjures up the passing world of the skilled blacksmith. The poem is grounded in local detail. The octet describes

discarded objects such as the untidy exterior, 'old axles and iron hoops rusting', all suggesting decay. The sestet describes the craftsmanship of the blacksmith, using onomatopoeic verbs, 'a flick to beat real iron out'. Sharp sounds bring the country forge to life, 'short-pitched ring', 'hiss'. Flashes of light erupt in a forceful image, 'The unpredictable fantail of sparks'. The blacksmith's anvil on which he works is in the centre of the forge. Heaney speaks in a reverential tone of its seeming magical properties, comparing its shape to the legendary medieval creature, 'horned as a unicorn'. He imagines the anvil as an 'altar' where rituals are performed.

3. But Heaney isn't just honouring his Irish rural roots, he is also exploring his identity as poet. He, like the blacksmith, is forging word patterns. Each man 'expends himself in shape and music', in the act of creation, changing something ordinary, iron or words, into something special. The use of this carefully crafted sonnet mirrors the traditional method of creating literature. The poet recognises where he belongs, claiming his place in literary tradition. He has opened 'a door into the dark', offering sights and sounds and insights to enrich readers.

4. In 'The Tollund Man', Heaney explores his heritage. Particularly the ancient conflicts throughout history. He imagines that 'some day I will go to Aarhus', the museum in Denmark, to see the preserved remains of the Iron Age man who had been ritually executed. Displacement and foreignness are central in this poem. Heaney's simple language recreates the humanity of the victim. His innocence is described in the visual imagery of 'The mild pods of his eye-lids'. Heaney has given him his individuality. The poet enables us to experience the man's alienation. In his imagination, he names the places he might pass through on his journey to Aarhus. Places that the unnamed victim has known, 'Tollund, Nebergard'. Both men are linked by this list. The poet imagines a strange connection with the Tollund Man.

5. The barbaric cruelty of the ritual killing of this man is highlighted by the harsh alliterative phrase, 'tightened her torc on him'. The man loses his identity while the peat bog transforms him over time into 'a saint's kept body'. Heaney compares the bog to a 'cauldron' holding the past alive. Concentrating on this victim enables the poet to examine other victims of the more recent conflict during the Troubles back home in Northern Ireland. Again, the jarring sounds recreate the painful truth of sectarian violence, the vicious murder of 'four young brothers' resulting in 'Tell-tale skin and teeth flecking the sleepers'. Heaney's poem raises many questions about whether or not national identity is worth fighting for. The tone of the last section is mournful – 'freedom' is 'sad'. The mood is downbeat, a man who is 'at home' must also be 'Unhappy'. The poet will feel 'lost' in the murderous bogs of Jutland, just as he does in the killing fields of Ulster.

6. 'Lightenings viii' retells the legend of a miraculous airship that appeared to the monks in their monastery at Clonmacnoise. Simple colloquial language frames this fantastic event. The physicality of the description of this dreamlike experience makes it more credible, 'hooked itself into the altar rails'. The vigorous activity of the crewman, captured in the dynamic verbs 'grappled', 'struggled' also add authenticity to this odd sight. Heaney completely up-ends our notions of belonging in the poem's conclusion. Viewing the sight from our perspective, we would regard the airship as 'marvellous', something out of the ordinary. But Heaney shows the sight from another perspective. The crewman regards our world as something 'marvellous'. The poet has challenged our sense of identity by making us understand that everything depends on point of view.

7. Heaney's poems explore identity and belonging through elegiac reconstructions of rural Irish life, through his detailed observations of people, places and agricultural implements. He examines his own identity as poet, yet is not content to remain rooted in Ireland, but soars upwards, truly getting to 'walk on air' while he challenges readers to be open to the wonder of new experiences.

(820 words)

EXAMINER'S COMMENT

A convincing critical response to the question, showing good engagement with the poetry of Heaney – both subject matter and style (especially sound effects, tone and imagery). Focused discussion supported by accurate quotation ranges widely over several key poems. Points are well-developed – although paragraph 4 is slightly unclear and disjointed. Overall, expression is fluent and assured (e.g. 'traditional sonnet nostalgically recreating a scene', 'jarring sounds recreate the painful truth of sectarian violence') adding to the top-grade standard of the essay.

GRADE: H1
P = 15/15
C = 14/15
L = 14/15
M = 5/5
Total = 48/50

 Revision Overview

'The Forge'
Sonnet celebrating traditional rural crafts and exploring the mysterious creative process of achieving poetic identity.

'Bogland'
Ireland's boglands function as a metaphor for the poet's search to find his national identity.

'The Tollund Man'
In responding to the violence in Northern Ireland during the 1970s, Heaney draws parallels with earlier victims in Jutland.

'Mossbawn: Sunlight'
Reflective recollection of the poet's childhood and the loving relationship he had with his Aunt Mary.

'A Constable Calls'
Coming-of-age experience illustrating the divisions between Northern Irish Catholics and the Protestant community.

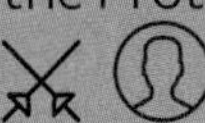

'The Skunk'
In this celebration of enduring love, the poet uses an affectionately teasing tone to express how he feels about his wife.

'The Harvest Bow'
A tender exploration of the father/son relationship and the unspoken understanding between them.

'The Underground'
Beautiful love poem that draws upon myth to revisit a hectic scene from the poet's honeymoon.

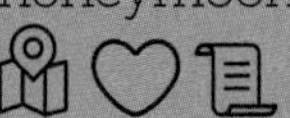

'Postscript'
The poet's description of experiencing transcendent beauty in the natural Irish landscape evokes powerful feelings.

'A Call'
Elegiac reflection on the passing of time and the poet's complex relationship with his father.

'Tate's Avenue'
Memories of particular places and moods are central to this poem which explores the theme of love in all of its richness.

'The Pitchfork'
Vivid recollection of rural life and the way everyday objects can become more than themselves through the power of the imagination.

'Lightenings viii'
In this curious and thought-provoking poem, Heaney makes room for everyday miracles and otherworldly wisdom.

Last Words

'A poet for whom sound is crucial, who relishes the way words and consonants knock around.'
Tim Nolan

'Heaney has achieved a hard-won clarity of vision.'
Heather Clark

'The best moments are those when your mind seems to implode and words and images rush of their own accord into the vortex.'
Seamus Heaney

 NATURE
 LOVE
 IDENTITY
 CREATIVITY
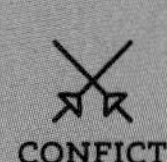 CONFICT
 PLACES
 HISTORY/ MEMORY
RELATIONSHIPS
 WONDER

Gerard Manley Hopkins 1844–1889

'Every poet must be original.'

Gerard Manley Hopkins, a priest and poet, was born in Stratford, outside London, in 1844. In 1863 he began studying classics at Balliol College, Oxford, where he wrote a great deal of poetry. Hopkins converted to Catholicism and was later ordained a Jesuit priest in 1877. It was while studying for the priesthood that he wrote some of his best-known religious and nature poems, including 'The Windhover' and 'Pied Beauty'. His compressed style of writing, especially his experimental use of language, sound effects and inventive rhythms, combined to produce distinctive and startling poetry. In 1884 Hopkins was appointed Professor of Greek at University College, Dublin. He disliked living in Ireland, where he experienced failing health and severe depression. In 1885 he wrote a number of the so-called 'terrible sonnets', including 'No Worst, There is None', which have desolation at their core. Hopkins died of typhoid fever in June 1889 without ever publishing any of his major poems. He is buried in Glasnevin Cemetery.

Investigate Further

To find out more about Gerard Manley Hopkins, or to hear readings of his poems, you could search some useful websites, such as YouTube, BBC Poetry, poetryfoundation.org and poetryarchive.org, or access additional material on this page of your eBook.

Prescribed Poems

○ **1 'God's Grandeur'**
Hopkins's sonnet welcomes the power of the Holy Ghost to rescue people from sin and hopelessness.
Page 296

○ **2 'Spring' (OL)**
This poem celebrates the natural beauty of springtime. However, Hopkins also regrets man's loss of innocence because of sin.
Page 300

○ **3 'As Kingfishers Catch Fire, Dragonflies Draw Flame'**
In recognising the uniqueness of everything that exists in the world, Hopkins praises God as the unchanging source of all creation.
Page 304

○ **4 'The Windhover'**
This was one of Hopkins's favourite poems and describes a bird in flight. Its powerful Christian theme focuses on the relationship between God and mankind.
Page 307

○ **5 'Pied Beauty'**
This short poem again celebrates the diverse delights of nature and human nature, all of which owe their existence to a changeless Creator. **Page 311**

○ **6 'Felix Randal'**
An engaging narrative poem about the life and death of one of Hopkins's parishioners. At a deeper level, it celebrates the significance of living a good Christian life.
Page 314

○ **7 'Inversnaid' (OL)**
Another nature poem rejoicing in the unspoiled beauty of the remote Scottish landscape. It concludes with the poet's heartfelt appeal to preserve the wilderness.
Page 318

○ **8 'I Wake and Feel the Fell of Dark, Not Day'**
One of the 'terrible sonnets' in which Hopkins reveals his personal torment, self-disgust and despair. Some critics argue that the poet is attempting to renew his own religious faith. **Page 321**

○ **9 'No Worst, There is None'**
Hopkins explores the experience of unbearable depression, guilt and the awful sense of feeling abandoned by God. Only sleep or death offer any relief. **Page 325**

○ **10 'Thou Art Indeed Just, Lord, if I Contend'**
In this intensely personal poem, Hopkins wonders why good people suffer while the wicked seem to prosper. He ends by pleading with God to strengthen his own faith. **Page 329**

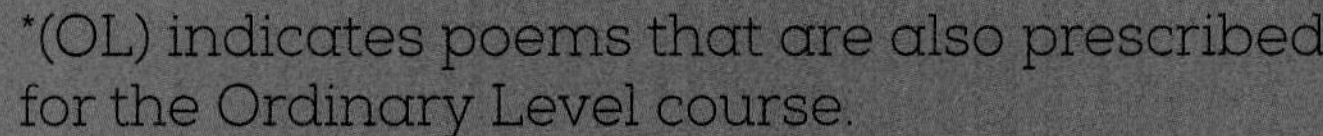

*(OL) indicates poems that are also prescribed for the Ordinary Level course.

1 God's Grandeur

The world is charged with the grandeur of God.
It will flame out, like shining from shook foil;
It gathers to a greatness, like the ooze of oil
Crushed. Why do men then now not reck his rod?
Generations have trod, have trod, have trod;
And all is seared with trade; bleared, smeared with toil;
And wears man's smudge and shares man's smell: the soil
Is bare now, nor can foot feel, being shod.

And for all this, nature is never spent;
There lives the dearest freshness deep down things;
And though the last lights off the black West went
Oh, morning, at the brown brink eastward, springs –
Because the Holy Ghost over the bent
World broods with warm breast and with ah! bright wings.

charged: powered; made responsible.
foil: shimmering gold or silver.

Crushed: compressed from olives or linseed.
reck his rod: pay heed to God's power.
seared: scorched; ruined.
bleared: blurred.
toil: industrialisation.
shod: covered; protected.

spent: exhausted.

last lights: the setting sun.

Note: Hopkins's philosophy emphasised the uniqueness of every natural thing, which he called inscape. He believed that there was a special connection between the world of nature and an individual's consciousness. Hopkins viewed the world as an integrated network created by God. The sensation of inscape (which the poet termed 'instress') is the appreciation that everything has its own unique identity. The concept is similar to that of epiphanies in James Joyce's writing.

Personal Response

1. Describe Hopkins's tone in the first four lines of this poem. Refer closely to the text in your answer.
2. How are human beings portrayed in the poem? Support your points with reference.
3. Select two unusual images the poet uses. Comment on the effectiveness of each.

Critical Literacy

Hopkins wrote many Italian (or Petrarchan) sonnets (consisting of an octave and a sestet). The form suited the stages in the argumentative direction of his themes. Like many other Christian poets, he 'found' God in nature. His poetry is also notable for its use of sprung rhythm (an irregular movement or pace which echoed ordinary conversation). 'God's Grandeur' is typical of Hopkins in both its subject matter and style. The condensed language, elaborate wordplay and unusual syntax – sometimes like a tongue-twister – can be challenging.

The poem's opening quatrain (four-line section) is characteristically dynamic. The **metaphor ('charged') compares God's greatness to electric power**, brilliant but hazardous. The visual effect of 'flame out' and 'shook foil' develops this representation of God's constant presence in the world. This image of oozing oil signifies a natural richness. The reference to electricity makes a subtle reappearance in line 4, where the 'rod' of an angry Creator is likened to a lightning bolt. The tone is one of energised celebration, but there is also a growing frustration: 'Why do men then now not reck his rod?' Hopkins seems mystified at human indifference to God's greatness.

The second quatrain is much more critical. We can sense the poet's own weariness with the numberless generations who have abandoned their spiritual salvation for the flawed material benefits of 'trade' and 'toil'. Hopkins's laboured repetition of 'have trod' is purposely heavy-handed. The internal rhymes of the negative verbs ('seared', 'bleared' and 'smeared') in line 6 convey his deep sense of disgust at a world blighted by industry and urbanisation. **Man's neglect of the natural environment is closely linked to the drift away from God**. Hopkins symbolises this spiritual alienation through the image of the 'shod' foot out of touch with nature and its Creator.

However, in response to his depression, the mood changes in the sestet (the final six lines of the sonnet). Hopkins's tone softens considerably and is aided by the gentle, sibilant effect in line 10: 'There lives the dearest freshness deep down things'. As in many of his religious poems, he takes comfort in conventional Christian belief. For him, 'nature is never spent'. The world is

filled with 'freshness' that confirms God's presence. This **power of renewal** is exemplified in the way morning never fails to follow the 'last lights' of dark night.

The reassuring image in the last line is of God guarding the world and promising rebirth and salvation. The source of this constant regeneration is 'the Holy Ghost' (God's grace) who 'broods' over a dependent world with the patient devotion of a bird protecting its young. In expressing his faith and surrendering himself to divine will, the poet can truly appreciate the grandeur of God. The final exclamations ('Oh, morning' and 'ah! bright wings') echo Hopkins's **sense of euphoria**.

Writing About the Poem

'Hopkins's original voice explores God's presence in this weary world.' Discuss this statement, with particular reference to the poem 'God's Grandeur'.

Sample Paragraph

Hopkins uses the Petrarchan sonnet form to examine man's lack of awareness of the beauty of God's world. A dynamic alliterative metaphor dramatically opens the poem, 'The world is charged with the grandeur of God'. His power and brilliance are conveyed through references to electricity, 'It will flame out, like shining from shook foil'. Yet man remains unconcerned at God's lightning bolt and does 'not reck his rod'. The tone in the second quatrain suggests the drudgery of man's mechanical world. The blight of industrialisation has 'smeared' God's glorious creation. The heavy repetition of 'have trod' coupled with the internally rhymed verbs ('seared' and 'bleared') show the horrendous effects of urbanisation on both man and landscape. Hopkins, in an innovative image, suggests that man is no longer in touch with his natural environment, the 'shod' foot can no longer feel the earth. A gentler tone emerges in the sestet. Hopkins realises the power of nature to regenerate itself, 'nature is never spent'. Unusual word order and a gentle sibilant effect stresses this ability to renew, 'There lives the dearest freshness deep down things'. I was impressed with Hopkins's religious belief expressed in the lovely natural image of the bird protecting its young, 'the Holy Ghost over the bent/World broods with warm breast'.

EXAMINER'S COMMENT

A very solid discussion on Hopkins's twin themes of God's power and man's indifference. There is a keen awareness of Hopkins's innovative use of language: 'A dynamic alliterative metaphor dramatically opens the poem'. Varied expressive language and accurate use of quotation also contribute to this top grade.

Class/Homework Exercises

1. Comment on Hopkins's use of sound in this poem. Refer closely to the text in your answer.
2. Hopkins is a poet of intense emotion, ecstasy and distress. Trace his expression of these emotions in your response. Support your answer with reference to 'God's Grandeur'.

Summary Points

- **Combination of conflicting emotions, ecstasy and distress.**
- **Natural world enlivened by God's presence.**
- **Assonance and alliteration emphasise despondency, man's neglect of natural environment associated with drift away from God.**
- **Belief in nature's ability to regenerate.**
- **Sonnet concludes with a benevolent image of Holy Ghost as benevolent mother bird.**
- **Tone becomes more reassuring in the sestet.**

2 Spring

Nothing is so beautiful as Spring –
  When weeds, in wheels, shoot long and lovely and lush;
  Thrush's eggs look little low heavens, and thrush
Through the echoing timber does so rinse and wring
The ear, it strikes like lightnings to hear him sing;
  The glassy peartree leaves and blooms, they brush
  The descending blue; that blue is all in a rush
With richness; the racing lambs too have fair their fling.

What is all this juice and all this joy?
  A strain of the earth's sweet being in the beginning
In Eden garden. – Have, get, before it cloy,
  Before it cloud, Christ, lord, and sour with sinning,
Innocent mind and Mayday in girl and boy,
  Most, O maid's child, thy choice and worthy the winning.

in wheels: radiating out like spokes; rampant; pivoting movement.
lush: growing thickly, luxuriantly.
Thrush's eggs: songbird's eggs, which are light blue.
rinse: wash out with fresh water.
wring: to twist or squeeze; drain off excess water.

have fair their fling: the lambs are enjoying their freedom.

strain: a trace; streak; a segment of melody.

cloud: darken; depress.

Mayday: innocence of the young.
Most: the best choice.
maid's child: Jesus, son of Mary.

'that blue is all in a rush'

Personal Response

1. Describe Hopkins's tone in the first eight lines of the poem. Refer to the text in your response.
2. What is the mood in the second section of the poem? What reasons would you give for this change in the sestet? Use reference or quotation to support your point of view.
3. Write your own personal response to this poem, commenting on both the subject matter and style.

Critical Literacy

'Spring' was written in May 1877. Hopkins had a special devotion to Mary, Queen of Heaven, and May is the month that is devoted to her. The poem was written after a holiday spent walking and writing poetry in Wales. Hopkins's emphatic language captures the exuberance of nature bursting into life.

The simple opening sentence in the first section, 'Nothing is so beautiful as Spring', is a deliberately exaggerated statement (hyperbole) used to emphasise a feeling. This Petrarchan sonnet's octet starts with an **ecstatic account of the blooming of nature in spring**. As we examine the poet's use of language, we can understand why it should be heard rather than read. Here in the second line – 'When weeds, in wheels, shoot long and lovely and lush' – the alliteration of 'w' and 'l', the assonance of 'ee' and the slow, broad vowels 'o' and 'u' add to this description of abundant growth. We can easily imagine the wild flowers growing before our eyes, as if caught by a slow-motion camera, uncurling and straightening to reach the heavens.

The **energy of the new plants** is contained in the verb 'shoot'. Just as the plants are shooting from the fertile earth, so one word seems to sprout out of another in the poem, e.g. 'thrush' springing from 'lush'. Now we are looking down, carefully examining a delicately beautiful sight among the long grasses: 'Thrush's eggs look little low heavens'. Note the speckled appearance of the eggs, similar to the dappling of blue and white in the sky. The oval shape is like the dome of the heavens.

The poet's **breathless excitement** at the sight of Heaven on earth is caught by the omission of the word 'like'. We hear the song of the bird as the assonance of 'rinse' and 'wring' fills our ears with strikingly rich sounds. It has a powerful effect, like a bolt of lightning. The focus shifts to the gleam on the leaves of the pear tree, as its 'glassy' appearance is observed. Hopkins looked closely at objects to try to capture their essence (inscape).

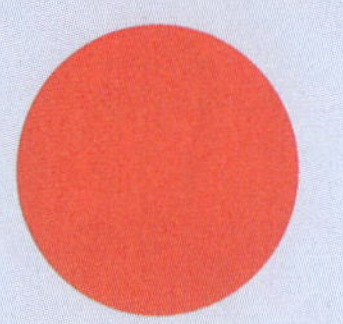

Hopkins **pushes language** to its boundaries as nouns become verbs ('leaves' and 'blooms'). The sky seems to bend down to reach the growing trees: 'they brush/The descending blue'. The blueness of the sky is captured in the alliteration of 'all in a rush/With richness'. Meanwhile, newborn lambs are frolicking happily, 'fair their fling'. This octet is a joyous exploration of a kaleidoscope of the colours, sounds and movement of spring. The poet's imagination soars as he strains language to convey the immediacy of the moment.

In the sestet, **the mood becomes reflective** as the poet considers the significance of nature: 'What is all this juice and all this joy?' As he meditates, he decides it is 'A strain of the earth's sweet being', a fleeting glimpse of a perfect world 'In Eden garden', before it was sullied with sin. Hopkins **had a deep love of God**, especially as the Creator. His tone becomes insistent as he urges God to grasp the world in order to preserve it in its perfect state. The hard 'c' sound of 'cloy' and 'cloud' shows how the beauty will become stained and imperfect if Christ does not act swiftly. Hopkins desires virtue and purity: 'innocence', 'Mayday in girl and boy'. He refers to Christ as Mary's child ('O maid's child') as he attempts to persuade God that this world is worth the effort ('worthy the winning').

The regular rhyme scheme adds to the music of the poem as well as emphasising key words: 'joy', 'cloy', 'boy', 'beginning', 'Sinning', 'winning'. The poet was influenced by reading the medieval theologian Duns Scotus, who said that the material world was an incarnation of God. Thus Hopkins felt justified in his preoccupation with the material world, as it had a sacramental value.

Writing About the Poem

'Hopkins uses poetry to speak of the glory of God.' Write a paragraph in response to this statement, using reference or quotation from 'Spring' to support your views.

Sample Paragraph

Hopkins had felt uneasy loving the natural world in case it distracted him from loving God, which was the main focus of his life. But after reading the theologian Duns Scotus, who maintained that the material world was a representation of God, Hopkins felt if he loved nature, he was loving its creator. So in giving us the glorious octet of this poem 'Spring', with the weeds 'long and lovely and lush', the blue of the sky in 'a rush/With richness', the thrush's eggs like 'little low heavens', Hopkins is worshipping

God. In the sestet he becomes more reflective as he more closely links the poem to the glory of God as he meditates on the meaning of all this 'juice' and 'joy'. He thinks we have seen a glimpse, 'A strain', of the earth before the Fall of Adam and Eve. He asks God to preserve the world in its sinless state. We also see his devotion to the Mother of God, Our Lady in this poem. The references to 'O maid's child' and 'Mayday' confirm this. May is the month associated with the worship of Mary, Queen of Heaven.

EXAMINER'S COMMENT

This confident answer has noted some of the key influences on Hopkins (Duns Scotus) in his decision to glorify God in his poetry. Personal engagement with the poem is evident in the lively language, e.g. 'in giving us the glorious octet of this poem'. Expression throughout is clear: 'He asks God to preserve the world in its sinless state.' The effective use of accurate quotation is central to this successful top-grade response.

Class/Homework Exercises

1. Hopkins employs language in an energetic, intense and religious way. Do you agree? Use reference to the poem 'Spring' in your answer.
2. Hopkins is fascinated by the uniqueness of things. How does Hopkins convey the wonder of the individuality of an object through his use of language in this poem?

Summary Points

- **Euphoric declaration of beauty of nature.**
- **Jubilant tone, rush of energy, one word sprouts from another.**
- **Rich visual detail and stunning sound effects.**
- **Religious impulse, reflection on innocence, God's beauty in nature and man.**
- **Sonnet form – descriptive octet and reflective sestet.**

3 As Kingfishers Catch Fire, Dragonflies Draw Flame

As kingfishers catch fire, dragonflies draw flame;
  As tumbled over rim in roundy wells
  Stones ring; like each tucked string tells, each hung bell's
Bow swung finds tongue to fling out broad its name;
Each mortal thing does one thing and the same:
  Deals out that being indoors each one dwells;
  Selves – goes itself; myself it speaks and spells,
Crying *What I do is me: for that I came.*

I say more: the just man justices;
  Keeps grace: that keeps all his goings graces;
Acts in God's eye what in God's eye he is –
  Christ. For Christ plays in ten thousand places,
Lovely in limbs, and lovely in eyes not his
  To the Father through the features of men's faces.

kingfishers: brilliantly coloured birds that hunt small fish.
dragonflies: brightly coloured insects with transparent wings.
tucked: plucked.
Bow: rim of bell that makes a sound when struck.

Selves: (used as a verb) defining or expressing its distinctiveness.

justices: (as a verb) acting justly.
Keeps grace: obeys God's will.

'dragonflies draw flame'

Personal Response

1. Comment on the nature images in the poem's opening line.
2. Select two interesting sound effects from the poem and briefly explain the effectiveness of each.
3. 'Celebration is the central theme in this poem.' Write your response to this statement, supporting your answer with reference to the text.

Critical Literacy

This sonnet is often cited as an example of Hopkins's theory of inscape, the uniqueness of every created thing as a reflection of God's glory. The poet believed that human beings had the uniqueness to recognise the divine presence in everything around us. The poem is written in an irregular ('sprung') rhythm that gives it a more concentrated quality.

The poem begins with two strikingly vivid images as Hopkins describes some of nature's most dazzling creatures. In line 1, he observes their vivid colour and dynamic movement (note the sharp alliteration and fast-paced rhythm) in the brilliant sunlight. The poet associates both the kingfisher and the dragonflies with fire. Aural images dominate lines 2–4. He takes **great delight in the uniqueness of existence** by listing a variety of everyday sounds: the tinkling noise of pebbles ('Stones ring') tossed down wells, the plucking of a stringed instrument and the loud ringing of a bell are all defined through their own distinctive sounds.

Hopkins is certain that the same quality applies to humans – 'Each mortal thing'. **We all express our unique inner selves**. Every individual does the same by presenting their inner essence (that dwells 'indoors'). The poet invents his own verb to convey how each of us 'Selves' (or expresses) our individual identity. The didactic tone of lines 7–8 clearly reflects his depth of feeling, summed up by his emphatic illustration about our god-given purpose on earth: 'What I do is me: for that I came'.

Hopkins's enthusiasm ('I say more') intensifies at the start of the sestet. His central argument is that **people should fulfil their destiny by being themselves**. Again, he invents a new verb to illustrate his point: 'the just man justices' (good people behave in a godly way). Acting 'in God's eye' and availing of God's grace is our purpose on earth. The poet focuses on his belief that human beings are made in God's image and have the capacity to become like the omnipresent Christ.

Hopkins's final lines are filled with the devout Christian faith that **God will redeem everyone who 'Keeps grace'**. The poet repeatedly reminds us of the 'Lovely' personal relationship between God and mankind. It is Christ's presence within every human being that makes 'the features of men's faces' lovely in God's sight. Typically, Hopkins is fully convinced of the reality of Christ and the existence of the spirit world. He sees his own role as a 'kingfisher' catching fire – reeling in souls with his mystical poems of hope and spirituality.

Some critics have commented that the poem is too instructive and that Hopkins was overly concerned with getting across his message at the expense of method. The poet himself did not consider it a success. Yet there is no denying the poetic language of feeling and excitement in every line of the poem.

Writing About the Poem

What aspects of this poem are typical of Hopkins's distinctive poetic style? Refer closely to the text in your answer.

Sample Paragraph

It seems to me that Hopkins the priest is the key speaker in 'As Kingfishers Catch Fire'. To me, the poem is not as typical as 'God's Grandeur' or 'Spring'. However, his writing is unique. It is full of energy and unusual language patterns. It starts with lively images drawn from nature – 'As kingfishers catch fire, dragonflies draw flame'. In my opinion, no other poet on our course could write as precisely as this. There is an immediacy about his images that demands attention. The alliteration of 'f' and 'd' sounds suggest blinding flashes of colour, darting flames and dramatic movements – exactly what fish and insects do in their natural habitats. Hopkins uses personification to show the vitality of the natural world – 'Stones ring'. He makes up new words of his own, such as 'justices'. Again, this is typical of his vibrant style. Hopkins does not bother with strict grammar either. He reduces sentences to childlike phrases to show his joy in being aware of the mystery of creation – 'For Christ plays in ten thousand places'. Even here, the alliteration adds energy to the rush of language. This is typical of so much of his poetry.

EXAMINER'S COMMENT

This answer is somewhat narrowly focused, lacking development of points raised, e.g. 'Hopkins does not bother with strict grammar either'. More thorough engagement with the body of the poem is expected for a top grade. This note-like response, listing significant elements of Hopkins's style, comes short of the highest grade.

Class/Homework Exercises

1. Hopkins admitted that his poetry had an 'oddness' about it. Comment on his management of language in this poem. Refer closely to the text in your answer.
2. Hopkins uses the Petrarchan sonnet form of an octet (eight lines) and sestet (six lines) in this poem. How does the poet's treatment of his theme of wonder change in these two sections? Support your answer with close reference to the text.

Summary Points

- **Distinctive quality of everything in the natural world.**
- **Invents verb, 'selves', to suggest unique quality of nature and man.**
- **Aural imagery, onomatopoeia, use of everyday sounds, sprung rhythm.**
- **Emphasises the importance of acceptance of God's will.**

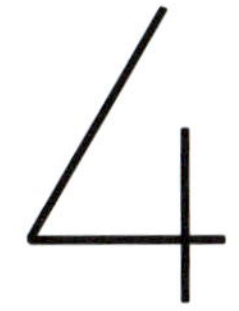

The Windhover

GERARD MANLEY HOPKINS

To Christ our Lord

I caught this morning morning's minion, kingdom
of daylight's dauphin, dapple-dawn-drawn Falcon, in his riding
Of the rolling level underneath him steady air, and striding
High there, how he rung upon the rein of a wimpling wing
In his ecstasy! then off, off forth on swing,
As a skate's heel sweeps smooth on a bow-bend: the hurl
and gliding
Rebuffed the big wind. My heart in hiding
Stirred for a bird, – the achieve of, the mastery of the thing!

Brute beauty and valour and act, oh air, pride, plume here
Buckle! AND the fire that breaks from thee then, a billion
Times told lovelier, more dangerous, O my chevalier!

No wonder of it: sheer plod makes plough down sillion
Shine, and blue-bleak embers, ah my dear,
Fall, gall themselves, and gash gold-vermilion.

Windhover: a kestrel or small falcon; resembles a cross in flight.

minion: favourite; darling.
dauphin: prince, heir to French throne.
dapple-dawn-drawn: the bird is outlined in patches of colour by the dawn light, an example of Hopkins's use of compression.
rung upon the rein: circling movement of a horse at the end of a long rein held by a trainer; the sound of the bird pealing like a bell as it wheels in the sky.
wimpling: pleated.
bow-bend: a wide arc.
Rebuffed: pushed back; mastered.
My heart in hiding: the poet is afraid, unlike the bird.

Buckle: pull together; clasp; fall apart.
chevalier: medieval knight; Hopkins regards God as a knight who will defend him against evil.
sheer plod: back-breaking drudgery of hard work, similar to Hopkins's work as a priest.
ah my dear: intimate address to God.
Fall, gall ... gash: a reference to the Crucifixion of Christ as He fell on the way to Cavalry, was offered vinegar and gashed by a spear on the cross.
gold-vermilion: gold and red, the colours of Christ the Saviour and also of the Eucharist, the Body and Blood of Christ which offers redemption.

'how he rung upon the rein of a wimpling wing'

Personal Response

1. In your opinion, has the poet been as daring in his use of language as the bird has been in its flight? Support your view by referring closely to the poem.
2. The sonnet moves from description to reflection. What does the poet meditate on in the sestet? Refer to the poem in your answer.
3. Write your own personal response to the poem, referring closely to the text in your answer.

Critical Literacy

'The Windhover' was Hopkins's favourite poem, 'the best thing I ever wrote'. It is dedicated to Christ – Hopkins wrote it in 1877, when he was thirty-three years old, the same age as Christ when he died. The poet celebrates the uniqueness of the bird and his own deep relationship with God the Creator.

The name of the bird comes from its custom of hovering in the air, facing the wind, as it views the ground for its prey. The opening lines of the octet are **joyful and celebratory** as Hopkins rejoices in the sight of the bird, 'daylight's dauphin'. The verb 'caught' suggests not just that the poet caught sight of the bird, but also that he 'caught' the essence of the bird on the page with words. This is an example of Hopkins's compression of language where he edges two meanings into one word or phrase. Hopkins shaped language by omitting articles, conjunctions and verbs to express the energy of the bird, 'off forth on swing'. **Movement fascinated the poet**. The bird is sketched by the phrase 'dapple-dawn-drawn'. A vivid image of the flecks of colour on his wings (as the dawn light catches him) is graphically drawn here.

The **momentary freshness** is conveyed by 'this morning', with the bird in flight beautifully captured by the simile 'As a skate's heel sweeps smooth on a bow-bend'. The 's' sound mimics the swish of the skater as a large arc is traced on the ice. This curve is similar to the strong but graceful bend of a bow stretched to loose its arrow, with all its connotations of beauty of line and deadly strength.

In the octet, there is typical **energetic language**: 'how he rung upon the rein of a wimpling wing/In his ecstasy!' This carries us along in its breathless description. The word 'wimpling' refers to the beautiful, seemingly pleated pattern of the arrangement of the outstretched wings of the bird. The capital 'F' used for 'Falcon' hints at its symbolism for Christ. This very personal poem uses 'I' in the octet and 'my' in the sestet. Hopkins lavishes praise on the bird: 'dauphin' (young prince, heir) and 'minion' (darling). Run-on lines add to the poet's excitement. He acknowledges that the bird

has what he himself does not possess: power, self-belief and grace ('My heart in hiding'). The lively rhyme, such as 'riding'/'striding', never becomes repetitive because of the varying line breaks. The octet concludes with Hopkins's admiration of 'the thing', which broadens the focus from the particular to the general. All of creation is magnificent.

This leads to the sestet, where **God the Creator becomes central to the poem**. The essence (inscape) of the bird is highlighted: 'air, pride, plume here'. The bird is strong, brave, predatory, graceful and beautiful. The word 'Buckle' is paradoxical, as it contains two contradictory meanings: clasp together and fall apart. The bird is holding the line when it rides the rolling wind and falls apart as it swoops down on its prey. Capital letters for the conjunction 'AND' signal a moment of insight: 'the fire that breaks from thee'. The pronoun refers to God, whose magnificence is shown by 'fire'. The Holy Spirit is often depicted as a bird descending with tongues of flame. A soft tone of intimacy emerges: 'O my chevalier!' It is as if Hopkins wants God to act as the honourable knight of old, to take up his cause and fight on his behalf against his enemy. God will be Hopkins's defender against evil.

The sestet concludes with **two exceptional images**, both breaking apart to release their hidden brilliance. The ploughed furrow and the 'bluebleak embers' of coal both reveal their beauty in destruction: 'sillion/Shine', 'gash gold-vermilion'. Christ endured Calvary and crucifixion, 'Fall, gall ... gash', and through his sacrifice, the 'Fall', achieved redemption for us. So too the priest embracing the drudgery of his service embraces his destiny by submitting to the will of God. In doing so, he reflects the greatness of God. Earthly glory is crushed to release heavenly glory. The phrase 'ah my dear' makes known the dominant force of Hopkins's life: to love God. The colours of gold and red are those of Christ the Saviour as well as the colours associated with the Eucharist, the Body and Blood of Christ. When Christians receive the sacrament of Holy Communion, they are redeemed. So, as the poem begins, 'dapple-dawn-drawn Falcon', it ends with 'gold-vermilion' in a triumph of glorious colour.

Writing About the Poem

'Hopkins's intense reflections on Christ in his poetry are always conveyed with visual energy.' Discuss this statement, with particular reference to 'The Windhover'.

Sample Paragraph

In 'The Windhover', Hopkins uses the image of the falcon, which hovers in a cross-shape on the wind, as an emblem of Christ. Using strong images, the poet describes the bird's magnificent beauty, 'dapple-dawn-drawn', and its strength, 'rebuffed the big wind'. In the sestet, Hopkins calls God 'O my chevalier'. This gives a vivid picture of a highly moral individual who was both strong-willed and who fought against evil. The verb 'Buckle' reminds me of the knight putting on his armour and stumbling in battle. Christ also fell on the way to Cavalry where he was crucified – out of which a great glory was given to man, 'the fire that breaks from thee'. Hopkins felt it was right to focus on nature as evidence of the power and beauty of God. In glorifying Him through the dramatic emblem of the windhover, he is glorifying divine creation, and therefore God Himself. The flash of red and gold, with which this visually powerful poem ends, 'gash gold-vermilion', reminds me that the priest carrying out his ordinary duties is also revealing the beauty of God's creation. I think Hopkins's reflections on Christ add a real spiritual dimension to his poetry.

EXAMINER'S COMMENT

Close reading of the poem is evident in this top-grade personal response: 'The verb "Buckle" reminds me of the knight putting on his armour'. Quotations are very well used here to highlight Hopkins's commitment to his Christian faith, 'The flash of red and gold, with which the poem ends, "gash gold-vermilion", reminds me that the lowly priest carrying out his ordinary duties is also revealing the beauty of God's creation.' Well-controlled language use throughout.

Class/Homework Exercises

1. Would you agree that 'The Windhover' illustrates much that is both spiritual and explicitly Christian in Hopkins's poetry? Give reasons for your response.
2. Hopkins creates a powerful sense of drama throughout 'The Windhover'. Discuss this view, using reference to the poem.

Summary Points

- **Deeply personal poem, engaging opening.**
- **Relationship with God accentuated by poet's ability to see the divine in nature.**
- **Medieval chivalric imagery.**
- **Bird's movement depicted by alliteration and assonance.**
- **Optimistic ending, illustrated by 'blue-black' becoming 'gold-vermilion'.**

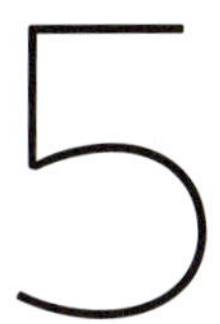

Pied Beauty

Pied: varied.

Glory be to God for dappled things –
For skies of couple-colour as a brinded cow;
For rose-moles all in stipple upon trout that swim;
Fresh-firecoal chestnut-falls; finches' wings;
Landscape plotted and pieced – fold, fallow, and plough;
And all trades, their gear and tackle and trim.

All things counter, original, spare, strange;
Whatever is fickle, freckled (who knows how?)
With swift, slow; sweet, sour; adazzle, dim;
He fathers-forth whose beauty is past change:
Praise him.

dappled: speckled, spotted.
brinded: streaked.
rose-moles: red-pink spots.
stipple: dotted.
Fresh-firecoal chestnut falls: open chestnuts bright as burning coals.
pieced: enclosed.
fold: sheep enclosure.
fallow: unused.
trades: farmwork.
gear: equipment.
tackle: implements.
trim: fittings.
counter: contrasting.
spare: special.
fickle: changeable.
He: God.
fathers-forth: creates.

'skies of couple-colour'

Personal Response

1. In your view, what is the central theme in this poem? Refer to the text in your answer.
2. Discuss the poet's use of sound effects in the poem. Support your answer with quotations.
3. Choose two striking images from the poem and comment on the effectiveness of each.

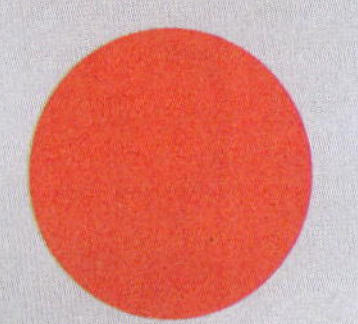

Critical Literacy

'Pied Beauty' is one of Hopkins's 'curtal' (or curtailed) sonnets, in which he condenses the traditional sonnet form. It was written in the so-called sprung rhythm that he developed, based on the irregular rhythms of traditional Welsh verse. The poem's energetic language – particularly its sound effects – reflects Hopkins's view of the rich, abundant diversity evident within God's creation.

The simplicity of the prayer-like opening line ('Glory be to God') is reminiscent of biblical language and sets the poem's devotional tone. From the start, Hopkins displays a **childlike wonder** for all the 'dappled things' around him, illustrating his central belief with a series of vivid examples from the natural world.

Included in his panoramic sweep of nature's vibrant delights are the dominant blues and whites of the sky, which he compares to the streaked ('brinded') patterns of cowhide. The world is teeming with contrasting colours and textures, captured in **detailed images**, such as 'rose-moles all in stipple upon trout' and 'Fresh-firecoal chestnut-falls'.

For the exhilarated poet, everything in nature is linked. It is ironic, of course, that what all things share is their god-given individuality. In line 4, he associates broken chestnuts with burning coals in a fire, black on the outside and glowing underneath. In turn, the wings of finches have similar colours. Condensed imagery and compound words add even greater energy to the description.

Hopkins turns his attention to human nature in lines 5–6. The farmland features he describes reflect hard work and efficiency: 'Landscape plotted and pieced – fold, fallow, and plough'. The range of man's impact on the natural world is also worth celebrating, and this is reinforced by the **orderly syntax and insistent rhythm**. Human activity in tune with nature also glorifies God.

Hopkins's final four lines focus on the **unexpected beauty of creation** and further reveal the poet's passionate Christianity. As though overcome by the scale and variety of God's works – 'who knows how?' – the poet meditates on a range of contrasting adjectives ('swift, slow; sweet, sour; adazzle, dim'), all of which indicate the wonderful diversity of creation. As always, the alliteration gives an increased dynamism to this image of abundance and variety in nature.

The poem ends as it began – with a shortened version of the two mottoes of St Ignatius of Loyola, founder of the Jesuits: *Ad majorem Dei* gloriam (to the greater glory of God) and *Laus Deo semper* (praise be to God always). For Hopkins, **God is beyond change**. The Creator ('He fathers-forth') and all the 'dappled' opposites that enrich our ever-changing world inspire us all to 'Praise him'.

Writing About the Poem

'Hopkins's appreciation of the energy present in the world is vividly expressed in his unique poetry.' Discuss this statement, with particular reference to 'Pied Beauty'.

Sample Paragraph

It seems to me that 'Pied Beauty' is more like a heartfelt prayer than an ordinary poem. It begins with the phrase 'Glory be to God' and continues to the final words 'Praise him'. In between, Hopkins lists a whole litany of examples of the variety of the 'dappled' natural environment, the 'brinded' patterns of cowhide, 'landscape plotted and pieced'. The pace of the poem is rapid as though he is in a rush to explain his astonishment: 'Fresh-firecoal chestnut-falls'. There is an overwhelming sense of God's mystery and greatness. This is partly due to the compound phrases, such as 'couple-colour' and 'rose-moles' which make us more aware of the varied appearances of natural things. The energetic rhythm builds to a climax in the last line. This is short, direct and almost breathless – just one simple monosyllabic phrase that sums up Hopkins's awareness of God's creation: 'Praise him'. From start to finish, I can easily appreciate Hopkins's personal sense of the overpoweringly beautiful world around him.

EXAMINER'S COMMENT

A short, focused response that ranges over a number of interesting features of Hopkins's style, particularly his description of nature's energy: 'The pace of the poem is rapid, as though he is in a rush to explain his astonishment'. The rapidity of Hopkins's verse is effectively explored, particularly in the reference to the lead-up to the climax in the poem's final line. A successful top-grade answer.

Class/Homework Exercises

1. Compare and contrast the views expressed in 'Pied Beauty' with any other 'religious' poem by Hopkins from your course. Support your answer with reference to both poems.
2. In your opinion, how does Hopkins express his attitude towards God in this poem? Refer to his use of imagery and pay particular attention to the concluding four lines.

Summary Points

- **Condensed version (ten and a half lines) of traditional sonnet form (fourteen lines).**
- **Anthem of praise to God for nature's variety.**
- **Catalogue of vibrant examples of 'dappled beauty'. Effective use of compound words.**
- **Alliteration conveys how man's activities are in harmony with God's design.**

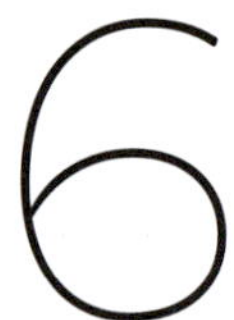

Felix Randal

Felix Randal: the parishioner's name was Felix Spenser. 'Felix' in Latin means 'happy'. Randal can also mean a lowly, humble thing or trodden on.

Felix Randal the farrier, O he is dead then? my duty all ended,
Who have watched his mould of man, big-boned and
  hardy-handsome
Pining, pining, till time when reason rambled in it, and some
Fatal four disorders, fleshed there, all contended?

Sickness broke him. Impatient he cursed at first, but mended
Being anointed and all; though a heavenlier heart began some
Months earlier, since I had our sweet reprieve and ransom
Tendered to him. Ah well, God rest him all road ever he offended!

This seeing the sick endears them to us, us too it endears.
My tongue had taught thee comfort, touch had quenched thy
  tears
Thy tears that touched my heart, child, Felix, poor Felix Randal;

How far from then forethought of, all thy more boisterous years,
When thou at the random grim forge, powerful amidst peers,
Didst fettle for the great grey drayhorse his bright and battering
  sandal!

farrier: blacksmith.
O he is dead then: reaction of priest at Felix's death.
hardy-handsome: compound word describing the fine physical appearance of the blacksmith.

disorders: diseases.
contended: competitively fought over Felix.

anointed: sacraments administered to the sick by a priest.
reprieve and ransom: the sacraments of confession and communion where Christians are redeemed from sin.
Tendered: offered.
all road ever: in whatever way (local dialect).

random: casual; irregular.
fettle: prepare.
drayhorse: big horse used to pull heavy carts.
sandal: type of horseshoe.

'at the random grim forge'

Personal Response

1. 'Hopkins is a poet who celebrates ordinary life and simple religious faith in his poem, "Felix Randal".' Discuss this statement with reference to the poem, illustrating your answer with quotations.
2. How does the octet differ from the sestet in this Petrarchan sonnet? Refer to theme and style in your response. Use quotations in support of your views.
3. Choose two aural images that you found interesting and give reasons for their effectiveness.

Critical Literacy

'Felix Randal' was written in Liverpool in 1880. The poem contrasts with others such as 'Spring'. Hopkins had been placed as a curate to the city slums of Liverpool, 'a most unhappy and miserable spot', in his opinion. He didn't communicate successfully with his parishioners and he didn't write much poetry, except this one poem about the blacksmith who died of tuberculosis, aged thirty-one.

The opening of the octet identifies the man with his name and occupation, 'Felix Randal the farrier'. Then the poet shocks us with the priest's reaction: 'O he is dead then? my duty all ended'. On first reading, this sounds both dismissive and cold. However, when we consider that the death was expected and that the priest had seen all this many times, we realise that the line rings with authenticity. For Hopkins, 'duty' was a sacred office. **The farrier is recalled in his physical prime**, using the alliteration of 'm', 'b' and 'h' in the phrase 'mould of man, big-boned and hardy-handsome'. The repetition of 'Pining, pining' marks his decline in health. His illness is graphically conveyed as his mental health deteriorated ('reason rambled') and the diseases attacked his body ('Fatal four disorders, fleshed there, all contended'). **The illnesses took possession of the body** and waged a horrific battle to win supremacy, eventually killing Felix.

The word 'broke' is suitable in this context, as in the world of horses it refers to being trained. Is Felix trained ('broke') through suffering? His realistic reaction to the news – 'he cursed' – changes when he receives the sacraments ('being anointed'). Felix was broken but is now restored by 'our sweet reprieve and ransom', the healing sacraments. **The tone changes** with the personal pronoun. The priest–patient relationship is acknowledged: we, both priest and layperson, are saved by God. A note of resigned acceptance, almost an anti-climax, is evident in the line 'Ah well, God rest him all road ever he offended!' The use of the Lancashire dialect ('all road') by the priest shows a developing relationship between the two men.

The detached priest's voice resurfaces in the sestet: 'seeing the sick'. This section of the sonnet focuses on the **reality of sickness** and its effects. Both Felix and the priest received something from the experience. We respond to the sick with sympathy ('the sick endears them to us'), but we also appreciate ourselves and our own health more ('us too it endears') as we face another's mortality. The priest comforted the dying man with words ('My tongue') and the Last Sacraments, anointing by 'touch' and becomes a father figure to 'child' Felix. Is there a suggestion that one must become like an innocent child to enter the kingdom of Heaven? The tercet (three-line segment) is intimate: 'thee', 'thy', 'Thy tears', 'my heart'. The last tercet explodes in a **dramatic flashback** to the energy of the young blacksmith in his prime, when there was little thought of death: 'How far from then forethought'. Onomatopoeia and alliteration convey the lifeforce (inscapes) of the young Felix, 'boisterous' and 'powerful amidst peers'.

Sprung rhythm adds to the force of the poem as the six main stresses are interspersed with an irregular number of unstressed syllables. Felix did a man's job at the 'grim forge' when he made the 'bright and battering sandal' for the powerful carthorse, powerfully conveyed in the assonance of 'great grey drayhorse'. The poem ends not with Felix in heavenly glory, but in his former earthly glory: 'thou ... Didst fettle'. God has fashioned Felix through his suffering just as Felix had fashioned the horseshoe. Both required force and effort to bend them to the shape in which they can function properly. The poem is a celebration of God's creation of the man.

Writing About the Poem

'Hopkins is a poet who celebrates unique identities and individual experiences, exploring their meaning and worth.' Discuss this statement in relation to one or more of the poems on your course, quoting in support of your points.

Sample Paragraph

In 'Felix Randal', Hopkins captures the unique essence of a great big strong man struck down by illness. He was 'big-boned and hardy-handsome', and the alliteration emphasises the magnificence of his physique. His understandable reaction to his own misfortune is evident in 'he cursed at first', the assonance echoing the deep guttural oaths. The repeated 'f' of 'Fatal four disorders, fleshed there' conveys the impossible odds stacked against the man. Here Hopkins has given us the unique identity of the man. He also gives us the dismissive voice of the weary priest: 'O he is dead then? my duty all ended'. Here is a man who has seen too much suffering. His use of the Lancashire expression 'all road' shows how he has tried to enter the world of his parishioners,

but he quickly reverts back to his professional capacity: 'This seeing the sick'. He has a strong belief that the sacraments will help: 'sweet reprieve and ransom'. So Hopkins also gives us the individual essence of the weary priest trying his best for the sick in his care. The poem leaves us feeling that the priest has received as much from the sick man as the sick man has received from the priest: 'Thy tears that touched my heart'.

EXAMINER'S COMMENT

As part of a full essay answer, this paragraph has dealt comprehensively with the various elements of the question. The close attention to the poet's use of language, assonance and alliteration, enhances the answer. Real personal engagement with the poem is evident in the in-depth discussion of the priest's transition from tiredness to his regained 'professional capacity'. A successful answer that merits the top grade.

Class/Homework Exercises

1. Hopkins deals with suffering in his poetry. Has this any relevance to the modern reader? Use reference to 'Felix Randal' in your answer.
2. Hopkins gives a vivid portrait of the farrier. Discuss how his changing tone conveys his view of Felix Randal. Support your answer with close reference to the text.

Summary Points

- **Inscape (essence captured) of blacksmith in this Petrarchan Sonnet.**
- **Focus on man's insignificance; glory only achieved through Christian faith.**
- **Sprung rhythm (many unstressed syllables) add to poem's energy.**
- **Simple everyday speech and colloquialisms root poem firmly in North of England.**
- **Final image is positive; 'b' sound accentuates energy.**

7 Inversnaid

Title: Inversnaid is a remote area located near Loch Lomond in the Scottish Highlands.

This darksome burn, horseback brown,
His rollrock highroad roaring down,
In coop and in comb the fleece of his foam
Flutes and low to the lake falls home.

A windpuff-bonnet of fawn-froth
Turns and twindles over the broth
Of a pool so pitchblack, fell-frowning,
It rounds and rounds Despair to drowning.

Degged with dew, dappled with dew
Are the groins of the braes that the brook treads through,
Wiry heathpacks, flitches of fern,
And the beadbonny ash that sits over the burn.

What would the world be, once bereft
Of wet and of wildness? Let them be left,
O let them be left, wildness and wet;
Long live the weeds and the wilderness yet.

burn: stream.
coop: hollow.
comb: moving freely.
Flutes: grooves; whistles.
twindles: spins.
fell: fiercely.
Degged: sprinkled about.
groins of the braes: sides of hills.
heathpacks: heather outcrops.
flitches: ragged tufts.
beadbonny: mountain ash tree with bright berries.
bereft: deprived.

'the fleece of his foam'

Personal Response

1. From your reading of the first stanza, explain how the poet conveys the stream's energy.
2. Sound effects play a key part in the second and third stanzas. Choose two aural images that convey Hopkins's excited reaction to the mountain stream. Comment on the effectiveness of each.
3. Write your own personal response to the poem, referring closely to the text in your answer.

Critical Literacy

'Inversnaid' was written in 1881 after Hopkins visited the remote hillsides around Loch Lomond. He disliked being in cities and much preferred the sights and sounds of the wilderness. The poem is unusual for Hopkins in that there is no direct mention of God as the source of all this natural beauty.

The opening lines of stanza one are dramatic. Hopkins compares the brown, rippling stream ('This darksome burn') to a wild horse's back. The forceful alliteration – 'rollrock highroad roaring' – emphasises the power of this small stream as it rushes downhill, its course directed by confining rocks. A sense of immediacy and energy is echoed in the **onomatopoeic effects**, including end rhyme ('brown', 'down'), repetition and internal rhyme ('comb', 'foam'). This is characteristic of Hopkins, as is his use of descriptive details, likening the foamy 'fleece' of the water to the fluted surface ('Flutes') of a Greek or Roman column.

Stanza two begins with another effective metaphor. The poet compares the yellow-brown froth to a windblown bonnet (hat) as the water swirls into a dark pool on the riverbed. The **atmosphere is light and airy**. Run-on lines reflect the lively pace of the noisy stream. However, the tone suddenly darkens with the disturbing image of the 'pitchblack' whirlpool which Hopkins sees as capable of drowning all in 'Despair'. The sluggish rhythm in lines 7–8 reinforces this menacing mood.

Nature seems much more benign in stanza three. The language is softer sounding – 'Degged with dew, dappled with dew' – as Hopkins describes the **steady movement of the water** through 'the groins of the braes'. Enclosed by the sharp banks, the stream sprinkles nearby branches of mountain ash, aflame with their vivid scarlet berries. As always, Hopkins delights in the unspoiled landscape: 'Wiry heathpacks, flitches of fern,/And the beadbonny ash'. Throughout the poem, he has also used traditional Scottish expressions ('burn', 'braes') to reflect the vigorous sounds of the Highlands.

The language in stanza four is rhetorical. Hopkins wonders what the world would be like without its wild qualities. The tone is personal and plaintive: 'O let them be left, wildness and wet'. While repetition and the use of the exclamation add a sense of urgency, his plea is simple: let nature remain as it is. The final appeal – 'Long live the weeds and the wilderness yet' – is reminiscent of his poem 'Spring'. Once again, there is no doubting Hopkins's **enthusiasm for the natural beauty of remote places** and the sentiments he expresses are clearly heartfelt. Although written in 1881, the poem has obvious relevance for today's generation.

Writing About the Poem

'Hopkins's deep appreciation of nature is a central feature of his striking poetry.' Discuss this statement, with particular reference to 'Inversnaid'.

Sample Paragraph

The most immediate thing that emerges about Hopkins is his extraordinary closeness to nature. This is evident in all his poems. He seems to have a heightened awareness of the sights and sounds of the remote mountain 'burn' in 'Inversnaid'. He details the colours of the water. It is 'darksome', 'horseback brown' and 'fawn-froth'. Hopkins is always excited by his natural environment. To him, the river is alive. It is 'roaring down'. He describes the rowan trees as 'the beadbonny ash', referring to their attractive red berries. In the last section of the poem, Hopkins openly states his fears for nature. He begs us to preserve the 'wildness and wet'. For him, all of nature deserves respect. He ends the poem with his own slogan, 'Long live the weeds and the wilderness'. Hopkins strikes me as being a lonely man who preferred the secluded Scottish hills where he could appreciate the natural world rather than being in a crowded city. He repeats the words 'wet' and 'wildness' a number of times in the final lines, leaving us in no doubt about how much the natural landscape meant to him.

EXAMINER'S COMMENT

Hopkins's awareness of the unruly aspects of nature is effectively explored: 'He details the colours of the water. It is "darksome"'. There is a convincing sense of close engagement with the body of the poem: 'Hopkins is always excited by his natural environment.' Accurate textual references and impressive, fluent expression ensure the top grade.

Class/Homework Exercises

1. In your opinion, does the poem 'Inversnaid' have relevance to our modern world? Support the points you make with reference to the text.
2. How does Hopkins reveal his intense love of nature in this poem? Refer to his subject matter and stylistic techniques in your response.

Summary Points

- **Celebration of nature's unruly beauty; unusually no reference to God.**
- **Colloquial Scots-English language locates poem in Scottish Highlands.**
- **Steady movement of water conveyed through onomatopoeic effects.**
- **Plea on behalf of unspoilt natural scenes.**

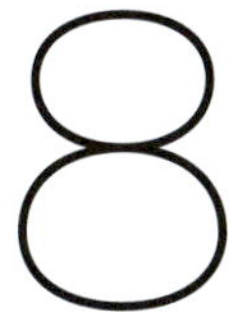

8 I Wake and Feel the Fell of Dark, Not Day

I wake and feel the fell of dark, not day.
What hours, O what black hours we have spent
This night! what sights you, heart, saw; ways you went!
And more must, in yet longer light's delay.
With witness I speak this. But where I say
Hours I mean years, mean life. And my lament
Is cries countless, cries like dead letters sent
To dearest him that lives alas! away.

I am gall. I am heartburn. God's most deep decree
Bitter would have me taste: my taste was me;
Bones built in me, flesh filled, blood brimmed the curse.
Selfyeast of spirit a dull dough sours. I see
The lost are like this, and their scourge to be
As I am mine, their sweating selves; but worse.

fell: threat; blow; knocked down; past tense of fall (fall of Adam and Eve cast into darkness); also refers to the mountain.

dead letters sent/To dearest him: communication which is of no use, didn't elicit a response.

gall: bitterness; anger; acidity; vinegar.

deep decree: command that cannot easily be understood.

Bones built in me, flesh filled, blood brimmed the curse: the passive tense of the verb might suggest how God created Man, yet Man has sinned.

Selfyeast of spirit a dull dough sours: yeast makes bread rise; Hopkins feels he cannot become good or wholesome.

The lost: those condemned to serve eternity in Hell with no hope of redemption, unlike the poet.

Personal Response

1. How is the oppressive atmosphere conveyed in this sonnet? Quote in support of your response.
2. How does the poem conclude, on a note of hope or despair? Illustrate your answer by referring closely to the text.
3. Comment on the use of alliteration to convey Hopkins's sense of dejection. Mention at least three examples.

Critical Literacy

'I Wake and Feel the Fell of Dark, Not Day' was written in Dublin, where Hopkins was teaching at UCD and was burdened by a massive workload of examination papers. After a long silence, he wrote the 'terrible sonnets'. Hopkins said of these, 'If ever anything was written in blood, these were.' This sonnet was discovered among his papers after his death.

The last three sonnets on the course are called the 'terrible sonnets Here Hopkins reaches the **darkest depths of despair**. The sonnet opens in darkness and the only mention of light in the whole poem is 'light's delay' in line 4, as it is postponed. He wakes to the oppressive blow of the dark ('the fell of dark'), not to the brightness of daylight. The heaviness of depression is being described, the oppressive darkness which Adam woke to after his expulsion from the Garden of Eden. Hopkins and his soul have shared these 'black hours' and they will experience 'more'. It is not just hours they have spent in darkness, but 'years', 'life'.

The formal, almost biblical phrase 'With witness I speak this' emphasises that what he has said is true. The hard 'c' sounds in 'cries countless' and the repetition of 'cries' keenly describe the **fruitless attempts at communication** ('dead letters'). There is no response: he 'lives alas! away'. We can imagine the poet in the deep dark of the night attempting to gain solace from his prayers to God ('dearest him'), but they go unanswered.

Hopkins feels this deep depression intensely. **Note the repetition of 'I'**: 'I wake', 'I speak', 'I am gall', 'I am heartburn', 'I see', 'I am'. He is in physical pain, bitter and burning. The language might well refer to Christ's Crucifixion, when he was offered a sponge soaked in vinegar to drink, and pierced through his side. However, the poet recognises that it is God's unfathomable decision that this is the way it should be: 'God's most deep decree'. **The poet is reviled by himself** in line 10: 'my taste was me'. He describes how he was fashioned: 'Bones built in me, flesh filled, blood brimmed'. The alliteration shows the careful construction of the body by the Creator, but Hopkins is full of 'the curse'.

Could this sense of revulsion be related to original sin emanating from the fall of Adam and Eve? The deadening 'd' sound of 'dull dough' shows that there is no hope of rising. The body is tainted, soured. It does not have the capacity to 'Selfyeast', to resurrect or renew. Is it being suggested that Hopkins needs divine intervention? Is there an overtone of the bread of Communion, the wholesome Body of Christ? The scope of the poem broadens out at the end as the poet gains an **insight into the plight of others**. All those condemned to Hell are like this and in fact are worse off: 'but worse'. The horrific atmosphere of Hell is conveyed in the phrase 'sweating selves'. For those 'lost', it is permanent. For Hopkins, perhaps it is just 'longer light's delay'. Some day **he will be redeemed**.

Writing About the Poem

'Hopkins's poetry displays a deeply personal and passionate response to the human condition.' Discuss with reference to the poems on your course, illustrating your answer with relevant quotations.

Sample Paragraph

Everyone can identify with Hopkins suffering from depression. This is evident in 'I Wake and Feel the Fell of Dark, Not Day'. To me he is describing waking over and over again at night. The long vowel sounds in 'O what black hours' give an idea of the man tossing and turning, trying to sleep. Hopkins's personal relationship with God was the focus of his life. His passionate pleas to God, 'To dearest him', are useless, 'dead letters'. So he is devastated and he uses the language of the Crucifixion to express that 'I am gall'. He despises himself: 'the curse', 'dull dough'. The poem is filled with self-disgust. The only slight glimmer for the poet is that those condemned to Hell are in a worse situation 'and their scourge to be ... their sweating selves; but worse'. Hopkins writes passionately about being human and the feeling of unworthiness.

EXAMINER'S COMMENT

This is a mature response to the assertion that Hopkins reacts deeply and passionately to the human condition: 'The poem seethes with self-disgust.' There is also in-depth exploration of the poem's sound effects: 'The long vowel sounds in "O what black hours" give an idea of the man tossing and turning'. Vocabulary and expression are impressive, adding to a successful, high-grade paragraph.

Class/Homework Exercises

1. 'Hopkins charts an extraordinary mental journey in "Wake and Feel the Fell of Dark, Not Day".' Give a personal response to this statement, quoting in support of your opinions.
2. Hopkins graphically explores his deep feeling of despair through light and dark imagery in 'I Wake and Feel the Fell of Dark, Not Day'. Pick one image of brightness and one of darkness which you considered effective and explain your choice.

Summary Points

- **Feeling of abandonment by God; spiritual suffering.**
- **Depressive's experience of waking into night vividly conveyed by imagery.**
- **Long vowel sounds and dragging repetition emphasise the prevailing darkness.**
- **Sense of self-disgust balanced by the poet's concluding empathy.**

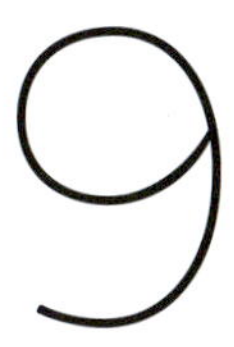

No Worst, There is None

GERARD MANLEY HOPKINS

No worst, there is none. Pitched past pitch of grief,
More pangs will, schooled at forepangs, wilder wring.
Comforter, where, where is your comforting?
Mary, mother of us, where is your relief?
My cries heave, herds-long; huddle in a main, a chief
Woe, world-sorrow; on an age-old anvil wince and sing –
Then lull, then leave off. Fury had shrieked 'No ling-
ering! Let me be fell: force I must be brief.'

O the mind, mind has mountains; cliffs of fall
Frightful, sheer, no-man-fathomed. Hold them cheap
May who ne'er hung there. Nor does long our small
Durance deal with that steep or deep. Here! creep,
Wretch, under a comfort serves in a whirlwind: all
Life death does end and each day dies with sleep

Pitched past pitch: pushed beyond.
pangs: sudden pains.
schooled at forepangs: prepared by earlier sorrows.
Comforter: the Holy Spirit.

main: crowd.

fell: harsh; cruel.
force: perforce; therefore.

Durance: endurance; determination.
whirlwind: turmoil.

'frightful, sheer, no-man-fathomed'

Personal Response

1. Comment on how Hopkins creates a sense of suffering and pessimism in the first four lines of the poem.
2. Discuss the effectiveness of the mountain images in lines 9–12.
3. In your opinion, is this a completely negative poem? Support your response by referring closely to the text.

Critical Literacy

This Petrarchan sonnet was written in Hopkins's final years, at a time when he suffered increasingly from ill health and depression. It was one of a short series of sonnets of desolation, now known as the 'terrible sonnets' or 'dark sonnets'. In 'No Worst, There is None', we see a man experiencing deep psychological suffering and struggling with his religious faith. The poem reveals a raw honesty from someone close to despair.

The opening is curt and dramatic, revealing the intensity of Hopkins's suffering: 'No Worst, There is None'. He is unable to imagine any greater agony. The emphatic use of monosyllables in line 1 reflects his **angry frustration**. Having reached what seems the threshold of torment, 'Pitched past pitch of grief', the poet dreads what lies ahead and the horrifying possibility that his pain ('schooled at forepangs') is likely to increase. The explosive force of the verb 'Pitched', combined with the harsh onomatopoeic and alliterative effects, heighten the sense of uncontrollable anguish. Both 'pitch' and 'pangs' are repeated, suggesting darkness and violent movement.

The rhythm changes in line 3. The three syllables of 'Comforter' slow the pace considerably. This is also a much softer word (in contrast to the harshness of the earlier sounds) and is echoed at the end of the line by 'comforting'. Hopkins's desolate plea to the Holy Spirit and the Virgin Mary emphasises **his hopelessness**: 'where, where is your comforting?' The tone, reminiscent of Christ's words on the Cross ('My God, why hast thou forsaken me?'), is both desperate and accusatory.

The poet likens his hollow cries for help to a herd of cattle in line 5. The metaphor highlights his lack of self-worth – his hopeless prayers 'heave' and 'huddle in a main'. He feels that his own suffering is part of a **wider universal 'world-sorrow'**. There is an indication here that Hopkins recognises that experiencing a crisis of faith can affect any Christian from time to time. This possibility is supported by the memorable image of the anvil being struck in line 6. He realises that the Christian experience involves suffering the guilt of sin and doubt to achieve spiritual happiness: 'on an age-old anvil wince and sing'.

But for the poet, any relief ('lull') from suffering is short-lived. His unavoidable feelings of shame and the pain of remorse are hauntingly personified: 'Fury had shrieked'. Once again, the severe sounds and the stretching of the phrase 'No lingering!' over two lines reinforce the relentlessness of Hopkins's troubled conscience.

This tormented tone is replaced by a more reflective one in the opening lines of the sestet, where Hopkins moves from the physical world of his 'cries' into the metaphorical landscape of towering mountains, with their dark, unknown depths. This **dramatic wasteland**, with its 'no-man-fathomed' cliffs, is terrifyingly portrayed. The poet reminds us that the terror of depression and separation from God cannot be appreciated by those 'who ne'er hung there'. The terror of being stranded on the 'steep or deep' rock face cannot be endured for long.

In the last two lines, Hopkins resigns himself to the **grim consolation** that all the depression and pain of this world will end with death, just as everyday troubles are eased by sleep. The final, chilling image of the wretched individual taking refuge from the exhausting whirlwind is less than optimistic. There is no relief from the terrible desolation and Hopkins's distracted prayers have yet to be answered.

Writing About the Poem

'Hopkins's deep despair is evident in the 'terrible sonnets'. Discuss this statement, with particular reference to 'No Worst, There is None'.

Sample Paragraph

At the start of 'No Worst, There is None', the tone is totally despondent. The first sentence is short and snappy, emphasising that Hopkins has reached rock bottom. Hopkins was a manic depressive and obsessed with religion. He also had issues with sexuality. In many ways he was caught between his role as a priest and his human desires. Rhetorical questions highlight his dependence on his religious faith – 'Comforter, where, where is your comforting?' This gives a heartfelt tone. Hopkins uses effective images which always make us feel sympathy for him, for example 'My cries heave, herds-long'. His tone is sorrowful and this is emphasised by comparisons. The prayers he offers to Heaven are just useless words which he intones:

EXAMINER'S COMMENT

This response includes a number of relevant examples of the varying tones throughout. Accurate quotations are effectively used in support and there is some good engagement with the poem. The expression was slightly awkward in places: 'This gives a heartfelt tone', and there is overuse of the verb 'emphasises'. Although hard-working, the answer does not merit the highest grade.

'My cries heave, herds-long'. He goes on to compare his sense of danger from sin with being trapped on a mountain – 'O the mind, mind has mountains'. The use of the 'O' punctuation mark emphasises the tone of desperation. The end of the poem is even more negative. Hopkins obviously had issues with his own faith in God. He uses a tone of despair as he compares himself to a stranded wanderer finding shelter from a 'whirlwind'. His only comfort is sleep and eventually death, which will silence his inner pain.

Class/Homework Exercises

1. Write your own personal response to 'No Worst, There is None'. Refer closely to the text in your answer.
2. The poet feels utterly abandoned by God in this poem. Trace the development of thought in 'No Worst, There is None' and discuss how Hopkins uses vivid description to explore his negative feelings. Support your answer with close reference to the text.

Summary Points

- **Most despairing and bleakest of 'terrible sonnets'.**
- **Alarming metaphors and powerful sound effects reveal inner suffering.**
- **Ups and downs of man's spiritual journey suggested by mountain imagery.**
- **Slightly optimistic end, death brings end to suffering for man.**

10 Thou Art Indeed Just, Lord, if I Contend

Justus quidem tu es, Domine, si disputem tecum: verumtamen justa loquar ad te: Quare via imporium prosperatur? &c.

Thou art indeed just, Lord, if I contend
With thee; but, sir, so what I plead is just.
Why do sinners' ways prosper? And why must
  Disappointment all I endeavour end?
    Wert thou my enemy, O thou my friend,
  How wouldst thou worse, I wonder, than thou dost
Defeat, thwart me? Oh, the sots and thralls of lust
Do in spare hours more thrive than I that spend,
Sir, life upon thy cause. See, banks and brakes
Now leaved how thick! laced they are again
With fretty chervil, look, and fresh wind shakes
Them; birds build – but not I build; no, but strain,
Time's eunuch, and not breed one work that wakes.
Mine, O thou lord of life, send my roots rain.

Latin quotation: Indeed you are just, O Lord, if I dispute with you; yet I would plead my case before you. Why do the wicked prosper? The first lines of the poem are a version of a Latin quotation that is taken from the Bible.
contend: dispute; argue; challenge.

sots: drunkards.
thralls: slaves.

brakes: thickets; groves of trees.

fretty: fretted; interlaced; the herb chervil has lacy leaves.
chervil: garden herb; the 'rejoicing leaf'.

eunuch: a castrated male, incapable of reproducing.

Personal Response

1. List the questions put to God. What tone is evident in each – anger, rebelliousness, reverence, resentment, trust, despair, etc.?
2. Is there a real sense of pain in the poem? At what point is it most deeply felt? How does the abrupt, jerky movement of the poem contribute to this sense of pain? Quote in support of your points.
3. Is the image of God in the poem stern or not? Do you think that Hopkins had a good or bad relationship with God? Illustrate your answer with reference to this poem.

Critical Literacy

'Thou Art Indeed Just, Lord, if I Contend' was written in 1889 at a time of great unhappiness for Hopkins in Dublin. He had written in a letter that 'all my undertakings miscarry'. This poem is a pessimistic yet powerful plea for help from God. It was written just three months before he died.

This sonnet opens with the **formal language of the courtroom** as the poet, in clipped tones, poses three questions in the octet. With growing frustration, he asks God to explain why sinners seem to prosper. Why is he, the poet, continually disappointed? If God was his enemy instead of his friend, how could he be any worse off? God, he allows, is just, but he contends that his own cause is also just. The language is that of a coherent, measured argument: 'sir', 'I plead'.

However, in lines 3–4, 'and why must/Disappointment all I endeavour end?', the inversion of the natural order makes the reader concentrate on the notable point that 'Disappointment' is the 'end' result of all the work the poet has done. But **the tone remains rational**, as Hopkins points out to 'sir' that the worst doing their worse 'more thrive' than he does. But his frustration at his plight makes the line of the octet spill over into the sestet, as the poet complains that he has spent his life doing God's will ('life upon thy cause').

The sestet has the ring of the real voice breaking through as Hopkins urgently requests God to 'See', 'look'. Here is **nature busily thriving**, producing, building, breeding, growing. The movement and pace of continuing growth and regrowth is caught in the line 'Now leaved how thick! laced they are again'. The **alliteration** of 'banks and brakes', 'birds build' vividly portrays the abundance of nature, as does the **assonance** of 'fretty' and 'fresh'. **Flowing run-on lines** describe the surge of growing nature. Hopkins is the exception in this fertile scene. The negatives 'not', 'no', the punctuation of semi-colon and comma and the inversion of the phrase 'but not I build; no, but strain' depict the **fruitless efforts of the poet to create**. The dramatic, sterile image of 'Time's eunuch', the castrated male, contrasts

the poet's unhappy state of unsuccessful effort with the ease of fruitful nature. Time is kind to nature, enabling it to renew, but the poet cannot create one work: 'not breed one work that wakes'.

The last line of the poem pleads for help and rescue. An image of a drought-stricken plant looking for life-giving water is used to describe the poet's plight of unsuccessful poetic creativity. **He looks to the 'lord of life'** for release. Hopkins had written in one of his final letters, 'If I could produce work ... but it kills me to be time's eunuch and never to beget'. It is intriguing that someone of such great faith can argue ('contend') so vehemently with God. Hopkins stretches the disciplined structure of the sonnet form to echo his frustration as he strains to create.

Writing About the Poem

'Hopkins's poetry deals with the theme that God's will is a mystery to us.' Discuss this statement, illustrating your response with relevant quotation from 'Thou Art Indeed Just, Lord, if I Contend'.

Sample Paragraph

How interesting to hear a man of great faith, a Jesuit priest, argue so openly and directly with God! As we see all the man-made and natural tragedies in the world, which of us has not thought, why has God allowed this to happen? Using the highly disciplined form of the sonnet, Hopkins charges God with accusations in the form of questions. How is it that sinners 'prosper'? Why 'must/Disappointment all I endeavour end?' The poet is frustrated, as we sometimes are; he does not know what is going on. God's will is a mystery to us. Hopkins cannot contain himself. The mood of puzzlement continues in the sestet as he urgently points out ('See', 'look') how nature is thriving ('fretty chervil', 'birds build'). But he, in contrast, is not. He concludes with the striking image of himself as the sterile 'Time's eunuch', a castrated slave unable to produce. He makes one final plea to God to nourish his parched 'roots' with 'rain'. The alliteration of 'roots rain' aligns him with the fertile world of nature, 'banks and brakes'. God is the 'lord of life', his divine plan a mystery to us, but we have the capacity to pray to Him.

EXAMINER'S COMMENT

Close reading of the text is evident here, particularly in the use of the rhetorical question, 'which of us has not thought, why has God allowed this to happen?' Assured use of language and accurate quotation: 'The mood of puzzlement continues in the sestet as he urgently points out ("See", "look") how nature is thriving ("fretty chervil", "birds build").' This guarantees an impressive top grade.

Class/Homework Exercises

1. Hopkins's innovative poetic style makes his work accessible to the modern reader. How true is this of 'Thou Art Indeed Just, Lord, if I Contend'? Use reference to the poem in your answer.
2. Hopkins complains and questions throughout this poem. What conclusion does he reach in the end? Did you find this ending satisfactory or not? Give reasons for your opinion.

Summary Points

- **Deeply personal and direct address to God.**
- **Hurt and frustration as poet wrestles with his religious faith.**
- **Struggle to control anger and frustration.**
- **Effective use of alliteration and vivid imagery.**
- **Contrast between abundance of nature and man's infertility.**
- **Concluding prayer to enable creativity to blossom.**

Sample Leaving Cert Questions on Hopkins's Poetry

1. **'Hopkins's poetry is defined largely by energetic language, dramatic tensions and a personal vision that is often anguished.' To what extent do you agree or disagree with this statement? Support your answer with reference to the poetry of Gerard Manley Hopkins on your course.**
2. **From your study of the poetry of Gerard Manley Hopkins on your course, select the poems that, in your opinion, best show his effective use of visual and aural effects to convey an imaginative response to the world of nature. Justify your selection by discussing Hopkins's effective use of visual and aural effects to convey an imaginative response to the world of nature.**
3. **'Hopkins uses sensual imagery and striking symbolism to highlight the significance of religious experience in his poetic world.' Discuss this statement, supporting your answer with reference to the poetry of Gerard Manley Hopkins on your course.**

How do I organise my answer?

(Sample question 1)

'Hopkins's poetry is defined largely by energetic language, dramatic tensions and a personal vision that is often anguished.' To what extent do you agree or disagree with this statement? Support your answer with reference to the poetry of Gerard Manley Hopkins on your course.

Sample Plan 1

Intro: (*Stance: agree with viewpoint in the question*) Hopkins 'looks hard' at life and his personal spiritual vision alters between deep depression and exuberant joy. His imaginative, innovative style uses natural rhythms, colloquialisms, aural music, compound phrases and poignant personification to convey this intimate – and often troubled – viewpoint.

Point 1: (*Resentment/resignation – vigorous repetition, alliteration, colloquialism*) 'Felix Randal' tragic narrative captures essence of strong man through compound expressions ('big-boned and hardy handsome'). Traces Felix's inner conflict. Authenticity achieved through colloquialism ('all road') and insistent tone ('he cursed'). Alliterative phrase soothes and restores ('our sweet reprieve and reason').

Understanding the Prescribed Poetry Question

Marks are awarded using the PCLM Marking Scheme: P = 15; C = 15; L = 15; M = 5 Total = 50

- **P** (Purpose = 15 marks) refers to the set question and is the launch pad for the answer. This involves engaging with all aspects of the question. Both theme and language must be addressed, although not necessarily equally.
- **C** (Coherence = 15 marks) refers to the organisation of the developed response and the use of accurate, relevant quotation. Paragraphing is essential.
- **L** (Language = 15 marks) refers to the student's skill in controlling language throughout the answer.
- **M** (Mechanics = 5 marks) refers to spelling and grammar.
- Although no specific number of poems is required, students usually discuss at least 3 or 4 in their written responses.
- Aim for at least 800 words, to be completed within 45–50 minutes.

NOTE

In keeping with the PCLM approach, the student has to take a stance by agreeing and/or disagreeing that Hopkins's poetry is defined largely by ...

- **an anguished personal vision** (intense conflicting emotions in his nature and devotional poems, desolation/ optimism, spiritual despondency/ regeneration, forceful feelings of self-disgust, empathy, frustration/prayer, redemption, etc.)

... through:

- **energetic language, dramatic tensions** (experimental expression, compressed compound words, enlivening sound effects, rich colloquialisms, emphatic repetition, vivid imagery, powerful rhythms, oratorical tones, contrasting poetic forms, etc.)

Point 2: (*Exuberance/reflection – aural music*) 'Spring' uses imaginative sound effects to convey joy – alliteration ('long and lovely and lush'), assonance ('weeds', 'wheels'), onomatopoeia ('wring'). Dramatic run-on lines express breathless excitement. Reflective sestet highlights the spiritual significance of the season's energetic growth.

Point 3: (*Elation – form, sound effects*) 'Pied Beauty' is a condensed sonnet (ten and a half lines instead of traditional fourteen) of hymn-like praise for God for the vibrancy and variety in nature using alliterative contrasts ('swift, slow', 'sweet, sour') and emphatic compound phrases ('couple colour', 'rose-moles'). Affirmative concluding phrase: 'Praise him'.

Point 4: (*Despair/optimism – dramatic opening, personification*) 'No Worst, There is None' explores force of suffering in sharp opening statement ('No worst, there is none'). Haunting personification ('Fury had shrieked') and urgent expression ('No lingering') intensify the bleak vision. Resigned conclusion acknowledges that anxieties end ('each day dies with sleep').

Conclusion: Dynamic language and stark contrasts depict a personal view of life in Hopkins's poetry varying from desolation, hurt and frustration to resignation, prayer and hope.

Sample Paragraph: Point 1

In 'Felix Randal', Hopkins narrates the moving dramatic story of a farrier, a simple blacksmith's life and death. He describes the workman in his prime using forceful language and compound expressions, 'big-boned and hardy handsome'. Felix's physical strength is suggested by the explosive alliterative phrase, 'bright and battering sandal' while he shoes a horse. Hopkins also captures the realism of the tragedy when the farrier is struck down by illness, 'Impatient, he cursed at first'. But Felix copes through his religious faith – the spiritual comfort of 'sweet reprieve and ransom'. The soothing alliterative phrase replaces his anger and despair. Hopkins uses Felix to show how every human being, no matter how strong, has to come to terms with sickness and death. The anecdote teaches how real strength comes from God. The language describing the blacksmith's 'boisterous years' is typically dynamic and uses emphatic repetition – describing Felix as being once 'powerful amidst peers'. The farrier's anguish changes to resignation and acceptance as he turns to God and the promise of spiritual happiness after death.

EXAMINER'S COMMENT

A reflective and analytical top-grade response that makes thoughtful use of selected text references to support points about the poet's central theme and language use. Quotes are skilfully interwoven into the main discussion. Expression throughout is varied and fluent. Phrases such as 'the realism of the tragedy' and 'typically dynamic' are impressive.

(Sample question 2)

From your study of the poetry of Gerard Manley Hopkins on your course, select the poems that, in your opinion, best show his effective use of visual and aural effects to convey an imaginative response to the world of nature. Justify your selection by discussing Hopkins's effective use of visual and aural effects to convey an imaginative response to the world of nature.

Sample Plan 2

Intro: (*Stance: agree with viewpoint in the question*) Hopkins's nature poems convey his personal religious vision of the natural world. He marvels, reflects and celebrates its magnificence, uniqueness, diversity and wildness through rich imagery, stunning sound effects, compound words and forceful rhythms.

Point 1: (*Appreciation/reflection – visual/aural effects*) 'Spring' uses hyperbolic language ('Nothing is so beautiful as Spring') to capture the poet's exuberant appreciation. Vigorous expression ('lush', 'rush') and delicate imagery evoke the season's beauty ('Thrush's eggs look little low heavens'). The bright birdsong is echoed through assonance ('rinse', 'wring'). An insistent prayer to preserve this beauty concludes ('Have, get, before it cloy').

Point 2: (*Celebration/uniqueness – compound words, alliteration, paradox*) 'The Windhover' celebrates uniqueness of the bird ('daylight's dauphin') through compound words ('dapple-dawn-drawn'). An alliterative phrase ('wimpling wing') describes the pleated appearance of its outstretched wing. The paradoxical verb 'Buckle' (pull together/fall apart) leads to a dramatic moment of epiphany. The bird is a symbol of Christ the Saviour who has to suffer ('Fall', 'gall') to provide redemption for man ('gash god-vermilion').

Point 3: (*Prayerful praise – compound worlds, sound effects*) 'Pied Beauty' is another powerful anthem of praise for God ('Glory be to God') for the variety of his creation, nature ('dappled things') using innovative emphatic language ('couple-colour', 'rose-moles'). The harmony of man and nature is conveyed through alliteration ('Landscape plotted and pieced – fold, fallow, plough'). Confident, monosyllabic conclusion ('Praise him').

Point 4: (*Delight in wilderness – colloquialism, onomatopoeia, run-on lines*) 'Inversnaid' uses dynamic Scots-English colloquialisms ('burn', 'flitches', 'beadbonny') to root the poem in the Highlands. Dashing run-on

NOTE

In keeping with the PCLM approach, the student has to justify the selection of poetry which shows Hopkins's:

- **effective use of visual and aural effects** (rich description, vivid imagery and symbols, evocative sound effects – alliteration, assonance, onomatopoeia, compound words, sprung rhythm, run-on lines, etc.)

... to convey:

- **an imaginative response to the world of nature** (deeply personal response to nature's spiritual significance, exuberant appreciation, celebration of diversity and uniqueness, reflective meditation, etc.)

lines and onomatopoeia convey the onward rush of fast streams ('Degged with dew, dappled with dew/Are the groins of the braes'). Alliteration evokes the essence of the unruly wildness in the plaintive plea ('O let them be, wildness and wet').

Conclusion: Hopkins was inspired by the orderly disorder of nature, 'counter, original, spare, strange'. Using detailed visual imagery, dazzling sound effects, compound phrasing, paradox, colloquialisms and energetic run-on lines, he creates engaging poetry to celebrate nature and praise God.

Sample Paragraph: Point 1

In 'Spring', Hopkins creates inspired pictures of the luxuriant growth of the season using alliteration and assonance, 'When weeds in wheels shoot long and lovely and lush'. The alliterative 'w' and 'l' combine with broad vowels to depict this new growth. The lively monosyllabic verb, 'shoots', captures the season's energy. By contrast, delicate imagery traces a tender scene of birth 'Thrush's eggs look little low heavens'. The omission of 'like' adds pace to the line and emphasises the poet's sense of wonder. The clear bright sound of the bird's song is heard in the assonant verbs, 'rinse' and 'wring'. Hopkins saw nature as evidence of God's existence. His poems often move from observing nature to recognising God's presence as creator. In the sonnet's reflective sestet, there is a fleeting glimpse from a more perfect world, 'a strain of the earth's sweet being'. This leads him to a final prayer that God will preserve the world and prevent it from going 'sour with sinning'. The poet's imaginative response ends on a positive note that human beings can put their trust in God. Gentle onomatopoeic effects reflect the harmonious tone and hopeful message, 'worthy the winning'.

EXAMINER'S COMMENT

Focused response that shows close engagement with both the question and the poem. Judicious use of selected reference and carefully interwoven quotations to explore the effectiveness of Hopkins's language – particularly in relation to sound. Assured, varied expression throughout add to the high-grade standard.

Leaving Cert Sample Essay

'Hopkins makes effective use of a variety of stylistic features to express intense feelings that range from delight to despair.' To what extent do you agree or disagree with this statement? Support your answer with reference to the poetry of Gerard Manley Hopkins on your course.

Sample Essay

INDICATIVE MATERIAL

Hopkins's variety of stylistic features:

- experimental language – sound, imagery, symbolism, repetition, dialect, sprung rhythm, inscape, compound words, various tones and poetic forms, etc.

... to express:

- intense feelings that range from delight to despair
- wonder, joy, celebration, excitement, appreciation, suffering, pessimism, loss, abandonment, dejection, etc.

1. Hopkins uses many different ways in his poems to express feelings of delight and despair. 'As Kingfishers Catch Fire', 'I Wake and Feel the Fell of Dark', 'No Worst' are good examples of these. He wrote mostly about his feelings about nature and God with an intense style. Hopkins found God in nature, for example 'Spring' is a sign how God created the world. Many of his poems are about his deep feelings connected with his beliefs as a priest. Religion meant everything to Hopkins.

2. Everything in nature was a sign that God created the world. The kingfishers are colourful birds and Hopkins is delighted by how they look and move so quickly. He uses detailed description to describe them and their bright fire colour. In nature, everything is exciting. This is a mystery to Hopkins who sees the hand of God in everything that is created. He notices things like the noise of little stones thrown down a well and says 'stones ring'. He thinks humans are also all different. He even invents words 'selves' to express this difference. He invents 'justices' to show how people should do what they're supposed to do, 'the just man justices'. I think the biggest thing about his style of writing is that the words are all condensed and he doesn't even use correct grammar because he is just so excited about finding God all around him in the beauty of nature.

3. 'I Wake and Feel' is the opposite. It is full of despair. Hopkins was teaching in a Dublin university and had exams to mark all the time. He suffered from depression and had all kinds of issues. He wrote what was called the terrible sonnets at this time and this one is all about his problems. He talks about being burdened by 'black hours'. Everything seems gloomy, 'the fell of dark'. I think the poem is filled with negativity and negative expressions and images, e.g. 'fell of darkness', 'dead letters', 'lost'. The poem is all about his doubts about God and Hopkins keeps repeating the word 'cries' to show his sadness. He can't get in contact with God because his letters are 'dead'. By this he means his prayers to God. He is disgusted with himself and feels that life is pointless without a religious faith.

4. 'No Worst' is full of depression too. Hopkins was ill when he wrote it 'pitched past grief'. He asks Mary, God's mother 'where is your relief?' He thinks of the mind as huge 'mountains'. He thinks they are frightful. This is a feeling of despair, Hopkins is so downhearted he wants to creep under a ledge out of the way of the storm. He makes affective use of repetition to show this, 'pangs', 'forepangs'. This is an old word meaning sorrow. The only comfort he seems to get is to remind himself that life ends with death in the same way as day ends with sleep. This is very depressing.

5. 'Thou Art Indeed Just' was written 3 months before he died. Hopkins was living in Dublin and unhappy. The year was 1889 and this was 3 months before his death at the age of just 45. He asks why sinners do well. Then he asks if God is supposed to be his freind, could he be any worse off if God was his enemy, seeing as he is not doing very well and is full of 'dissappointment'. He is full of frustration 'thwart'. He asks why nature is doing well, the 'the birds build', the weeds are growing but he is 'not'. He also asks God to make it rain on him so he can be productive. Hopkins is struggling to keep in his anger under control. The tone ends like a prayer in which he prays to God, 'send my roots rain'.

EXAMINER'S COMMENT

Uneven response that touches slightly on some aspects of poetic style, such as repetition, imagery and tone. These need to be much more developed and analysed to show how such features are effective in conveying Hopkins's feelings. Unnecessary biographical background adds little to the answer. Expression is note-like and repetitive. There are also several misquotes, grammar and spelling errors which have reduced the quality of the answer.

GRADE: H4
P = 10/15
C = 9/15
L = 8/15
M = 4/5
Total = 31/50

6. Hopkins's poetry changes from happiness to sadness. He is very sad when he is living in Dublin because he has stacks of work and he is sick. He is disappointed that God is not doing more to help him while he cannot 'build'. Many elements of style are used to describe these different feelings. I think Hopkins is a poet with plenty to say. I agree that he makes affective use of a variety of features to express intense feelings that range from delight to despair.

(725 words)

Class/Homework Exercise

1. **Rewrite paragraph 5. (Aim for at least 130 words.)**

PROMPT!

- *Maintain the focus on the full question.*
- *Identify the central feeling in the poem and focus on aspects of style.*
- *Key features of style might include emphatic alliteration and vivid imagery.*
- *Use full titles when referring to the poems.*
- *Check that the quotations are accurate.*
- *Vary expression for 'asks' e.g. 'wonders', 'demands to know'.*

Revision Overview

'God's Grandeur'
In this dramatic sonnet, Hopkins explores how God's reassuring presence is infused in the world of nature.

'Spring'
A beautifully crafted reflection on the beauty, innocence and spiritual significance of nature.

'As Kingfishers Catch Fire, Dragonflies Draw Flame'
Central themes include nature's beauty, variety and uniqueness. Hopkins relates mankind's ultimate spiritual purpose to the natural world.

'The Windhover'
The sense of religious wonder is a key feature of this striking sonnet in which Hopkins presents the beauty of nature as a compelling metaphor for Christ's beauty.

'Pied Beauty'
Another hymn to creation. Hopkins praises the variety and beauty of the world, glorifying the infinite power of God and the hope that can be found in faith.

'Felix Randal'
Italian sonnet tracing the relationship between a spiritual healer and the sufferer. Both complement each other in the act of attaining eternal salvation.

'Inversnaid'
Hopkins wonders what would become of the world without unspoiled remote landscapes and he urges people to retain such beautiful places.

'I Wake and Feel the Fell of Dark, Not Day'
In this 'dark sonnet', Hopkins explores the theme of exile from God, the personal doubt that many believers feel at times.

'No Worst, There is None'
Another of the 'terrible sonnets'. As a Christian, Hopkins is intensely aware of the spiritual torment of feeling alienated from God.

'Thou Art Indeed Just, Lord, if I Contend'
Another powerful examination of the mystery of faith. Hopkins questions the existence of evil in the world but concludes by placing his own trust in God.

Last Words

'What you look hard at seems to look hard at you.'
G. M. Hopkins

'Hopkins is more concerned with 'putting across his perceptions than with fulfilling customary expectations of grammar.'
Robert Bernard Martin

'Design, pattern, or what I am in the habit of calling inscape is what I above all aim at in poetry.'
G. M. Hopkins

NATURE

MEANING OF LIFE

SUFFERING

RELIGION/ SPIRITUALITY

TRANSIENCE

John Keats
1795–1821

'I have loved the principle of beauty in all things.'

John Keats is one of the most widely recognised and loved English poets. Born in London in 1795, he was not expected to have poetic aspirations, considering his ordinary background. Nevertheless, from his boyhood he had an acute sense of beauty and chose to make a career as a poet.

Keats is best known for his series of odes, filled with lush images of nature. These display an assured poetic instinct and a remarkable ability to appeal powerfully to the senses by the brilliance of his diction. Many of his poems are noted more for their strength of feeling than for thought, often reflecting the poet's intense inner conflicts.

In 1818, Keats met eighteen-year-old Frances (Fanny) Brawne and a close friendship developed between them. In 1819, they became engaged and he dedicated his sonnet 'Bright Star' to her. However, the relationship was cut short by the effects of the poet's consumption (tuberculosis).

As his medical condition worsened, Keats was advised to move to a warmer climate and in November 1820, he arrived in Rome. Unfortunately, his health continued to deteriorate and he died there on 23 February 1821.

Investigate Further

To find out more about John Keats, or to hear readings of his poems, you could do a search some useful websites, such as YouTube, BBC Poetry, poetryfoundation.org and poetryarchive.org, or access additional material on this page of your eBook.

Prescribed Poems

○ **1 'To One Who Has Been Long in City Pent'**
This Italian sonnet describes the delights of the English countryside while reflecting poignantly on the passing of time. Keats disliked living in the city and was firmly convinced about nature's restorative power. **Page 342**

○ **2 'Ode to a Nightingale'**
Unhappy with the real world, Keats attempts to escape into the ideal by entering the mysterious world of the nightingale's song. The poem begins by describing the song of an actual nightingale, but the bird quickly becomes a symbol of the immortality of nature. In the end, the poet is left with an intense self-awareness and returns to reality. **Page 345**

○ **3 'On First Looking into Chapman's Homer' (OL)**
This Petrarchan sonnet conveys the sheer sense of excitement and wonder which Keats found after reading the ancient works of Homer. The poet uses dramatic imagery to describe the revelation of Chapman's English translation comparing it to an astronomer who has discovered a new planet, or to Cortez's first sighting of the Pacific Ocean. **Page 352**

○ **4 'Ode on a Grecian Urn'**
Keats's famous ode explores the paradoxical relationship between the immortal world of art and transient reality. The enigmatic Grecian urn excites his imagination. It is a powerful symbol of timeless perfection which provokes by silently posing questions. **Page 356**

○ **5 'When I Have Fears That I May Cease to Be'**
In this Shakespearean sonnet, Keats expresses his fear of dying young before he has time to fulfil his potential. He also reflects on the transience of life, love and fame. The poem is a good example of Keats's use of archaic language and his distinctive musical sound effects. **Page 362**

○ **6 'La Belle Dame Sans Merci' (OL)**
A highly dramatic ballad set in the medieval era, this mysterious poem tells the tragic tale of a lovesick knight and his 'Beautiful Lady without Mercy'. The haunting story of love and loss in a bleak wintry landscape is dominated by images of death. **Page 365**

○ **7 'To Autumn'**
Characteristically filled with wonderful images and sensuous detail, this celebrated poem describes the beauty of nature, highlighting autumn's abundant fruitfulness and ultimate decline. This is achieved through Keats's rich language, personification and evocative sound effects. **Page 371**

○ **8 'Bright Star, Would I Were Steadfast as Thou Art'**
Another Shakespearean sonnet focusing primarily on the differences between eternity and mortality. As in many of his well-known odes, Keats is fascinated by the idea of a perfect, unchanging world – but is forced to accept that his dream is impossible. **Page 375**

*(OL) indicates poems that are also prescribed for the Ordinary Level course.

1 To One Who Has Been Long in City Pent

Title: closely echoes a line from John Milton's epic poem, 'Paradise Lost': 'As one who long in populous city pent'.

To one who has been long in city pent,
'Tis very sweet to look into the fair
And open face of heaven, – to breathe a prayer
Full in the smile of the blue firmament.
Who is more happy, when, with heart's content,
Fatigued he sinks into some pleasant lair
Of wavy grass, and reads a debonair
And gentle tale of love and languishment?
Returning home at evening, with an ear
Catching the notes of Philomel, – an eye
Watching the sailing cloudlet's bright career,
He mourns that day so soon has glided by:
E'en like the passage of an angel's tear
That falls through the clear ether silently.

pent: confined, imprisoned.
firmament: sky.
lair: sheltered hideaway.
debonair: pleasing, sophisticated.
languishment: yearning, desire.
Philomel: legendary nightingale.
cloudlet: small cloud.
career: movement.
ether: upper air, atmosphere.

Personal Response

1. Describe the contrasting moods in the poem's octave and sestet. Support your answer with suitable reference to the poem.
2. Comment on Keats's use of sound effects throughout the sonnet in describing the natural world.
3. In your opinion, how relevant is this poem to modern life? Briefly explain your response.

Critical Literacy

Written in the summer of 1816 when Keats was 21 and a medical student in London, this poem follows the Petrarchan (or Italian) sonnet structure. The octave (first eight lines) describes the delights of the English countryside while the sestet (last six lines) reflects poignantly on the passing day.

The opening section of the octave immediately reveals Keats's preference for nature over city life. Line 1 is marked by an insistent rhythm and a series of heavy monosyllables which echo the dull monotony of urban routine: 'To one who has been long in city pent'. The emphatic verb 'pent' is particularly effective in highlighting Keats's

frustrated sense of confinement. But we soon see his obvious excitement as he considers the 'fair' countryside, personifying its natural beauty as the 'open face of heaven' (line 3). The energetic run-on lines and celebratory tone (''Tis very sweet') add to the upbeat mood. For Keats, however, there is more to the unspoilt country than just its beauty and sense of release. He also finds a reverential kind of spiritual peace when he is able to 'breathe a prayer' and reaffirm the joys of existence in such a natural setting. This worshipful tone is reinforced in various religious references to 'heaven' and the 'firmament', a biblical term often used to describe the sky.

Keats continues to praise nature's virtues in lines 5–8 by appealing directly to the reader's likely sympathy for 'happy' country living and the joy of relaxing to one's 'heart's content'. He illustrates this with the image of finding a 'pleasant lair' and sinking into the 'wavy grass' to read a 'gentle tale of love and languishment'. Characteristically, **Keats's musical language is filled with rich sibilant, assonant and alliterative sounds**. At ease in this tranquil rural landscape, he can enjoy reading a favourite 'tale of love'. This defines his notion of perfect contentment. As always, the most important Romantic qualities of Keats's poetry are the imagination, a love of nature, and the sense of beauty to which a strangeness has been added.

The sestet, however, is largely dominated by a **tender sense of loss**. As in so many of his poems, Keats can only escape from the real world for a limited time. Returning home in the evening, he hears the nightingale singing ('the notes of Philomel'). This elevated reference to a tragic mythical figure who was turned into a bird reflects the pervading atmosphere of serenity. The imagery Keats uses is equally mellow. He observes 'the cloudlet's bright career' and 'mourns that day so soon has glided by'. Again, broad assonant vowels enhance the sense of melancholy. Does his brief visit to the countryside symbolise the transience of all human life? Lines 13–14, comparing the onset of evening to the falling of 'an angel's tear' are particularly evocative. There is a clear suggestion of some underlying sense of a divine presence existing within nature's mysterious beauty.

Keats's journey from confinement in the city to finding peace in the quiet meadows and finally to **reflective nostalgia** all takes place over a single day. The concise sonnet form is ideally suited to the poet's meditative subject matter. Readers are left with a thought-provoking poem whose deft use of metaphorical language illustrates the poet's heartfelt views on nature's restorative power and human mortality.

Writing About the Poem

'The rejuvenating force of nature is a central theme in many of Keats's poems.' Discuss this statement in relation to 'To One Who Has Been Long in City Pent', using suitable reference to the text.

Sample Paragraph

In 'To One Who Has Been Long in City Pent', the poet describes the experience of a city-dweller who visits the countryside. He is cheered up at once as he breathes in the open atmosphere. Keats uses simple child-like language – ''Tis very sweet'. The sight of the clear blue sky fills his heart with joy. I felt that he almost discovered God in nature which he personifies – 'face of heaven'. This image suggests a personal relationship between Keats and nature. I liked the contrast between his lack of freedom in the city where he felt 'pent' and his happiness in the country – 'some pleasant lair'. His mood is so much brighter under the 'blue firmament' where he can lie on a bed of soft 'wavy grass' and reads a sweet romantic story. At that moment he feels as if he is the happiest man on earth. Keats's language is much more positive when he describes the rejuvenating force of nature – 'more happy', 'gentle tale of love'. In the end, he must face reality again. But thanks to nature, he is prepared for city life. He has happy memories of a day that has 'glided by'.

EXAMINER'S COMMENT

This is a competent response which includes some worthwhile discussion of the poet's themes and language use. Comments on stylistic features, such as contrast and mood, are well supported by apt reference: 'Keats's language is much more positive when he describes the rejuvenating force of nature'. There is evidence of genuine engagement with the poem, for example in the last sentence. However, the expression is awkward at times: 'His mood is so much brighter under the "blue firmament" where he can lie on a bed of soft "wavy grass" and reads a sweet romantic story'. This prevents the paragraph from achieving the top grade.

Class/Homework Exercises

1. 'John Keats's poetry focuses some of life's mysterious elements.' Discuss this view, with particular reference to the poem, 'To One Who Has Been Long in City Pent'.
2. 'Keats often makes effective use of metaphors and personification in his poems.' To what extent is this true of 'To One Who Has Been Long in City Pent'? Support your answer with suitable reference to the poem.

Summary Points

- **Nature's power to delight, life's transience, the joy of literature.**
- **Varying moods and atmospheres.**
- **Effective personification, vivid images and metaphors.**
- **Musical sound effects, alliteration, broad assonant vowels.**
- **Complementary use of octave and sestet creates unity.**

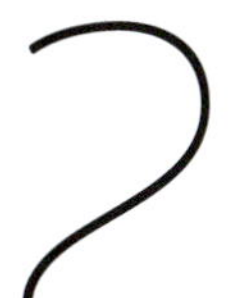

2 Ode to a Nightingale

Title: the nightingale has always been considered a secretive bird known for singing very beautifully. It is also associated with romantic love.

JOHN KEATS

I

My heart aches, and a drowsy numbness pains
My sense, as though of hemlock I had drunk,
Or emptied some dull opiate to the drains
One minute past, and Lethe-wards had sunk:
'Tis not through envy of thy happy lot,
But being too happy in thine happiness, –
That thou, light-winged Dryad of the trees,
In some melodious plot
Of beechen green, and shadows numberless,
Singest of summer in full-throated ease.

hemlock: poisonous plant.

opiate: sleep-inducing drug.

Lethe-wards: forgetfulness. (In Greek mythology, the dead drank from the River Lethe to forget their human lives.)

Dryad: beautiful woodland maiden; tree nymph.

II

O, for a draught of vintage! that hath been
Cooled a long age in the deep-delved earth,
Tasting of Flora and the country green,
Dance, and Provençal song, and sunburnt mirth!
O for a beaker full of the warm South,
Full of the true, the blushful Hippocrene,
With beaded bubbles winking at the brim,
And purple-stained mouth;
That I might drink, and leave the world unseen,
And with thee fade away into the forest dim:

draught of vintage: drink of good wine.

Flora: Roman goddess of flowers.

Provençal: South-eastern France.

South: the warm Mediterranean.

blushful Hippocrene: red wine of the Greek gods, associated with inspiration.

III

Fade far away, dissolve, and quite forget
What thou among the leaves hast never known,
The weariness, the fever, and the fret
Here, where men sit and hear each other groan;
Where palsy shakes a few, sad, last gray hairs,
Where youth grows pale, and spectre-thin, and dies;
Where but to think is to be full of sorrow
And leaden-eyed despairs,
Where Beauty cannot keep her lustrous eyes,
Or new Love pine at them beyond tomorrow.

palsy: wasting disease.

spectre-thin: ghostly.

lustrous: radiant, bright.

pine: yearn for.

IV

Away! away! for I will fly to thee,
Not charioted by Bacchus and his pards,
But on the viewless wings of Poesy,
Though the dull brain perplexes and retards:
Already with thee! tender is the night,
And haply the Queen-Moon is on her throne,
Clustered around by all her starry Fays;
But here there is no light,
Save what from heaven is with the breezes blown
Through verdurous glooms and winding mossy ways.

Bacchus: god of wine in Roman legend.
pards: leopards were used to draw Bacchus's chariot.
Poesy: poetry
Queen-Moon: Diana, the Roman moon-goddess.
Fays: fairy attendants.
verdurous: grassy green.

V

I cannot see what flowers are at my feet,
Nor what soft incense hangs upon the boughs,
But, in embalmed darkness, guess each sweet
Wherewith the seasonable month endows
The grass, the thicket, and the fruit-tree wild;
White hawthorn, and the pastoral eglantine;
Fast fading violets covered up in leaves;
And mid-May's eldest child,
The coming musk-rose, full of dewy wine,
The murmurous haunt of flies on summer eves.

incense: pleasant fragrance.
embalmed: heavy-scented
endows: enriches.
eglantine: sweet briar, a beautiful wild rose.

VI

Darkling I listen; and, for many a time
I have been half in love with easeful Death,
Called him soft names in many a mused rhyme,
To take into the air my quiet breath;
Now more than ever seems it rich to die,
To cease upon the midnight with no pain,
While thou art pouring forth thy soul abroad
In such an ecstasy!
Still wouldst thou sing, and I have ears in vain –
To thy high requiem become a sod.

Darkling: in the darkness.
mused: bemused, uncertain.
requiem: liturgical funeral song.
sod: clump of earth; grassy soil.

VII

Thou wast not born for death, immortal Bird!
No hungry generations tread thee down;
The voice I hear this passing night was heard
In ancient days by emperor and clown:
Perhaps the self-same song that found a path
Through the sad heart of Ruth, when, sick for home,
She stood in tears amid the alien corn;
The same that oft-times hath
Charmed magic casements, opening on the foam
Of perilous seas, in faery lands forlorn.

emperor and clown: the highest and lowest in society.
Ruth: Biblical character who was exiled.
casements: windows.
faery: fairy (early spelling).
forlorn: abandoned, despondent.

VIII

Forlorn! the very word is like a bell
  To toll me back from thee to my sole self!
Adieu! the fancy cannot cheat so well
  As she is fam'd to do, deceiving elf.
Adieu! adieu! thy plaintive anthem fades
  Past the near meadows, over the still stream,
    Up the hillside; and now 'tis buried deep
      In the next valley-glades:
  Was it a vision, or a waking dream?
    Fled is that music: – Do I wake or sleep?

toll: call.
sole self: personal loneliness.
fancy: imagination.

plaintive anthem: bittersweet song.

'in faery lands forlorn'

Personal Response

1. Comment on the effectiveness of Keats's language throughout the second stanza in conveying his longing to escape from reality.
2. Select two memorable images from the poem that you find particularly effective. Explain your choice in each case.
3. Describe Keats's mood in the poem's final stanza.

Critical Literacy

'Ode to a Nightingale' is considered one of the finest poems in English literature and reveals John Keats's highest imaginative powers. The beautiful song of the nightingale fills him with a desire to escape from the cares of life. This highly passionate ode illustrates Keats's intense perception of human experience. Written in a single day in May 1819, the poem explores themes of transience, mortality and nature. It is a typical Romantic ode which emphasises powerful emotions and the importance of imagination. Keats also makes effective use of synaesthesia (the mixing of sense impressions) which is a characteristic of his rich imagery.

The ode begins with an expression of the poet's acute self-awareness and his deep desire to escape. The initial mood of the opening stanza combines ecstatic joy and pain – almost to the point of completely dulling the senses. Keats declares his own brooding heartache. He feels 'a drowsy numbness' that he associates with hemlock or opium. Sibilant sounds echo this wistful trance-like feeling. Overwhelmed by the rich music of the nightingale's song, **he appears to be in a meditative dream**, attempting to identify himself with the bird. Heavy alliterative 'd' and 'n' sounds add to the weary tone. Monosyllables ('pains', 'drunk', 'drains') create a slow, deliberate rhythm, reflecting the poet's dejected mood. Lines 9–10 focus directly on the nightingale and are less lethargic. The mood lightens here, in contrast to the earlier exhausted atmosphere. Vowel sounds sharpen and the sibilance becomes noticeably more energetic ('Singest of summer', 'full-throated ease').

In stanza two, Keats longs for the oblivion of alcohol, calling for 'a draught of vintage' that tastes of 'the country-green'. The exclamatory 'O' emphasises his sense of yearning. In his wildly imaginative state, the wine tastes of the French Mediterranean 'Dance, and Provençal song'. But the poet longs for more than just being carefree. He also wishes the wine to inspire him when he refers to the 'Hippocrene', a sacred fountain that was said to bring poetic inspiration to those who drank from it. There is **an abundance of vigorous imagery** throughout these lines and an atmosphere of warmth predominates. The phrase 'sunburnt mirth' combines the idea of sunshine with the joy of young people celebrating. Repeated references to dancing and the 'blushful' wine with its 'beaded bubbles winking at the brim' are enriched by vibrant onomatopoeic sounds. Keats's compressed images

often overlap. The senses of sight, hearing and touch are closely associated with tasting the wine as a pleasurable escape from harsh reality.

Ironically, the poet's awareness of the real world makes it impossible for him to 'Fade far away'. Much of the third stanza is preoccupied with the human condition at its worst: the 'weariness, the fever, and the fret' of everyday life is illustrated with a **graphic image of physical suffering** where 'youth grows pale, and spectre-thin, and dies'. Assonance emphasises this tragic view of illness and decay. Keats sees time itself as the greatest of all sorrows, worse than any terrible disease. Everything decays and 'Beauty cannot keep her lustrous eyes'. Only the nightingale's singing transcends mortality.

In stanza four, the poet orders the nightingale to fly away, and he will follow, not through being intoxicated ('Not charioted by Bacchus'), but through poetry, which will give him 'viewless wings'. As Keats imagines himself joining the nightingale's magical world, the **atmosphere becomes dreamlike**: 'tender is the night'. The personified 'Queen-Moon' is surrounded by 'her starry Fays'. This majestic image is typical of the exaggerated senses which heighten the poet's fantasy. An underlying air of excitement pervades the darkness. The imaginary woodland setting is mysterious with the heavenly breeze blowing through 'verdurous glooms and winding mossy ways'. Soft sibilance and consonant 'm' sound effects are used here to further invigorate the poet's ecstatic mood.

Stanza five consists of a single flowing sentence describing Keats's close union with the nightingale. A vivid impression of smell is created to serve his exuberant imagination. The poet becomes acutely aware of the sweet fragrances around him. Yet even here, it is impossible to avoid the presence of death within the 'embalmed darkness'. He lists the intoxicating forest smells of fresh grass, fruit-trees and flowers. **Aural imagery enhances the magical quality of the visual details**. Recurring sibilant effects emphasise the beauty of 'White hawthorn', 'pastoral eglantine' and 'Fast fading violets'. In his visionary journey, Keats makes remarkable use of sensory language – and particularly elegant assonance – to create a truly languid atmosphere: 'The murmurous haunt of flies on summer eves.'

Much of the focus in the sixth stanza is on **escaping painful reality through death**. Keats again addresses the nightingale directly: 'Darkling I listen'. He then makes a somewhat unsettling revelation that he has often been 'half in love' with the idea of dying. His use of personification ('Called him soft names') implies that death has seemed like a friend, offering comfort to the poet. He feels that the present moment would be the ideal time to ease into a new spiritual life now that the bird is singing in 'such an ecstasy'. The enthusiastic tone suddenly changes, however, as Keats realises the irony that the bird would continue singing while the poet's lifeless body lies buried in the earth.

Throughout stanza seven, he continues to contrast the nightingale (as a symbol of immortality) with his own mortal self. **The forceful tone seems almost celebratory**: 'Thou wast not born for death'. Indeed, the bird's stirring voice has always been heard, by ancient 'emperor and clown'. He considers how such birdsong once consoled the lonely biblical figure of Ruth when she 'stood in tears amid the alien corn'. Always the Romantic poet, Keats traces the nightingale's comforting song back to 'faery lands', both magical and tragic. For him, the beauty of nature has fascinated humanity throughout generations.

At the start of stanza eight, the emphatic word 'Forlorn' rings like a bell to wake Keats from his deep preoccupation back to his 'sole self'. The nightingale has ceased to be a symbol and is again the actual bird the poet heard at the outset. As Keats emerges from his hypnotic state to say farewell, he realises that the bird's song (even if it is immortal) will not always be within his range of hearing: 'thy plaintive anthem fades/Past the near meadows, over the still stream'. This marks a crucial development for the poet, who until now has yearned to leave the physical world and follow the nightingale into a higher realm. The bird flies farther away from him, however, becoming a faint memory and **Keats laments that his imagination has failed him**. In the last two lines, he wonders whether he has had a true insight or whether he has been daydreaming: 'Was it a vision, or a waking dream?'

Throughout the ode, Keats has been caught between a yearning to escape into a permanent ideal world and an acceptance of transient reality. But has he been changed by his visionary experience? Critics have disagreed about the poem's ending, so readers are left to interpret the final tone for themselves. Is it happy, hopeful, sad, excited, despairing or resigned? Only the individual reader can decide.

Writing About the Poem

'Tensions and contrasts are central elements of Keats's poetry.' To what extent is this true of 'Ode to a Nightingale'? Support your answer with reference to the text of the poem.

Sample Paragraph

'Ode to a Nightingale' is structured around the poet, who is aware of his own mortality and the bird, which is free. Keats's mood is of longing, but 'not through envy'. The tension is within the poet himself. He is caught between celebrating the nightingale's 'happy lot' and wishing to be part of this ideal existence. His tone reflects this yearning – 'That I might drink ... And with thee fade away'. Keats desires dying as an escape from the pain of this world and admits to being 'half in love with easeful Death'. The mood keeps changing throughout, at times deliriously joyful when enjoying the bird singing 'In such an ecstasy'. But the poet is often downbeat – 'to think is to be full of sorrows'. While Keats reluctantly returns to reality at the end of the poem and accepts that his imagination will not provide a lasting escape from life's suffering, he never seems truly at ease as the nightingale's 'plaintive anthem fades'. For me, this was the most heartbreaking moment in the poem. The last two lines summed up Keats's dilemma, as if he was stranded between longing and disappointment, not even sure if the nightingale was part of 'a vision or a waking dream'.

EXAMINER'S COMMENT

A very assured and controlled answer that addressed both elements of the task, 'tensions' and 'contrasts'. Supportive points made excellent use of accurate quotation and reference ranging over the poem. Expression was also very impressive – fluent and varied: 'The mood keeps changing throughout, at times deliriously joyful'. The brief personal engagement, 'For me this was the most heartbreaking moment in the poem', also enhanced this very successful top-grade answer.

Class/Homework Exercises

1. 'A deep and disturbing sense of unhappiness often pervades Keats's poetry.' To what extent do you agree with this view of 'Ode to a Nightingale'? Support your answer with reference to the poem.
2. 'Sensuous imagery is a key feature of Keats's distinctive language use.' Discuss this statement with close reference to 'Ode to a Nightingale'.

Summary Points

- **Themes include the conflicted nature of human life, imagination, the natural world and escapism.**
- **Contrasting tones and moods: sorrow and joy, the real and ideal.**
- **Keats's sensuous language and symbols are characteristic of the ode.**
- **Dense concentration of sense impressions and use of synaesthesia.**
- **Memorable sound effects – alliteration, assonance, siblance.**

3 On First Looking into Chapman's Homer

Chapman: the writer George Chapman (1559–1634) who translated Homer's epic poems into English.
Homer: Greek epic poet (circa 750–650 BC); author of *The Iliad* and *The Odyssey*.

Much have I travell'd in the realms of gold,
   And many goodly states and kingdoms seen;
   Round many western islands have I been
Which bards in fealty to Apollo hold.
Oft of one wide expanse had I been told
   That deep-brow'd Homer ruled as his demesne;
   Yet did I never breathe its pure serene
Till I heard Chapman speak out loud and bold:
Then felt I like some watcher of the skies
   When a new planet swims into his ken;
Or like stout Cortez when with eagle eyes
   He star'd at the Pacific – and all his men
Looked at each other with a wild surmise –
   Silent upon a peak in Darien.

realms of gold: majestic worlds of the imagination and poetry.
goodly states: wonderful works of literature.
western islands: poems from the British Isles and Ireland.
bards in fealty to Apollo: poets dedicate their work to the Greek god of the arts.
wide expanse: undiscovered world of great literature.
deep-browed: wise; scholarly.
demesne: private kingdom.
serene: clear air.

watcher of the skies: astronomer.
ken: knowledge; understanding.
stout: fearless.
Cortez: The explorer Cortez reached Mexico in 1518. Another Spaniard, Balboa, was the first European to glimpse the Pacific Ocean in 1513.
surmise: surprise; wonder.
Darien: old name for the narrow stretch of land (now called Panama).

'He stared at the Pacific'

Personal Response

1. In your opinion, what is the central theme of this poem? Support your response with reference to the text.
2. There are several striking metaphors in the octave (first eight lines) of the poem. Choose one that you consider particularly interesting and comment on its effectiveness.
3. Explain how Keats uses language to convey his feelings in the sestet (final six lines).

Critical Literacy

Written in October 1816, this famous sonnet expresses the intensity of John Keats's experience while reading the translated works of Homer. For the twenty-year-old Keats, there was nothing to equal the excitement of Greek poetry. To show how deeply Homer's genius affected him, Keats uses dramatic images of exploration and discovery. In a sense, the reading experience itself becomes a great voyage, leading to creative writing both for the poet and the reader.

Keats's intense love of poetry is evident from the start. He addresses the reader directly, comparing himself to a traveller who enjoys visiting exotic places. For him, reading is an adventure. The exclamatory opening lines establish his enthusiasm for literature. **Keats makes effective use of vivid comparisons, travel imagery and a vigorous tone to express his feelings**. The vivid phrase 'realms of gold' implies world riches – the power of creativity and the imagination.

Keats develops the metaphor of exploration, reflecting on the many wonderful poems ('goodly states' and 'western islands') that he has already read. In the second quatrain, he identifies the 'wide expanse' of Homer's epic works with a vast ocean. Throughout the octave, there is **an unmistakable impression of restlessness** and eager anticipation. The poet is heartfelt in his praise of Chapman whose 'loud and bold' translation of Homer's poetry allows him to enjoy its invigorating atmosphere ('pure serene').

The sense of fresh discovery brings the reader to the sonnet's volta (or change in the train of thought): 'Then felt I ...' (line 9). Keats uses two similes that are both beautiful and appropriate to convey the astonishment of finally reading Homer: 'Then felt I like some watcher of the skies/When a new planet swims into his ken'. Just as the astronomer is excited to discover a newly found world among the stars, Keats is similarly thrilled to finally read the poems of Homer. The swimming metaphor is part of the many **recurring water images which add to the poem's cohesive structure**.

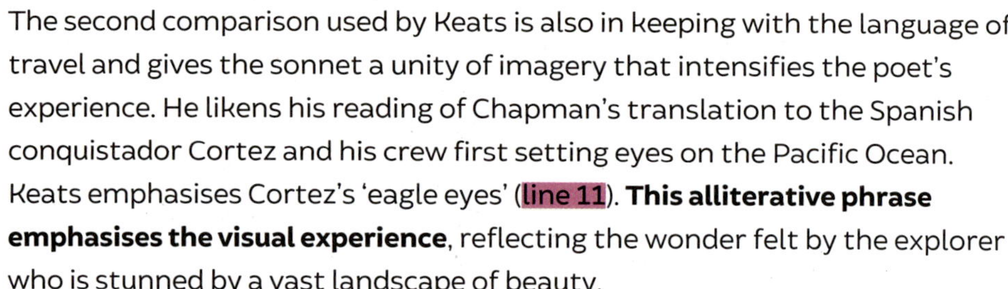

The second comparison used by Keats is also in keeping with the language of travel and gives the sonnet a unity of imagery that intensifies the poet's experience. He likens his reading of Chapman's translation to the Spanish conquistador Cortez and his crew first setting eyes on the Pacific Ocean. Keats emphasises Cortez's 'eagle eyes' (line 11). **This alliterative phrase emphasises the visual experience**, reflecting the wonder felt by the explorer who is stunned by a vast landscape of beauty.

Cortez's men stand in silent amazement, looking 'at each other with a wild surmise'. The emotion is carefully controlled, with a sureness of diction and sound. The sense of openness to a wide sea of wonder is suggested by long vowels ('wild', 'surmise', 'silent'), tapering off to hushed astonishment in the weak syllables of the final words, 'upon a peak in Darien'. There is no need for overstatement as Keats's **restrained ending** leaves the reader with a lingering sense of breathtaking exhilaration.

All through the sestet, run-on lines intensify the rhythm to convey a wide-sweeping sense of movement – of planets circling the heavens, and ships circumnavigating the earth. In this way, Keats makes the subtle point that discovery is part of what makes us all human. The **poem typifies much of his Romantic style**. Internal rhymes and sibilant sound effects give it a rich, sensuous, musical quality. But primarily, this dramatic sonnet expresses the power of Keats's personal experience and reveals his passion for poetry.

Writing About the Poem

'Keats makes effective use of the Petrarchan sonnet form in "On First Looking into Chapman's Homer".' Discuss this view, using suitable reference to the poem.

Sample Paragraph

'On First Looking into Chapman's Homer' is a Petrarchan sonnet, clearly divided into an octave and a sestet, with a tightly controlled rhyme scheme. In the first eight lines, Keats presents the idea of his lifelong desire to read the poetry of 'deep-brow'd Homer'. The tone is emphatic: 'Much have I travell'd in the realms of gold'. He uses various travel images to explain his great love of books, such as 'Round many western islands have I been'. In line nine, the word 'Then' marks the break or turn in his thought and the sestet records his delight after discovering Chapman's English version of Homer's epic poems. This is a characteristic of Italian sonnets and Keats develops the subject of his response to Homer through the use of vibrant imagery and similes which convey his sense of surprise. Comparing himself to a successful astronomer who finds 'a new planet' and the explorer Cortez adds energy. The sensation of shock and joy is evident in the final image, 'Silent, upon a peak in Darien'. There is a sense of unity throughout the poem. Keats uses the condensed sonnet form very effectively to convey the intensity of his feelings – and I could relate to this.

EXAMINER'S COMMENT

An informative and well-focused response which addresses the question directly throughout. Suitable – and accurate – quotations are integrated successfully, offering valuable support: 'In line nine, the word "Then" marks the break or turn in his thought and the sestet records his delight.' Key points are expressed with confidence in a clear, fluent style: 'This is a characteristic of Italian sonnets and Keats develops the subject of his response to Homer through the use of vibrant imagery and similes'. A top-grade paragraph.

Class/Homework Exercises

1. Trace the progress of thought in 'On First Looking into Chapman's Homer', using suitable reference to the poem.
2. Comment on the changes of tone between the octave and sestet, supporting your points with apt reference to the text.

Summary Points

- **Central themes include the excitement of literature and the power of imagination.**
- **Superbly sustained metaphors of exploration.**
- **Petrarchan or Italian sonnet form (octave and sestet).**
- **Sensuous language, vivid imagery patterns, contrasting tones.**
- **Powerful sound effects, run-on lines, contrasting rhythms and moods.**

POETRY FOCUS

4 Ode on a Grecian Urn

Ode: celebratory poem addressed to a person or a thing.
Urn: tall vase with stem and base used for storing a person's cremated ashes.

I

Thou still unravish'd bride of quietness,
Thou foster-child of silence and slow time,
Sylvan historian, who canst thus express
A flowery tale more sweetly than our rhyme:
What leaf-fring'd legend haunts about thy shape
Of deities or mortals, or of both,
In Tempe or the dales of Arcady?
What men or gods are these? What maidens loth?
What mad pursuit? What struggle to escape?
What pipes and timbrels? What wild ecstasy?

II

Heard melodies are sweet, but those unheard
Are sweeter; therefore, ye soft pipes, play on;
Not to the sensual ear, but, more endear'd,
Pipe to the spirit ditties of no tone:
Fair youth, beneath the trees, thou canst not leave
Thy song, nor ever can those trees be bare;
Bold Lover, never, never canst thou kiss,
Though winning near the goal – yet, do not grieve;
She cannot fade, though thou hast not thy bliss,
For ever wilt thou love, and she be fair!

III

Ah, happy, happy boughs! that cannot shed
Your leaves, nor ever bid the Spring adieu;
And, happy melodist, unwearied,
For ever piping songs for ever new;
More happy love! more happy, happy love!
For ever warm and still to be enjoyed,
For ever panting, and for ever young;
All breathing human passion far above,
That leaves a heart high-sorrowful and cloyed,
A burning forehead, and a parching tongue.

still: as yet, unmoving.
unravish'd: untouched.
Sylvan historian: storyteller from the woods.
legend: myth, tale.
Tempe: Greek valley.
Arcady: rural district in Greece.
loth: unwilling.
timbrels: tambourines.
sensual: physical.
spirit ditties of no tone: poems from another dimension which have no earthly sound.
Bold: confident, fearless.
cloyed: overfull.
parching: dried up, thirsty.

IV

Who are these coming to the sacrifice?
  To what green altar, O mysterious priest,
Lead'st thou that heifer lowing at the skies,
  And all her silken flanks with garlands dresst?
What little town by river or sea shore,
  Or mountain-built with peaceful citadel,
    Is emptied of this folk, this pious morn?
And, little town, thy streets for evermore
  Will silent be; and not a soul to tell
    Why thou art desolate, can e'er return.

V

O Attic shape! Fair attitude! with brede
  Of marble men and maidens overwrought,
With forest branches and the trodden weed;
  Thou, silent form, dost tease us out of thought
As doth eternity: Cold Pastoral!
  When old age shall this generation waste,
    Thou shalt remain, in midst of other woe
Than ours, a friend to man, to whom thou say'st,
  'Beauty is truth, truth beauty' – that is all
    Ye know on earth, and all ye need to know.

heifer: young cow.

citadel: stronghold protecting a city.
pious: God-fearing.

desolate: deserted.

Attic: from Athens.
brede: decoration, embroidery.
overwrought: frantic, overworked.

tease: provoke, tantalise.

Cold Pastoral: passionless story of idealised rural life.

'Cold Pastoral'

Personal Response

1. In your opinion, what is the main theme of this poem?
2. Select one image from the poem that you found particularly effective. Briefly explain your choice.
3. Comment on the final two lines of the poem.

Critical Literacy

Keats's famous ode explores the paradoxical relationship between the permanent world of art and transient reality. The poet believed that despite being mortal, human beings must strive to make themselves immortal. The mysterious Grecian urn enables the imagination to operate. It is a symbol of timeless perfection that provokes by silently posing questions. This symbol of eternal beauty is in eternal repose.

The poet stands before an ancient Grecian vase and addresses it in a series of vivid metaphors – 'bride of quietness ... foster-child of silence'. Keats is immediately engrossed in the artistic images which are frozen in time. Respectfully, he considers the **meaning of the urn**. The word 'still' establishes an atmosphere of ambiguity ('as yet' or 'not moving'). This 'unravish'd' urn has not been affected by the destructive power of time. Although it does not speak, this 'Sylvan historian' clearly tells a story. Indeed, it can relate a tale from the countryside much better than the poet – 'thus express/A flowery tale more sweetly than our rhyme'. Keats wonders about the scene that is depicted on the side of the vase: 'What leaf-fring'd legend haunts about thy shape?' He speculates that it is an ancient saga about groups of men – or possibly gods – enjoying themselves in the scenic Greek countryside. Several rapid questions close the first stanza capturing all the frenzied excitement associated with lovers. The 'mad pursuit' involves unwilling maidens who 'struggle to escape'. This headlong dash is accompanied by wild music on 'pipes and timbrels' and concludes with the climactic phrase, 'wild ecstasy'. In this stanza, Keats has drawn a sharp contrast between the dynamic pursuit portrayed on the urn and the stillness of its own form.

Stanza two opens quietly. The poet makes effective use of a memorable paradox to argue that music heard on earth is 'sweet' but that the music of the imagination is 'sweeter'. He urges the musicians on the urn to 'play on' – even though their other-worldly music cannot be experienced in the mortal world: 'Pipe to the spirit ditties of no tone'. Keats directly addresses one particular young man, 'Fair youth, beneath the trees, thou canst not leave/ Thy song'. The breathless run-on lines suggest suspended time – the immediacy of being preserved at a precise moment, forever singing to his beloved. In this idyllic place, the trees will never shed their leaves. **Keats has become deeply engrossed in the urn's images**. Paradoxically, all the characters are immortal, but not living. Although the young lover is very

near to the girl he loves, she is just out of reach: 'never, never canst thou kiss'. The double negative reinforces the poignant reality. Nonetheless, the poet offers a consoling insight. Even though the youth cannot embrace his beloved, she can never grow old. Within the permanent reality of art, their love and beauty will live on: 'For ever wilt thou love, and she be fair'.

In the third stanza, Keats focuses on the sublime joy of the pastoral scene pictured on the urn where nothing is subject to transience. The poet's mood is ecstatic and he evidently delights in the 'happy, happy boughs' that will not lose their leaves with the passing seasons. Repetition and vibrant rhythm echo his enjoyment. Within the ideal artistic world, it will always be springtime. The 'unwearied' musician will constantly play songs which will stay 'for ever new'. **Time does not exist here**. The pace of the stanza becomes more urgent as the poet immerses himself in the urn's narrative. Emphatic alliteration conveys the joy of escaping the tyranny of ageing: 'More happy love! more happy, happy love!' In contrast to this blissful state of endless 'warm' and 'panting' emotion on the beautiful vase, Keats acknowledges the stark truth of everyday human feeling with its 'burning forehead' and 'parching tongue'. In the real world, people suffer the pain of unreturned love which leaves them with 'a heart high-sorrowful and cloyed'. Is the poet suggesting that romantic love between human beings is always flawed?

Stanza four describes another of the urn's dramatic images – the ritual sacrifice of an animal. Keats inquires about the images of people approaching a 'green altar': 'Who are these coming to the sacrifice?' Readers are also drawn into the scene by the poet's fascination with the festivities recorded on the urn. Keats's **imagery is characteristically sensuous**. A 'mysterious priest' leads in a ceremonial heifer – 'her silken flanks with garlands dresst'. Meanwhile, the nearby village remains strangely deserted, its silent streets desolate 'for evermore'. Like everything else on the urn, its inhabitants are frozen in time and will never return home.

In the final stanza the poet steps back from his close observation and looks at the vase in its entirety, 'O Attic shape'. He is completely in awe at its beauty, 'Fair attitude'. Keats acknowledges that the urn confuses mere mortals with its intriguing narrative – 'tease us out of thought'. Human beings cannot ever comprehend the concept of 'eternity'. He refers to the urn as a 'Cold Pastoral' which tells its inanimate story of romance and religious rites. It is eternal and far removed from the living, breathing, imperfect world of those on earth. The urn remains 'in midst of other woe/ Than ours'. Others will look at it. It is a 'friend to man' showing beautiful images on its exquisite form which contains the ashes of the dead.

The concluding two lines have long been debated. The urn seems to be addressing man, 'Beauty is truth, truth beauty'. What is beautiful is real and genuine. Keats clearly seems to be celebrating the transcendent powers of art which can offer a glimpse of the unchanging happiness to be realised in eternity. Like all great works of art, the Greek vase will always be 'a friend to man'. Did the sculptor who created it recognise the limited capabilities of humans to comprehend the mysteries of life and death? While we must make up our own minds about the poet's meaning, at the very least, Keats has made us consider these important questions through his reflections on the beautiful urn and its enigmatic images.

Writing About the Poem

'Keats explores the transient and immortal through striking and sensual imagery.' Discuss this view, with reference to 'Ode on a Grecian Urn'.

Sample Paragraph

The poem, 'Ode on a Grecian Urn', does indeed 'tease' the reader 'out of thought'. The cold marble of this 'Attic shape' was originally used to store ashes. Yet it is decorated with dynamic images of a 'mad pursuit' of maidens by 'men or gods'. Rapid-fire questions mimic the frantic chase, 'What pipes and timbrels? What wild ecstasy?' Keats captures the essence of young love, 'For ever panting', 'For ever warm'. The sensuality of young love is effectively conveyed through the assonance of the long 'a', almost like a young lover's sigh. Yet this is not human love, there is no 'For ever'. It is vividly described in the alliterative phrase, 'heart high-sorrowful and cloyed'. Human love is subject to change, whereas the urn shows a love yet to be enjoyed where the 'Bold lover' will always love and his beloved will always be fair, 'She cannot fade'. The immortality of the images on the urn is depicted by the 'desolate' image of the little town which will never know where its inhabitants have gone because they will never return and the town will remain 'silent'. The 'Cold Pastoral' of the urn will puzzle its viewers through the ages with its idealised pictures of rural life as it silently relates its never-ending message that 'Beauty is truth, truth beauty'. Through the use of sensuous imagery, Keats has provided an interesting exploration of the transience of human life, which he contrasts with the permanence of art.

EXAMINER'S COMMENT

This is a very assured response engaging closely with the poem's main themes of mortality and immortality. Quotations are effectively interwoven to support discussion points: 'Rapid-fire questions mimic the frantic chase, "What pipes and timbrels? What wild ecstasy?"' The expression throughout is both varied and controlled, ensuring the top grade.

Class/Homework Exercises

1. Keats becomes deeply involved in the story told on the urn. What questions does he consider? Support your response with close reference to the poem.
2. How does Keats create a mood of excitement in 'Ode on a Grecian Urn'? Comment on his use of questions, the exclamation marks, sentence length and use of repetition in your answer.

Summary Points

- **Key themes include transience, immortality, art, reality and the desire to escape.**
- **Innovative use of the ode enables readers to reflect on the subject matter.**
- **Distinctive moods – contrasting images of the lovers and little town.**
- **Sensuous language, metaphors, paradoxes, recurring questions, emphatic repetition.**
- **Variety of tones; effective use of assonance, alliteration, sibilance.**

5 When I Have Fears That I May Cease to Be

When I have fears that I may cease to be
Before my pen has gleaned my teeming brain,
Before high-piled books, in charactery,
Hold like rich garners the full ripen'd grain;
When I behold, upon the night's starr'd face,
Huge cloudy symbols of a high romance,
And think that I may never live to trace
Their shadows, with the magic hand of chance;
And when I feel, fair creature of an hour,
That I shall never look upon thee more,
Never have relish in the faery power
Of unreflecting love; – then on the shore
Of the wide world I stand alone, and think
Till love and fame to nothingness do sink.

gleaned: gathered; made use of.
teeming: full (of ideas).
charactery: print; writing.
garners: granaries; stores.

high romance: noble poetic themes.

relish: pleasure.
faery: magical.

unreflecting: spontaneous, natural.

'the wide world'

Personal Response

1. In your opinion, what are the main fears expressed by Keats in the poem?
2. Choose one image from the poem that you found particularly interesting. Briefly explain your choice.
3. Comment on the change of tone and mood in lines 12–14.

Critical Literacy

In this carefully crafted Shakespearean sonnet, consisting of a long single sentence, Keats describes his fear of dying young before he has time to fulfil his artistic potential. He is also fearful of never experiencing the joy of being truly in love. This makes him feel that he is utterly alone in the world. However, he finally resolves his anxiety in the poem's concluding lines by asserting the unimportance of romance and literary fame.

The sombre tone reflecting Keats's fear of failure is evident from the start. Striking images convey the poet's personal confession about his deepest concerns. Throughout the first quatrain, he emphasises the dreadful possibility that he may never achieve his full creative potential. His anxiety is typical of dissatisfied artists throughout time. The **extended autumn harvest imagery** – 'gleaned', 'garners', 'full ripen'd grain'– suggests the fertility of Keats's youthful mind and reinforces his heightened sense of frustration. The adjectives, 'high-piled' and 'rich', clearly indicate how acutely aware he is of his own poetic power ('teeming brain').

In the second quatrain, Keats reveals that he is also anxious about not having sufficient time to explore more of life's great mysteries. The strange beauty of creation is symbolised by his **dramatic personification** of the sky – 'night's starr'd face'. Sadly, there is a suggestion of the unattainable in the poet's dreamlike desire to sit under the stars hoping for inspiration. He recognises the wonders of the natural world and its countless mysteries ('Huge cloudy symbols') masking undiscovered delights. If he is fortunate enough, then such 'shadows' might well prompt him to be creative – depending on the 'magic hand of chance'.

The focus throughout the poem, however, is on **the unstoppable passing of time**, emphasised by Keats's repetitive use of 'When' and 'never'. Its corrosive effects are further considered in the third quatrain where the poet is clearly saddened by the thought of losing his lover – 'fair creature of an hour'. Characteristically, he is likely to be using personification here as a poetic technique to highlight the effects of time. For Keats, all of human experience is beautiful but short-lived. Romantic love is also transient, but has 'faery power' or some curious magical quality because it is 'unreflecting' and allows lovers to momentarily escape reality.

As the sonnet builds to a climax in the rhyming couplet, Keats achieves some distancing from his own feelings and this enables him to reach a resolution. He considers his own solitary destiny ('I stand alone') and the more general reality of human insignificance. The stark image of being stranded on the shore of 'the wide world' (a traditional image of eternity) signifies an important development of thought from his initial terrors to an acceptance of life's unimportance. **He ceases to fear and yearn**. Some critics have interpreted Keats's view of death as finding freedom from suffering and dread. However, the concluding tone includes both submission and despair – echoed by broad assonant vowels and the final word 'sink'. The slow, deliberate rhythm further reflects the poet's stark realisation that neither love nor poetry can ever challenge mortality.

Overall, this sonnet offers readers **an interesting insight into Keat's personal perspective on transience and death**. There is a remarkable contrast between the poet's early energetic mood and his eventual acknowledgment of life's brevity. The poem is distinguished by Keats's

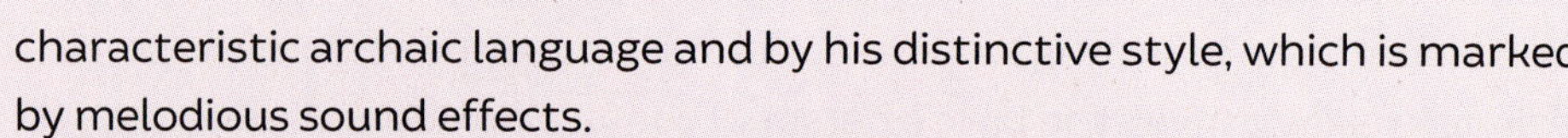

characteristic archaic language and by his distinctive style, which is marked by melodious sound effects.

Writing About the Poem

'John Keats's poems often portray the conflict between the poet's personal feelings and the stark realities of life.' Discuss this view, with reference to 'When I Have Fears That I May Cease to Be'.

Sample Paragraph

The title of 'When I Have Fears That I May Cease to Be' immediately brings us into Keats's private world which is filled with anxiety and uncertainty. Time is seen as the great enemy of his 'teeming brain'. The poet's urgent tone reflects his sense of panic about the certainty of death. The disturbing awareness of his own mortality is seen in the repetition of key words, such as 'When', 'before' and 'never'. Keats compares his creative potential for producing new poems to a farmer harvesting 'the full-ripen'd grain'. He uses metaphorical language to describe the mysterious universe – 'the night's starr'd face' which he 'may never live to trace'. This sense of inner conflict and frustration is expressed in the final lines in a memorable image where Keats imagines himself alienated between the land and the sea in transition from this life to the next. He is on the edge 'of the wide world'. The poet's troubled self-analysis has been resolved as he now sees himself as insignificant – 'I stand alone'. In accepting the truth about how short human life is, Keats has come to terms with the fact that his fears about missing out on 'love and fame' are unimportant. In relief and dismay, he faces the reality that his fears 'to nothingness do sink'.

EXAMINER'S COMMENT

This impressive top-grade response makes effective use of apt quotations to address the question directly. The conflict between Keats's feelings and the growing awareness of his mortality is central to the answer. There is also some very good discussion of the poet's language use in developing key themes: 'The poet's troubled self-analysis has been resolved as he now sees himself as insignificant – "I stand alone".' Controlled fluent expression confirms the high standard.

Class/Homework Exercises

1. Outline the central themes in 'When I Have Fears', carefully tracing the progress of thought in the poem.
2. Comment on the effectiveness of Keats's vibrant language in this sonnet. Refer to the text in your answer.

Summary Points

- **Transience, immortality, poetry and love are central themes.**
- **Concise Shakespearean sonnet form intensifies Keats's feelings.**
- **Effective use of language – extended harvest metaphor.**
- **Vivid imagery, recurring personification, contrasting tones.**

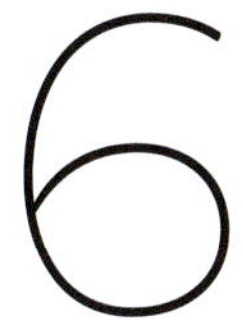

La Belle Dame Sans Merci

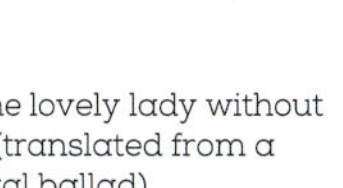

Title: the lovely lady without mercy (translated from a medieval ballad).

JOHN KEATS

I

O what can ail thee, knight-at-arms,
Alone and palely loitering?
The sedge has withered from the lake
And no birds sing.

ail: make you unwell.

sedge: marsh plant (resembling coarse grass).

II

O what can ail thee, knight-at-arms,
So haggard and so woe-begone?
The squirrel's granary is full,
And the harvest's done.

haggard: looking exhausted and unwell.

woe-begone: miserable in appearance.

granary: storehouse for grain.

III

I see a lily on thy brow,
With anguish moist and fever-dew,
And on thy cheeks a fading rose
Fast withereth too.

IV

I met a lady in the meads,
Full beautiful – a faery's child,
Her hair was long, her foot was light,
And her eyes were wild.

meads: flat grassland meadows.

V

I made a garland for her head,
And bracelets too, and fragrant zone;
She looked at me as she did love,
And made sweet moan.

fragrant zone: flower-filled belt.

VI

I set her on my pacing steed
And nothing else saw all day long.
For sidelong would she bend, and sing
A faery's song.

steed: horse.

VII

She found me roots of relish sweet,
And honey wild, and manna-dew,
And sure in language strange she said –
'I love thee true.'

VIII

She took me to her elfin grot,
And there she wept and sighed full sore,
And there I shut her wild wild eyes
With kisses four.

IX

And there she lulled me asleep,
And there I dreamed – Ah! woe betide!
The latest dream I ever dreamt
On the cold hill side.

X

I saw pale kings and princes too,
Pale warriors, death-pale were they all;
They cried – 'La Belle Dame sans Merci
Hath thee in thrall!'

XI

I saw their starved lips in the gloam,
With horrid warning gaped wide,
And I awoke and found me here,
On the cold hill's side.

XII

And this is why I sojourn here,
Alone and palely loitering,
Though the sedge is withered from the lake,
And no birds sing.

relish: delight.

manna: food (God's food to the Israelites in the wilderness).

elfin: small and delicate.

grot: cave, grotto.

in thrall: in another's power, enslaved.

gaped: open-mouthed.

sojourn: remain.

'And there I dreamed'

Personal Response

1. How does Keats establish a dreamlike or eerie atmosphere in this poem? In your response consider the effect of medieval references, the use of archaic words and the supernatural elements.
2. How effective is Keats in conveying the message of doomed love? Support your answer with suitable reference to the poem.
3. In your opinion, what moral lesson can be learned from this poem? Briefly explain your answer.

Critical Literacy

Keats has set his dramatic ballad in the medieval era. This mysterious poem can be interpreted in several ways. Is it a tale of human yearning for eternal love? Is Keats warning against the seductive physical attractions of the deadly femme fatale who loves only to destroy? Does the storyline demonstrate the loss of freedom that comes with falling in love? The Romantic poets, such as Keats, were interested in nature, art, freedom, love and equality. They usually wrote about these themes in lyrical, descriptive language.

This ballad plunges the reader into a conversation between an unidentified speaker and a dying knight. The first three stanzas contain the sequence of questions which the speaker puts to the knight. The next nine stanzas are the knight's reply. He is unlike the stereotypical heroic figures who appear in legends. This is no chivalrous warrior intent on overcoming enormous challenges to win his fair lady. Instead, the knight is 'alone and palely loitering'. From the start, he is portrayed as vulnerable, 'O what can ail thee, knight-at-arms'? **The desolate autumn setting is sketched in a few well-chosen details**. The land is arid and the birds have already flown away: 'The sedge has withered from the lake'. The emphatic monosyllables of 'And no birds sing' reinforce the dismal scene. Throughout stanza one, Keats makes effective use of pathetic fallacy – almost personifying the bleak landscape – to underline the plight of the unfortunate knight.

Stanza two focuses on the knight's bedraggled appearance: 'So haggard and so woe-begone'. Nature has completed its annual cycle, 'The squirrel's granary is full,/ And the harvest's done'. This natural world is in order, and is one of plenty and ease, unlike the disordered predicament of the distraught knight. In stanza three, Keats continues to use descriptive imagery to paint a vivid picture of the lonely, listless knight. **Broad vowel sounds ('brow', 'anguish moist') echo his despondent mood**. The lily is a flower which is traditionally associated with death and even the rose – usually a symbol of beauty and passion – is 'fading'. The onomatopoeic verb 'withereth' also suggests that the helpless knight is trembling in his death throes.

In stanza four, the knight remembers how he met a beautiful and enchanting lady: 'a faery's child'. He describes her **alluring appeal**: 'Her hair was long, her foot was light'. But this mysterious woman's 'wild' eyes suggest a creature not of this world. He courts her in the time-honoured tradition and she appears to return his ardour: 'She looked at me as she did love'. He is completely obsessed and 'nothing else saw all day long' (stanza six). He helps her onto his 'pacing steed', seemingly placing her on a pedestal to be worshipped while she holds him spellbound by her 'faery's song'.

Almost immediately, this enigmatic lady seduces him with exotic food: 'relish sweet', 'honey wild' and 'manna-dew'. The focus is on the intense physical attraction between the couple and she cannot hide her feelings – 'I love thee true'. But once again, a note of disquiet appears when she begins to speak in 'language strange' – another suggestion of her otherworldliness. **The suspense increases** further in stanza eight when the couple arrive at her 'elfin grot'. Suddenly the lady indulges in an uncontrolled outburst of emotion: 'there she wept and sighed full sore'. Was this because she knew what she was about to do, but was unable to reverse it? The knight attempts to calm her: 'I shut her wild wild eyes/With kisses four'. Repetition and run-on line give emphasis to the turbulent scene.

However, the romantic mood seems dimmed by her weeping and the knight is 'lulled' to sleep in stanza nine. His **dreams instantly descend into nightmares** as a haunting procession of 'pale kings, and princes too' utter dire warnings: 'La Belle Dame sans Merci/Hath thee in thrall'. The horrific state of these unfortunates is emphasised by the compound word, 'death-pale'. Their grotesque appearance of 'starved lips' that 'gaped wide' show the consequences of becoming involved with this merciless creature.

The poem concludes as it began beside the remote lake. Keats's use of the present tense raises interesting questions. Can the knight ever really escape the dire consequences of his passionate romance with 'La Belle Dame'? The repetition of details from the opening lines give a sense of finality. **An ominous aura of mystery lingers**. Keats has composed a thought-provoking poem which cautions against the risks of being carried away by impulsive desire.

The Romantic poets revived the medieval ballad genre, a form of poetry which simply tells its tale largely through dialogue. The hypnotic alternating rhythm of four and three beats to a line weaves its spell on readers. This unsettling story slowly and deliberately moves to its inevitable tragic ending. The deluded knight who invested so much in pursuing ideal love is left trapped on the 'cold hill's side' (stanza eleven). Is Keats issuing a stark warning about the dangers of obsessive love?

Writing About the Poem

Keats explores themes of transience and death in richly emotional and symbolic poetry. Discuss this statement in relation to 'La Belle Dame Sans Merci', supporting your points with suitable reference to the poem.

Sample Paragraph

The poet explores the divide between human mortality and eternity which can never be bridged in the medieval ballad, 'La Belle Dame Sans Merci'. In this puzzling narrative of the knight and his lady, Keats examines the difficulties of seeking never-ending romantic love. Various voices are heard in the story, the unidentified speaker, 'O what can ail thee knight-at-arms', the lovesick knight, 'I met a lady in the meads', and the bewitching woman, 'I love thee true'. The timeless landscape is richly dramatised with a few well-chosen details, 'The sedge has withered' and 'no birds sing'. I thought this was symbolic of the knight's predicament, facing up to a life without hope. The description of his physical and mental state was caught very effectively through the image of flowers, the lily a symbol of death and the decaying rose. How different this was to the lovely garlands he had given to his love when he first fell for her. The nightmarish consequences of his doomed affair is detailed in the procession of former lovers of this bewitching creature, 'pale

EXAMINER'S COMMENT

A mature and insightful reaction to a challenging question, addressing both the poet's subject matter and language use. Quotations are used to effectively support key discussion points: 'The nightmarish consequences of his doomed affair is explicitly detailed in the procession of former lovers of this bewitching creature, "pale warriors, death-pale were they all".' Worthwhile personal engagement and fluently expressed ideas contribute to this successful top-grade paragraph.

warriors, death-pale were they all'. The repetition of the adjective, 'Pale' suggests how they were tricked by this enchantress. Readers are left wondering if this strange lady will continue to captivate other unsuspecting men with her dangerous promise of perfect love.

Class/Homework Exercises

1. Comment on the effectiveness of Keats's imagery in this ballad. Refer closely to the text in your answer.
2. 'Keats's use of contrast in "La Belle Dame Sans Merci" is an important part of the poem's fascination.' Discuss this view, supporting your points with suitable reference to the text.

Summary Points

- **Reality, the supernatural, and romantic love are key themes.**
- **Archaic language adds to the mysterious world of the poem.**
- **Evocative imagery intensifies the timeless scene.**
- **The ballad form is effectively used to relate the story of the knight and his lady.**
- **Effective use of setting, contrasting atmospheres, onomatopoeia and repetition.**

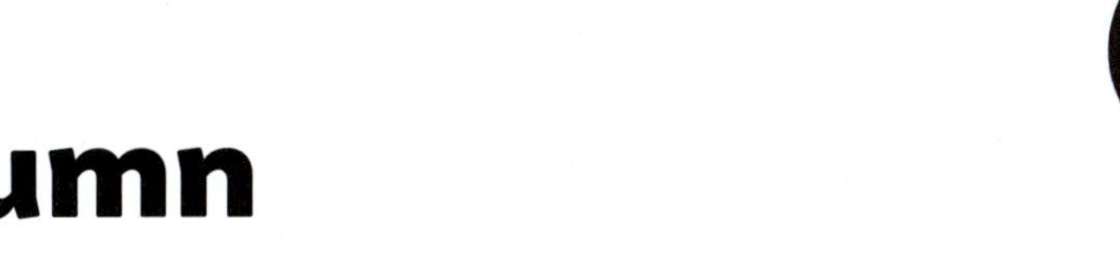

7 To Autumn

I

Season of mists and mellow fruitfulness,
Close bosom-friend of the maturing sun;
Conspiring with him how to load and bless
With fruit the vines that round the thatch-eaves run;
To bend with apples the moss'd cottage-trees,
And fill all fruit with ripeness to the core;
To swell the gourd, and plump the hazel shells
With a sweet kernel; to set budding more,
And still more, later flowers for the bees,
Until they think warm days will never cease,
For Summer has o'er-brimm'd their clammy cells.

mellow: pleasantly smooth, soft to taste and in colour.
Conspiring: making secret plans.
thatch-eaves: overhanging roof of straw.
core: centre.
gourd: large fleshy fruit.
kernel: soft part of nut.
clammy: unpleasantly damp.

II

Who hath not seen thee oft amid thy store?
Sometimes whoever seeks abroad may find
Thee sitting careless on a granary floor,
Thy hair soft-lifted by the winnowing wind;
Or on a half-reaped furrow sound asleep,
Drowsed with the fume of poppies, while thy hook
Spares the next swath and all its twined flowers:
And sometimes like a gleaner thou dost keep
Steady thy laden head across a brook;
Or by a cider-press, with patient look,
Thou watchest the last oozings, hours by hours.

abroad: over a large expanse.
sitting careless: seated unconcerned.
winnowing: removing chaff (the dry outer covering of grain).
poppies: flower, cutter.
swath: strip of corn cut by scythe.
twined: twisted around.
gleaner: gatherer of leftover grain after harvest has been cut.

III

Where are the songs of Spring? Ay, where are they?
Think not of them, thou hast thy music too, –
While barred clouds bloom the soft-dying day,
And touch the stubble-plains with rosy hue;
Then in a wailful choir the small gnats mourn
Among the river sallows, borne aloft
Or sinking as the light wind lives or dies;
And full-grown lambs loud bleat from hilly bourn;
Hedge-crickets sing, and now with treble soft
The red-breast whistles from a garden-croft;
And gathering swallows twitter in the skies.

bloom: give a glow to.
stubble-plains: field after harvest is cut.
gnats: small flies.
sallows: young willows.
bourn: small stream.
Hedge-crickets: shrill, chirping insect.
garden-croft: cultivated area near to country cottage.

'Season of mists'

Personal Response

1. In your opinion, what is the main theme of the poem?
2. Choose one image from the poem which appealed to you and comment on its effectiveness.
3. How does Keats create a mood of peace and calm in this poem? Refer to aspects of his content and style in your response.

Critical Literacy

In a letter written in September 1819, Keats says: 'How beautiful the season is now – How fine the air ... I never liked stubble-fields so much as now – Aye better than the chilly green of the spring. Somehow, a stubble-field looks warm – in the same way that some pictures look warm. This struck me so much in my Sunday's walk that I composed upon it.' What he composed was the ode, 'To Autumn'. This was written at a time when Keats knew he was seriously ill. Yet, in this poem, he achieves a great serenity. Acutely aware that moments of intense pleasure do not last, he sets his love of the beautiful against the uncontrollable reality of suffering and death.

This is Keats's final ode in his celebrated sequence of 'Great Odes'. It is a valediction, a farewell to the season of abundance and fruition. The poet absents himself from this poem, unlike his very obvious presence in his other two odes. There is no use of the personal pronoun, 'I'. Nonetheless, the reader is very much aware of the presence of the poet who is delighting in this rich 'Season of mists and mellow fruitfulness'. Keats does not even include the term 'ode' in the title. Indeed, a low- key invocation begins the poem. He is enabling us to enter into the season itself' thanks to his rich description of its pleasures.

Stanza one concentrates on the imagery of touch. In stanza two, he focuses on the visual while the third stanza appeals to the ear. Over the course of the poem, Keats examines various aspects of the season – including vegetation, human activity, animals, birds and insects. The ode moves slowly from the ripeness just before the harvest to the activities associated with harvest-time and its aftermath. In its broad structure, the poem follows the pattern of a typical autumn day, progressing from the 'maturing sun' to the actual harvesting to the evening's 'soft-dying day'.

Lines 1–11 invite us to experience the season directly, through concrete images of ripeness and fulfilment, 'fruit the vines', 'bend with apples'. The **wonderful excess of the season** is represented through repetition – 'budding more,/And still more'. The endless pleasure of the season is vividly conveyed by the soft alliterative 'm', 'For summer has o'er-brimmed their clammy cells'. Even the bees are deceived into thinking this warm

atmosphere will last. Personification of autumn as a co-conspirator with the sun adds to the season's enigmatic image. Precise and onomatopoeic verbs ('load', 'bend', 'fill', 'swell', 'plump', 'o'er-brimm'd') trace the ongoing quiet activity of growth and maturity. There is even a sacred quality (implied by the word 'bless') to this creative world of nature. Keats's tactile imagery focuses on this seemingly endless abundance, 'swell'. The essence of the season is conveyed in one long sentence and there is little to suggest that this season is going to end.

Stanza two personifies the season as several youthful workers engaged in bringing in the harvest. A beautiful picture of a young girl with her hair blowing softly in the autumn breeze is portrayed in the phrase 'soft-lifted by the winnowing wind'. Even the breeze is busy harvesting. The image of the exhausted granary labourer is suggestive of a lingering season, work as yet incomplete, 'half-reaped furrow sound asleep'. Keats skilfully conjures up an air of lethargy in the deep peace of this rich time of year. The gleaner is described as balancing a load on her head as she crosses the brook unhurried. Finally, autumn is portrayed as the patient watcher, the cider-maker who ensures that he gets the 'last oozings' of the apples. The slow movement is caught in the sibilant 's' sounds, reminding us that autumn is indeed a season of **sensuous profusion**.

Somewhat surprisingly, stanza three does not proceed directly to winter, but instead returns to spring: 'Where are the songs of Spring?' The poet is untroubled by that and listens to the mournful sounds of autumn. Its **melancholic music** is wistfully relayed in the 'wailful choir' of gnats who 'mourn', as they rise and fall on the 'light wind'. We can imagine hearing the grown lambs in the onomatopoeic 'bleat', adding to the mood of nostalgia. The chirping of the hedge-crickets joins the melodic ensemble. Finally, the robin 'whistles', contributing its distinctively shrill tone to the choir – and suddenly the reality of autumn is upon us. Robins are usually associated with winter. The migrating swallows 'twitter', but will soon be heard no more – it is a 'soft-dying day'. This final stanza – with its many suggestions of death contrasts sharply with the vitality and excess of the first. But even the poem's open and closing rhyme scheme reinforces the natural symmetry and sense of finality. In his mature ode, Keats has succeeded in blending 'beauty' and 'truth'. This magnificent season must end because the world is governed by time and mortality. Having experienced the delights of autumn, the poet is now quietly resigned to the cycle of nature.

Writing About the Poem

'Keats explores the beauty of the world with sensuous passion, but he also views it honestly.' Discuss this view, with reference to the subject matter and style of 'To Autumn'.

Sample Paragraph

Keats appealed to my senses with a dazzling display of imagery in 'To Autumn'. He combined a picture into both tactile and visual imagery, 'touch the stubble-plains with rosy hue'. I could see the rich reddish colour of the setting sun and feel the sharp bristles of the cut corn in the harvested field. The visual image of a girl's hair lifted by a light breeze, 'Thy hair soft-lifted by the winnowing wind' is portrayed in sensuous detail. But it is not just poetic imagery, there is the reality of the actual harvesting, the heavy lifting, the exhaustion of cutting, 'on a half-reaped furrow sound asleep' and the sheer grind, 'last oozings'. Similarly, Keats does not shy away from the reality of the dying year. In the last stanza, he faces the transience of the season unlike the bees who 'think warm days will never cease'. There are many melancholy words and phrases, 'wailful', 'mourn', 'soft-dying', 'sinking', all contributing to the truth that winter inevitably follows autumn. There is also an inherent sadness which cannot be denied in the long vowel sounds of 'mourn', 'borne' and 'bourn'. The lavish sumptuousness of autumn, its 'mellow fruitfulness', is slowly receding into the mists. Keats has examined the beauty of this season, but truthfully.

EXAMINER'S COMMENT

An assured personal response engaging closely with the question. Quotations are well integrated into the commentary to support discussion points. A highly commendable detailed analysis of aural effects and tone: 'There is also an inherent sadness which cannot be denied in the long vowel sounds of "mourn", "borne" and "bourn"'. Expression throughout is varied, fluent and controlled: 'the lavish sumptuousness of autumn, its "mellow fruitfulness" is slowly receding into the mists'. An excellent top-grade paragraph.

Class/Homework Exercises

1. The first eight lines deal with the process of watching and contemplating. How do you think Keats watches and contemplates the season in this poem? Support your response with close reference to the poem, 'To Autumn'.
2. How does Keats create a mood of serenity in the poem? Refer to his use of imagery and sound effects in your answer.

Summary Points

- **Key themes of this great ode include rich abundance of the season, the reality of transience.**
- **Sensuous visual, tactile and aural imagery.**
- **Sound effects – alliteration, assonance, sibilance, repetition, rhyme.**
- **Distinctive moods – elation, melancholy.**

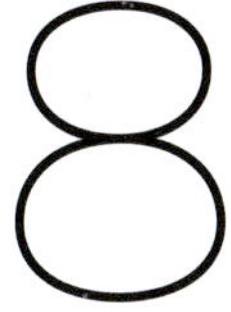

Bright Star, Would I Were Steadfast as Thou Art

JOHN KEATS

Bright star, would I were steadfast as thou art –
Not in lone splendour hung aloft the night
And watching, with eternal lids apart,
Like nature's patient, sleepless Eremite,
The moving waters at their priestlike task
Of pure ablution round earth's human shores,
Or gazing on the new soft-fallen mask
Of snow upon the mountains and the moors –
No – yet still steadfast, still unchangeable,
Pillow'd upon my fair love's ripening breast,
To feel for ever its soft fall and swell,
Awake for ever in a sweet unrest,
Still, still to hear her tender-taken breath,
And so live ever – or else swoon to death.

steadfast: steady, unswerving, resolute.
aloft: above.
lids: eyelids.
Eremite: hermit, recluse.
ablution: the act of cleansing.
Pillowed: cushioned.
tender: youthful, warm, romantic.
swoon: faint, pass out.

'still steadfast, still unchangeable'

Personal Response

1. Outline the contrasts that Keats draws between himself and the star. Illustrate your answer with close reference to the poem.
2. Keats uses repetition extensively throughout this poem. In your opinion, what is its effect on the reader? Support your answer with reference to the text.
3. Choose one image from the poem that you found particularly effective. Briefly explain your choice.

Critical Literacy

In 1820 when Keats was setting sail to Italy to find a cure for his worsening ill-health, he inscribed this sonnet into a book of Shakespearean poetry belonging to a friend. It is thought to be one of the last poems he ever composed. The poet focuses primarily on the differences between eternity and mortality.

This well-known poem consists of a single sentence and is divided into an octet and sestet from the Italian sonnet form. Line 1 begins with the arresting exclamation, 'Bright star'. Keats is startled by the brilliance of a distant star's 'splendour'. A heartfelt wish swiftly follows and he desires to be as dependable as the faraway star, 'hung aloft the night'. But in line 2, the emphatic 'Not' conveys his misgivings about the star's detached situation. Its isolation is implicit in its solitary occupation which consists of 'watching', 'gazing' on the earth. But the poet does not wish to be 'lone'. Personification emphasises the star's solitary existence. It observes, but does not participate. Existing on the periphery, there is no rest for this star because it continually views the ocean 'with eternal lids apart'. However, its sleeplessness is non-human, so the poet's wishes seem already to be futile.

Line 4 adds to the reclusive image of the star which Keats likens to 'nature's patient, sleepless Eremite'. The sea's restless stirrings are presented as a stately religious ceremony, a 'priestlike' ritual. It cleanses 'earth's human shores'. The poet's focus has now changed from contemplating the permanence of the star to the flux and flow of life here on earth. The rise and fall of the sea is beautifully expressed in the gentle run-on lines 5–6. Broad 'u' and 'o' vowels create a serene, flowing movement which is in contrast to the still star. Line 7 reveals another transient image of life on earth. The blanket of snow covering all in its white purity is regarded as a temporary 'mask'. It conceals – but only for a time. Keats uses the compound word, 'soft-fallen' to mimic the snowfall's silent arrival. The tranquillity of the newly transformed landscape is suggested by the alliterative phrase, 'the mountains and the moors', diverse places encased in a harmonious covering. The octet concludes with positive suggestions of life on earth – 'pure', 'new' and 'soft'.

However, the sharp monosyllabic negative, 'No', marks the turning-point of this sonnet. Is Keats rejecting the cold, eternal life of the star? Or is he refusing to accept the transience of human life? The adverb 'still' is repeated, announcing his desire to spend eternity frozen in a special moment, 'Pillow'd upon my fair love's ripening breast'. He clearly desires the permanence of the star's life, but not its cold, isolated existence. He also wants the warmth of a human relationship. This is evocatively conveyed in the rich imagery and sound effects of line 11. The intimate sensuality of human love is shown in the rise and fall of his lover's breath: 'To feel for ever its soft fall and swell'. This is reminiscent of an incoming, outgoing tide. A sharp contrast with the passive star is evident with the poet's wish to be 'Awake for ever in a sweet unrest'. More than anything, he wants to be constantly aware of his blessed state.

Unfortunately what he desires is impossible. All moments on this earth end. They will not last 'for ever' (line 12). His lover's mortality is conveyed in her even breathing which resonates in the compound word 'tender-taken'. This personal search for an ideal ('And so live ever') cannot be achieved by a human being whose world is one of change and ending. The poem's final phrase accepts this inescapable inevitability. If Keats cannot live forever, he will have to 'swoon to death' and pass into another kind of eternity. The sonnet's couplet provides a conclusive finish to the poem: 'breath' ceases on 'death'.

Writing About the Poem

'John Keats often expresses profound concern for life's deepest questions in poetry of rich description and sensual language.' Discuss this view, with reference to 'Bright Star'.

Sample Paragraph

In 'Bright Star', Keats explores the unobtainable, but much sought-after goal of enjoying the pleasures of this life forever. The permanence of the star is greatly admired by Keats as he addresses some important questions about life. He quickly rejects the star's solitary existence, not once but twice, 'Not', 'No'. The poet does not wish for its 'lone splendour' nor its 'Eremite' life. Instead, Keats paints dynamic pictures of life on earth, 'the moving waters', 'the mask/Of snow'. Although these are temporary, the poet glorifies the tides which cleanse 'round earth's human shores'. The broad

EXAMINER'S COMMENT

This is an excellent response to a challenging question. There is close engagement with the viewpoint and language in the poem: 'The snow is a unifying influence on "mountains and the moors".' Points are clearly expressed and supported by useful and accurate quotation. The analysis of the poet's technique in using aural imagery is particularly impressive: 'The explosive "p" and "b" together with the lyrical "l" sounds suggest a sensual picture of warmth.' A top-grade answer.

vowels, 'u' and 'o', create a mood of calmness. The snow is a unifying influence on 'mountains and the moors'. Keats also presents us with the significance of human intimacy where the lovers embrace: 'Pillow'd upon my fair love's ripening breast'. The explosive 'p' and 'b' together with the lyrical 'l' sounds suggest a sensual picture of warmth. How different from the reclusive, distant star! The soft rise and fall of his beloved's breathing is heard in the alliterative word, 'tender-taken'. Keats desperately wishes to remain in this moment endlessly. But that is not human destiny. So he accepts reality and death, but even here he conveys a graceful, sensual action – he will 'swoon' to death.

Class/Homework Exercises

1. 'Tensions between the transient and the immortal are often found in Keats's poetry.' Discuss this view, using suitable reference to 'Bright Star, Would I Were Steadfast as Thou Art'.
2. Keats led a 'life of sensation' and also a 'life of thoughts'. Discuss this statement in relation to the poem. Support your points with close reference to the text in your answer.

Summary Points

- **Eternity and mortality are central themes.**
- **Precise descriptions convey contrasts between the star and transient human life.**
- **Distinctive imagery patterns reinforce the tensions within the poem.**
- **Sonnet forms frame Keats's intense feelings.**
- **Repetition, musical language and personification enhance the sensual experience.**

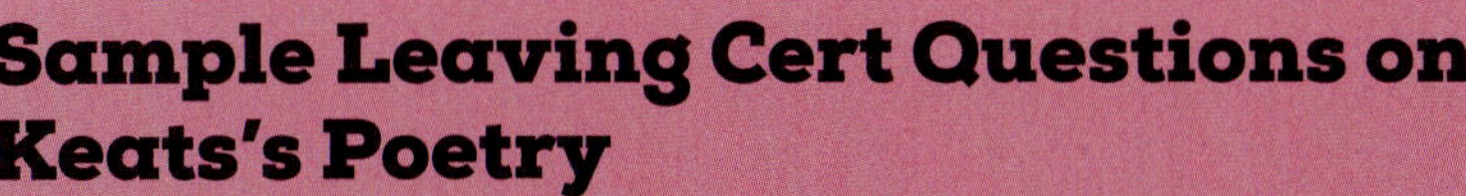

Sample Leaving Cert Questions on Keats's Poetry

1. **From your study of the poetry of John Keats on your course, select the poems that, in your opinion, best show his effective use of sensuous language to convey his preoccupation with transience and mortality. Justify your response by discussing Keats's effective use of sensuous language to convey his preoccupation with transience and mortality.**
2. **'Keats's poetry is defined largely by rich imagery, striking symbolism and a deeply felt belief in the importance of the imagination.' Discuss this statement, supporting your answer with reference to the poetry of John Keats on your course.**
3. **'Keats makes effective use of a variety of stylistic features to express an intense awareness of both the joys and sorrows of human experience.' To what extent do you agree or disagree with this statement? Support your answer with reference to the poetry of John Keats on your course.**

How do I organise my answer?

(Sample question 1)

From your study of the poetry of John Keats on your course, select the poems that, in your opinion, best show his effective use of sensuous language to convey his preoccupation with transience and mortality. Justify your response by discussing Keats's effective use of sensuous language to convey his preoccupation with transience and mortality.

Sample Plan 1

Intro: (*Stance: agree with viewpoint in the question*) Keats explores the paradoxical relationship between immortal worlds of art and nature and the transience of human life through language that appeals to the senses.

Point 1: (*Immortality/transience – visual and aural imagery*) 'Ode to a Nightingale' contrasts human suffering and death with immortal world of nature. Vivid visual and aural imagery show the difference between man ('youth grows pale, and spectre-thin, and dies') and bird ('Singest of summer', 'full-throated ease'). Dreamlike evocation of idyllic world of nightingale ('Queen-Moon ... Clustered around by all her starry Fays').

Understanding the Prescribed Poetry Question

Marks are awarded using the PCLM Marking Scheme: P = 15; C = 15; L = 15; M = 5 Total = 50

- **P** (Purpose = 15 marks) refers to the set question and is the launch pad for the answer. This involves engaging with all aspects of the question. Both theme and language must be addressed, although not necessarily equally.
- **C** (Coherence = 15 marks) refers to the organisation of the developed response and the use of accurate, relevant quotation. Paragraphing is essential.
- **L** (Language = 15 marks) refers to the student's skill in controlling language throughout the answer.
- **M** (Mechanics = 5 marks) refers to spelling and grammar.
- Although no specific number of poems is required, students usually discuss at least 3 or 4 in their written responses.
- Aim for at least 800 words, to be completed within 45–50 minutes.

NOTE

In keeping with the PCLM approach, the student has to justify the choice of Keats's poems on the course that show:

- **a preoccupation with transience and mortality** (comparisons between immortal worlds of art and nature and harsh finite mortal existence, potential and failure of escapism, advantages and disadvantages of eternity, etc.)

... conveyed through:

- **effective use of sensuous language** (vivid visual imagery, musical sound effects, synaesthesia, paradox, repetition, personification, innovative use of ode and sonnet forms, etc.)

Point 2: (*Immortality/transience – questions, repetition, paradox*) 'Ode on a Grecian Urn' conveys the immortal world of art through a powerful symbol of silence ('unravish'd bride of quietness') posing enigmatic questions ('Who are these coming to the sacrifice?'). Repetition depicts joyful pastoral scene ('happy, happy love'). Puzzling paradox of immortal world ('For ever wilt thou love'/'never, never canst thou kiss').

Point 3: (*Immortality/transience – symbol, paradox*) 'Ode on a Grecian Urn' explores troubling mortal life through compound words and onomatopoeia ('heart high sorrowful and cloyed'). Symbol of eternity teases human beings. 'Cold Pastoral' of romance and religious rites shows beautiful images, yet contains ashes of dead.

Point 4: (*Immortality/transience – metaphor, personification, sonnet*) 'When I Have Fears That I May Cease to Be' portrays poet's fears of dying young ('I may never live to trace') and not achieving potential through extended harvest imagery ('gleaned', 'garners', 'full-ripen'd grain'). Reversal of viewpoint in concluding couplet expresses acceptance of human fate through assonance vowels and a stark monosyllable ('Till love and fame to nothingness do sink').

Conclusion: Rich, powerful poetry connects two opposing views – the immortal worlds of nature and art and the transient mortal world of human beings. Submission to the reality of human fate.

Sample Paragraph: Point 4

The sonnet, 'When I Have Fears That I May Cease to Be', uses its first quatrain to reveal the poet's concerns about the future. Human transience and mortality are recurring themes in his poetry. Using characteristically sensual language, Keats compares his creative potential as a poet to the natural world through several harvest images ('garners', 'full ripen'd grain'). His 'teeming brain' is shown through vivid adjectives 'high-piled', 'rich'. The second quatrain symbolises life's wonders, using dramatic personification, 'night's starr'd face'. The poet expresses his deep frustration that he 'may never live to trace' these wonders because he may 'cease to be' too soon. A memorable image of his isolation 'on the shore/Of the wide world I stand alone' exposes his stark realisation that he is unimportant in the vast eternal universe. The poem is filled with rich musical sound effects – and the concluding assonance adds a poignant quality to Keats's sense of reality that human existence is brief, 'love and fame to nothingness do sink'.

EXAMINER'S COMMENT

Well-written top-grade response addresses both aspects of the question (transience and sensual language). There is close engagement with the poem, particularly in the analysis of how Keats's concerns are conveyed through stylistic features, including rich imagery and evocative sound effects. Supportive accurate quotations are carefully integrated into the discussion throughout.

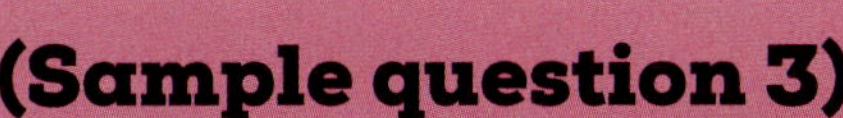

(Sample question 3)

'Keats makes use effective use of a variety of stylistic features to express an intense awareness of both the joys and sorrows of human experience.' To what extent do you agree or disagree with this statement? Support your answer with reference to the poetry of John Keats on your course.

Sample Plan 2

Intro: (*Stance: agree with viewpoint in the question*) Keats explores the joys and sorrows of the human experience through an effective use of sensuous language, rich imagery, personification, vivid contrasts and the use of various poetic forms.

Point 1: (*Joy/sorrow – sonnet, personification, musical imagery*) 'To One Who Has Been Long in City Pent' uses the sonnet's octet to compare the frustration of confined urban lifestyle ('long in city pent') to delight of the open countryside ('look into the fair/And open face of heaven') using dynamic personification. Contrasting sestet conveys loss and transience through evocative verbs ('mourns', 'glided by', 'falls'). Broad-vowelled assonance suggests melancholy.

Point 2: (*Joy – imagery, run-on lines*) 'On First Looking into Chapman's Homer' expresses the joy and richness of imagination in reading. Effective use of vivid imagery ('realms of gold'). Exhilarated sense of discovery compared to awe of astronomer ('When a new planet swims into his ken') or the shock of an explorer ('He star'd at the Pacific'). Run-on lines convey movement – planet circling, ships circumnavigating – expressing Keats's intense reaction to Homer's writing.

Point 3: (*Joy/sorrow/romantic love – ballad, imagery*) 'La Belle Dame Sans Merci' is a dramatic ballad using dialogue and haunting imagery to trace the dire consequences of unrequited love ('the sedge has withered'). The enchanting attraction of the fascinating lady is conjured up through alliteration ('hair was long, her foot was light'). Nightmare consequences of doomed love depicted through shocking procession of former lovers ('starved lips in the gloam').

Point 4: (*Joy/sorrow – visual, tactile, aural imagery, personification*) 'To Autumn' is a farewell to the season of abundance evoked though alliteration and sibilance ('Season of mists and mellow fruitfulness'). Dynamic images of ripeness ('fruit the vines') contrasts with the passing evening ('soft-dying day'). Vivid personification of the transient season as a young girl ('Thy hair soft-lifted by the winnowing wind'). Long vowels capture the sad reality of the transient season ('mourn', 'bourne').

NOTE

In keeping with the PCLM approach, the student has to take a stance by agreeing or disagreeing that Keats expresses:

- **an intense awareness of both the joys and sorrows of human experience** (restorative power of nature contrasted with confinement of city life, the power of the imagination and literature, the joy and sorrow of romantic love, beauty and transience of the human world, etc.)

... through an effective use of:

- **a variety of stylistic features** (visual, aural and tactile imagery, personification, varying moods, contrasts, archaic language, setting, repetition, run-on lines, ballad, ode and sonnet forms, etc.)

Conclusion: Keats presents the wonder and sadness of the human experience through contrasting views of urban and rural life, the joy of the imagination, the reality of transience and death, the consequences of doomed love and the celebration of the paradoxical nature of autumn, both its abundance and inevitable decline. Effective use of poetic forms, rich imagery, personification and contrasts engage readers.

Sample Paragraph: Point 1

In 'To One Who Has Been Long in City Pent', Keats uses sonnet form effectively. The octet and sestet are skilfully unified to create a satisfying poem that glorifies nature and the open landscape. The oppressiveness of city life is described in the heavy monosyllables of the first line, concluding in the monosyllabic verb 'pent'. In contrast, lively personification and dashing run-through lines reveal Keats's enthusiastic reaction to the wide countryside, 'in the smile of the blue firmament'. The sestet strikes a poignant note, however, as he accepts that all this beauty will pass. Despondent broad-vowelled verbs list the inevitable change, 'mourns', 'glided by'. An evocative image of 'an angel's tear' which 'falls through the clear ether silently' acknowledges the divine mystery behind nature's beauty. The changing tone from confinement in the city to contentment in nature is echoed by various poetic devices that reveal the joy and sorrow of the human world.

EXAMINER'S COMMENT

An insightful response that tackles the question directly and shows excellent understanding of the sonnet form. Discussion of Keats's skilful use of sound effects and tone are well developed. Confident expression throughout. Suitable references and quotes are skilfully worked into the answer. A well-deserved top grade.

Leaving Cert Sample Essay

'Keats often expresses a desire to escape from everyday reality, combined with a longing for artistic fulfilment, in a poetic style that is both dramatic and beautiful.' Discuss this statement, supporting your answer with reference to the poetry of John Keats on your course.

Sample Essay

(Desire to escape and longing for fulfilment expressed through a dramatic, beautiful style.)

1. From the poems of Keats that we have studied, it is clear that there is a constant tension between what he imagines and everyday reality. This theme is clearly seen in 'Ode on a Grecian Urn' and 'Ode to a Nightingale'. The world of nature seems to represent a kind of paradise in Keats's imagination. His wish for escape and to find happiness clearly reflects his experience of real life filled with pain and sorrow. But Keats never fully escapes into this ideal world of beauty and perfection. His writing is characterised by intense feelings. Some of the poems contain characters and conflict – and many of them reflect the inner tensions in Keats's own life.

2. The gap between transience and immortality is clearly explored in 'Ode on a Grecian Urn'. Keats underlines the temporary nature of our lives, contrasting it with the permanence of art as typified by the marble urn. The pictures painted on the Greek vase are never-changing, unlike the decay and change of real human life. A major theme is that a beautiful work of art brings constant joy. The scenes portrayed on the urn show a pagan springtime festival with musicians and young lovers about to kiss. As Keats becomes caught up in this artistic paradise, he becomes more and more ecstatic. It will always be springtime there, the leaves will always be on the trees, the lovers will be young and carefree forever, the musicians will never stop playing their tunes. The poet's enthusiasm to be part of this freedom reaches a climax in the third stanza when he repeats the word 'happy' – 'Ah, happy, happy boughs' and 'more happy, happy love'. Repetition is used throughout the poem to add to the drama being played out on the urn and to clearly highlight his own excitement – 'What pipes and timbrels? What wild ecstasy?'

3. To Keats, the scene on the vase clearly captures immortality and eternal youth. These are his own deep desires. The lovers will be 'for ever young'. The beautiful urn symbolises a timeless ideal world. He ends by saying that when his own generation is old and gone, the urn will still remain and bring delight to future generations. The poet's conclusion – 'Beauty is truth; truth, beauty' – may not be completely clear, but it seems that he is making a final statement that celebrates the arts and emphasises how essential true beauty is to human beings.

4. 'Ode to a Nightingale' is another intense reflection on the contrast between the painful mortality of human existence and the immortal beauty found in the bird's hypnotic song. At the start, Keats is clearly in an entranced hallucinatory state, experiencing 'a drowsy numbness'. The sibilant 's' sounds and sensuous language add to the intensity of his mood. He feels a bittersweet happiness at the thought of the nightingale's untroubled life. The poet celebrates the way 'vintage' wine evokes the sun-drenched countryside of the 'warm South' of France. The imagery appeals to different senses – the taste of the wine, the sound of the birdsong and the sight of the 'purple-stained mouth'. Wine also offers Keats temporary release from the horrific realities described in the middle section of the poem – the 'weariness, the fever, and the fret' of real life. The graphic images of illness – 'youth grows pale and spectre thin' – are clearly disturbing.

INDICATIVE MATERIAL

- Keats often desires to escape reality, combined with a longing for artistic fulfilment (recurring wish to free himself from transient reality into imagination and an ideal state of being, yearning for aesthetic beauty, nature seen as restorative and symbolising immortality, etc.)

... expressed in:

- a poetic style that is both dramatic and beautiful (intense narratives, vibrant sensuous imagery, compelling archaic language, evocative musical sound effects, vivid flights of fancy, hauntingly imaginative odes, melodramatic ballads, striking sonnets, etc.)

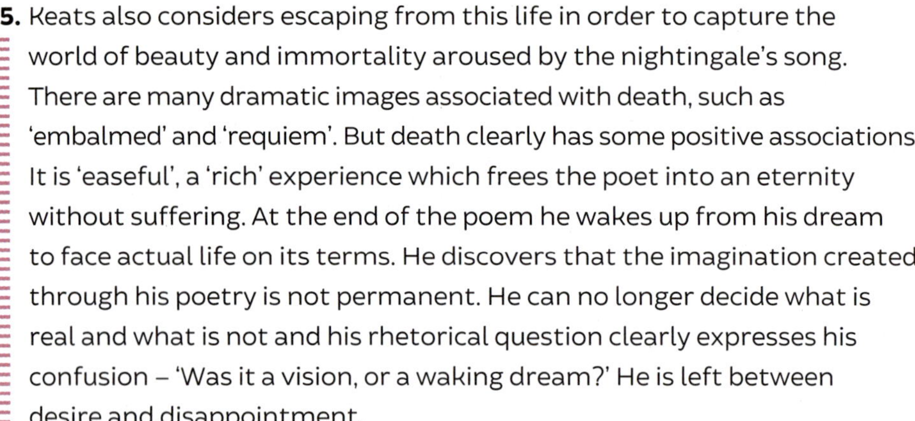

5. Keats also considers escaping from this life in order to capture the world of beauty and immortality aroused by the nightingale's song. There are many dramatic images associated with death, such as 'embalmed' and 'requiem'. But death clearly has some positive associations. It is 'easeful', a 'rich' experience which frees the poet into an eternity without suffering. At the end of the poem he wakes up from his dream to face actual life on its terms. He discovers that the imagination created through his poetry is not permanent. He can no longer decide what is real and what is not and his rhetorical question clearly expresses his confusion – 'Was it a vision, or a waking dream?' He is left between desire and disappointment.

6. In 'On First Looking into Chapman's Homer', Keats describes the excitement of discovering the 'pure serene' of great literature. This beautifully written sonnet uses the extended metaphor of discovery to suggest that wonderful moment when he first read Chapman's translation of Homer's writing – 'Then felt I like some watcher of the skies'. The poem's image of the explorer 'stout Cortez' transfixed in silence and 'wild surmise' at the scale of the Pacific Ocean is vividly dramatic. The experience symbolises artistic perfection and reflects Keats's intense emotional state. The sense of openness to wonder is suggested by assonant vowels ('wild', 'surmise') and the sounds become more hushed in the final awestruck line, 'Silent upon a peak in Darien'. Keats associates escaping painful reality with the desire for perfection – and this pursuit of beauty is evident in his celebration of poetry and the human imagination.

(835 words)

EXAMINER'S COMMENT

A reflective and analytical response to a challenging question. Good overview in the opening paragraph followed by an insightful treatment of the two odes. Relevant points are supported by apt reference highlighting the dramatic elements and poetic qualities of both poems. The discussion is appropriately selective in commenting upon these long texts. Good varied expression in general – although the adverb 'clearly' is overused.

GRADE: H1
P = 14/15
C = 14/15
L = 13/15
M = 5/5
Total = 46/50

Revision Overview

'To One Who Has Been Long in City Pent'
Nature's beauty and its powers of regeneration are central themes in this Petrarchan (Italian) sonnet.

'Ode to a Nightingale'
Keats tries to free himself from suffering and the world of change by identifying with the nightingale's song.

'On First Looking into Chapman's Homer'
Celebrates the imaginative vision of great literature which Keats experienced when he first read a translation of Homer's *The Iliad*.

'Ode on a Grecian Urn'
Addresses the complexities of art and its impact on people's lives. Keats claims that the most powerful truths are to be found in art.

'When I Have Fears That I May Cease to Be'
Fearful about the inevitability of death, Keats feels anxious about his own poetic achievement and reputation.

'La Belle Dame Sans Merci'
In this haunting ballad, romantic love is entangled with pain, and pleasure is intertwined with death.

'To Autumn'
Keats celebrates the beauty of autumn by focusing on its passing and the transitory nature of human existence.

'Bright Star, Would I Were Steadfast as Thou Art'
In this compelling sonnet, Keats reflects on romantic love and the appreciation of things that are unchanging.

Last Words

'I am certain of nothing, but of the holiness of the Heart's affections and the truth of Imagination.'
John Keats

'Keats's poetry is "an ark of the covenant between language and sensation".'
Seamus Heaney

'Keats's important poems are related to, or grow directly out of ... inner conflicts.'
Douglas Bush

NATURE

ART

JOY/HOPE

TRANSIENCE

SUFFERING

DEATH

LOVE

BEAUTY

Sylvia Plath
1932–1963

'Out of the ash
I rise with my red hair
And I eat men like air.'

Born in Boston, Massachusetts, in 1932, Sylvia Plath is a writer whose best-known poems are noted for their intense focus and vibrant, personal imagery. Her writing talent – and ambition to succeed – was evident from an early age. She kept a journal during childhood and published her early poems in literary magazines and newspapers. After studying Art and English at college, Plath moved to Cambridge, England, in the mid-1950s. Here she met and later married the poet Ted Hughes. The couple had two children, Frieda and Nicholas, but the marriage was not to last. Plath continued to write through the late 1950s and early 1960s. During the final years of her life, she produced numerous confessional poems of stark revelation, channelling her long-standing anxiety and doubt into poetic verses of great power and pathos. At her creative peak, Sylvia Plath took her own life on 11 February 1963.

Investigate Further

To find out more about Sylvia Plath, or to hear readings of her poems, you could search some useful websites, such as YouTube, BBC poetry, poetryfoundation.org and poetryarchive.org, or access additional material on this page of your eBook.

Prescribed Poems

Note that Plath uses American spellings and punctuation in her work.

*(OL) indicates poems that are also prescribed for the Ordinary Level course.

1 Black Rook in Rainy Weather

On the stiff twig up there
Hunches a wet black rook
Arranging and rearranging its feathers in the rain.
I do not expect a miracle
Or an accident

To set the sight on fire
In my eye, nor seek
Any more in the desultory weather some design,
But let spotted leaves fall as they fall,
Without ceremony, or portent.

Although, I admit, I desire,
Occasionally, some backtalk
From the mute sky, I can't honestly complain:
A certain minor light may still
Lean incandescent

Out of kitchen table or chair
As if a celestial burning took
Possession of the most obtuse objects now and then –
Thus hallowing an interval
Otherwise inconsequent

By bestowing largesse, honour,
One might say love. At any rate, I now walk
Wary (for it could happen
Even in this dull ruinous landscape); skeptical,
Yet politic; ignorant

Of whatever angel may choose to flare
Suddenly at my elbow. I only know that a rook
Ordering its black feathers can so shine
As to seize my senses, haul
My eyelids up, and grant

desultory: unexceptional, oppressive.

portent: omen.

incandescent: glowing.

hallowing: making holy.
inconsequent: of no importance.

largesse: generous, giving.

skeptical: wary, suspicious.

politic: wise and likely to prove advantageous.

A brief respite from fear
Of total neutrality. With luck,
Trekking stubborn through this season
Of fatigue, I shall
Patch together a content

Of sorts. Miracles occur,
If you care to call those spasmodic
Tricks of radiance miracles. The wait's begun again,
The long wait for the angel,
For that rare, random descent.

spasmodic: occurring in bursts.

Personal Response

1. What is the mood of the poet? How does the weather described in the poem reflect this mood?
2. Select one image from the poem that you find particularly striking or dramatic. Briefly explain your choice.
3. What do you think the final stanza means? Consider the phrase 'The wait's begun again'. What is the poet waiting for?

Critical Literacy

'Black Rook in Rainy Weather' was written while Plath was studying in Cambridge in 1956. It contains many of her trademarks, including the exploration of emotions, the use of weather, colour and natural objects as symbols, and the dreamlike world. She explores a number of themes: fear of the future, lack of identity and poetic inspiration.

Stanza one begins with the straightforward description of a bird grooming itself, which the poet observes on a rainy day. But on closer inspection, the mood of the poem is set with the words 'stiff' and 'Hunches'. The bird is at the mercy of the elements ('wet') and there is no easy movement. **This atmospheric opening is dull and low key**. The black rook is a bird of ill omen. But the bird is presenting its best image to the world as it sits 'Arranging and rearranging its feathers'. Plath longed to excel in both life and art. If she were inspired by poetry, the rook would take on a new light as if on fire. Yet she doesn't see this happening. Even the weather is 'desultory' in the fading season of autumn. Poetic inspiration is miraculous; it is not ordinary. The world is experienced in a heightened way. Notice the long line, which seems out of proportion with the rest as she declares that she doesn't expect any order or 'design' in the haphazard weather. The decaying leaves will fall with no ritual, without any organisation. **This is a chaotic world**, a random place with no design, just as poetic inspiration happens by chance. It is also accidental, like the falling leaves.

After this low-key opening, the poem starts to take flight in stanzas three and four when the poet states: 'I desire'. Plath employs a witty metaphor as she looks for 'some backtalk' from the 'mute sky'. **She would like to connect with it**. It could happen on her walk, or even at home if she were to experience a 'certain minor light' shining from an ordinary, everyday object like a chair. The association of fire and light makes an ordinary moment special. It is 'hallowing'; it is giving generously ('largesse'). She is hoping against hope. Plath may be sceptical, but she is going forward carefully in case she misses the magic moment. **She must stay alert and watchful**. She must also be 'politic', wise.

Stanzas six, seven and eight explore poetic inspiration. Plath doesn't know if it will happen to her or how it will happen. Two contrasting attitudes are at loggerheads: hope and despair. The rook might inspire her: '**Miracles occur**'. If she were motivated, it would relieve 'total neutrality', this nothingness she feels when living uninspired. Although she is tired, she is insistent, 'stubborn'. The poet will have to 'Patch' something together. She shows human vulnerability, but she is trying. This new-found determination is a very different tone to the negative one at the beginning.

Literature was as important to Plath as friends and family. What she can't live without, therefore, is inspiration – her life would be a dark, passionless existence. **Depression** is an empty state with no feeling or direction, yet her view of creativity is romantic. It is miraculous, available only to a chosen few. 'The long wait for the angel' has begun. Notice the constant use of the personal pronoun 'I'. This is a poet who is very aware of self and her own personal responses to events and feelings. The outside world becomes a metaphor for her own interior world.

Plath uses both archaic language and slang, as if reinforcing the randomness of the world. This is also mirrored in the run-on lines. All is haphazard, but carefully arranged, so even the extended final sentence stretches out as it waits for the 'random descent' of inspiration. Throughout the poem's **carefully arranged disorder**, two worlds are seen. One is negative: 'desultory',

'mute', 'dull', 'stubborn', 'fatigue'. This is indicative of Plath's own bleak mood. The other world is positive: 'light', 'celestial', 'largesse', 'love', 'shine'. This offers the possibility of radiance.

Writing About the Poem

'Plath's poems are carefully composed and beautifully phrased.' Write a paragraph in response to this statement, illustrating your answer with close reference to the poem 'Black Rook in Rainy Weather'.

Sample Paragraph

Just like the rook, Plath 'arranges and rearranges' her words with infinite care to communicate the contrast between the dull life of 'total neutrality' which occurs when she is not inspired, when nothing sets 'the sight on fire'. I particularly admire how she arranges disorder in the poem. This mirrors the chance of poetic inspiration. Long lines poke untidily out of the first three stanzas, seeking the 'minor light' to 'Lean incandescent' upon them. I also like how the lines run in a seemingly untidy way into each other, as do some stanzas. Stanza three goes into four, as it describes the chance of a light coming from an ordinary object, such as a kitchen chair, which is seen only if the poet is inspired. The alliteration of 'rare, random' in the last line mirrors the gift of poetic technique which will be given to the poet if she can receive the blessed benediction of poetic inspiration: 'Miracles occur'.

EXAMINER'S COMMENT

Close reading of the poem is evident in this top-grade original response to Plath's poetic technique. Quotations are very well used here to highlight the poet's ability to create anarchic order.

Class/Homework Exercises

1. Plath criticised the poem, 'Black Rook in Rainy Weather' for its 'glassy brittleness'. In your opinion, what does she mean? Refer to both the content and style of the poem, supporting your answer with reference to the text.
2. In your opinion, has the poet given up hope of being inspired? Use reference to the poem in your answer.

Summary Points

- **Waiting for poetic inspiration, the hope for something better.**
- **Despondency – negative adjectives, harsh verbs.**
- **Miracle of inspiration, contrasting imagery of fire and light.**
- **Careful rhyme patterns echo design of the rook's plumage.**
- **Language – colloquial and formal, slang and religious terminology.**

The Times Are Tidy

Unlucky the hero born
In this province of the stuck record
Where the most watchful cooks go jobless
And the mayor's rôtisserie turns
Round of its own accord.

There's no career in the venture
Of riding against the lizard,
Himself withered these latter-days
To leaf-size from lack of action:
History's beaten the hazard.

The last crone got burnt up
More than eight decades back
With the love-hot herb, the talking cat,
But the children are better for it,
The cow milks cream an inch thick.

province: a remote place.
stuck record: the needle would sometimes get jammed on a vinyl music album.

rôtisserie: meat on a rotating skewer.

lizard: dragon.

crone: old witch.

'riding against the lizard'

Personal Response

1. What is suggested by the poem's title? Is Plath being cynical about modern life? Develop your response in a short paragraph.
2. Select one image from the poem which suggests that the past was much more dangerous and exciting than the present. Comment on its effectiveness.
3. Do you agree or disagree with the speaker's view of modern life? Give reasons for your answer.

Critical Literacy

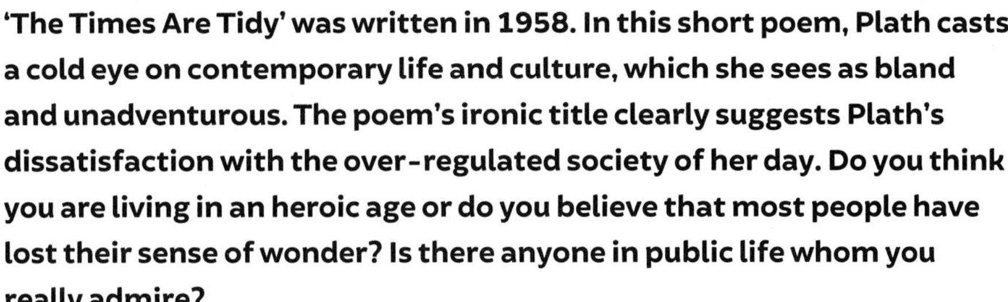

'The Times Are Tidy' was written in 1958. In this short poem, Plath casts a cold eye on contemporary life and culture, which she sees as bland and unadventurous. The poem's ironic title clearly suggests Plath's dissatisfaction with the over-regulated society of her day. Do you think you are living in an heroic age or do you believe that most people have lost their sense of wonder? Is there anyone in public life whom you really admire?

Stanza one is dominated by hard-hitting images reflecting how the world of fairytale excitement has disappeared. From the outset, **the tone is scornful and dismissive**. Plath believes that any hero would be totally out of place amid the mediocrity of our times. True talent ('the most watchful cooks') is largely unrewarded. The unexpected imagery of the 'stuck record' and the mayor's rotating spit symbolise complacent monotony and lack of progress, particularly during the late 1950s, when Plath wrote the poem. Both images convey a sense of purposeless circling, of people going nowhere. It seems as though the poet is seething with frustration at the inertia and conformity of her own times.

Plath's **darkly embittered sense of humour** becomes evident in stanza two. She laments the current lack of honour and courage – something which once existed in the world of fairytales. Unlike the past, contemporary society is compromised. There are no idealistic dragon-slayers any more. The worker who dares to stand up and criticise ('riding against the lizard') is risking demotion. The modern dragon – a metaphor for the challenges we face – has even been reduced to a mere lizard. Despite this, we are afraid of confrontation and prefer to retreat. The verb 'withered' suggests the weakness and decay of our safe, modern world. The poet openly complains that 'History's beaten the hazard'. Over time, we have somehow defeated all sense of adventure and daring. These qualities belong in the distant past.

In stanza three, Plath continues to contrast past and present. Witches are no longer burned at the stake. This might well suggest that superstition has disappeared, and with it, all imagination. The last two lines are ironic in tone, reflecting the poet's deep **disenchantment with the excesses of our consumer society**. The final image – 'the cow milks cream an inch thick' – signifies overindulgence.

The poet clearly accepts that **society has changed for the worse**. Children may have everything they want nowadays, but they have lost their sense of wonder and excitement. Plath laments the loss of legendary heroism. Medieval dragons and wicked witches (complete with magic potions and talking cats) no longer exist. Her conclusion is that life today is unquestionably less interesting than it used to be. Unlike so much of Plath's work, the personal pronoun 'I' is not used in this poem. However, the highly contemptuous views and weary, frustrated tone clearly suggest that Plath feels unfulfilled.

Writing About the Poem

Write a paragraph in which you comment on Plath's critical tone in 'The Times Are Tidy'.

Sample Paragraph

The tone of voice in 'The Times Are Tidy' is almost irrationally critical of modern life. Plath has nothing good to say about today's world as she sees it. The poem's title is glib and self-satisfied, just like the neatly organised society that Plath seems to despise. The opening comment – 'Unlucky the hero born/In this province' – emphasises this negative tone. The poet's mocking attitude becomes increasingly disparaging as she rails against the unproductive images of easy living – 'the stuck record' and 'the mayor's rôtisserie'. Plath goes on to contrast today's apathetic society with the more spirited medieval era, when knights in armour existed. The poet omits all the positive aspects of modern life and chooses to give a very one-sided view of the world. Plath ends on a sarcastic note, sneering at the advances of our world of plenty – 'cream an inch thick'. The voice here – and indeed, throughout the entire poem – is both critical and superior.

EXAMINER'S COMMENT

This short top-grade paragraph demonstrates strong analytical skills and is firmly focused on Plath's judgmental tone. The supporting references range widely and effectively illustrate the poet's critical attitude. Quotations are particularly well integrated and the management of language is assured throughout.

Class/Homework Exercises

1. Outline the main theme in 'The Times Are Tidy'. In your answer, trace the way the poet develops her ideas during the course of the poem.
2. Trace the changing tones in the poem, 'The Times Are Tidy'. Support your answer with close reference to the text.

Summary Points

- **Poet's distaste for pursuit of materialism prevalent in 1950s American society.**
- **Collapse of moral standards in public life.**
- **Death of the spirit of adventure, no challenge to society's smugness.**
- **Humour and irony, derisive tone, entertaining images and sound effects.**
- **Contrast between modern 'tidy' times and 'untidy' times of legend.**

Morning Song

SYLVIA PLATH

Love set you going like a fat gold watch.
The midwife slapped your footsoles, and your bald cry
Took its place among the elements.

Our voices echo, magnifying your arrival. New statue.
In a drafty museum, your nakedness
Shadows our safety. We stand round blankly as walls.

I'm no more your mother
Than the cloud that distils a mirror to reflect its own slow
Effacement at the wind's hand.

All night your moth-breath
Flickers among the flat pink roses. I wake to listen:
A far sea moves in my ear.

One cry, and I stumble from bed, cow-heavy and floral
In my Victorian nightgown.
Your mouth opens clean as a cat's. The window square

Whitens and swallows its dull stars. And now you try
Your handful of notes;
The clear vowels rise like balloons.

midwife: a person trained to assist at childbirth.
elements: primitive, natural, atmospheric forces.

Effacement: gradual disappearance.

pink roses: images on the wallpaper.

vowels: speech sounds made without stopping the flow of the breath.

'clear vowels rise'

Personal Response

1. Comment on the suitability and effectiveness of the simile in line 1.
2. What is the attitude of the mother to the new arrival? Does her attitude change in the course of the poem? Refer to the text in your answer.
3. A metaphor links two things so that one idea explains or gives a new viewpoint about the other. Choose one interesting metaphor from the poem and comment on its effectiveness.

Critical Literacy

'Morning Song' was written in 1961. Plath explores the complex issues of the relationship between a mother and her child, celebrating the birth of the infant but also touching on deep feelings of loss and separation.

Do all mothers immediately welcome and fall in love with a new baby? Are some of them overwhelmed or even depressed after giving birth? Are parents often anxious about the new responsibilities a baby brings? Plath wrote this poem after two intensely personal experiences, celebrating the birth of her daughter, Frieda, who was 10 months old, and shortly after a miscarriage. The poem is realistic and never strays into sentimentality or cliché. The title 'Morning' suggests a new beginning and 'Song' a celebration.

Stanza one describes the arrival of the child into the world in a confident, rhythmic sentence announcing the act of creation: 'Love set you going'. The simile comparing the child to a 'fat gold watch' suggests a plump baby, a rich and precious object. Broad vowel effects emphasise the physical presence of the infant. The 'ticking' sound conveys action and dynamism, but also the passage of time. Plath's child is now part of the mortal world where change and death are inevitable. At this moment of birth, the baby is the centre of attention as the midwife and parents surround her. But this is a cruel world, as we see from the words 'slapped' and 'bald'. The infant is part of the universe as she takes her place among the 'elements'. The verbs in this stanza are in the past tense – **the mother is looking back at the event**. The rest of the poem is written in the present tense, which adds to the immediacy of the experience.

Stanza two has a feeling of disorientation, as if the mother feels separated from the child now that she has left the womb. There is a nightmarish, surreal quality to the lines 'Our voices echo, magnifying your arrival'. Plath sees the child as a new exhibit ('New statue') in a museum. Commas and full stops break up the flow of the lines and **the tone becomes more stilted and detached**. The child as a work of art is special and unique, but the museum is 'drafty', again a reference to the harshness of the world. The baby's vulnerability is stressed by its 'nakedness'. The midwife's and parents' frozen response is caught in the phrase 'blankly as walls'. They anxiously observe, unsure about their ability to protect. This baby also represents a threat to

the parents' relationship as she 'Shadows' their safety. The child is perceived as having a negative impact on them, perhaps driving them apart rather than uniting them.

Stanza three focuses on the **complex relationship between child and mother**. Plath feels she can't be maternal ('no more your mother'). This is vividly shown in the image of the cloud that rains, creating a puddle. **But in the act of creation, it destroys itself and its destruction is reflected in the pool of water**. Throughout her life, the poet was haunted by a fear of her own personal failure. Does she see a conflict between becoming a mother and remaining a writer? She also realises as the child grows and matures that she will age, moving closer to death, and this will be reflected in the child's gaze. The mood of this stanza is one of estrangement and powerlessness. Notice how the three lines of the stanza run into each other as the cloud disappears.

In stanza four, the tone changes to one of intimate, maternal love as the caring mother becomes alert to her child's needs. The situation described is warm and homely – the 'flat pink roses' are very different to the chill 'museum' of a previous stanza. The fragile breathing of the little child is beautifully described as 'your moth-breath/Flickers'. **Onomatopoeia in 'Flickers' mimics the tiny breathing noises of the child**. The mother is anticipating her baby's needs as she wakes ('listen'). The breathing child evokes happy memories of Plath's seaside childhood ('A far sea moves in my ear').

The infant cries and the attentive mother springs into action. She laughs at herself as she describes the comical figure she makes, 'cow-heavy and floral' in stanza five. She feels awkward as she 'stumble[s]' to tend her child, whose eager mouth is shown by a startling image ('clean as a cat's') when it opens wide to receive the night feed of milk. **The stanza flows smoothly** over into stanza six, just as nature flows to its own rhythm and does not obey clocks or any other man-made rules. Night becomes morning as the child swallows the milk and the window swallows the stars.

Children demand a parent's time and energy. **This child now defines herself** with her unique collection of sounds ('Your handful of notes'). This poem opened with the instinctive, elemental 'bald' cry of a newborn, but closes on a lovely, happy image of music and colour, as the baby's song's notes 'rise like balloons'.

Writing About the Poem

'Morning Song' begins with the word 'Love'. How does Plath treat the theme of love over the course of the poem? Support your answer with reference to the text.

Sample Paragraph

'Morning Song' treats the theme of love by addressing both the joy of parental love and also the shock new parents experience. It opens with a tender statement that the poet's daughter was conceived in love – 'Love set you going'. This warm tone changes, however, to the curiously disengaged voice of the second stanza where the parents 'stand round blankly as walls'. The enormity of the event of the birth of their child into a harsh world, 'drafty museum', seems to overwhelm them, particularly the mother who is unable to express natural maternal feelings. In the third stanza, the sense of separation deepens and Plath admits that she does not really feel like the child's mother at all. Instead, she explores her feelings of annihilation through the complex image of the disintegrating cloud, which creates only to be destroyed in the act of creation. The poem ends on a more affectionate note as the attentive mother feeds her child while listening to her baby's song 'rise like balloons'. For me, the gentle effect of this image suggests the innocence of the infant. Overall, I found Plath's mixed emotions interesting as she takes a realistic approach to the complicated emotions that new parents can experience.

EXAMINER'S COMMENT

A succinct, focused and well-supported response showing good personal engagement with the poem. The central point about Plath's conflicting emotions is clearly stated and the development of thought is traced throughout the poem. Excellent language control and impressive vocabulary (e.g. 'curiously disengaged voice', 'complex image of the disintegrating cloud') are in keeping with the top-grade standard.

Class/Homework Exercises

1. 'The sense of alienation is often agonisingly evoked in Plath's poetry.' To what extent is this true of 'Morning Song'? Support your answer with reference to the poem.
2. 'Sylvia Plath makes effective use of unusual and startling imagery to explore deeply personal themes.' Discuss this view with particular reference to the poem, 'Morning Song'.

Summary Points

- **Poet's ambivalent attitude to motherhood: loss of individual identity conflicting with deep love.**
- **Striking, unexpected imagery: contrasts between the child's delicacy and the mother's clumsiness.**
- **Development from inanimate objects (the watch, statue, mirror, cloud) to animate objects (moth, cow, cat, singer).**
- **Varying tones: tender, anxious, alienated, reflective, caring, fulfilled.**
- **Intense feelings of dislocation replaced by increasing sense of inter-connectedness.**

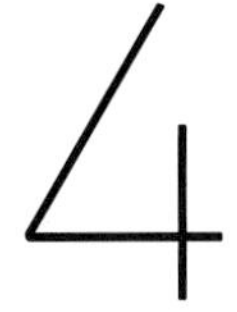

Finisterre

SYLVIA PLATH

This was the land's end: the last fingers, knuckled and rheumatic,
Cramped on nothing. Black
Admonitory cliffs, and the sea exploding
With no bottom, or anything on the other side of it,
Whitened by the faces of the drowned.
Now it is only gloomy, a dump of rocks –
Leftover soldiers from old, messy wars.
The sea cannons into their ear, but they don't budge.
Other rocks hide their grudges under the water.

The cliffs are edged with trefoils, stars and bells
Such as fingers might embroider, close to death,
Almost too small for the mists to bother with.
The mists are part of the ancient paraphernalia –
Souls, rolled in the doom-noise of the sea.
They bruise the rocks out of existence, then resurrect them.
They go up without hope, like sighs.
I walk among them, and they stuff my mouth with cotton.
When they free me, I am beaded with tears.

Our Lady of the Shipwrecked is striding toward the horizon,
Her marble skirts blown back in two pink wings.
A marble sailor kneels at her foot distractedly, and at his foot
A peasant woman in black
Is praying to the monument of the sailor praying.
Our Lady of the Shipwrecked is three times life size,
Her lips sweet with divinity.
She does not hear what the sailor or the peasant is saying –
She is in love with the beautiful formlessness of the sea.

Gull-colored laces flap in the sea drafts
Beside the postcard stalls.
The peasants anchor them with conches. One is told:
'These are the pretty trinkets the sea hides,
Little shells made up into necklaces and toy ladies.
They do not come from the Bay of the Dead down there,
But from another place, tropical and blue,
We have never been to.
These are our crêpes. Eat them before they blow cold.'

land's end: literally 'Finisterre'; the western tip of Brittany.

Admonitory: warning.

trefoils: three-leaved plants.

paraphernalia: discarded items.

doom-noise: hopeless sounds.

Our Lady of the Shipwrecked: the mother of Christ prayed for sailors.

conches: shells.

trinkets: cheap jewellery.

crêpes: light pancakes.

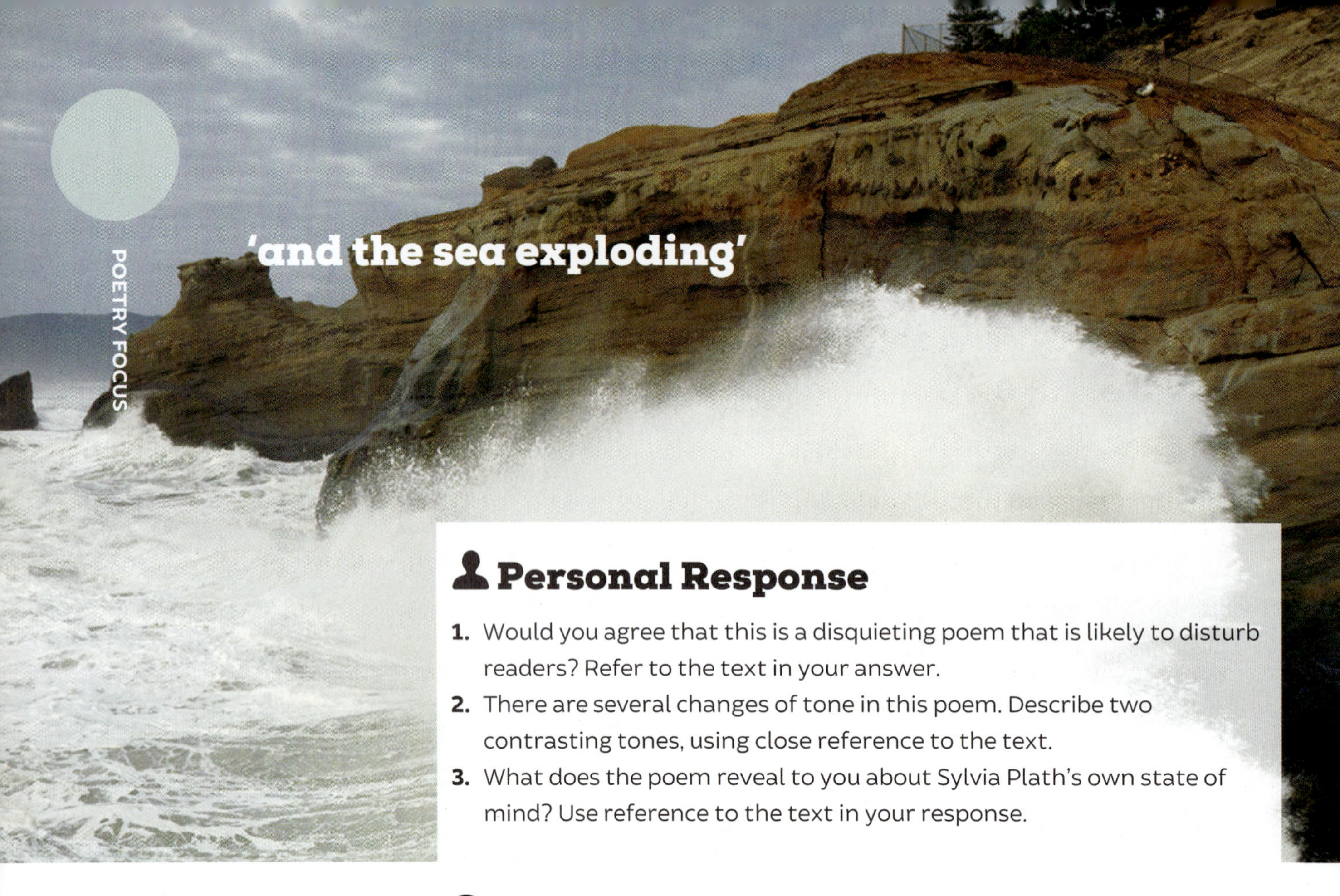

Personal Response

1. Would you agree that this is a disquieting poem that is likely to disturb readers? Refer to the text in your answer.
2. There are several changes of tone in this poem. Describe two contrasting tones, using close reference to the text.
3. What does the poem reveal to you about Sylvia Plath's own state of mind? Use reference to the text in your response.

Critical Literacy

'Finisterre' was written in 1960 following Plath's visit to Brittany, France. As with many of her poems, the description of the place can be interpreted both literally and metaphorically.

The sea has always inspired poets and artists. It is at times welcoming, menacing, beautiful, peaceful and mysterious. Throughout her short life, Sylvia Plath loved the ocean. She spent her childhood years on the Atlantic coast just north of Boston. This setting provides a source for many of her poetic ideas. Terror and death loom large in her descriptive poem 'Finisterre', in which the pounding rhythm of storm waves off the Breton coast represents **Plath's inner turmoil**.

Stanza one opens dramatically and immediately creates a disturbing atmosphere. Plath describes the rocky headland as being 'knuckled and rheumatic'. In a series of powerful images ('Black/Admonitory cliffs', 'the sea exploding'), the poet recreates the uproar and commotion of the scene. The **grisly personification** is startling, linking the shoreline with suffering and decay. There is a real sense of conflict between sea and land. Both are closely associated with death ('the faces of the drowned'). The jagged rocks are compared to 'Leftover soldiers' who 'hide their grudges under the water'. There is a noticeable tone of regret and protest against the futility of conflict, which is denounced as 'old, messy wars'.

Plath's **negative imagery** is relentless, with harsh consonant sounds ('knuckled', 'Cramped') emphasising the force of raging storm waves. The use of contrasting colours intensifies the imagery. As the 'sea cannons' against the headland, the atmosphere is 'only gloomy'. It is hard not to see the bleak seascape as a reflection of Plath's own unhappy state of mind.

In stanza two, the poet turns away from the cruel sea and focuses momentarily on the small plants clinging to the cliff edge. However, these 'trefoils, stars and bells' are also 'close to death'. If anything, they reinforce the **unsettling mood** and draw the poet back to the ocean mists, which she thinks of as symbolising the souls of the dead, lost in 'the doom-noise of the sea'. Plath imagines the heavy mists transforming the rocks, destroying them 'out of existence' before managing to 'resurrect them' again. In a **surreal sequence**, the poet enters the water ('I walk among them') and joins the wretched souls who lie there. Her growing sense of panic is suggested by the stark admission: 'they stuff my mouth with cotton'. The experience is agonising and leaves her 'beaded with tears'.

Plath's thoughts turn to a marble statue of 'Our Lady of the Shipwrecked' in stanza three. Once again, in her imagination, she creates a **dramatic narrative** around the religious figure. This monument to the patron saint of the ocean should offer some consolation to the kneeling sailor and a grieving peasant woman who pray to the mother of God. Ironically, their pleas are completely ignored – 'She does not hear' their prayers because 'She is in love with the beautiful formlessness of the sea'. Is the poet expressing her own **feelings of failure and despondency here**? Or is she also attacking the ineffectiveness of religion? The description of the statue is certainly unflattering. The figure is flighty and self-centred: 'Her marble skirts blown back in two pink wings'. In contrast, the powerful ocean remains fascinating.

In the fourth stanza, Plath turns her attention to the local Bretons who sell souvenirs to tourists. Unlike the previous three stanzas, **the mood appears to be much lighter** as the poet describes the friendly stall-keepers going about their business. It is another irony that their livelihood (selling 'pretty trinkets') is dependent on the sea and its beauty. Like the statue, the locals seem unconcerned by the tragic history of the ocean. Indeed, they are keen to play down 'the Bay of the Dead' and explain that what they sell is imported 'from another place, tropical and blue'. In the final line, a stall-holder advises the poet to enjoy the pancakes she has bought: 'Eat them before they blow cold'. Although the immediate mood is untroubled, the final phrase brings us back to the earlier – and more disturbing – parts of the poem where Plath described the raging storms and the nameless lost souls who have perished at sea.

Writing About the Poem

Write a paragraph commenting on Sylvia Plath's use of detailed description in 'Finisterre'.

Sample Paragraph

The opening images of the rocks – 'the last fingers, knuckled and rheumatic' – are of decrepit old age. The strong visual impact is a regular feature of Plath's writing. The first half of the poem is filled with memorable details of the windswept coastline. In her careful choice of descriptive terms, Plath uses broad vowels to evoke a pervading feeling of dejection. Words such as 'drowned', 'gloomy' and 'doom' help to create this dismal effect. The dramatic aural image, 'The sea cannons', echoes the roar of turbulent waves crashing onto the rocks. Plath's eye for close observation is also seen in her portrait of the holy statue – 'Her lips sweet with divinity'. The poem ends with a painstaking sketch of the traders selling postcards and 'Little shells made up into necklaces and toy ladies'. The local people seem to have come to terms with 'the Bay of the Dead' and are getting on with life. Overall, the use of details throughout the poem leaves readers with a strong sense of place and community.

EXAMINER'S COMMENT

Quotations are very well used here to highlight Plath's ability to create specific scenes and moods through precise description. The examples range over much of the poem and the writing is both varied and controlled throughout. A top-grade response.

Class/Homework Exercises

1. It has been said that vivid, startling imagery gives a surreal quality to 'Finisterre'. Using reference to the poem, write a paragraph responding to this statement.
2. 'Plath's unique imagination addresses unhappiness and hopelessness.' To what extent do you agree with this statement? Support your answer with suitable reference to 'Finisterre', referring to the poem's content and style.

Summary Points

- **Fearful, ominous description of ordinary place.**
- **Disquieting tone of Our Lady of the Shipwrecked as aloof and self-absorbed.**
- **Ironic contrast between sweet appearance of statue and grim reality of shipwrecks in bay.**
- **Formal structure of poem contrasts with terror of situation.**
- **Striking images and sounds, personification, rich symbolism.**

5 Mirror

I am silver and exact. I have no preconceptions.
Whatever I see I swallow immediately
Just as it is, unmisted by love or dislike.
I am not cruel, only truthful –
The eye of a little god, four-cornered.
Most of the time I meditate on the opposite wall.
It is pink, with speckles. I have looked at it so long
I think it is part of my heart. But it flickers.
Faces and darkness separate us over and over.

Now I am a lake. A woman bends over me,
Searching my reaches for what she really is.
Then she turns to those liars, the candles or the moon.
I see her back, and reflect it faithfully.
She rewards me with tears and an agitation of hands.
I am important to her. She comes and goes.
Each morning it is her face that replaces the darkness.
In me she has drowned a young girl, and in me an old woman
Rises toward her day after day, like a terrible fish.

exact: accurate, giving all details; to insist on payment.
preconceptions: thoughts already formed.

reaches: range of distance or depth.

agitation: shaking, trembling.

'The eye of a little god, four-cornered

Personal Response

1. Select two images that suggest the dark, sinister side of the mirror. Comment briefly on your two choices.
2. What, in your opinion, is the main theme or message of this poem?
3. Write your own personal response to this poem, referring closely to the text in your answer.

Critical Literacy

'Mirror' was written in 1961 as Sylvia Plath approached her twenty-ninth birthday. In this dark poem, Plath views the inevitability of old age and death, our preoccupation with image and our search for an identity.

Do you think everyone looks at themselves in a mirror? Would you consider that people are fascinated, disappointed or even obsessed by what they see? Does a mirror accurately reflect the truth? Do people actually see what is reflected or is it distorted by notions and ideals which they or society have? Consider the use of mirrors in fairytales: 'Mirror, mirror on the wall, who's the fairest of them all?' Mirrors are also used in myths – like the story of Narcissus, who drowned having fallen in love with his reflection – and in children's books such as *Through the Looking Glass*. Mirrors are also used in horror films as the dividing line between fantasy and reality.

In this poem, Plath gives us a startling new angle on an everyday object. The function of a mirror is to reflect whatever is put in front of it. Stanza one opens with a ringing declaration by the mirror: 'I am silver and exact'. This **personification has a sinister effect** as the mirror describes an almost claustrophobic relationship with a particular woman. The dramatic voice of the mirror is clear and precise. It announces that it reports exactly what there is without any alteration. We have to decide if the mirror is telling the truth, as it says it has no bias ('no preconceptions'). It does not judge; it reflects the image received. The mirror adopts the position of an impartial observer, but it is active, almost ruthless ('I swallow').

Yet how truthful is a mirror image, as it flattens a three-dimensional object into two dimensions? The image sent out has no depth. The voice of the mirror becomes smug as it sees itself as the ruler of those reflected ('The eye of a little god'). Our obsession with ourselves causes us to worship at the mirror that reflects our image. In the modern world, people are often disappointed with their reflections, wishing they were thinner, younger, better looking. But **the mirror insists it tells the truth**; it doesn't flatter or hurt. The mirror explains how it spends its day gazing at the opposite wall, which is carefully described as 'pink, with speckles'. It feels as if the wall is part of itself. This reflection is disturbed by the faces of people and the dying light. The passage of time is evoked in the phrase 'over and over'.

In stanza two, the tension increases and the mirror announces that it is 'a lake'. Both are flat surfaces that reflect. However, a lake is another dimension, it has depth. **There is danger**. The image is now drawn into its murky depths. The woman is looking in and down, not just at. It is as if she is struggling to find who she really is, what her true path in life is. Plath frequently questioned who she was. Expectations for young women in the 1950s were limiting. Appearance was important, as were the roles of wife, mother and homemaker. But Plath also wanted to write: 'Will I submerge my embarrassing desires and aspirations, refuse to face myself?' The mirror becomes irritated and jealous of the woman as she turns to the deceptive soft light of 'those liars, the candles or the moon'. **The woman is dissatisfied with her image**. In her insecurity, she weeps and wrings her hands. Plath always tried to do her best, to be a model student, almost desperate to excel and be affirmed. Is there a danger in seeking perfection? Do we need to love ourselves as we are? Again, the mirror pompously announces 'I am important to her'.

The march of time passing is emphasised by 'comes and goes', 'Each morning' and 'day after day'. The woman keeps coming back. The mirror's sense of its significance is shown by the frequent use of 'I' and the repetition of 'in me'. As time passes, the woman is facing the truth of her human condition as her reflection changes and ages in the mirror. Her youth is 'drowned', to be replaced by a monstrous vision of an old woman 'like a terrible fish'. **The lonely drama of living and dying is recorded with a nightmarish quality**. There is no comforting rhyme in the poem, only the controlled rhythm of time. The mirror does not give what a human being desires: comfort and warmth. Instead, it impersonally reminds us of our mortality.

Writing About the Poem

What is your personal response to the relationship between the mirror and the woman? Support your views with reference to the poem.

Sample Paragraph

I feel the mirror is like an alter ego, which is coolly appraising the woman in an unforgiving way. The mirror is 'silver'. This cold object is heartless. Although the mirror repeatedly states that it does not judge, 'I have no preconceptions', the woman feels judged and inadequate: 'She rewards me with tears and an agitation of hands.' I think the relationship between the woman and the mirror is dangerous. She does indeed 'drown' in the mirror, as she never feels good enough. The complacent mirror rules her like a 'little god, four-cornered'. It reminds me of how today we are never satisfied with our image, always wanting something else, more perfect. Plath also tried to be perfect. This relationship shows a troubled self, a lack of self-love. Who is saying that the older woman is 'like a terrible fish'? I think the mirror has become the voice of a society which values women only for their looks and youth, rather than what they are capable of achieving.

EXAMINER'S COMMENT

In this fluent and personal response, close analysis of the text contributes to a distinctive and well-supported, high-grade account of the uneasy relationship between the mirror and the woman.

Class/Homework Exercises

1. 'Plath's use of dramatic monologue is an unsettling experience for readers.' Discuss this statement with reference to 'Mirror'.
2. 'All who share the human condition have a bright and dark side.' Discuss Plath's exploration of this theme in her poem 'Mirror'. In your response, pay particular attention to her use of imagery.

Summary Points

- **Key themes include transience and mortality.**
- **Chilling personification of the mirror.**
- **Exploration of identity, duality of being.**
- **Startlingly shocking imagery and drama convey frightening tone.**

Pheasant

SYLVIA PLATH

You said you would kill it this morning.
Do not kill it. It startles me still,
The jut of that odd, dark head, pacing

Through the uncut grass on the elm's hill.
It is something to own a pheasant,
Or just to be visited at all.

I am not mystical: it isn't
As if I thought it had a spirit.
It is simply in its element.

That gives it a kingliness, a right.
The print of its big foot last winter,
The tail-track, on the snow in our court –

The wonder of it, in that pallor,
Through crosshatch of sparrow and starling.
Is it its rareness, then? It is rare.

But a dozen would be worth having,
A hundred, on that hill – green and red,
Crossing and recrossing: a fine thing!

It is such a good shape, so vivid.
It's a little cornucopia.
It unclaps, brown as a leaf, and loud,

Settles in the elm, and is easy.
It was sunning in the narcissi.
I trespass stupidly. Let be, let be.

You: probably addressed to Plath's husband.

jut: extending outwards.

mystical: spiritual, supernatural.

pallor: pale colour.

crosshatch: criss-cross trail.

cornucopia: unexpected treasure.

narcissi: bright spring flowers.

'in its element'

Personal Response

1. Comment on Sylvia Plath's attitude to nature based on your reading of 'Pheasant'.
2. Compile a list of the poet's arguments for not killing the pheasant.
3. Write a paragraph on the effectiveness of Plath's imagery in the poem.

Critical Literacy

'Pheasant' was written in 1962 and reflects Plath's deep appreciation of the natural world. Its enthusiastic mood contrasts with much of her more disturbing work. The poem is structured in eight tercets (three-line stanzas) with a subtle, interlocking rhyming pattern (known as terza rima).

The poem opens with an urgent plea by Plath to spare the pheasant's life: 'Do not kill it'. In the first two stanzas, the tone is tense as the poet offers a variety of reasons for sparing this impressive game bird. She is both shocked and excited by the pheasant: 'It startles me still'. Plath admits to feeling honoured in the presence of the bird: 'It is something to own a pheasant'. The broken rhythm of the early lines adds an abruptness that heightens the sense of urgency. **Plath seems spellbound by the bird's beauty** ('The jut of that odd, dark head') now that it is under threat.

But the poet is also keen to play down any sentimentality in her attitude to the pheasant. Stanza three begins with a straightforward explanation of her attitude: 'it isn't/As if I thought it had a spirit'. Instead, **she values the bird for its graceful beauty and naturalness**: 'It is simply in its element.' Plath is keen to show her recognition of the pheasant's right to exist because it possesses a certain majestic quality, 'a kingliness'.

In stanza four, the poet recalls an earlier winter scene when she marvelled at the pheasant's distinctive footprint in the snow. The bird has made an even greater impression on Plath, summed up in the key phrase 'The wonder of it', at the start of stanza five. She remembers **the colourful pheasant's distinguishing marks against the pale snow**, so unlike the 'crosshatch' pattern of smaller birds, such as the sparrow and starling. This makes the pheasant particularly 'rare' and valuable in Plath's eyes.

The poet can hardly contain her regard for the pheasant and her tone becomes increasingly enthusiastic in stanza six as she dreams of having first a 'dozen' and then a 'hundred' of the birds. In a few **well-chosen details**, she highlights their colour and energy ('green and red,/Crossing and recrossing') before adding an emphatic compliment: 'a fine thing!' Her delight continues into stanza seven, where Plath proclaims her ceaseless admiration for the pheasant: 'It's a little cornucopia', an inspirational source of joy and surprise.

Throughout the poem, the poet has emphasised that the pheasant rightly belongs in its natural surroundings, and this is also true of the final lines. Stanza eight is considered and assured. From the poet's point of view, **the pheasant's right to live is beyond dispute**. While the bird is 'sunning in the narcissi', she herself has become the unwelcome intruder: 'I trespass stupidly'. Plath ends by echoing the opening appeal to spare the pheasant's life: 'Let be, let be.' The quietly insistent repetition and the underlying tone of unease are a final reminder of the need to respect nature.

It has been suggested that the pheasant symbolises Plath's insecure relationship with Ted Hughes. For various reasons, their marriage was under severe strain in 1962 and Plath feared that Hughes was intent on ending it. This interpretation adds a greater poignancy to the poem.

Writing About the Poem

There are several mood changes in 'Pheasant'. What do you consider to be the dominant mood in the poem? Refer to the text in your answer.

Sample Paragraph

The mood at the beginning of 'Pheasant' is nervous and really uptight. Plath seems to have given up hope about the pheasant. It is facing death. She repeats the word 'kill' and admits to being shocked at the very thought of what the bird is facing. She herself seems desperate and fearful. This is shown by the short sentence, 'Do not kill it'. But the outlook soon changes. Plath describes the pheasant 'pacing' and 'in its element'. But she seems less stressed as she describes the 'kingliness' of the pheasant. But the mood soon settles down as Plath celebrates the life of this really beautiful bird. The mood becomes calmer and ends in almost a whisper, 'Let be, let be'. The dominant mood is calm and considered in the poem.

EXAMINER'S COMMENT

This is a reasonable middle-grade answer to the question, pointing out the change of mood following the first stanza. Some worthwhile references are used to show the poem's principal mood. The expression, however, is flawed in places (e.g. repeatedly using 'But' to start sentences). This response requires more critical analysis and development to raise the standard.

Class/Homework Exercises

1. Plath sets out to convince the reader of the pheasant's right to life in this poem. Does she succeed in her aim? Give reasons for your answer.
2. 'Sylvia Plath's deep appreciation of the harmonious order of the natural world is expressed through vivid imagery.' To what extent is this true of her poem, 'Pheasant'? Support your answer with reference to the text.

Summary Points

- **Heartfelt plea on behalf of the rights of wild creatures.**
- **Graphic description of beauty of bird.**
- **Tension, poet as intruder.**
- **Imperatives (verbal commands) inject urgency.**
- **Subtle music, casual flow of the rhythm of normal speech.**

Elm

SYLVIA PLATH

Title: the wych elm is a large deciduous tree, with a massive straight trunk and tangled branches. It was once a favourite timber of coffin makers. Plath dedicated the poem to a close friend, Ruth Fainlight, another American poet.

For Ruth Fainlight

I know the bottom, she says. I know it with my great tap root:
It is what you fear.
I do not fear it: I have been there.

the bottom: lowest depths.
tap root: the main root.

Is it the sea you hear in me,
Its dissatisfactions?
Or the voice of nothing, that was your madness?

Love is a shadow.
How you lie and cry after it
Listen: these are its hooves: it has gone off, like a horse.

All night I shall gallop thus, impetuously,
Till your head is a stone, your pillow a little turf,
Echoing, echoing.

Or shall I bring you the sound of poisons?
This is rain now, this big hush.
And this is the fruit of it: tin-white, like arsenic.

arsenic: poison.

I have suffered the atrocity of sunsets.
Scorched to the root
My red filaments burn and stand, a hand of wires.

atrocity: massacre, carnage

filaments: fibres, nerves.

Now I break up in pieces that fly about like clubs.
A wind of such violence
Will tolerate no bystanding: I must shriek.

The moon, also, is merciless: she would drag me
Cruelly, being barren.
Her radiance scathes me. Or perhaps I have caught her.

scathes: injures, scalds.

I let her go. I let her go
Diminished and flat, as after radical surgery.
How your bad dreams possess and endow me.

I am inhabited by a cry.
Nightly it flaps out
Looking, with its hooks, for something to love.

I am terrified by this dark thing
That sleeps in me;
All day I feel its soft, feathery turnings, its malignity.

Clouds pass and disperse.
Are those the faces of love, those pale irretrievables?
Is it for such I agitate my heart?

I am incapable of more knowledge.
What is this, this face
So murderous in its strangle of branches? –

Its snaky acids hiss.
It petrifies the will. These are the isolate, slow faults
That kill, that kill, that kill.

malignity: evil.

disperse: scatter widely.

irretrievables: things lost forever.

snaky acids: deceptive poisons.

petrifies: terrifies.

'I am terrified by this dark thing'

Personal Response

1. There are many sinister nature images in this poem. Select two that you find particularly unsettling and comment on their effectiveness.
2. Trace and examine how love is presented and viewed by the poet. Support the points you make with reference to the text.
3. Write your own individual response to this poem, referring closely to the text in your answer.

Critical Literacy

Written in April 1962, 'Elm' is one of Sylvia Plath's most intensely dramatic poems. Plath personifies the elm tree to create a surreal scene. It 'speaks' in a traumatic voice to someone else, the 'you' of line 2, the poet herself – or the reader, perhaps. Both voices interact throughout the poem, almost always expressing pain and anguish. Critics often associate these powerful emotions with the poet's own personal problems – Plath had experienced electric shock treatment for depression. However, this may well limit our understanding of what is a complex exploration of many emotions.

The opening stanza is unnerving. The poet appears to be dramatising an exchange between herself and the elm by imagining what the tree might say to her. The immediate effect is eerily surreal. From the start, **the narrative voice is obsessed with instability and despair**: 'I know the bottom'. The tree is described in both physical terms ('my great tap root' penetrating far into the ground) and also as a state of mind ('I do not fear it'). The depth of depression imagined is reinforced by the repetition of 'I know' and the stark simplicity of the chilling comment 'It is what you fear'.

The bizarre exchange between the two 'speakers' continues in stanza two. The elm questions the poet about the nature of her **mental state**. Does the wind blowing through its branches remind her of the haunting sound of the sea? Or even 'the voice of nothing' – the numbing experience of madness?

Stanzas three and four focus on the dangers and disappointments of love – 'a shadow'. The tone is fearful, emphasised by the comparison of a wild horse that has 'gone off'. The relentless sounds of the wind in the elm will be a bitter reminder, 'echoing' this loss of love 'Till your head is a stone'. **Assonance** is effectively used here to heighten the sense of hurt and abandonment. For much of the middle section of the poem (stanzas five to nine), the elm's intimidating voice continues to dramatise a series of horrifying experiences associated with insanity. The tree has endured extreme elements – rain ('the sound of poisons'), sunshine ('Scorched to the root'), wind ('of such violence') and also the moon ('Her radiance scathes me'). **The harsh imagery and frenzied language** ('burn', 'shriek', 'merciless') combine to create a sense of shocking destructiveness.

Stanzas ten and eleven mark a turning point where the voices of the tree and the poet become indistinguishable. This is achieved by the seemingly harmless image of an owl inhabiting the branches, searching for 'something to love'. The speaker is haunted by 'this dark thing'. The **poet's vulnerability** is particularly evident in her stark admission: 'I feel its soft, feathery turnings, its malignity'. Plath has come to relate her unknown demons to a deadly tumour.

In the last three stanzas, the poet's voice seems more distant and calm before the final storm. The image of the passing clouds ('the faces of love') highlight the notion of rejection as the root cause of Plath's depression. The poem ends on a visionary note when she imagines being confronted by a 'murderous' snake that appears in the branches: 'It petrifies the will'. The scene of **growing terror builds to a hideous climax** until her own mental and emotional states (her 'slow faults') end up destroying her. The intensity of the final line, 'That kill, that kill, that kill', leaves readers with a harrowing understanding of Plath's paralysis of despair.

Writing About the Poem

Do you think that 'Elm' has a surreal, nightmarish quality? In your response, refer to the text to support your views.

Sample Paragraph

I agree that Sylvia Plath has created a disturbing mood in the poem, 'Elm'. Giving the tree a speaking voice of its own is like something from a child's fairy story. Plath compares love to a galloping horse. The poem is mainly about depression and madness. So it's bound to be out of the ordinary. The speaker in the poem is confused and asks weird questions, such as 'Is it the sea you hear in me?' She is obsessive and totally paranoid. Everything is against her, as far as she imagines it. The weather is an enemy even, the rain is 'tin-white like arsenic'. The end is as if she is having a dream and imagines a fierce snake in the tree coming after her. The dramatic scene unnerves the reader. This represents Plath's deepest nightmare, the fear of loneliness. Violent verbs such as 'suffered' disturb the reader and images – 'a hand of wires', 'snaky acids hiss' – create a surreal atmosphere. The poem is hectic and confusing – especially the images.

EXAMINER'S COMMENT

This short mid-grade paragraph includes some worthwhile references to the poem's disturbing aspects. The points are note-like, however, and the writing style lacks control in places. Effective use of apt quotations.

Class/Homework Exercises

1. What evidence of Plath's deep depression and hypersensitivity is revealed in the poem 'Elm'? Refer closely to the text in your answer.
2. Plath said of her later poetry, 'I speak them to myself ... aloud'. In your opinion, how effective are the sound effects and use of direct speech in the poem 'Elm'? Support your views with accurate quotation.

Summary Points

- **Inner torment, awful fear of being oneself.**
- **Terrifying personification of elm.**
- **Rich symbolism and imagery, effective sounds.**
- **Nightmare world, surreal mood, paralysis of fear, threat of madness.**
- **Simple unvarnished style, poem overflows with poet's feelings of lost love.**

SYLVIA PLATH

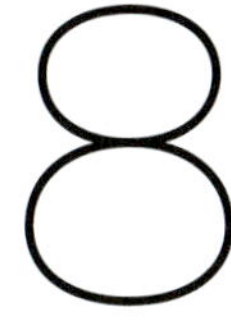

Poppies in July

Little poppies, little hell flames,
Do you do no harm?

hell flames: most poppies are red, flame-like.

You flicker. I cannot touch you.
I put my hands among the flames. Nothing burns.

And it exhausts me to watch you
Flickering like that, wrinkly and clear red, like the skin of a mouth.

A mouth just bloodied.
Little bloody skirts!

There are fumes that I cannot touch.
Where are your opiates, your nauseous capsules?

fumes: the effects of drugs.

opiates: sleep-inducing narcotics.
nauseous: causing sickness.

If I could bleed, or sleep! –
If my mouth could marry a hurt like that!

Or your liquors seep to me, in this glass capsule,
Dulling and stilling.

liquors: drug vapours.
capsule: small container.

But colorless. Colorless.

colorless: drained, lifeless.

Personal Response

1. Comment on the title, 'Poppies in July'. Is the title misleading? Explain your answer.
2. What evidence can you find in 'Poppies in July' that the speaker is yearning to escape?
3. Colour imagery plays a significant role in the poem. Comment on how effectively colour is used.

Critical Literacy

Like most confessional writers, Sylvia Plath's work reflects her own personal experiences, without filtering any of the painful emotions. She wrote 'Poppies in July' in the summer of 1962, during the break-up of her marriage.

The first stanza is marked by a sense of unease and foreboding. The speaker (almost certainly Plath herself) compares the blazing red poppies to 'little hell flames' before directly confronting them: 'Do you do no harm?' **Her distress is obvious** from the start. The poem's title may well have led readers to expect a more conventional nature poem. Instead, the flowers are presented as being highly treacherous, and all the more deceptive because they are 'little'.

Plath develops the fire image in lines 3–6. However, even though she places her hands 'among the flames', she finds that 'Nothing burns' and she is forced to watch them 'Flickering'. It almost seems as though she is so tired and numb that **she has transcended pain** and can experience nothing: 'it exhausts me to watch you'. Ironically, the more vivid the poppies are, the more lethargic she feels.

The uncomfortable and disturbed mood increases in the fourth stanza with two **startling images**, both personifying the flowers. Comparing the poppy to 'A mouth just bloodied' suggests recent violence and physical suffering. The 'bloody skirts' metaphor is equally harrowing. There is further evidence of the poet's overpowering weariness in the prominent use of broad vowel sounds, for example in 'exhausts', 'mouth' and 'bloodied'.

In the fifth stanza, Plath's disorientated state turns to a distracted longing for escape. Having failed to use the vibrancy of the poppies to distract her from her pain, she now craves the feeling of oblivion or unconsciousness. But although she desires the dulling effects of drugs derived from the poppies, her **tone reflects her feelings of helplessness** as she describes the 'fumes that I cannot touch'.

The mood becomes even more distraught in lines 11–12, with the poet begging for any alternative to her anguished state. 'If I could bleed, or sleep!'

is an emphatic plea for release. It is her final attempt to retain some control of her life in the face of an overwhelming sense of powerlessness. Plath's **growing alienation** seems so unbearably intense at this point that it directly draws the reader's sympathy.

The last three lines record the poet's surrender, perhaps a kind of death wish. Worn down by her inner demons and the bright colours of the poppies, Plath lets herself become resigned to a 'colorless' world of nothingness. Her **complete passivity** and vulnerability are emphasised by the dreamlike quality of the phrase 'Dulling and stilling'. As she drifts into a death-like 'colorless' private hell, there remains a terrible sense of betrayal, as if she is still being haunted by the bright red flowers. The ending of 'Poppies in July' is so dark and joyless that it is easy to understand why the poem is often seen as a desperate cry for help.

Writing About the Poem

'Poppies in July' is one of Plath's most disturbing poems. What aspects of the poem affected you most?

Sample Paragraph

'Poppies in July' was written at a time when Plath was struggling with the fact that her husband had deserted her. This affected her deeply and it is clear that the poppies are a symbol of this difficult time. Everything about the poem is negative. The images of the poppies are nearly all associated with fire and blood. Plath's language is alarming when she compares the poppies to 'little hell flames' and also 'the skin of a mouth'. The most disturbing aspect is Plath's own unstable mind. She seems to be in a kind of trance, obsessed by the red colours of the poppies, which remind her of blood. I got the impression that she was nearly going insane in the end. She seems suicidal – 'If I could bleed'. For me, this is the most disturbing moment in the poem. I can get some idea of her troubled mind. Plath cannot stand reality and seeks a way out through drugs or death. The last image is of Plath sinking into a dull state of drowsiness, unable to cope with the world around her.

EXAMINER'S COMMENT

Overall, a solid middle-grade response which responds personally to the question. While some focus is placed on the disturbing thought in the poem, there could have been a more thorough exploration of Plath's style and how it enhances her theme of depression.

Class/Homework Exercises

1. Would you agree that loneliness and pain are the central themes of 'Poppies in July'? Refer to the text of the poem when writing your response.
2. Discuss how the poet uses vivid description in this poem to explore her negative feelings. Support your answer with reference to the text.

Summary Points

- **Desire to escape into oblivion.**
- **Personal aspect, engaged in inner conflict.**
- **Compelling drama, upsetting imagery, intense mood of despair.**
- **Despairing mood conveyed in downward motion of poem.**
- **Contrast between dynamic, vivid flowers, a symbol of vibrancy of life, and longed-for dullness of oblivion.**

SYLVIA PLATH

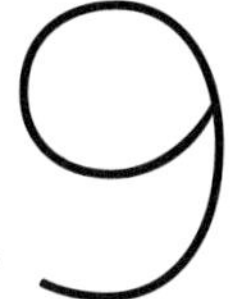

The Arrival of the Bee Box

I ordered this, this clean wood box
Square as a chair and almost too heavy to lift.
I would say it was the coffin of a midget
Or a square baby
Were there not such a din in it.

The box is locked, it is dangerous.
I have to live with it overnight
And I can't keep away from it.
There are no windows, so I can't see what is in there.
There is only a little grid, no exit.

grid: wire network.

I put my eye to the grid.
It is dark, dark,
With the swarmy feeling of African hands
Minute and shrunk for export,
Black on black, angrily clambering.

swarmy: like a large group of bees.

How can I let them out?
It is the noise that appalls me most of all,
The unintelligible syllables.
It is like a Roman mob,
Small, taken one by one, but my god, together!

I lay my ear to furious Latin.
I am not a Caesar.
I have simply ordered a box of maniacs.
They can be sent back.
They can die, I need feed them nothing, I am the owner.

Caesar: famous Roman ruler.

I wonder how hungry they are.
I wonder if they would forget me
If I just undid the locks and stood back and turned into a tree.
There is the laburnum, its blond colonnades,
And the petticoats of the cherry.

laburnum: tree with yellow hanging flowers.
colonnades: long groups of flowers arranged in a row of columns.

They might ignore me immediately
In my moon suit and funeral veil.
I am no source of honey
So why should they turn on me?
Tomorrow I will be sweet God, I will set them free.

The box is only temporary.

moon suit: protective clothing worn by beekeepers; all-in-one suit.

'It is the noise that appalls me'

Personal Response

1. How would you describe the poet's reaction to the bee box – fear or fascination, or a mixture of both? Write a paragraph for your response, referring to the poem.
2. Select two surreal images from the poem and comment on the effectiveness of each.
3. Would you describe this poem as exploring and overcoming one's fears and anxieties? Is the ending optimistic or pessimistic, in your opinion?

Critical Literacy

'The Arrival of the Bee Box' was written in 1962, shortly after Plath's separation from her husband. Her father, who died when she was a child, had been a bee expert and Plath had recently taken up beekeeping. She explores order, power, control, confinement and freedom in this deeply personal poem.

The poem opens with a simple statement: 'I ordered this'. Straightaway, the emphasis is on order and control. The poet's tone in stanza one seems both matter-of-fact and surprised, as if thinking: 'Yes, I was the one who ordered this' and also 'Did I really order this?' **This drama has only one character, Plath herself.** We observe her responses and reactions to the arrival of the bee box. Notice the extensive use of the personal pronoun 'I'. We both see and hear the event.

The box is described as being made of 'clean wood' and given a homely quality through the simile 'Square as a chair'. But then a surreal, dreamlike metaphor, 'the coffin of a midget/Or a square baby', brings us into a **nightmare world**. The abnormal is suggested by the use of 'midget' and 'square baby'. The coffin conveys not only death, but also entrapment and confinement, preoccupations of the poet. The box has now become a sinister object. A witty sound effect closes the first stanza, as 'din in it' mimics the sound of the bees. The noisy insects are like badly behaved children.

Stanza two explores the **poet's ambivalent attitude to the box**. She is curious to see inside ('I can't keep away from it'). Yet she is also frightened by it, as she describes the box as 'dangerous'. She peers in. The third stanza becomes claustrophobic with the repetition of 'dark' and the grotesque image of 'the swarmy feeling of African hands/Minute and shrunk for export'. The milling of the bees/slaves is vividly captured as they heave around in the heat amid an atmosphere of menace and oppression, hopelessly desperate.

We hear the bees in stanza four. The metaphor of a Roman mob is used to show how they will create **chaos and danger if they are let loose**. The assonance of 'appalls' and 'all' underlines the poet's terror. The phrase

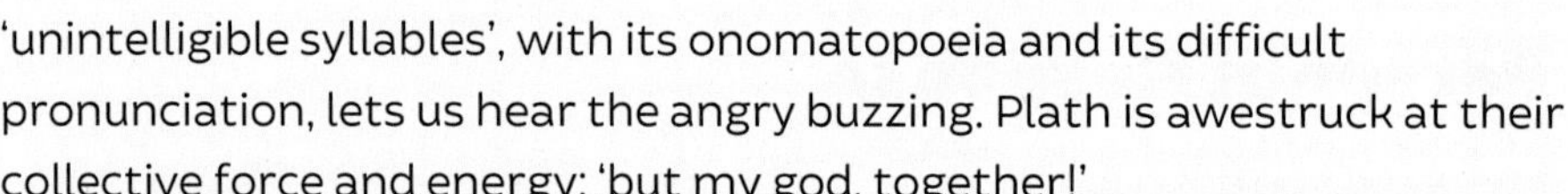

'unintelligible syllables', with its onomatopoeia and its difficult pronunciation, lets us hear the angry buzzing. Plath is awestruck at their collective force and energy: 'but my god, together!'

In stanza five the poet tries to listen, but only hears 'furious Latin' she does not understand. She doubts her capacity to control them, stating that she is 'not a Caesar', the powerful ruler of the Romans. She regards them as 'maniacs'. Then she suddenly realises that if she has ordered them, she can return them: 'They can be sent back'. **She has some control of this situation**. Plath can even decide their fate, whether they live or die: 'I need feed them nothing'. She has now redefined the situation as she remembers that she is 'the owner'. They belong to her.

The poet's feminine, nurturing side now emerges as she wonders 'how hungry they are'. The stereotype of the pretty woman surfaces in the description of the bees' natural habitat of trees in stanza six. Plath thinks that if she releases them, they would go back to the trees, 'laburnum' and 'cherry'. She herself would then merge into the landscape and become a tree. This is a reference to a Greek myth where Daphne was being pursued by Apollo. After begging the gods to be saved, they turned her into a tree.

The poet refers to herself in her beekeeping outfit of veil and boiler suit in stanza seven. She rhetorically asks why the bees would attack her, as she can offer no sustenance ('I am no source of honey'). **She decides to be compassionate**: 'Tomorrow I will be sweet God, I will set them free'. She realises that they are imprisoned for the time being: 'The box is only temporary'.

This poem can also be read on more than one level. The box could represent the poet's attempt to be what others expect, the typical 1950s woman – pretty, compliant, nurturing. The bees could symbolise the unstable side of her personality, which both fascinated and terrified Plath. **The box is like Pandora's box**: safe when locked, but full of danger when opened. Although she finds this disturbing, she also feels she must explore it in the interests of developing as a poet. The references to the doomed character of Daphne and the 'funeral veil' echo chillingly. Would these dark thoughts, if given their freedom, drive her to suicide? The form of this poem is seven stanzas of five lines. One final line stands alone, free like the bees or her dark thoughts. If the box represents Plath's outside appearance or body, it is mortal, it is temporary.

Writing About the Poem

How does this poem address and explore the themes of order and power? Write a paragraph in response. Support your views with reference to the text.

Sample Paragraph

The poem opens with a reference to order, 'I ordered this'. It is an assertion of power, a deliberate act by 'I'. Throughout the poem the repetition of 'I' suggests a person who consciously chooses to act in a certain way. 'I put my eye to the grid'. It is as if the poet wishes to confront and control her fears over the contents of the box. This box contains live bees, whose well-being lies in the hands of the poet. 'I need feed them nothing, I am the owner'. The box metaphor suggests a lack of freedom – 'locks', 'little grid' enhance this atmosphere of claustrophobic control. Although she realises that she is not 'Caesar', the mighty Roman ruler, she can choose to be 'sweet God'. She alone has the power to release the bees, 'The box is only temporary'. This poem can also be read as referring to the control a person exercises when confronting their innermost fears and desires. These thoughts can be ignored or faced. The person can choose to contain them or confront them. Plath feared her own dark side, but felt it should be explored to enable her to progress as a poet. For her 'The box is only temporary'.

EXAMINER'S COMMENT

This is an assured top-grade response which focuses well on the central themes of order and power. Apt and accurate quotations are used effectively. The opening point on Plath's use of the personal pronoun is particularly impressive.

Class/Homework Exercises

1. How does Plath create a dramatic atmosphere in 'The Arrival of the Bee Box'?
2. Plath examines repression in 'The Arrival of the Bee Box'. Why do you think she fears a loss of control? In your response, refer to both the subject matter and stylistic techniques evident in the poem.

Summary Points

- **Central themes include power, control, freedom, self-expression.**
- **Innovative use of metaphor, contrasting moods.**
- **Unusual personification, startling images and drama.**
- **Clever word-play, witty sound effects, internal rhyme.**
- **Disconcerting ending emphasised by single stand-alone line.**

10 Child

Your clear eye is the one absolutely beautiful thing.
I want to fill it with color and ducks,
The zoo of the new

Whose name you meditate –
April snowdrop, Indian pipe,
Little

Stalk without wrinkle,
Pool in which images
Should be grand and classical

Not this troublous
Wringing of hands, this dark
Ceiling without a star.

meditate: reflect.

Indian pipe: American woodland flower.

Stalk: plant stem.

classical: impressive, enduring.

troublous: disturbed.

Personal Response

1. What was your own immediate reaction after reading 'Child'? Refer to the poem in your answer.
2. Which images in the poem are most effective in contrasting the world of the child and the world of the adult?
3. Plath uses various sound effects to enhance her themes in 'Child'. Comment briefly on two interesting examples.

'The zoo of the new'

Critical Literacy

Sylvia Plath's son was born in January 1962. A year later, not long before the poet's own death, she wrote 'Child', a short poem that reflects her intense feelings about motherhood.

The opening line of stanza one shows the **poet's emphatic appreciation of childhood innocence**: 'Your clear eye is the one absolutely beautiful thing'. The tone at first is hopeful. Her love for the new child is generous and unconditional: 'I want to fill it with color'. The childlike language is lively and playful. Plath plans to give her child the happiest of times, filled with 'color and ducks'. The vigorous rhythm and animated internal rhyme in the phrase 'The zoo of the new' are imaginative, capturing the sense of **youthful wonder**.

In stanza two, the poet continues to associate her child with all that is best about the natural world. The baby is like the most fragile of flowers, the 'April snowdrop'. The assonance in this phrase has a musical effect, like a soft lullaby. Yet her own fascination appears to mask a deeper concern. Plath feels that such a perfect childhood experience is unlikely to last very long. Despite all her positive sentiments, what she wants for **the vulnerable child** seems directly at odds with what is possible in a **flawed world**.

Run-on lines are a recurring feature of the poem and these add to the feeling of freedom and innocent intensity. Stanza three includes two **effective comparisons**, again taken from nature. Plath sees the child as an unblemished 'Stalk' that should grow perfectly. A second quality of childhood's pure innocence is found in the 'Pool' metaphor. We are reminded of the opening image – the child's 'clear eye', always trusting and sincere.

The poet would love to provide a magical future for her young child, so that the pool would reflect 'grand and classical' images. However, as a loving mother, she is trapped between her **idealism** – the joy she wants for her child – and a **distressing reality** – an awareness that the child's life will not be perfectly happy. This shocking realisation becomes clear in stanza four and overshadows her hopes completely. The final images are stark and powerful – the pathetic 'Wringing of hands' giving emphasis to her helplessness. The last line poignantly portrays the paradox of the tension between Plath's dreams for the child in the face of the despair she feels about the oppressive world: this 'Ceiling without a star'. The intensely dark mood is in sharp contrast with the rest of the poem. The early celebration has been replaced by anguish and an overwhelming sense of failure.

Writing About the Poem

Do you think 'Child' is a positive or negative poem? Refer to the text in explaining your response.

Sample Paragraph

Plath's poem, 'Child', is about a mother's inadequacy. The poet wants the best for her innocent son. Although the first half of the poem focuses on her wishes to protect him, this changes. Plath starts off by wanting to fill the boy's life with happy experiences (bright colours and toys) and keep him close to nature. There are references to nature right through the poem and Plath compares her son to an 'April snowdrop'. This tender image gave me a very positive feeling. Everything about the child is wonderful at first. He is 'absolutely beautiful'. This all changes at the end. The mood turns negative. Plath talks of being confined in a darkened room that has a 'Ceiling without a star'. This is in total contrast with the images early on which were of the bright outdoors. The poet was positive at the start. This has been replaced with negative feelings. The ending is dark and 'troublous' because Plath knows her child will grow up and experience pain just as she has.

EXAMINER'S COMMENT

This paragraph addresses the question well and offers a clear response. There is some good personal engagement which effectively illustrates the changing mood from optimism to pessimism and uses apt quotations in support. A mid-grade response. The style of writing is a little note-like and pedestrian. Fresher expression and more development of points would have raised the standard from its present average middle grade.

Class/Homework Exercises

1. Write a paragraph comparing 'Child' with 'Morning Song'. Refer to theme and style in both poems.
2. 'Plath explores the changing nature of parental love in her poem, 'Child'. How does she reveal her sense of inadequacy in providing for her child? Support your response by reference to the poem.

Summary Points

- **One of several poems about children, moving from tenderness to anxiety.**
- **Lullaby, easy flowing movement, images of light and darkness.**
- **Contrast between love of child and poet's own depression.**
- **Appropriate style, clear, simple language.**
- **Juxtaposition of joyful, colourful world of child and dark despair of poet.**

Sample Leaving Cert Questions on Plath's Poetry

1. **'Sylvia Plath makes effective use of various stylistic features to express a range of intense and compelling feelings.' Discuss this view, supporting your answer with reference to both the themes and poetic style in the poetry of Sylvia Plath on your course.**
2. **'Sylvia Plath's confessional and introspective poems are largely defined by a disturbing sense of drama and underlying feelings of dread.' Discuss this view, supporting your answer with reference to both the thematic concerns and writing style in the poetry of Sylvia Plath on your course.**
3. **'Plath's powerful portrayal of the world of nature is conveyed through verbal energy and strikingly vivid symbolism.' To what extent do you agree or disagree with this view? Support your answer with reference to Plath's subject matter and writing style in her prescribed poems.**

How do I organise my answer?

(Sample question 1)

'Sylvia Plath makes effective use of various stylistic features to express a range of intense and compelling feelings.' Discuss this view, supporting your answer with reference to both the themes and poetic style in the poetry of Sylvia Plath on your course.

Sample Plan 1

Intro: (*Stance: agree with viewpoint in the question*) Plath uses a range of stylistic devices, including striking personification, vivid imagery and powerful sound effects to explore various feelings of self-doubt, wonder, angst and alienation.

Point 1: (*Torment – personification, repetition*) 'Elm' uses surreal personification to express poet's inner torment creating a nightmarish scene ('I must shriek'). Repetition conveys both deep depression ('I know') and the paralysis of despair ('That kill, that kill, that kill'). Atmosphere of extreme destructiveness established by frenzied verbs ('burn', 'drag', 'scathes').

Understanding the Prescribed Poetry Question

Marks are awarded using the PCLM Marking Scheme:
P = 15; C = 15; L = 15; M = 5
Total = 50

- **P** (Purpose = 15 marks) refers to the set question and is the launch pad for the answer. This involves engaging with all aspects of the question. Both theme and language must be addressed, although not necessarily equally.
- **C** (Coherence = 15 marks) refers to the organisation of the developed response and the use of accurate, relevant quotation. Paragraphing is essential.
- **L** (Language = 15 marks) refers to the student's skill in controlling language throughout the answer.
- **M** (Mechanics = 5 marks) refers to spelling and grammar.
- Although no specific number of poems is required, students usually discuss at least 3 or 4 in their written responses.
- Aim for at least 800 words, to be completed within 45–50 minutes.

NOTE

In keeping with the PCLM approach, the student has to take a stance by agreeing and/or disagreeing that Plath makes skilful use of:

- **various stylistic features** (her poetic style is noted for startling complex imagery, unsettling symbolism, contrast, repetition, surreal personification, dynamic verbs, disquieting sound effects, etc.)

... to express:

- **intense compelling feelings** (deep self-awareness, inner torment, uncertainty, longing to escape, depression, wonder, conflicted love, disillusionment, sense of loss, etc.)

Point 2: (*Despair – contrast, imagery*) 'Child' explores complex mother-child relationship, moving from tenderness to anxiety. Effective comparisons establish love of child ('Little/Stalk without wrinkle'). Poet's depression conveyed through disturbing imagery ('dark/Ceiling without a star').

Point 3: (*Alienation – sound effects*) 'Morning Song' again explores complex mother–child relationship, focusing on loss and separation. Passing time is created through onomatopoeia ('ticking'). Cruelty of world conveyed through harsh monosyllables ('slapped', 'bald'). Fragile child captured through onomatopoeia ('Flickered'). Menacing sibilant phrasing suggests threat to parents' relationship by child's arrival ('Shadows our safety').

Point 4: (*Disillusionment – imagery, tone*) 'The Times Are Tidy' uses a contemptuous tone to criticise the monotony of 1950s America, conveyed through derisory images ('stuck record', 'mayor's rotisserie'). Materialistic world of excess expressed though imagery of over-indulgence ('the cow milks cream an inch thick'). Poet bemoans how decadent modern world has 'withered' sense of adventure and heroism.

Conclusion: Effective use of stylistic devices communicates poet's intense feelings of alienation wonder, torment, disillusionment, etc.

Sample Paragraph: Point 2

In 'Child', Plath writes about the innocence of her young son. She expresses despair at her overwhelming feelings of inadequacy as a mother. She longs to provide a wonderful world for her little child whose 'clear eye is the one absolutely beautiful thing'. His innocent world is effectively conveyed in delicate imagery from nature, 'Stalk without wrinkle'. But this magical, idealistic impression soon implodes as the poet succumbs to negative feelings. The onomatopoeic image 'Wringing of hands' is multi-layered. It foreshadows the trouble the child will inevitably encounter in later life and also it graphically describes Plath's own helpless mental state. The final image is damning both for her and her young son, 'Ceiling without a star'. She feels confined in a situation without hope because her son will have to live in a flawed, oppressive world. The startling contrast between the ideal life which the poet wishes to give her child, 'grand and classical' and the grim reality for both of them makes this poem intensely disturbing.

EXAMINER'S COMMENT

Succinct and successful commentary that engages well with the poem. Focused well on how various aspects of style evoke and emphasise the poet's conflicted feelings about her child and his future. Good use of relevant supportive quotes that are integrated into the critical analysis. Expression is controlled and effective throughout this top-grade response.

(Sample question 2)

'Sylvia Plath's confessional and introspective poems are largely defined by a disturbing sense of drama and underlying feelings of dread.' Discuss this view, supporting your answer with reference to both the thematic concerns and writing style in the poetry of Sylvia Plath on your course.

Sample Plan 2

Intro: (*Stance: agree with viewpoint in the question*) Plath's revelatory and self-analytical poems are characterised by a distressing sense of turmoil and suspense, deep feelings of anxiety and an intensely dramatic poetic style.

Point 1: (*Poetic inspiration – negative language*) 'Black Rook in Rainy Weather' explores the problem of random poetic inspiration ('certain minor light') through pessimistic adjectives ('desultory', 'obtuse') and harsh verbs ('flare', 'hauls'). Chaos of world conveyed through forceful language and religious terminology ('hallowing an interval').

Point 2: (*Introspection on place – personification, contrast*) 'Finisterre' offers both a literal and metaphorical description of a visit to Brittany. Dramatic personification conveys the endless struggle between land ('Admonitory cliffs') and water ('sea exploding'). Imaginative, tense narrative created by the statue of Our Lady starkly contrasting her 'sweet' appearance with the harsh reality of shipwrecks ('souls, rolled in the doom-noise of the sea').

Point 3: (*Appreciation of nature – imperatives, repetition*) 'Pheasant' examines poet's appreciation of nature through the imperative phrase ('Do not kill it'). Insistent repetition increases Plath's clamour on behalf of nature ('Let be, let be'). Tone of admiration ('kingliness', 'such a good shape') replaced by underlying tone of unease at human intrusion ('I trespass stupidly').

Point 4: (*Personal experience – imagery, repetition*) 'Poppies in July' addresses personal trauma of separation through disturbing imagery ('little hell flames'). Downward spiral of poet's mental state emphasised by poem's rhythm. Plath wishes to escape hurt by descending into oblivion ('Dulling and stilling'). Dynamism of opening replaced by downbeat repetition ('colorless. Colorless').

NOTE

In keeping with the PCLM approach, the student has to agree or disagree that Plath's poems are:

- **confessional and introspective** (poet is concerned with self-awareness, exploration of personal emotions, conflicting feelings, fear of the future, lack of identity, poetic inspiration, appreciation of nature, inner turmoil, desire to escape, etc.)

... largely defined by:

- **a disturbing sense of drama and underlying feelings of dread** (ominous descriptive details, dramatic narratives, striking contrast, disturbing imagery, vivid symbolism, powerful sound effects, menacing personification, intense tones, moods and atmospheres, etc.)

Conclusion: Poet discloses deep feelings which she examines through disturbing imagery, personification, strong verbs and insistent repetition. Readers can relate to the poet on her tumultuous personal journey.

Sample Paragraph: Point 4

Plath reveals the personal trauma of marital separation in 'Poppies in July'. We are jolted from the deceptively joyful title into a surreal world of shocking imagery, 'little hell flowers', 'bloody skirts'. Her suffering is conveyed through laden assonance and broad vowels, 'exhausts', 'mouth', 'bloodied'. The poet is so traumatised that she has no longer the capability to feel anything, 'I cannot touch you', 'Nothing burns'. Yet she longs to feel even pain, 'If I could bleed', or to escape 'sleep'. Anything is preferable to her present state. She desires oblivion from the opiates, 'Dulling and stilling'. The repetitive double 'l' sound is effective, slowing down the pace of the poem. Plath's images are vivid and dramatic. The dynamism of the red poppies which 'flicker' is replaced in the last line by a feeling of lifelessness conveyed by dreary repetition, 'colorless. Colorless'. The final sense is of complete separation – perhaps signifying the separation of the poet from her husband or even the loss of consciousness.

EXAMINER'S COMMENT

This is a reflective and analytical top-grade response that shows a close understanding of the poem. Points are focused directly on both aspects of the question (introspective approach and disturbing drama). There is close engagement with the text, particularly in the discussion of how Plath's concerns are conveyed through surreal imagery, evocative assonance and repetition. Supportive, accurate quotations are carefully integrated into the commentary throughout.

Leaving Cert Sample Essay

From your study of the poetry of Sylvia Plath on your course, select the poems that, in your opinion, best demonstrate her skilful use of language and imagery to explore extremes of human experience. Justify your selection by demonstrating Plath's skilful use of language and imagery to explore extremes of human experience in the poems you have chosen.

Sample Essay

1. Sylvia Plath once wrote 'It is so much safer not to feel, not to let the world touch me'. Yet, her poetry enables the reader to feel extreme moments of the human experience. The poems, 'Mirror', 'Morning Song', 'The Arrival of the Bee Box' and 'Elm' make a powerful impact on the reader's mind. Plath explores the inevitability of old age, the problems affecting motherhood and personal identity, the tension between power and freedom and the awful fear of being oneself. She uses a variety of stylistic features, including sinister personification, surreal imagery, dramatic narrative and a wide variety of tones.

2. Plath's anguished voice expresses her unceasing search for identity in the dramatic poem, 'Mirror'. Here, she imagines the cool critical tone of the mirror, 'the eye of a little god, four-cornered'. The poet's sinister personification portrays the mirror as a living being which has an almost claustrophobic relationship with the speaker in the poem, scrutinising her 'day after day'. It announces that it is 'silver and exact' with 'no preconceptions', 'unmisted by love or dislike'. Yet in the chilling metaphor there is a suggestion of danger for the woman. She is clearly dissatisfied with the image of herself reflected 'faithfully' in the mirror, standing 'with tears and an agitation of the hands'. 1950s America placed extreme pressure on young women to conform to a strict stereotype of being attractive and to perform the conventional roles of wife, mother and homemaker. Plath shows with real honesty how there is no escape from this life with its relentless and terrifying march of time, 'Each morning'. She uses startling personification to show how society cruelly views women as worthless once their youth is spent.

3. 'Elm' also effectively uses this technique of terrifying personification to present the poet's view of the dark side of life. There is even a sense of being thrust by pressures to the edge of insanity. A series of horrific experiences linked with madness is dramatised by the fearful 'voice' of the tree which is being pushed to its limits, 'Scorched to the root'. Plath explores unnerving feelings of despair through the confessional lines, 'I am terrified by this dark thing that sleeps in me'. She expresses her trauma as a malignant growth, quietly and ominously increasing inside, 'all day I feel its soft, feathery turnings'. As in 'Mirror', there is a suffocating sense of being confined. The ending is highly dramatic – a visionary moment where the speaker imagines being attacked by a vicious snake. The repetition of 'kill' in the final line highlights the awful realisation of being completely overwhelmed.

4. Even an event like the birth of a little baby in 'Morning Song' is presented in a style that leaves the reader feeling uneasy. Plath must have been experiencing post-natal depression. This is a common thing in our society today and is not taken seriously enough because of our patriarchal society in my view. Plath describes new parents standing 'round blankly as walls'. The tone here is detached, 'New statue'. Yet the opening dynamic image uses personification to imitate the wonderful act of creation, 'Love set you going like a fat gold watch'. However, her tender description of the baby's 'moth-breath' contrasts sharply with her negative view of motherhood as a cloud which disappears after producing rain, 'the cloud that distils a mirror to reflect its own slow effacement'. The poem is filled with conflicted feelings. Again, Plath addresses the realities of life, exploring the ambivalent attitudes to motherhood which many new parents can experience.

INDICATIVE MATERIAL

Plath makes effective use of a range of stylistic features, including:

- striking imagery, heightened surreal scenes, rich metaphors and similes, sinister dramatic language, searing tones, disturbing sound effects, poetic forms, etc.

... to explore:

- extremes of human experience
- intense expression of mother-child relationship, penetrating insights into human life, self-analysis, fear, joy, conflicted love, preoccupation with life's darker aspects, nature, transience, etc.

5. 'The Arrival of the Bee Box' examines other extremes – the tension between control and freedom. The confident, emphatic statement, 'I ordered this, this clear wood box'. The speaker appears to be in control, yet almost immediately this changes, slipping into a surreal world which contradicts through the disturbing image, 'the coffin of a midget'. Plath focuses on the bees' confinement through a series of stifling images which seem to mirror her own experience of human society. She likens the bees to African slaves through vibrant visual and aural imagery, 'the swarmy feeling of African hands ... Black on black, angrily clambering'. The innovative use of the sibilant adjective 'swarmy' vividly conveys the sweltering conditions of the bee-box and a slave ship. The poet suggests the clamour of the trapped bees, the 'unintelligible syllables, it is like a Roman mob'. Her urgent search for perfection is shown by her desperate wish to do what is right for them. In the end, she vows 'Tomorrow I will be sweet God, I will set them free'.

6. Plath's poetry reveals a brutal world in which she struggles with her own idealism and her deep desire to do her very best in everything. She echoes the challenges human beings face in their journey through life by various poetic devices, particularly shocking personification, rich imagery and searing honesty.

(810 words)

EXAMINER'S COMMENT

Good clear introduction. Overall, the essay shows genuine engagement with the question, with most discussion rooted in the texts of the poems (although Paragraph 4 drifts away at the start). Discussion is insightful throughout and points are succinct but sufficiently developed and supported with an impressive range of embedded quotations. Good use of critical terms and controlled, varied expression all contribute to the top-grade standard.

GRADE: H1
P = 14/15
C = 13/15
L = 14/15
M = 5/5
Total = 46/50

Revision Overview

'Black Rook in Rainy Weather'
Life-affirming poem in which Plath explores the mystery of poetic inspiration and the importance of appreciating everyday life as it is.

'The Times Are Tidy'
Focuses on political themes and the poet's personal dissatisfaction with the materialistic and unheroic era she lived in.

'Morning Song'
Feeling estranged from her own child, the poet addresses themes of motherhood, alienation and human frailty.

'Finisterre'
Dramatic seascape depicting a turbulent scene that reflects the poet's troubled state of mind and her thoughts on the futility of conflict.

'Mirror'
In this chilling poem, the personified mirror reflects Plath's own thoughts about identity and people's fixation with their inevitable mortality.

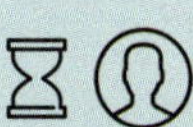

'Pheasant'
The poet is embarrassed by her unwitting intrusion into a natural scene, yet she enjoys and appreciates the beauty of the pheasant in its element.

'Elm'
Plath invents a demon in her subconscious that gives her a self-destructive vision. Shocked by this powerful, violent and uncontrolled experience, she surrenders to mental exhaustion.

'Poppies in July'
Expresses the longing to escape from deep depression. The poet is so emotionally drained that she struggles to find any feeling that connects her to reality.

'The Arrival of the Bee Box'
Plath explores various feelings of power and powerlessness associated with bee-keeping. The poet's indecisiveness seems to reflect her own chaotic state of mind.

'Child'
This dark yet beautiful poem captures Plath's personal insecurity concerning her marriage and her conflicted feelings as a mother.

Last Words

'Her poems have that heart-breaking quality about them.'
Joyce Carol Oates

'Artists are a special breed. They are passionate and temperamental. Their feelings flow into the work they create.'
J. Timothy King

'I am a genius of a writer. I have it in me. I am writing the best poems of my life.'
Sylvia Plath

CREATIVITY

REGRET

NATURE

WONDER

LOVE

AGEING

IDENTITY

ESCAPE

CHILDHOOD

FREEDOM

The Unseen Poem

'Students should be able ... to read poetry conscious of its specific mode of using language as an artistic medium.'
(DES English Syllabus, 4.5.1)

Note that responding to the unseen poem is an exercise in aesthetic reading. It is especially important, in assessing the responses of the candidates, to guard against the temptation to assume a 'correct' reading of the poem.

Reward the candidates' awareness of the patterned nature of the language of poetry, its imagery, its sensuous qualities, and its suggestiveness.

SEC Marking Scheme

In the Unseen Poem 20-mark question, you will have 20 minutes to read and respond to a short poem that you are unlikely to have already studied. Targeted reading is essential. **Read over the questions** first to focus your thoughts and feelings.

In your **first reading** of the poem:

- Aim to get an initial sense of what the poet is saying and think about why the poet is writing about that particular subject.
- What is happening? Who is involved? Is there a sense of place and atmosphere?
- Underline interesting words or phrases that catch your attention. Avoid wasting time worrying about any words that you don't understand. Instead, **focus on what makes sense** to you.

Read through the poem **a second time:**

- Who is speaking in the poem? Is it the poet or another character?
- Is the poet describing a scene?
- Or remembering an experience?
- What point is the poet making?
- What do you notice about the poet's language use?
- How does the poem make you feel?
- Did it make you wonder? Trust your own reaction.

Check the **'Glossary of Common Literary Terms'** on GillExplore.ie.

- **Theme** (the central idea or message in a poem ... There may be more than one theme)
- **Imagery** (includes similes, metaphors, symbols and personification)
- **Sound (aural) effects** – often referred to as onomatopoeia (includes alliteration, assonance, sibilance, rhyme and repetition)
- **Tone** (nostalgic, happy, sad, reflective, angry, optimistic, etc.)
- **Mood** (atmosphere can be relaxed, mysterious, poignant, uneasy, etc.)
- **Rhythm** (slow, steady, rapid, uneven, etc.)
- **Persona** (the speaker or 'voice' in the poem ... This may or may not be the poet)
- **Personification** (where a thing is treated as a living being, e.g. 'his brown skin hung in strips' - Elizabeth Bishop's description of the fish she caught)
- **Enjambment** (when a line doesn't have punctuation at the end. The resulting run-on lines usually add emphasis)
- **Irony** (when there is a different meaning to what is stated, e.g. the title of Plath's poem, 'The Times Are Tidy')
- **Emotive language** (language that affects the reader's feelings, e.g. 'our times have robbed your cradle' in Eavan Boland's 'Child of Our Time')
- **Contrasts**
- **Structure and layout**

REMEMBER!

'This section [Unseen Poetry] was often not answered, resulting in a loss of 20 marks. Omitting questions or parts of questions has a deleterious effect and is often due to poor time management.'
Chief Examiner's Report

Unseen Poem – Practice 1

Read the following poem by Alan Bold and answer **either** Question 1 **or** Question 2 which follow.

1 Autumn

Autumn arrives
Like an experienced robber
Grabbing the green stuff
Then cunningly covering his tracks
With a deep multitude
Of colourful distractions.
And the wind,
The wind is his accomplice
Putting an air of chaos
Into the careful diversions
So branches shake
And dead leaves are suddenly blown
In the faces of inquisitive strangers.
The theft chills the world,
Changes the temper of the earth
Till the normally placid sky
Glows red with a quiet rage.

Alan Bold

1. (a) What do you learn about the poet's attitude to autumn in the above poem? Support your answer with reference to the poem. (10)

(b) Identify two images from the poem that make an impact on you and give reasons for your choice. (10)

OR

2. Discuss the appeal of this poem, commenting on its theme, tone and the poet's use of language and imagery. Support your answer with reference to the poem. (20)

Sample Answer 1

Q1. (a) (Poet's attitude to autumn)
(Basic response)

The poet's attitude to autumn is not good at all because he calls autumn an experienced robber which is a negative thing. Alan does not compare the beauty in which nature is full of descriptive scenery of leaves falling in countryside areas. I think he's wrong about autumn to call it a theif in the night because this is not the whole picture at all and he only sees the negative side like storms and trees shaking. There is another story to the beauty of autumn's nature other than the dead leaves which are a reminder of the image of death which is a totally negative side. Alan has a pesimmistic attitude and this is too narrow to be true to life.

EXAMINER'S COMMENT

- *Makes one valid point about negativity.*
- *Little development or use of reference.*
- *No focus on the varied aspects of autumn.*
- *Expression is awkward and repetitive.*
- *Incorrect spellings ('theif', 'pesimmistic').*

Marks awarded: 3/10

Sample Answer 2

Q1. (a) (Poet's attitude to autumn)
(Top-grade response)

Alan Bold has a very playful outlook towards the season of autumn. In comparing it to a cunning 'experienced' robber who sneaks in every year to steal 'the green stuff' that grows in summer, he seems fascinated by the way nature changes so secretively. Bold develops the metaphor throughout the poem, closely observing how the wind (autumn's 'accomplice') creates chaos, tossing colourful leaves across the ground. Autumn is depicted as a powerful natural force which not only changes the landscape, but also affects how people feel. This is evident in the poem's final lines where he suggests that autumn marks the transition into winter and is a reminder that nature can be destructive – and even something to be feared. The poet's overall attitude is that the season of autumn warns human beings about our fragile relationship with the natural world.

EXAMINER'S COMMENT

- *Insightful answer that engages closely with the poem.*
- *Interesting final point about nature's destructive power.*
- *Good use made of supportive quotations throughout.*
- *Varied sentence length, fluent expression.*
- *Grammar and spellings are excellent.*

Marks awarded: 10/10

Sample Answer 3

Q1. (b) (Two images that make an impact)
(Basic response)

'the faces of inquisitive strangers' This is the first image that makes an impact on me and my reasons for my choice is that it is just exactly as it would happen in reality when people are in parks. This when we see the leaves are blown around into your face during October. If people have young children with them they never stop asking questions about the weather and everything.

'normally placid sky' The second image from the poem that made an impact on me and my reason for my choice is because this is that it is pure Irish weather in which the clouds are grey. It is usually about to rain in Ireland just like the calm before the storm. It does not exactly stay placid for long in this country. This image is detailed and true to life.

EXAMINER'S COMMENT

- *Little engagement with the poem's language.*
- *Limited point about the realism of both images.*
- *Needs more developed discussion.*
- *Drifted into general commentary.*
- *Repetitive, flawed expression throughout.*

Marks awarded: 4/10

Sample Answer 4

Q1. (b) (Two images that make an impact)
(Top-grade response)

I thought the 'experienced robber' image was very powerful. The simile immediately suggests that autumn is sly – disturbing the peace of summer. Alan Bold cleverly develops the comparison, emphasising the criminal image of the season, with associated words, such as 'covering his tracks' and 'cunningly'. The effect is playful – autumn is ingenious, fooling everyone into a false sense of security by disguising the changes that are happening to the climate. This lively colourful season is not to be fully trusted.

In a second striking image, the poet personifies the wind, describing it as autumn's 'accomplice' in creating widespread havoc. It creates an air of chaos – literally. This gives nature a human characteristic, which only strengthens its awesome power. The wind shows autumn to be even more terrifying because something so strong is merely its accomplice.

EXAMINER'S COMMENT

- *Perceptive analysis of the poet's inventive language.*
- *Good understanding of the extended metaphor.*
- *Effective use of apt textual reference.*
- *Excellent expression throughout.*

Marks awarded: 9/10

Unseen Poem – Practice 2

Read the following poem by Grace Nichols and answer **either** Question 1 **or** Question 2 which follow.

2 Roller-Skaters

Flying by
on the winged-wheels
of their heels

Two teenage earthbirds
zig-zagging
down the street

Rising
unfeathered –
in sudden air-leap

Defying law
death and gravity
as they do a wheely

Landing back
in the smooth swoop
of youth

And faces gaping
gawking, impressed
and unimpressed

Only mother watches – heartbeat in her mouth

Grace Nichols

1. (a) What do you think the poet is saying about the relationships between parents and their children in the above poem? Support your answer with reference to the poem. (10)

(b) Identify two images from the poem that make an impact on you and give reasons for your choice. (10)

OR

2. Discuss the language, including the imagery, used by the poet throughout this poem. Make detailed reference to the poem in support of your answer. (20)

Sample Answer 1

Q2. (Poet's language use)
(Basic response)

The poet's language including the imagry used by the poet throughout this poem is very detailed. It shows a street where roller skaters are taking place. The details show they are brave doing the wheely and zig zags as they are actually risking their lives for the sport they love. I myself have mixed feelings about the imagry because it shows how they jump in the air and amazing tricks. Like leaps but on the other hand their mother is afraid that he will be hurt. The language describes the danger involved in this daredevil sport.

People out in the street are looking at the image of these skaters. This is an image of risking life or just to show off to attract attention on the street. The language and images make me think of the danger involved behind the first impressions of an exciting sport that attracts kids in every city. At the start of the poem it is very exciting because no one is injured so far but as Grace protrays the skaters more in a detailed way the language becomes more dangerous for example when she says that there is a risk of death during the wheely. No wonder the mother watching has an image of her heart in her mouth because it is a dangerous situation and she is not too impressed.

EXAMINER'S COMMENT

- *Makes some points about detailed description.*
- *Little development or use of close reference to language.*
- *Minimal focus on the effectiveness of imagery.*
- *Expression is awkward and repetitive at times.*
- *Mechanical errors ('imagry', 'protrays').*

Marks awarded: 6/20

Sample Answer 2

Q2. (Poet's language use)
(Top-grade response)

Vivid imagery and energetic language are key features in this poem. Grace Nichols describes the young roller skaters 'Flying by' and having 'winged-wheels'. Both of these descriptions are metaphors as the skaters are not actually 'flying' nor do they have real 'wings' on their heels. The whole poem can be seen as one developed metaphor that suggests the breakneck actions of the skaters who seek thrills and excitement. Short lines and dynamic verbs, such as 'zig-zagging' and 'Rising' suggest their speed.

The skaters are compared to 'earthbirds' which is very effective. I can almost imagine that they will take off into the air at any minute. Later on, they are described as 'unfeathered', which links back to the same idea that they are defying 'death and gravity'. Towards the end, the poet mentions the 'smooth sweep of youth' and suggests that the skaters are really enjoying their freedom because they are happy-go-lucky and youthful.

The poem's rhythm is lively throughout and not interrupted by punctuation. This highlights the reckless moves the skaters make. Run-on lines (enjambment) create a sense of their continuous movement. Sound effects also play a huge part in the poem. There is a pattern of slender 'i' and 'e' vowels – e.g. 'winged-wheels' – in the opening lines which increases the pace. The alliteration suggests the repeated actions of the skaters.

The lay-out is arranged in a series of very short lines and this also highlights the skaters' lively movement. The final separate line cleverly suggests how the mother is outside of the action and can only watch helplessly from a distance as her child takes risks.

EXAMINER'S COMMENT

- *Focused on the effectiveness of language throughout.*
- *Ranges over various aspects, including imagery and sound.*
- *Well-developed discussion of the bird metaphor.*
- *Insightful comments on rhythm and structure.*
- *Good expression (although 'suggests' is overused).*

Marks awarded: 18/20

REMEMBER!

There is no single 'correct' reading of the poem. Respond to the poem honestly. How does it make you feel? Trust your own reaction.

Unseen Poem – Practice 3

Read the following poem by David Harmer and answer **either** Question 1 **or** Question 2 which follow.

At Cider Mill Farm

I remember my uncle's farm
Still in mid-summer
Heat hazing the air above the red roof tops
Some cattle sheds, a couple of stables
Clustered round a small yard
Lying under the hills that stretched their long back
Through three counties.

I rolled with the dogs
Among the hay bales
Stacked high in the barn he built himself
During a storm one autumn evening
Tunnelled for treasure or jumped with a scream
From a pirate ship's mast into the straw
Burrowed for gold and found he'd buried
Three battered Ford cars deep in the hay.

He drove an old tractor that sweated oil
In long black streaks down the rusty orange
It chugged and whirred, coughed into life
Each day as he clattered across the cattle grids
I remember one night my cousin and I
Dragging back cows from over the common
We prodded them homeward through the rain
And then drank tea from huge tin mugs
Feeling like farmers.

He's gone now, he sold it
But I have been back for one last look
To the twist in the lane that borders the stream
Where Mary, Ruth and I once waded
Water sloshing over our wellies
And I showed my own children my uncle's farm
The barn still leaning over the straw
With for all I know three battered Ford cars
Still buried beneath it.

David Harmer

1. (a) What is your impression of the poet's experiences on the farm in the above poem? Support your answer with reference to the poem. (10)

(b) Select two images from the poem that appeal to you and give reasons for your choice. (10)

OR

2. Discuss the language used by the poet, commenting on imagery, tone and sound effects. Support your answer with reference to the poem. (20)

Sample Answer 1

Q1. (a) (Poet's experiences on the farm)

(Basic response)

My first impression of David harmer is that he remembers spending a lot of happy times on his school holidays in cider mill farm. It belonged to his uncle who was the farm owner during his childhood, so he would have been there in the holidays. He had a lot of happy experiences splashing about in the river and messing with the dogs but his best experience is of the one time he drank tea from the big tin mugs belonging to the proper farmers after working with the cattle one evening. But the boy was dissapointed after the farm was sold, any child would naturally suffer from dissapointment by loosing their freedom. Up to then the farm life was very appealing, a good break away from school for a child during the holidays.

EXAMINER'S COMMENT

- *Some references to the poet's happy experiences.*
- *These could have been more effectively supported by quotes.*
- *Lacks discussion on stylistic features, e.g. nostalgic tone.*
- *Capital letter errors and misspellings ('dissapointed', 'loosing').*

Marks awarded: 4/10

Sample Answer 2

Q1. (a) (Poet's experiences on the farm)

(Top-grade response)

David Harmer's reminiscences are of exciting childhood days spent on his uncle's farm. From the start, his tone is nostalgic, 'Heat hazing the air above the red roof tops'. The broad vowel sounds and gentle alliteration emphasise the poet's happy memories of far-off times. He uses very little punctuation, suggesting that the memories are distant and all grouped together. The images of rural scenes show the impact that the countryside 'under the hills' had on him. I think it's almost as if the changing seasons matched the change in the poet's life as he grew up. The poem's overall mood is enthusiastic, however. The boy's sense of adventure is seen when exploring new sensations among the farm animals, 'We prodded

EXAMINER'S COMMENT

- *Intuitive response focusing on the poet's idyllic childhood.*
- *Good range of discussion points.*
- *Well supported by suitable quotations.*
- *Effective reference to imagery, tone and sound effects.*
- *Confident expression and excellent mechanics.*

Marks awarded: 10/10

them homeward through the rain'. He seems fascinated by the 'rusty orange' tractor – and its unusual noises which still appear to excite his imagination, 'It chugged and whirred'. As a child, he delighted in creating his own world of pirates and buried treasure. It's clear that the time on the farm was an important period, so much so that he wants to pass on his memories to his own children.

Sample Answer 3

Q1. (b) (Two appealing images)

(Basic response)

The first appealing image is of 'one night dragging back cows' because this shows the way cows don't hurry and have to be prodded with sticks to make them move. They nearly have to get dragged along as the image says, so this is the reason why this is a good image as it really shows that farmers totally have their hands full trying to get animals to go anywhere at night. It's just the way cows are. The next image is 'three battered Ford cars'. This is the second appealing image of cars lying rusting in a field like a scrapyard. This can be seen in some parts of the country where rusting cars are dumped without a second thought and they are a complete and total eyesore to the public who have to look at them, day and night. So in one way this is not appealing as an image because some people just dump rubbish anywhere. It's not a very appealing thing either for the public to have to put up with in this day and age, is it?

EXAMINER'S COMMENT

- *Slight points that need to be much more developed.*
- *Drifts into irrelevant general commentary.*
- *No attempt to examine the effectiveness of the language.*
- *Repetitive expression lacks fluency.*

Marks awarded: 3/10

Sample Answer 4

Q1. (b) (Two appealing images)

(Top-grade response)

There are many appealing images in this poem. I liked the ones that focused on the poet's carefree childhood, such as 'Heat hazing the air above the red roof tops'. The summer setting has strong associations with warmth and happiness. The poet remembers the haze of bright sunlight and the vivid red colours of the farm buildings. This vibrant imagery suggests an exaggerated childlike memory which is reinforced by the 'h' and 'r' alliteration. The line has a dreamlike quality, suggesting the wonder of the experience.

Some of the feelings the poet recalls are reinforced by sound images, for example, 'Water sloshing over our wellies'. The onomatopoeic effect of 'sloshing' echoes the squelching noises made by the children as they splashed through the water. Again, the repetition of sound in 'Water' and 'wellies' mimics their repeated actions as they stomped in the stream. This all contributes to the upbeat fairytale mood of the poem. Harmer is re-living a moment when he was totally happy-go-lucky on his uncle's farm.

EXAMINER'S COMMENT

- *Perceptive analysis of visual and aural imagery.*
- *Well-developed discussion examining language closely.*
- *Points supported by relevant textual reference.*
- *Excellent expression and varied vocabulary throughout.*

Marks awarded: 10/10

Unseen Poem – Practice 4

Read the following poem by Rosita Boland and answer **either** Question 1 **or** Question 2 which follow.

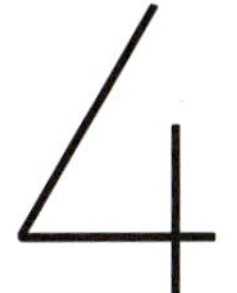

Lipstick

Home from work one evening,
I switched the radio on as usual,
chose a knife and started to slice
red peppers, scallions, wild mushrooms.

I started listening to a programme about Iran.
After the Shah fled, Revolutionary Guards
patrolled the streets of Teheran
looking for stray hairs, exposed ankles
and other signs of female disrespect.

The programme ended.
I was left standing in my kitchen
looking at the chopped vegetables on the table;
the scarlet circles of the peppers
delicate mouths, scattered at random.

When they discovered a woman wearing lipstick
they razor-bladed it off:
replaced one red gash with another.

Rosita Boland

1. (a) What do you learn about the kind of person the poet is from reading this poem? Explain your answer with reference to the poem. (10)

(b) Identify a mood or feeling evoked in the above poem and explain how the poet creates this mood or feeling. Support your answer with reference to the poem. (10)

OR

2. What impact did this poem make on you? Refer closely to the text in discussing its theme, tone and the poet's use of language and imagery. (20)

Sample Answer 1

Q2. (Impact of the poem)

(Basic response)

This was a hard to understand poem about a worker who comes home to make a meal. But she starts to listen to the radio news about what is happening in the war. I think she imagines the soilders running wild attacking people. One soilder uses a knife and attacks an innocent woman who is just dressed up and wearing lipstick which is her basic human right and just out for the evening. 'They patrolled the street'. This guard should of known better. This is the part of the poem that made the most impact on me personally. I am totally against armies running wild out of control.

This is the theme of war and the tone of this poem is showing up what happens on the back streets in some parts of the world. If your not doing any harm you should be left in peace. I think the poet uses language very well to get the whole point across. There is a big difference between the image of the innocent woman out to enjoy herself on a night out as she is intitled and the angry language of the soilder out on patrol who attacks her for no good reason. This is also at the end of the poem where I think there is a big difference between the two women. Unfortunately it is not a state of peace everywhere else which is the main impact of the poem.

EXAMINER'S COMMENT

- *Makes one reasonable point about the impact of violence.*
- *Only slight engagement with the poem.*
- *No convincing analysis of the poet's language use.*
- *Expression could have been much more controlled.*
- *Mechanical errors ('soilder', 'intitled', 'should of', 'your').*

Marks awarded: 6/20

Sample Answer 2

Q2. (Impact of the poem)
(Top-grade response)

Although the language is simple in this poem, it actually makes the point that routine violence against women is still common in some societies, such as Iran. This makes a greater impact as the poem develops because the poet's tone is almost relaxed in the first stanza – 'I switched the radio on as usual'. The radio programme is truly shocking. Boland points out the stark difference between what we take for granted as normality here at home and the grotesque reality of life in conflict areas, such as the Middle East.

The vivid image of the attack on the civilian is horrific. I can imagine that most people would have found it as disturbing as I did. The poet creates a dramatic effect by contrasting the girl's fragile beauty and the brutal violence she experiences. There are also some subtle echoes within the poem. The guard's vicious action is foreshadowed by the earlier image of the poet herself using a kitchen knife to slice vegetables. I can relate to her sense of physical revulsion as she imagines the Iranian policeman's use of a razor blade to replace 'one red gash with another'.

I was also struck by the emphasis on the innocence of victims and the helplessness that the poet feels. The quiet tone of the final stanza reflects her sense of failure, 'left standing there in my kitchen'. Vivid images of the half-chopped vegetables, particularly the 'scarlet circles of the peppers', are closely associated with the 'Delicate mouths' of vulnerable women who suffer vicious abuse and injustice. The ending has a stark clarity that sums up the savage regime in Tehran.

EXAMINER'S COMMENT

- *Convincing personal response to the question.*
- *Points are clear, incisive and aptly supported.*
- *Links theme and stylistic features very well.*
- *Perceptive analysis of tone, imagery and contrast.*
- *Excellent expression, fluent and varied.*

Marks awarded: 20/20

REMEMBER!

Avoid wasting time worrying about any words that you don't understand. Instead, focus on what makes sense to you.

Unseen Poem Revision Points

- **Study the wording of questions** to identify the task that you have to do.
- Express your **key points** clearly.
- Include **supportive reference or quotation** (correctly punctuated).
- Refer to both the poet's **style** (how the poem is written) as well as the **themes** (what the poet is writing about).
- **Select interesting phrases** that give you an opportunity to discuss subject matter and use of language.
- **Avoid summaries** that simply repeat the text of the poem.
- **Engage with the poem** by responding genuinely to what the poet has written.

Unseen Poem – Practice 5

Read the following poem by Pat Boran and answer **either** Question 1 **or** Question 2 which follow. (Allow 20 minutes to complete the answer.)

Stalled Train

In the listening carriage, someone's
phone
cries out for help. A student frisks
himself,
a woman weighs her handbag
then stares into space. Our train
is going nowhere. We've stood here
so long now the cattle in this field
have dared come right up close
to chew and gaze. We tell ourselves
that somewhere down the line
things we cannot understand
are surely taking place – the future
almost within reach – and into each
small telephone that rings
or shudders now, like doubt,
we commit (if still in whispers)
our hopes and fears, our last known
whereabouts.

Pat Boran

1. (a) In your opinion, is the dominant mood in the poem positive or negative? Explain your answer with reference to the poem. (10)

(b) Identify two images from the poem that you find interesting and give reasons for your choice. (10)

OR

2. Discuss the impact of this poem, with reference to its theme and the poet's use of language and imagery. Refer closely to the text in support of your answer. (20)

PROMPT!

- *Think about the poet's attitude to modern life.*
- *Imagery is vivid, graphic, cinematic.*
- *Surreal, mysterious, dreamlike atmosphere.*
- *Effective use of personification and symbols.*
- *Final lines are disturbing.*
- *Poem raises many interesting questions.*

Acknowledgements

The authors and publisher are grateful to the following for permission to reproduce copyrighted material:

'The Fish', 'The Bight', 'At the Fishhouses', 'The Prodigal', 'Questions of Travel', 'The Armadillo', 'Sestina', 'First Death in Nova Scotia', 'Filling Station', and 'In the Waiting Room' from *Poems by Elizabeth Bishop.* Copyright © 2011 by The Alice H. Methfessel Trust. Publisher's Note and compilation copyright © 2011 by Farrar, Straus and Giroux. Reprinted by permission of Farrar, Straus and Giroux.

'The War Horse', 'Child of Our Time', 'The Famine Road', 'The Shadow Doll', 'White Hawthorn in the West of Ireland', 'Outside History', 'The Black Lace Fan my Mother Gave Me', 'This Moment', 'The Pomegranate', 'Love' from *New Selected Poems* by Eavan Boland. Copyright © Eavan Boland, 2005, Carcanet Press Limited.

'The Tuft of Flowers', 'Mending Wall', 'After Apple-Picking', 'The Road Not Taken', 'Birches', '"Out, Out–"', 'Spring Pools', 'Acquainted with the Night', 'Design', 'Provide, Provide' from *Poetry of Robert Frost* by Robert Frost. Published by Jonathan Cape. Reprinted by permission of The Random House Group Limited.

'The Forge', 'Bogland', 'The Tollund Man', 'Mossbawn: Sunlight', 'A Constable Calls', 'The Skunk', 'The Harvest Bow', 'The Underground', 'Postscript', 'A Call', 'Tate's Avenue', 'The Pitchfork', 'Lightenings viii' by Seamus Heaney. Copyright © Seamus Heaney, reproduced by permission of Faber and Faber Ltd.

'Black Rook in Rainy Weather', 'The Times are Tidy', 'Morning Song', 'Finisterre', 'Mirror', 'Pheasant', 'Elm', 'Poppies in July', 'The Arrival of the Bee Box', 'Child' by Sylvia Plath. Copyright © Sylvia Plath, reproduced by permission of Faber and Faber Ltd.

'Autumn' by Alan Bold. Copyright © Alan Bold. Reproduced with permission of Alice Bold.

'Roller-Skaters' from *Give Yourself A Hug* © Grace Nichols, 1994. Reproduced with permission of Curtis Brown Group Limited, London on behalf of Grace Nichols.

'At Cider Mill Farm' by David Harmer, from *The Works 3* chosen by Paul Cookson, Macmillan Children's Books, 2004. Copyright © David Harmer. Used by permission of the author.

'Lipstick' from *Dissecting the Heart* by Rosita Boland. Copyright © Rosita Boland, 2013, reproduced by kind permission of the author and The Gallery Press, Loughcrew, Oldcastle, County Meath, Ireland.

'Stalled Train' from *Then Again* by Pat Boran, 2019, Dedalus Press. Copyright © Pat Boran, reproduced by kind permission of Dedalus Press.

The authors and publisher have made every effort to trace all copyright holders, but if any have been inadvertently overlooked we would be pleased to make the necessary arrangement at the first opportunity.